SAGE was founded in 1965 by Sara Miller McCune to support the dissemination of usable knowledge by publishing innovative and high-quality research and teaching content. Today, we publish over 900 journals, including those of more than 400 learned societies, more than 800 new books per year, and a growing range of library products including archives, data, case studies, reports, and video. SAGE remains majority-owned by our founder, and after Sara's lifetime will become owned by a charitrust that secures our continued independence.

Los Angeles | London | New Delhi | Singapore | Washington DC | Melbourne

Introduction to Political Economy

Introduction to Political Economy

Contexts, Issues and Challenges

Peu Ghosh
Faculty, Department of Political Science,
Lady Brabourne College, Kolkata

SAGE | TEXTS

Los Angeles | London | New Delhi
Singapore | Washington DC | Melbourne

First published in 2022 by

SAGE | TEXTS

SAGE Publications India Pvt Ltd
B1/I-1 Mohan Cooperative Industrial Area
Mathura Road, New Delhi 110 044, India
www.sagepub.in

SAGE Publications Inc
2455 Teller Road
Thousand Oaks, California 91320, USA

SAGE Publications Ltd
1 Oliver's Yard, 55 City Road
London EC1Y 1SP, United Kingdom

SAGE Publications Asia-Pacific Pte Ltd
18 Cross Street #10-10/11/12
China Square Central
Singapore 048423

Published by Vivek Mehra for SAGE Publications India Pvt. Ltd. Typeset in 10/12 pt Cambria by Zaza Eunice, Hosur, Tamil Nadu, India.

Library of Congress Control Number: 2021054214

ISBN: 978-93-5479-231-1 (PB)

SAGE Team: Amit Kumar, Anandadeep Roy, Shruti Gupta, Sonam Rana and Anupama Krishnan

Contents

Detailed Contents

List of Figures

List of Tables

List of Abbreviations

AEC	ASEAN Economic Community
AITUC	All India Trade Union Congress
APEC	Asia-Pacific Economic Cooperation
ASEAN	Association of Southeast Asian Nations
ASSOCHAM	Associated Chambers of Commerce and Industry of India
BPO	Business process outsourcing
BRI	Belt and Road Initiative
BRICS	Brazil, Russia, India, China and South Africa
CARE	Cooperative for Assistance and Relief Everywhere
CEPs	Comprehensive Economic Partnerships
CGA	Controller General of Accounts
CII	Confederation of Indian Industry
CMIE	Centre of Monitoring Indian Economy
CSO	Central Statistics Office
CU	Customs union
CUFTA	Canada–United States Free Trade Agreement
DPIIT	Department for Promotion of Industry and Internal Trade
ECLAC	Economic Commission for Latin America and the Caribbean
ECOSOC	Economic and Social Council
ECSC	European Coal and Steel Community
ECU	European Currency Unit
EEC	European Economic Community
EFTA	European Free Trade Association
EIU	Economic Intelligence Unit
EMU	Economic and monetary union
EU	European Union
FDI	Foreign direct investment
FICCI	Federation of Indian Chambers of Commerce and Industry
FII	Foreign institutional investment
FPI	Foreign portfolio investment
FTA	Free trade area
FTC	Free Trade Commission

GAB	General Arrangements to Borrow
GATS	General Agreement on Trade in Services
GATT	General Agreement on Tariffs and Trade
GDI	Gender Development Index
GDP	Gross domestic product
GEM	Gender empowerment measure
GII	Gender inequality index
GNP	Gross national product
GST	Goods and services tax
GVA	Gross value added
HDI	Human Development Index
HPI	Human Poverty Index
IBRD	International Bank for Reconstruction and Development
ICSID	International Centre for Settlement of Investment Disputes
ICT	Information and communication technology
IDA	International Development Association
IDPs	Internally displaced persons
IFC	International Finance Corporation
IIP	Index of Industrial Production
ILO	International Labour Organization
IMF	International Monetary Fund
IPE	International political economy
IPR	Intellectual property rights
IT	Information technology
JSCs	Joint stock companies
LDCS	Least Developed Contracting States
LFPR	Labour force participation rate
LINKS	Local and Indigenous Knowledge Systems
M&A	Merger and acquisition
MDGs	Millennium Development Goals
MEPs	Members of the European Parliament
MFA	Multi-fibre Agreement
MFN	Most favoured nation
MIC	Military–industrial complex
MIGA	Multilateral Investment Guarantee Agency
MNCs	Multinational corporations
MRTP	Monopolies and restrictive trade practices
NAFTA	North American Free Trade Agreement
NATO	North Atlantic Treaty Organization's
NDB	New Development Bank
NEP	New Economic Policy
NGOs	Non-governmental organizations
NIEO	New International Economic Order
NLDCS	Non-Least Developed Contracting States
NYSE	New York Stock Exchange
ODA	Official development assistance

OECD	Organisation for Economic Co-operation and Development
OPEC	Organization of the Petroleum Exporting Countries
PPP	Purchasing power parity
PTA	Preferential trade agreements
R&D	Research and development
RBI	Reserve Bank of India
SAARC	South Asian Association for Regional Cooperation
SAFTA	South Asian Free Trade Area
SAPs	Structural adjustment programmes
SAPTA	SAARC Preferential Trade Agreement
SDGs	Sustainable Development Goals
SDRs	Special drawing rights
SEA	Single European Act
SIPRI	Stockholm International Peace Research Institute
SMC	SAFTA Ministerial Council
TAC	Treaty of Amity and Cooperation
TINA	There is no alternative
TLP	Trade Liberalization Programme
TNCs	Transnational corporations
TRIMS	Trade-related Investment Measures
TRIPS	Trade-related Aspects of Intellectual Property Rights
UN	United Nations
UNCTAD	UN Conference on Trade and Development
UNDP	United Nations Development Programme
UNHCR	United Nations High Commissioner for Refugees
USMCA	United States–Mexico–Canada Agreement
WHO	World Health Organization
WTO	World Trade Organization

Preface

The timing of the book *Introduction to Political Economy: Contexts, Issues and Challenges* is quite significant. In the years 2020 and 2021, humans have confronted an attack from a virus, COVID-19. Since the outbreak of the pandemic, life has not been normal. Rather, humans had to adapt themselves to the 'new normal' of masks, sanitizers and social distancing. Economies were hard hit by lockdowns or complete closures to break the chain of infection. Living and making a living became tough with recession, unemployment and diminished growth rate. COVID-19 not only posed before us sets of challenges, but it also raised questions on a number of issues which had taken a back seat in the functioning of the real-world affairs. The COVID-19 pandemic has ignited debates around the agendas of globalization, market forces, human welfare, human development and exclusion, environmental protection and sustainable development, which are matters of interest for the discipline of international political economy (IPE). The health sector even in developed countries was not geared up to meet the exigencies, let aside the developing and poor/er countries.

It was thought, therefore, by the author and the publisher to bring out a book which will address the issues of political economy. Since the 1970s, liberalization, globalization and financialization of economies have caught momentum across the globe. The entire texture of global economy has undergone changes with movement of capital, services, multinational corporations (MNCs), trade and so on. Communication is faster in terms of information as well as transportation and travel. We now live in an interconnected world where breaking the chain of interconnectedness has become difficult. IPE helps to understand the difficult facets of developments, role of state, actors and their impact on global economy as well as globalization and its overreaching influence. IPE as a discipline attempts to bring together international politics and economics and give an integrated view of the working of global political economy.

The present book is a comprehensive coverage of topics/issues which are of great interest to students of international politics, economics as well as those pursuing their specialization in IPE or global political economy. The curriculum requirements of the Indian universities have been dealt in this book with utmost care and in a student-friendly manner for Core and Discipline Specific Elective subjects in international relations, political science and economics. The book addresses theoretical perspectives of political economy, more precisely IPE; globalization and functioning of states; approaches to development; issues and challenges to development and Indian political economy of reforms.

The book is divided into 11 chapters, which give an expansive view of the working of the IPE.

Chapter 1 covers theories of IPE. It deals with realism and liberalism, with emphasis on liberal interdependence theory, hegemonic stability theory and dependency theory. **Chapter 2** gives a broad idea about capitalist transformation. It discusses about the transition from feudalism to capitalism along with basic features of capitalism, capitalist accumulation, rise of modern corporations, monopoly capitalism and imperialism. It also focuses on the 'golden age' of capitalism of the post-Second World War. **Chapter 3** discusses post-Second World War developments in IPE. It also examines the changing trade regimes, Bretton Woods system, the International Monetary Fund, the World Bank, the General Agreement on Tariffs and Trade, the World Trade Organization, MNCs and issues related with trade and security. **Chapter 4** covers the changing dynamics of capitalist production, organizational form and labour process from Fordist to post-Fordist production, markets and labour process, changing nature of job security and labour rights. **Chapter 5** analyses the State in the era of globalisation from the aspects of welfare, development and autonomy. It also engages in the discussion on the development–democracy debate. **Chapter 6** is quite expansive in scope. It covers topics such as the changing role of finance during globalization with emphasis on globalization and changing role of finance in capital accumulation and corporate structure. It also deals with globalization and financialization with emphasis on financial liberalization, structural adjustment programmes, foreign direct investment and financial crisis. **Chapter 7** is wholly dedicated to the theories of development. It discusses the theories of classical liberalism, Marxism, welfarism, neoliberalism, Gandhian approach and post-development paradigm. **Chapter 8** covers a number of issues in development having social dimensions. It examines topics such as globalization and uneven development; human development; UN Millennium Development Goals; non-governmental organizations; culture, media and television; big dams and environmental concerns; global arms industry and arms trade and knowledge systems. **Chapter 9** covers issues of globalization and development dilemmas. The chapter discusses issues like information technology revolution and debates on sovereignty, gender including Gender Development Index, gender empowerment measure, gender inequality index, racial and ethnic problems, migration and displacement, environment and sustainability and Sustainable Development Goals. **Chapter 10** deals with the regional economic formation: the European Union, Association of Southeast Asian Nations, Asia-Pacific Economic Cooperation, North American Free Trade Agreement, South Asian Free Trade Area, BRICS (Brazil, Russia, India, China and South Africa) and their significance in regional cooperation. **Chapter 11** gives an overview of the political economy of India from the planned period, the reforms and the post-reform era.

Acknowledgements

I am thankful to my colleagues of Lady Brabourne College for their inspiration and encouragement in all my endeavours and my friends, who have always been very helpful and inspiring in my academic projects. My sincere thanks to my father, Shri Subhas Kumar Ghosh, and my mother, Smt. Krishnashree Ghosh, for their rock-solid support in my entire academic career. I must also acknowledge the editorial and production team of my publisher, SAGE, for their encouraging and continuous cooperation. As for the students, who are our future, we give them best wishes from the entire team involved in this project of the book on political economy. The students will immensely benefit as they will come to know about international politics and economics integrated into IPE.

About the Author

Peu Ghosh is an Associate Professor in the Department of Political Science, Lady Brabourne College, Kolkata, West Bengal. She is an MA PhD in international relations from Jadavpur University, Kolkata, and has done a certificate course in human rights from IGNOU.

She has special interest in international relations, IPE, politics of South Asia, migration and refugee issues and international humanitarian law.

She is the author of the books titled *International Relations* and *Indian Government and Politics*. She has a monograph titled *Bhutanese Refugees: A Forgotten Saga*, which is based on rigorous research work and visit to the Bhutanese refugee camps in Nepal.

The book titled *International Relations*, 5th edition, received the Award of Excellence in the year 2020 in the category of Textbooks: College (English) from the Federation of Indian Publishers, the representative body of the publishers in India and affiliate member of International Publishers Association, Geneva.

She has a number of articles published in reputed journals and chapters in edited books to her credit. She has worked as an intern with the United Nations High Commissioner for Refugees, New Delhi. She has gone through training in peace studies in the Institute of Peace and Dialogue, Vienna, Austria, under pioneer teachers such as Professor Johan Galtung, Dietrich Fischer, Patrice Brodeur and Sara Clarke-Habibi, who had illuminated her with their knowledge on conflict and conflict resolution.

She has delivered lectures in several national and international seminars including an invited lecture in the Department of Islamic Political Science, Academy of Islamic Studies, University of Malaya, Kuala Lumpur, Malaysia. She has been a speaker at the plenary at the 1st International Conference of Africa-Asia Development University Network and the Africa's Asian Options (AADUN–AFRASO) Project, 2014, Malaysia, and at the Congress of the Humanities and Social Sciences (2014), Brock University, St Catharines, Ontario, Canada.

She is actively involved in the formulation of fundamentals of political science, glossary of political science from English to Bengali under the Commission for Scientific & Technical Terminology, Department of Higher Education, Ministry of Education, Government of India.

She is member of the International Editorial Board of *International Journal of Political Science* since 2020.

1 Theories of International Political Economy

LEARNING OBJECTIVES

- Introducing international political economy (IPE)
- Knowing the theories
- Learning about realism and its way of examining IPE from a power perspective
- Getting to know about liberalism and liberal interdependence model of IPE
- Grasping the theory of hegemonic stability with its emphasis on the presence of a hegemon to maintain stability in the world economic order
- Finally, learning about the process of functioning of global economic structures from the perspective of domination and subordination, dependency and control from the angle of dependency theory as well as modern world systems theory

Introduction

It is quite interesting to note the growing engagement of the academicians with international political economy (IPE). What makes IPE a central point of attention needs a little examination. The main question is who influences whom. Is it economics which impacts politics or vice versa? For long, the two disciplines had a kind of compartmentalized study of their individual disciplines. Only lately as of the 1970s, academicians from both the disciplines began to show interest in IPE. Many international events that took place in the international economic and political scenario around this time started to draw their attention.

The post-Second World War political and economic developments saw the rise of the USA and the emergence of the Bretton Woods system (Chapter 3) which continued till the beginning of the 1970s. Later from the beginning of the 1970s, the US power declined comparatively and the world was becoming multipolar with emerging powers such as China, Japan and the European Union (EU). Along with this, there was a significant presence of a large number of newly developing economies which were former colonies and belonged to the category of developing, underdeveloped and poor. Therefore, IPE was thought to be a tool to understand the process in which world economic system worked. The demand of New International Economic Order (NIEO) on the part of the Global South (the developing, underdeveloped and poor countries) made scholars think about the dependency syndrome in these countries. Further, in the 1990s, the march of globalization around the world with the mantra of economic liberalization unleashed a host of forces that needed rigorous academic research (Chapters 8 and 9). This clearly meant that some serious thinking from a politico-economic angle was needed and this augmented interest in IPE.

IPE which was neglected till the 1970s quickly came to the forefront. Since the Great Depression years, 1929, the 20th century witnessed a study of economics as a compartmentalized discipline. Since the 1970s again, there was a resurgence of interest in political economy as pointed above. The politico-economic development around this time could not be explained by the existing theories solely from the perspective of economics or politics. Scholars questioned the intellectual justifications for a division between economics and politics. The decline of the Bretton Woods system (Chapter 3) which ended the two decades of stability globally in every sphere compelled social scientists to comprehend how politics and economics interact in contemporary IPE. The need was felt to take account of political tendencies as well as economic trends by both political scientists and economists. This was thought to enable them to get a wholesome picture of political and economic affairs in an integrated way. IPE is, therefore, a confluence of politics and economics. The politico-economic matrix gives a key to understand the international economic order and power game in the global theatre. With works of Robert Keohane and Joseph Nye, who proposed the model of complex interdependence, IPE started gaining ground. Demand for NIEO also created a brand of scholars who forwarded their theories of dependency and modern world system. The post-Second World War international scenario influenced scholars to come up with theories like hegemonic stability which reflected the kind of world order that was created by the USA as a hegemon. Apart from these, the reigning theory of realism based on statism, national interest and self-help model had been there which still has a great influence among IPE scholars.

Francis Fukuyama, in his *The End of History and the Last Man* (1992), opined that with the collapse of Communism after the disintegration of the USSR or the erstwhile Soviet Union, there has been a triumph of liberalism. There is no alternative to it. History has reached its goal of free markets and consumer culture reinforced by liberal institutions such as representative governments and international organizations. There has been a universalization of democratic ideals. Revolutionary technologies have reinvigorated the forces of globalization which has created a homogenizing world—a 'global village'. The globe is connected through various regimes, be it political, strategic, security or economic and trade. It has created an interconnected world almost on the model of complex interdependence. Has this interconnectedness and interdependence created a picture that is bright or uneven development, inequality and exclusion persists (Chapter 8)? Issues that have come to the foreground are connected with the role of states, multinational corporations (MNCs), development dilemmas, financialization, liberalization, globalization and the ever-changing world economic scenario. IPE takes up the job of examining issues like these which are being the focal point of discussion in the working of the global political economy.

The COVID-19 pandemic has put the world into challenges. Not only it is costing lives but also taking its toll upon the economy. The economic shutdown or lockdown has put the economies out of gear. It has posed a lot of questions before the governments of all countries. Do the States have to rethink about globalization? Does the social sector matter? How tenable is the argument for minimum state intervention? COVID-19 has also pointed out the glaring inequality which remains or made rather invisible in normal times. Unemployment, hunger, poverty and job loss are following the pandemic and will continue in the future too. This coronavirus crisis also exposed the vulnerabilities of different sections of societies such as migrant workers/interstate workers, women and children to mention a few. Thomas Piketty had talked about (*Capital in the Twenty-first Century*, 2014) a 'social state' rather than a 'welfare state' (Chapter 5). At this juncture, we are confronted with the question that what kind of fiscal and social state will emerge in the post-COVID times in the developing world which is the most affected by the pandemic and the economic crisis following it. All questions may not be answerable at this juncture but COVID crisis has pushed us to introspect the theories of IPE and examine their viabilities.

This chapter clearly gives an idea about the prominent IPE theories which provide analytical perspectives on the functioning of IPE. There have been four major trends of theories in IPE—**realism, liberalism and liberal interdependence theory, hegemonic stability theory** and **dependency theory.** Each of these theories has been examined and effort has been made to point out their relevance or their functioning during the COVID times.

Realism

Realism has been a dominant school of thought and still rules the roost with its continuing significance and variations. This strand of thinking is nothing new. Classical realism has its roots in the thinking of Thucydides, Machiavelli, Hobbes, Carl Von Clausewitz and not to forget about Chanakya, the great Indian expert in statecraft. Each one of them underpinned the necessity of a strong state and a capable ruler. The realists view the international political scenario as anarchy where each state pursues its own national interest. To fulfil this necessity, states are engaged in pursuit of increasing national power on the basis of national capabilities. This results in an incessant struggle for power. There is no place for morality or legality of state action. The state/statesmen have to ultimately adapt, manoeuvre and change to the emergent power-political configuration in international politics.

Till the outbreak of the Second World War, more precisely in the interwar period, liberal thinking with its emphasis on harmony of interest and achievement of free movement of goods across national borders was the predominant school of thought. The liberals underpinned the importance of universal free trade which will lead every country to the highest level of utility, ultimately removing the economic basis of international conflict and war. International regimes would help the states to achieve such a condition where no unfair competition would be present. On the international level in 1918, just before the end of the First World War, President Woodrow Wilson placed his 'Fourteen Points' of world peace, world organization and free trade among countries who accept the peace. However, the outbreak of the Second World War gave a jolt to such liberal ideas and aroused the need for a deeper understanding of international politics and economics of that time.

Therefore, branding the liberals as utopians arose another school of thought identified as political realism/realism. The basic ideas were reflected in a more vigorous way in the wake of the outbreak of the Second World War in the writings of E. H. Carr (*Twenty Years' Crisis, 1919–1939: An Introduction to the Study of International Relations*, 1939) and in the post-Second World War in the seminal work of the most prominent realist thinker, Hans. J. Morgenthau (*Politics among Nations: The Struggle for Power and Peace*, 1948).

E. H. Carr saw the world as composed of oligarchical configuration of powerful states who control wealth and influence others who are too weak to make themselves visible in the world politics. There is, therefore, a division between the 'haves' and the 'have-nots'. World politics becomes a struggle between revisionist power who represents the 'have-nots' and the status quoits power who are the 'haves'. The liberal assumption of harmony of interests and world peace is, therefore, utopian.

Hans J. Morgenthau was the chief proponent of realism. To him, international politics like all politics is a struggle for power. His expositions are contained in the six signposts or principles given in Table 1.1. The main signpost which helps in understanding international politics is the concept of interest defined in terms of power. This is true for every state and every action of every state is guided towards defending its national interest.

Neo-realism another variant of realism was propounded by Kenneth Waltz in his famous works *Man, the State and War* (1959) and *Theory of International Politics* (1979). He opines that the problem is the very structure of international system which results in anarchy. In the absence of higher authority in the international system, the states can only secure themselves through **self-help model** which is discussed in Figure 1.1. This self-help model creates **security dilemma** among states because security build-up of one creates insecurity of others. In a self-help system, the logic of self-interest provides a basis for understanding the problem of coordinating the interests of individual versus the interests of common good and the pay-off between short-term and long-term interests. Therefore, cooperation is not overlooked but in such cooperative efforts, each will try to maximize their relative power and preserve their autonomy.

Neoclassical realism which somewhat tries to work a middle path between classical realism and neo-realism adds choices available to the states in the situation of anarchy. International structures do constrain the states but there are also other factors which determine the choices of the leaders. They refer to the internal characteristics of the state in this regard. The leaders have to weigh their options, on the one hand, keeping in mind the international structure and, on the other, in the domestic sphere, the influence of the politico-military institutions, societal factors, interest groups, autonomy of state from society and elite/social cohesion. This might be seen an addition to the earlier thoughts but under the influence of the liberal thinking in world politics.

Table 1.1 Hans. J. Morgenthau, *Politics among Nations: The Struggle for Power and Peace*: Six Signposts

1. Politics like society in general is governed by objective laws that have their roots in human nature which is unchanging.
2. National interest defined in terms of power makes the theoretical understanding of politics possible.
3. Interest defined as power is an objective category which is universally valid but not with a meaning that is fixed once for all.
4. Universal moral principles cannot be applied to state action.
5. Moral aspirations of a particular state cannot be identified with moral laws that govern the universe.
6. Politics is an autonomous sphere distinct from and not subordinate to the standards of economics, law and morality.

Figure 1.1 A Realist Self-help Model

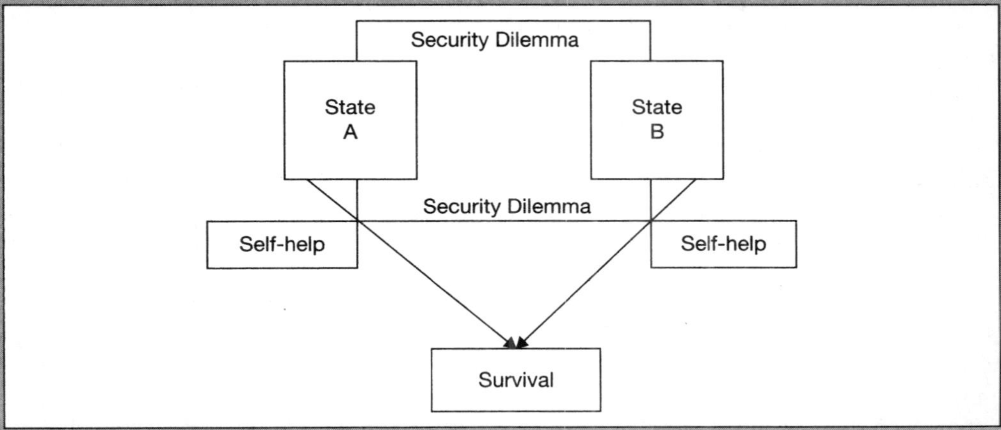

The basic assumptions of realism were shared by the mercantilist tradition of IPE which saw competition among states in world economy to maximize relative strength and power and almost toed the realist exposition of world politics. As we have got an overview of realism and its variation, now it is pertinent to understand the functioning of the world order from a realist/neo-realist perspective.

E. H. Carr criticizes liberal propositions of harmony of interest and world peace as utopian. The liberals upheld that overall majority of interactions among nations are co-operative and non-conflictual as they see a harmony of interests in these. As opposed to this, Carr sees a divergence of interest between states desiring maintenance of the status quo and states desiring to change it.

For the realists, states are the most important unit of analysis. States are the predominant actors in world politics from a realist standpoint. Given the anarchic situation in the world politics with consequential insecurities, dangers and threats to survival, the states are intended upon to accumulate more power. This pursuit for power makes the states to compete with one another for ensuring survival and security, control over market, access to raw materials and spreading influence. This, as Waltz points out, can be done by increasing capabilities. Capabilities might include population, resources, geographical location, territory, degree of economic development, military strength, political stability and competence.

Capabilities can reinforce power. When power is backed by capabilities, the crucial thing that must be ensured first of all is the survival of the states. Survival is the precondition which will enable states to attain other goals. According to Waltz, there are varied goals beyond the survival motive but survival is the prime goal.

This brings us to the question of security of the states and here the realists divulge into two groups—**defensive realists** and **offensive realists.** Defensive realists like Kenneth Waltz stated that international system is anarchic. The motive driving states is survival. It is unwise for states to maximize their share of world power but advisable to maintain balance of power and status quo. Pursuit of hegemony is foolish. On the other hand, John Mearsheimer (*The*

Tragedy of Great Power Politics, 2001) was of the opinion that international system fosters conflict and states should gain as much power as possible. Overwhelming power is the best way to ensure one's own survival. States should pursue hegemony where possible. In the case of survival, defensive realists suggest aversion of competition for power, while offensive realists are keen on competition for power. Offensive realists see this competition between revisionist states and aspiring hegemons who are always ready to take risks with the aim of improving their position in the international system.

The understanding is that states need to protect themselves at any cost. The ethic of responsibility of states is different from legal and moral responsibility. As we have seen from the discussion of Morgenthau's realism for preservation of national interest or for greater good, acts of an immoral kind may have to be taken up for pre-empting or removing threats to national security. Examples of US intervention in Afghanistan and Iraq in the name of War on Terror, recent USA–Iran bitterness in 2019, North Atlantic Treaty Organization's (NATO) intervention in Libya and external power interferences such as the USA, Russia and Turkey in Syria and Yemen can be used to supplement the above principle which is highly questionable from the humanitarian point of view.

When each state operates on the basis of such assumptions and makes every effort to maximize power, then there arises a security dilemma. There is no one to help the states in the world of power struggle. In the absence of any international body, this can only be achieved through **self-help.** As Waltz points out, in an anarchic structure, **self-help** is necessarily the principle of action. The atmosphere of security dilemma arises as one state embarks upon military preparedness which sends shocks to another. The other state then suffers from insecurity. It then tries to match with the military preparedness of the previously mentioned state. This will eventually lead to arms race as we see in case of India–Pakistan and the USA and the USSR during the Cold War days. Figure 1.1 gives a brief idea of the self-help model.

What then is the realist road map to security? What can be the way/s to resolve such anarchical conditions and restore order in the absence of international body to mediate? To this, the realists have forwarded the concept of **balance of power** as a key to the restoration of stability in a world of anarchy that can be best done by forming alliances and counter alliances. Balance of power can ensure the sovereignty and independent existence of a state from an aggressor or a hegemon. A balancer most often is a dominant state and it provides stability to the system through its domination which can be detrimental to weaker and small states. Thus, a hegemon may be present in the realist scheme of thinking who can establish political equilibrium. However, there can be counterbalances in the form of counter alliances but most often the recalcitrant or revisionist state is punished to maintain the status quo. The First World War and the Second World War are the examples where Germany and then Germany and Japan were curbed so that there were no future threats from them. However, in a nuclear age, this often becomes a **balance of terror** as states develop nuclear capabilities and threaten the existence of one another by use of nukes. **Mutual assured destruction** prevents an all-out war and thereby stability to some extent can be restored but can never be guaranteed. The Cuban Missile Crisis of 1962 almost took the world to the verge of nuclear war. Diplomacy, negotiations and communication are an essential part of retaining the stability in international system. Whatever it may be, offensive or defensive, realists and neo-realists prescribe self-preservation as the ultimate goal in international politics, be it alone or in alliance with others.

The liberal thinkers prescribe a complex interdependence model of economic cooperation. The dependency theorists examine the international economic process through the lens of a structural exploitative relationship between the core and the periphery. The realists propose a self-help model of survival in the struggle for power in world politics. As Friedman and Lake opine, the hegemonic stability theory visualizes a world order being established and maintained by a dominant state—the hegemon is an offshoot of realism. This theory, according to them, tries to address the question of distribution of international power in such a way that the form of IPE comes to be dominated by a single hegemon. Free trade and a stable and strong regime can be ensured by a hegemon. Therefore, unlike the liberal or the dependency theorists, the realists see the pursuit of power by states at international level as shaping the IPE.

Liberalism and Liberal Interdependence Theory

As diametrically opposed to realism, liberalism gives a different kind of world view. The realists, as discussed above, give a statist version of world politics. Realists assume each state to be against the other which causes anarchy in world politics. Survival is the core agenda of every state. Deterrence and even nuclear deterrence can ensure survival but is no guarantee to stability in international politics. Therefore, international politics becomes an unending struggle for power. Quite opposed to this is the view put forward by the liberal thinkers. Before going into the liberal perspective of IPE, it would be pertinent to look back at the classical liberal tradition of political philosophy. The classical liberal tradition was championed by Immanuel Kant (*Perpetual Peace: A Philosophical Sketch,* 1795), John Locke (*Two Treatises of Government,* 1690), John Stuart Mill (*On Liberty,* 1859) and Adam Smith (*Wealth of Nations,* 1776), among others.

The key propositions forwarded by Kant were that sustained peace can be brought by republican constitutions and commercial exchanges which would be embodied in cosmopolitan law. This does not prevent him from seeing the states being far from self-interest. He opined that self-interest would compel the states to bring a just peace and he visualized a federation of interdependent republics to be a goal for sustaining peace. In short, Kant believed that war and conflict can be overcome by concerted changes in the domestic and international structures of governance. Prudent search for establishment of pacific federation will contribute to a more peaceful world where individual freedom will get full expression and democracy and trade will expand which in turn will facilitate the evolution of international law and international organizations.

John Locke also in his *Two Treatises* talked about liberty and right to property. Liberty meant the absence of restraint and violence from others which was to be secured through law. This extended to the enjoyment of property also. Mill in his *On Liberty* (1859) talks about the limits to the power of the rulers through constitutional checks and guarantees of liberties and rights to individuals. Adam Smith in his *Wealth of Nations* forwarded the themes of division of labour, free trade and the working of the 'invisible hand' of the market.

These liberal traditions were taken forward by contemporary liberal theorists of international politics. As opposed to the realist pursuit for balance of power as a path to peace, the liberals like Michael Doyle ('Kant, Liberal Legacies, and Foreign Affairs' [1983] and 'Liberalism and World Politics' [1986]) forwarded the democratic peace theory. The assumptions of this exposition are that democratic sovereign states do not wage war against another democratic state. Such democratic sates are believed to comprise market economies, rule of law and democratic representation. The other proposition being liberal democracies exercising such restraint form separate zones of peace among themselves. They find liberal reasons of aggression to fight against non-liberal and non-democratic states. These have been widely contested as US actions in Iraq and Afghanistan and, currently, the US advocacies against Iran are blatant aggression or threats of aggression by a liberal democracy.

Now liberalism has not been a singular kind of exposition from scholars. There have been several lines of thinking on liberal world view. Prominent among them were the champions of institutionalism. The pioneering figures were David Mitrany (*A Working Peace System,* 1943) and Ernst B. Haas (*Beyond the Nation State: Functionalism and International Organization and the Uniting of Europe—Political, Social, and Economic Forces, 1950–1957,* 1964). They talked about integration through international and regional institutions. Such integration would help to solve common problems of humanity. If David Mitrany thought about the United Nations (UN), then Haas forwarded his exposition on the basis of the integration process in Europe. Mitrany had forwarded the concept of 'spillover' effect or ramification of cooperation. This meant cooperation in one field would lead to collaboration among other sectors. As states would become more integrated through such cooperation, they would be rendered meaningless. The emergence of a functional society focusing on functions rather than territory will gradually evolve and in this way international peace can be established. Haas looked at integration from the regional perspective. The aim being formation of a political union through phases beginning from a common market to economic union and finally to the political union. A true reflection of his proposition has been the EU though it is going through some trouble due to BREXIT.

This strand of liberal institutionalism was further reinforced by Robert Keohane (*After Hegemony: Cooperation and Discord in the World Political Economy,* 1984) and David Lake ('Anarchy, Hierarchy and the Variety of International Relations', 1996) and came to be identified as neoliberal institutionalism in response to the reaffirmation of neo-realism of Kenneth Waltz and other realists. The underlying belief of liberal institutionalism is that institutions contribute to peace by fostering habits of cooperation and a sense of common interests. For example, in the field of economic relations, extensive cooperation has been worked out through international intuitions such as the International Monetary Fund (IMF) and the World Bank and political and social ones through the UN. Institutions devise means and ways through which common goals can be achieved and costs can be kept low. Overall, the emphasis of liberal institutionalist thinkers has been that norms, conventions and cooperation are core to working of the world order leading towards a peaceful world.

Institutions often understood as organizations have been broadened to include international regimes also. These can be economic regimes such as the General Agreement on Tariffs and Trade (GATT)/World Trade Organization (WTO), nuclear non-proliferation regimes (NPT), disarmament regimes and the like. Stephen Krasner ('Structural Causes and Regime Consequences', 1982) while elucidating the concept of international regimes upheld that regime-governed activity enforced through principles and norms creates a kind of behaviour which unlike the realists is not governed by narrow calculations of self-interest. Though self-interest prevails, neoliberals see institutions and regimes creating patterns of cooperation among states. It can be said to be like coordinating collective responses to diverse global problems. Two other lines of liberal thinking have been commercial liberalism and embedded liberalism. Richard Rosecrance (*The Rise of the Trading State: Commerce and Conquest in the Modern World,* 1986) opined that international trading system has shifted the focus of global politics from military-politico agenda to interdependent world of trading states. The underlying belief is that extensive economic linkages would prevent war among those involved in the economic interdependent relations. Embedded liberalism as forwarded by John Ruggie (*International Regimes, Transactions, and Change: Embedded Liberalism in the Post-War Economic Order,* 1982) underscored a balanced approach to liberal reconstruction. The balance was to be sought between liberalizing trade, on the one hand, and social equity, political stability, employment, development and so on, on the other. However, this was just pushed aside with the Reagan and Thatcher brand of economic neoliberalism which was an extended version of commercial liberalism.

Neoliberals had put forward their proposition as opposed to state-centric realist expositions. The pluralist brand of neoliberals put forth that the world not only comprises states as actors but also non-state actors. Working of world politics is no longer interactions/interrelations among states. It is more than that. The word process is now permeated by non-state actors who influence domestic and international politics. According to Keohane and Nye (*Transnational Relations and World Politics,* 1977), the emerging scenario saw transnational relations which transcend the states pursuing unilateral policies. Though the neoliberals accepted that the world order is an anarchic environment of self-interested egoistic state actors, they say that cooperation is not impossible under such situation as well. Neoliberals see anarchy as a vacuum which was being gradually filled up by human-created processes and institutions which might act as cross-purposes with the governmental institutions. Such transnationalism was depicted by Keohane and Nye's **complex interdependence model** which has been the most striking contribution of the neoliberals put forth by Robert Keohane and Joseph Nye in *Power and Interdependence* (1977, 1989) and Robert Keohane in *After Hegemony: Cooperation and Discord in the World Political Economy,* 1984.

Figure 1.2 is an exposition of complex interdependence model. To explain it, the starting point would be the presence of various communication channels which connect societies. The figure depicts not only interstate communications but also trans-governmental and transnational communications. When such communications take place, the agenda is not topped by military and security issues. Economic, non-military, food, environment, climate change, displacement and the like can become a prime agenda. Therefore, the realist hierarchy of agenda putting military and security first was repudiated in this model of complex interdependence. Keohane and Nye also contended that military force was expensive and, in some cases, cannot be used.

The traditional model of world politics which worked on the basis of congruence of military interest might have helped dominant states to create linkages with other states and thereby prevail over the weaker ones. In the complex interdependence model, there is no such congruence of interest; as a result, there will be variety of patterns of interactions among states comprising political bargaining, construction of rules and associated institutions, international organizations and international regimes which would guide the interactions. Therefore, there will be increased transnational activities and trans-governmental relations. However, since there is no super-ordinate authority to enforce such interactions, voluntarism becomes core of the complex interdependence model. An increase of interdependence in

Figure 1.2 Model of Complex Interdependence

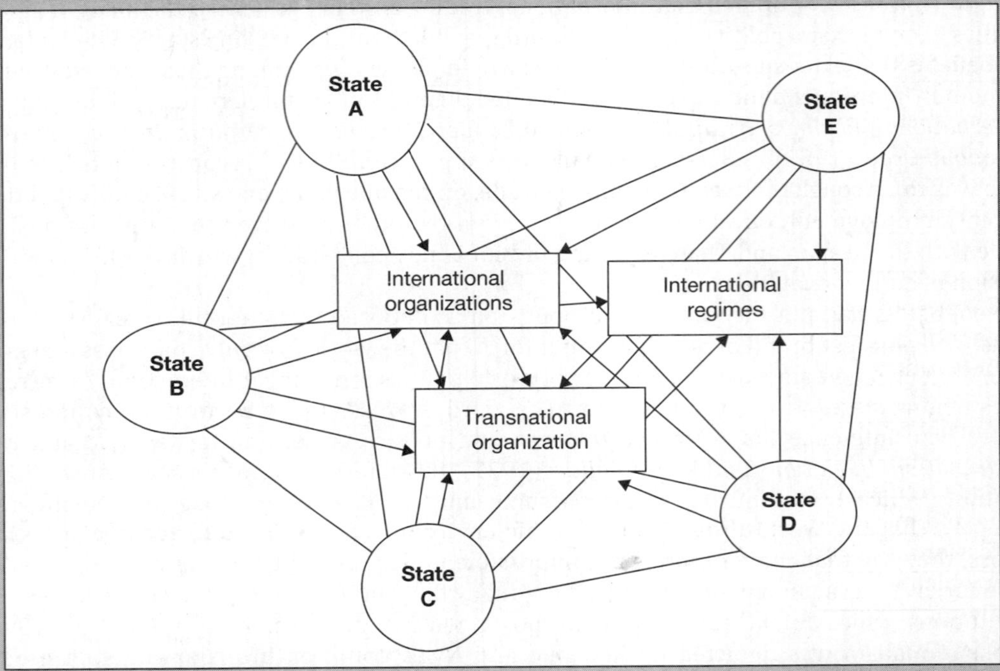

Note: Complex interdependence among states, international organizations, international regimes and transnational organizations.

trade, technology transfer, investment, migration, climate change cooperation, environmental concerns, migration and refugee movement, and student and cultural exchanges become the agenda for such complex interdependence.

Hegemonic stability (discussed in the next section) has also helped in the emergence of international institutions and regimes. The US hegemony in the post-Second World War era has created almost a war-free environment and regimes which have expanded the complex interdependence among states. Keohane (1984) also opines that even if there is a hegemonic decline, this cooperation will continue as interdependence provides a rational strategic incentive for states to continue cooperating with each other.

Discussion on liberalism will be incomplete if we do not mention about neoliberalism. It has been discussed in detail in Chapter 7. We will discuss in brief about neoliberalism over here which underpins the working of the IPE. The economic principles put forward by Adam Smith were reformulated by David Ricardo. He argued that when each country produces those commodities for which by its own situation, climate and other natural or artificial advantages it is adapted, and exchanges them for the commodities of other countries', this would result in an increase in global production and the 'universal good of the whole'. Free trade created domination by economically and politically powerful countries like England in the 18th and the 19th centuries.

As the Great Depression of 1939 set in, it required more state intervention as we see Franklin D. Roosevelt coming up with the 'New Deal' in the USA and more interventionist policies by states in Western Europe. Therefore, the economic theory of liberalism gave a new kind of perspective and is identified with John Maynard Keynes. Among his line of thinking, the most striking was deficit spending. He saw this as an effective measure with the liberal part being that deficit could be used by the state to improve social and welfare services. So in the event of depression, the government should spend and spend. In the post-Second World War period, Keynesian economics was further elaborated in Professor Roy Harrod and Evsey Domar's model. The Harrod–Domar model focused on Keynesian theory on the relations between savings, investment and output.

In the period following the decline in American hegemony in the 1970s, there was the abandonment of Keynesian economics and renewal of classical liberal ideas in the form of neoliberalism. The ideas could be found in the writings of Friedrich von Hayek and his work, *The Road to Serfdom* (1956). He argued that without markets, means of production cannot be optimally combined. Another proponent of neoliberal ideas was Karl Polanyi. Polanyi's main point as summarized by Mark Blyth (*Great Transformations: Economic Ideas and Institutional Change in the Twentieth* Century, 2002) was that state intervention was 'at best a waste of time and money … [and] more likely downright dangerous … [indeed] governments cause recessions and depressions by their very actions'. Besides this, there was also revival of Say's law which underpins that supply creates its own demand. On the other hand, tax cuts especially for the rich seemed to be self-financing through tax revenues, and as per the public choice theory, politicians are analogs of market actors and their aim of maximizing votes by providing goods to constituents/public make democratic governments prone to generating inflation. This in nutshell means government intervention will disturb the naturally self-equilibrating economy and bring in social crisis which cannot be solved by Keynesian economics but by neoliberal free market economy.

This neoliberal economic thinking was quickly adapted by President Ronald Reagan and Prime Minister Margaret Thatcher in the 1980s. Thereafter, neoliberalism became the governing principle of the IPE and the Hayekian principles were infused into the international financial institutions such as the IMF and the World Bank. There was also the rise of the 'Washington Consensus' (discussed in Chapter 7) encouraging fiscal discipline, tax reform, trade liberalization, foreign direct investment (FDI) and so on which also became the guiding principles of the IMF and the World Bank.

Through the several propositions put forward by liberal scholars, it becomes evident that they seem to convey a liberal world order based on economic liberalism enforced through economic interdependence. A statist and power-centric approach of the realists has not been absolutely shunned by the neoliberals, but they did not overlook cooperation in an anarchical situation. However, in their pursuit for extending economic liberalism in a globalizing era, they have overlooked the inequality created in the world. The rich countries become richer and the poor ones poorer. They have not been able to take into account how homogenizing tendency of globalization has given rise to crisis in developing countries. It has also unleashed the Pandora's box of identity politics being fought along ethnic, religious and racial lines which neoliberals did not take into their scheme of thinking. States still continue to be the most important actors in world politics and their role is increasing in the face of economic crises. States had come, in a major way after the 2008 financial crisis, with bailout packages. In 2020, facing a global economic recession due to COVID-19 outbreak, governments are being forced to announce economic packages to mitigate economic hardships arising out of corona outbreak. US President Donald Trump signed a $2 trillion bailout package, the largest after President Barack Obama signed a $800 billion bailout package during the 2008 economic crisis. India declared a ₹20 lakh crore package for all segments of the economy in 2020. States are coming forward in a big way in playing their role and the future courses of economic transactions may not be conducted in the same way as proposed by the liberals in the post-COVID era.

Hegemonic Stability Theory

To understand hegemonic stability theory, we have to begin our discussion from the period following the Second World War. The post-Second World War scenario will be conducive to comprehend the basics of this theory. A quick reading of Chapter 3 will give an idea of the instability that prevailed during the interwar period and stability that was worked out in the post-Second World War era in 1944 at the Bretton Woods Conference.

The central point of the economic instability has been the exchange rate system (explained in Chapter 3). It was in the Bretton Woods Conference of 1944 that 44 states came together to prepare a design for a future international economic regime. Following the Bretton Woods Conference, the IMF was established to force compliance with the rules of international trade and finance. A fixed exchange rate was devised by fixing the exchange rates to the dollar which in turn was tied to gold ($35/oz). This was thought to be bringing about stability in the global economic system. Once currencies were pegged to dollar, the dollar supremacy was established and with it began the hegemony of the USA. Working on neoliberal principles of free market ensured through international economic institutions and regimes such as the IMF, the World Bank and the GATT (now WTO) sought to provide stability in the international monetary system till the 1970s. The Americans and the British understood the requirement of such stability in the international arena through the UN, on the one hand, and the international economic regimes, on the other, to reconstruct their economy in the post-war period (Chapter 3).

The USA being a major economy and dollar being as good as gold, the hegemony of the USA was established and till the 1970s, the stability in the global economy could be maintained to some extent. However, decline of the hegemon began in the 1970s with devaluation of dollars and introduction of float exchange rates. Other currencies became powerful in the global economy and the hegemon also faced a multipolar world.

In this backdrop of the emergence of the hegemon post-Second World War, the hegemonic stability theory became quite popular. It was thought that a hegemon was necessary for states to have confidence in and engage in free market economy in an anarchic international environment. The forced participation of other countries for collective good under the hegemon further created an atmosphere for international cooperation whether political or economic. Undoubtedly, the normative basis of the hegemonic stability provided by the USA in the post-Second World War period as a hegemon caught the attention of the scholars of this theory. Political scientists such as Stephen Krasner ('State, Power and the Structure of International

Trade', 1976), Robert Gilpin (*The Political Economy of International Relations*, 1987) and Robert Keohane (1984) tried to examine the IPE of the 20th century from this perspective.

With the failure of Britain to act as a hegemon in the interwar period, the need to stabilize the system after the Great Depression was felt. As Charles P. Kindleberger (*The World in Depression: 1929–1939,* 1973) has observed that for the world economy to be stabilized, a stabilizer is needed who would be a hegemon and who would fulfil the requirement of a liberal economic order. Usually, a hegemon is the most dominant and powerful state with a great political, military and economic clout. Robert Keohane further opined that order in world politics can be brought about by a single dominant power by the creation of international regimes. According to Keohane and Nye, hegemony is a situation in which one state has the power and capability to maintain essential rules governing the interstate relations. The hegemon must also have the willingness to do so.

To be a hegemon, the dominant state must have an economic preponderance in every aspect from controlling access of raw materials to being a major source of capital flow globally with technological superiority and major entry in the world market along with a decisive role in the international economic regimes. In short, in the global political and economic system, the hegemon will act as a stabilizer. It will foster and facilitate international cooperation and prevent defection by enforcing the rules of international regimes. These might include sanctions, rupture of communication, peaceful methods of reconciliation and sometimes quasi-military to full military actions. These efforts are made to force the defectors to toe the line of the hegemon. Figure 1.3 illustrates the hegemonic stability theory.

From the example of US hegemony, it can be discerned that the chief motive is the maintenance of an international economic system based on neoliberal ideology. This can be done by encouraging free trade and enforcing international trade rules through international economic regimes such as the IMF, the World Bank and the WTO. Now, the question which arises is that whether this hegemony will continue for time immemorial or will it decline? The answer will be no and yes. In the long run, the hegemonic power of the hegemon is bound to decline. This happened in the case of the USA in the 1970s with the devaluation of dollar and end of Bretton Woods System (explained in Chapter 3).

Figure 1.3 Hegemonic Stability Theory

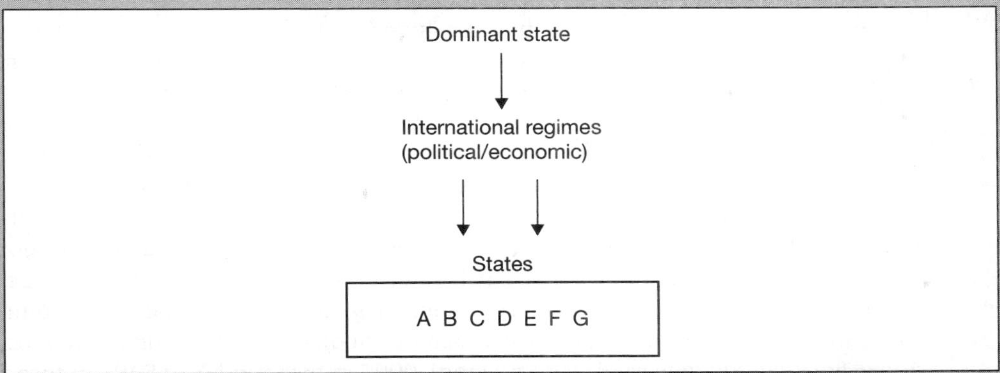

The significant cause for a hegemonic decline is the cost of burden that the hegemon has to bear to maintain the system over time. In the international political sphere, the US involvement globally like in the UN as well as interventions in the non-conformist states will at the end make it weary. The hegemon then would most likely try to relinquish its responsibilities. Former President Donald Trump withdrew from the Paris Climate Accord, cut the funding of the UN and its bodies, withdrew from Trans-Pacific Partnership, withdrew troops from Afghanistan and recently during the ongoing COVID-19 crisis gave an ultimatum of stopping the funding of the World Health Organization (WHO). It is being assumed that post-COVID-19, the leading state would be pursuing a more nationalist economic policy. Unilateralism is often an option for a hegemon and even a declining hegemon.

As the hegemon retracts under the burden of economic crisis in the post-COVID-9 scenario, the rest of the world will be supposed to be carrying out its political and economic activities in the absence of a hegemon who would be a powerful state but no longer a hegemon most likely. The world tends to become multipolar. There is the European Union, Japan and the BRICS (Brazil, Russia, India, China and South Africa) countries which most likely would determine their way of doing things in the world politics. China already has posed a great threat to the existing declining hegemon. The tariff war between the USA and China was a beginning and the blame game of coronavirus crisis of 2020 shows the challenges of rising power and declining power. India is also an emerging power. How it deals with the economic recession brought about by the corona crisis will determine its economic position in the international arena. President Joe Biden who succeeded President Donald Trump has expressed his willingness to engage with the world. The USA also engaged itself with a new alliance—the Quad or the Quadrilateral grouping—to contain the rising challenges from economic, political and security spheres from China. There is an attempt, therefore, to restore balance of power in IPE and global politics.

COVID-19 crisis of 2020 will determine the course of future global order, both political and economic, and whether there will be another hegemon or the old one will continue to dominate by using allies and likeminded states. Neoliberal thinkers like Keohane have opined that hegemony has created an atmosphere of interdependence in IPE. This will continue even if the power of the hegemon like the USA declines. The regimes created by the hegemon whether economic or political serve as a platform of expanding cooperation among self-interested actors. So in the absence of the hegemon, economic cooperation in particular will survive. Asia moved on even though the USA withdrew from the Trans-Pacific Partnership which is a multilateral economic agreement. COVID-19 has posited before the world community such issues which make cooperation in medical field, economic field and, obviously, political field inevitable.

Dependency Theory

'Dependency' literally means 'dependence' or 'reliance' on someone or something. In the realm of IPE, this dependence has to be viewed from an economic perspective. Such an examination reveals the economic dependence of some countries on the other. Such dependence is one of exploitation and creation of underdevelopment in the dependent countries. The actors concerned are obviously developed countries and the others being the developing world often identified as the 'Third World' countries. Figure 1.4 gives pictorial depiction of dependence.

Figure 1.4 Creation of Underdevelopment

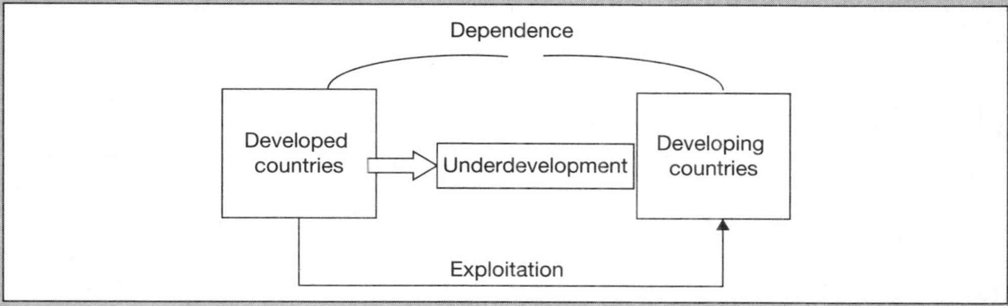

Brandt Line is an imaginary line demarcating the socio-economic and political division of the world into the Global North and the Global South. The Global North comprises the wealthy and rich countries and the Global South are the poor and developing countries of Asia, Africa and Latin America who have a legacy of colonial exploitation and subordination to a foreign rule. Because of the subordination and economic exploitation by the colonial masters and after that the neo-colonial masters, they face acute problems of underdevelopment. The resulting underdevelopment creates an unequal world. After a comparison of economic development among the developed and developing countries, the glaring inequality becomes evident (Table 1.2). The rich countries such as the USA, the UK, France and Germany have higher gross domestic product (GDP) than countries of Africa, Asia and Latin America.

An exception to this categorization in the recent times is the rise of the BRICS countries. Except Russia, the rest are part of the Global South but have shown steady economic progress.

The Global North represents the rich countries with high GDP, advanced technologies, research and development (R&D) and capabilities to influence global economy through

Table 1.2 A Comparative Analysis of GDP 2019

Developed Countries	GDP	Developing Countries	GDP
USA	$21.43 trillion	Colombia	$327.895 billion
UK	$2.74 trillion	Honduras	$23.803 billion
France	$2.07 trillion	Guatemala	$81.318 billion
Germany	$3.86 trillion	Nigeria	$446.543 billion
Italy	$2.014 trillion	Somalia	$7.70 billion
Switzerland	$703,165 million	Pakistan	$284.214 billion
Sweden	$531,408 million	Nepal	$29.813 billion
Canada	$1.741 trillion	Bhutan	$2.842 billion

international economic regimes. On the other hand, the Global South are the poor/poorer countries with unstable political regimes which are mostly non-democratic, high population, low welfare services, low GDP, high external borrowings and lack of advanced and sophisticated technologies.

It is this widening gap and inequalities of economic development between the Global South and the Global North that the dependency theorists hinted at. The unjust and unequal situation of extreme underdevelopment was the result of creation of dependence of the Global South on the Global North, first by colonization and thereafter by neo-colonization. To find out the creation of such dependence has been the central concern of the dependency theorists. The pioneers of dependency theory are Andre Gunder Frank (*Capitalism and Underdevelopment in Latin America,* 1967), Raul Prebisch (*Towards a Dynamic Development Policy for Latin America,* 1963) and Dos Santos ('The Structure of Dependence', 1970), among others.

Incorporating certain Marxist concepts, dependency theory went further to explain the dependence syndrome perpetuated by developed countries. Dos Santos points out that the dependence in the underdeveloped countries is caused by the development and expansion of economies of other country/ies which subject/s them to perpetual exploitative relation. The concepts that the dependency theorists introduce in their formulation of their proposition are that of 'core' and 'periphery'. Core countries are the developed countries and 'periphery' are the underdeveloped countries.

The IPE perpetuates an international capitalist system of which these are a part. There is an international division of labour between the two tiers of world economy—the core and the periphery, the 'haves' and the 'have-nots'. Since the peripheral countries have been the subject of exploitation of their formal colonial rulers, they continue to lag behind in their development process. Since these countries do not have adequate resources for bringing about economic development, poverty alleviation, welfare services and host of other developmental activities, they have to rely on the core countries for such supplies. As nothing comes for free, so when capital moves or technology is transferred from core to periphery, there are certain conditionalities that are attached. In the current international economic scenario, they are in the nature of structural adjustment programmes (SAPs) which underpin the necessity of opening markets, bringing down tariffs and encourage free trade. There is an overall subordination of indigenous productive capabilities due to high penetration of FDI, foreign institutional investment (FII) and advanced technologies from the core. High imports and rather low exports create a Balance of Payments deficit from institutions like the IMF and the World Bank, and this may put the peripheral countries at perpetual indebtedness and create debt crises in these countries.

Santos another proponent has further clarified that dependency is a common feature of the peripheral countries. This dependence is on the core countries. He opines that the relation of interdependence assumes the form of dependence between the dominant ones and the dependent ones. The dominant economies through this expansion in world economy can become self-sustaining, whereas the dependent ones can only do so by depending on the dominant ones. This can have either a positive or a negative impact on their immediate development.

Andre Gunder Frank puts forward some basic assumptions of dependency theory. The so-called developed countries were once undeveloped but never underdeveloped like the peripheral countries. The underdevelopment of the periphery is the consequence of relationship between metropolitan countries and their satellite countries in a capitalist world system.

Figure 1.5 International Economic Process and Creation of Dependence

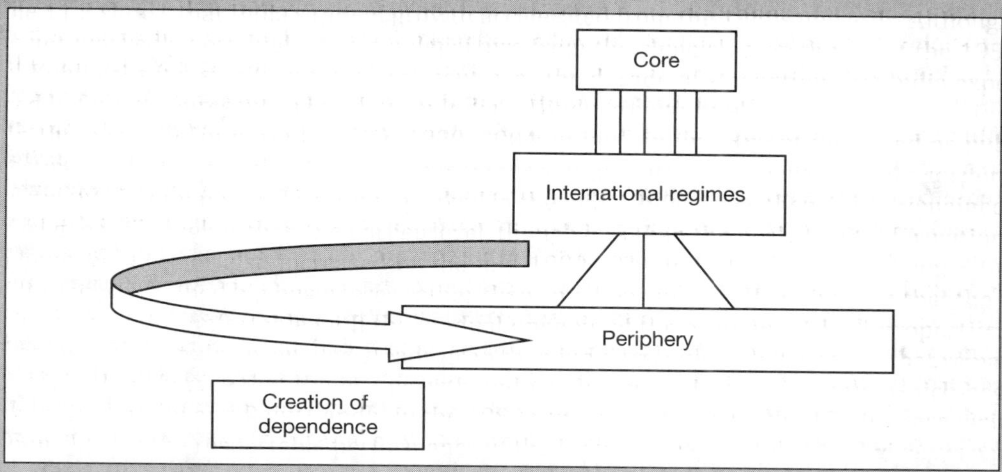

Underdevelopment in the periphery is the product of historical process of capitalist development in the core. The satellite countries are the colonies or neocolonial countries which connect all parts of the world system with the core countries and the regimes created by them. Regions such as Asia, Africa and Latin America have experienced colonial and neo-colonial exploitation previously by colonial countries and currently by advanced economies of the world and their established world economic order. Figure 1.5 gives a brief idea about the process of exploitation and domination in the international economic system.

Raul Prebisch, an Argentine economist, who was the executive director of UN Economic Commission for Latin America and the Caribbean (ECLAC) formed after the Second World War in 1948, was another proponent of dependency theory. The ECLAC examined the underdevelopment of Latin American countries and opined that the wealthy West European countries and the USA have created dependency vis-à-vis resource extraction from these countries. It can be deduced from the above propositions that as there is dependency in one part, there is domination on the other part. The dominance is perpetuated by external forces like unequal terms of trade, MNCs, international commodity market, FDI, FII, external debt and international economic regimes or any other means through which the unequal relationship is reinforced, consequently widening the inequality.

Dependency theory should also be read along with modern world systems theory which also has its roots in the Marxist tradition. The chief proponent has been Immanuel Wallerstein (*Modern World System: Capitalist Agriculture and the Origins of the European World-Economy in the Sixteenth Century,* 1974). He traces the origin of the current modern world system in the capitalist mode of production originating in Europe in the 16th century after the Industrial Revolution in Europe. The world before that was organized into world empires and the current world system as world economies. Wallerstein considers this capitalist mode of production as a system of production for sale in a market with the motive of profit-making and appropriation of this profit. He divided the world system spatially into regions. To the dual division of the world by the dependency theorists, he added another tier or division—semi-periphery. Semi-periphery region is characterized by features of core and periphery. It, like the periphery, is exploited by the core and, unlike the periphery, has a vibrant indigenous productive system. The core is advanced economies of the world which have sophisticated technologies, R&D, and capital along with access to world markets with control over resources of other countries of the periphery and semi-periphery. The periphery supplies raw materials and cheap labour. Semi-peripheral countries are attractive destinations of capital flows from the core countries and MNCs. However, these distinctions are not permanent. The countries can gravitate between core, periphery and semi-periphery. BRICS countries are a pointer in this direction. They cannot be classified as periphery and at the upper echelon of the semi-periphery. The relationship between core with the periphery and semi-periphery is one of domination and subordination reinforced by exploitation (Figure 1.6).

Samir Amin (*Unequal Development: An Essay on the Social Formations of Peripheral Capitalism,* 1976) said that the capitalist mode of production is made exclusive to the core rather than the periphery. Unevenness in the modes of production in the periphery is best exploited by the core countries. The rush of foreign capital and MNCs leads to the destruction of the pre-capitalist modes of production of the periphery as they cannot match up to the challenges posed by the external forces from the core countries. Therefore, growth is blocked and underdevelopment is accentuated. This hinders the autonomous development of the peripheral countries. The post-colonial scholarship also suggests the continuance of the persistent form of colonial forms of power in contemporary world politics, which is seen in social construction of race, gender, class and relation of power and subordination.

The shortcomings of the dependency theory are that they generalize the experiences of the periphery. The peripheral countries may be at different levels of economic development and

Figure 1.6 **Modern World System Theory**

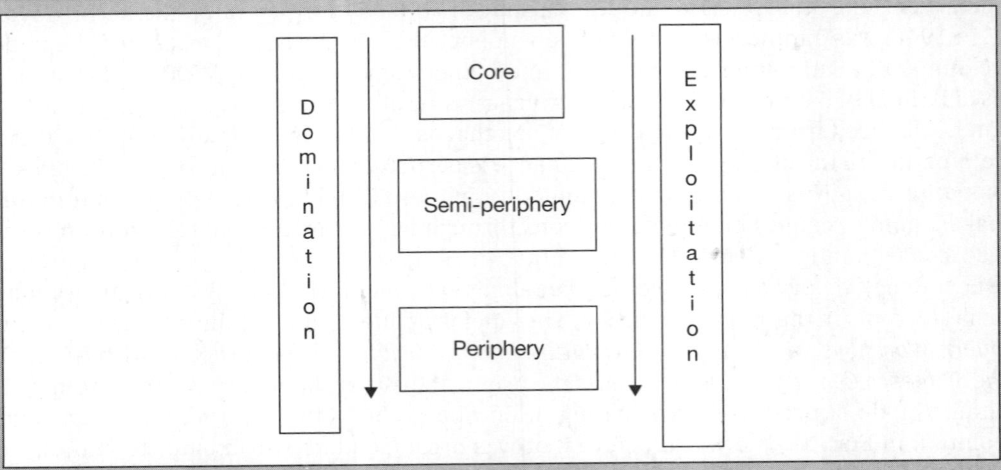

their relations with the other peripheral states may not be equitable. Dependency theorists have not given insights into the domestic structure of the states which influence their economic policies. Domestic factors such as political ruling elites, bureaucrats, pressure groups and social factors have not been dealt by the dependency theorists. Moreover, the peripheral countries of Eastern Europe integrated into the EU contributing to the Union's southward and eastward expansion. This reflected that these peripheral and semi-peripheral countries embraced similar economic pattern of the rich West European countries, which is market economy. Besides countries like those members of the Organization of the Petroleum Exporting Countries (OPEC) have rich oil resources but the pricing is greatly determined by politicking with the USA and the fixation of global oil price. Now, they have been caught in the politics of pricing between Russia, the USA and Saudi Arabia plus the other OPEC members. The year 2020 saw the lowest international crude price following the outbreak of the COVID-19 pandemic. The financial recession that has set in 2020 due to the pandemic is further going to push the poor and the developing countries into financial hardships and widen the great divide between the rich and the poor countries. This may lead to more dependency on foreign aid and external borrowing which might augment another round of debt crisis and underdevelopment. The countries of Africa are finding it hard to fight the pandemic in the absence of resources and infrastructure.

Conclusion

Theories are helpful tools in understanding any discipline. Theory is essential for any discipline to help in research and for providing the basis for explanation, analysis and prediction. So it is not strange that IPE will also have theories of its own to help in understanding the working of economic order, questions of development, challenges before states, newer dimensions of development, factors such as globalization, liberalization and financialization, and so on.

Realism, liberalism and liberal interdependence theory, hegemonic stability theory and **dependency theory** are the most dominant theories of IPE. Realism gives a statist view with national power and national interest playing a role in international politics as well as international economics. They also offer a model of an IPE with a reigning hegemon to provide stability to the IPE.

Liberalism and neoliberalism focus on less intervention of state and more reliance on laissez-faire. Free market economy and liberalization in place of heavy state interference are the cult of liberalism and neo-liberalism. Hegemonic stability theory views that order in world politics can be brought about by a single dominant power by the creation of international regimes. A hegemon who is a dominant power in global politics, having the willingness to maintain the stability of world order, is needed to bring about order in international system. Finally, both the dependency theory and the modern world systems theory look at dependence of the developing and poor countries as a creation of the developed countries. These theories singularly try to give an idea of the world economic order and functioning in their own way. If these theories are combined, then an integrated world view on the processes of IPE can be acquired.

Summary

There have been four major trends of theories in IPE: **realism, liberalism and liberal interdependence theory, hegemonic stability theory** and **dependency theory.**

The **realists** view the international political scenario as anarchy where each state pursues its own national interests. To fulfil this necessity, states are engaged in the pursuit of increasing national power on the basis of national capabilities. This results in an incessant struggle for power. Neo-realism advocated the self-help model and security dilemma. The realists have forwarded the concept of **balance of power** as a key to the restoration of stability in a world of anarchy that can be best done by forming alliances and counter alliances. Realism tries to address the question of distribution of international power in such a way that the form of IPE comes to be dominated by a single hegemon.

The classical liberalism's assumptions are that democratic sovereign states do not wage war against another democratic state. Such democratic sates are believed to comprise market economies, rule of law and democratic representation. There have been various strands of liberalism such as liberal institutionalism and complex interdependence model. The latter talks about interstate communications, and trans-governmental and transnational communications, creating an interdependent world. **Neoliberalism** emerged in the post-Second World War period with the abandonment of Keynesian economics and renewal of classical liberal ideas which emphasized less state intervention and working of free market economies.

Hegemonic stability theory views that order in world politics can be brought about by a single dominant power by the creation of international regimes. Hegemony is a situation in which one state has the power and capability to maintain essential rules governing the interstate relations as well as the willingness to do so.

Dependency theory contends that the unjust and unequal situation of extreme underdevelopment was the result of creation of dependence of the Global South on the Global North, first by colonization and thereafter by neo-colonization. It sees the world divided into core and periphery, and creation of dependence of periphery on core.

Modern world systems theory proposes a three-tier division of the world into core, semi-periphery and periphery countries. The core or the advanced economies exploit the semi-periphery and periphery and create underdevelopment.

REVIEW AND REFLECTION QUESTIONS

1. We have studied four theories of IPE. Which one do you think corresponds to the real functioning of global economy?
2. Realism works on the propositions of national interest and national power. Following the basic assumptions of the political realist approach examine the understanding of IPE.
3. Liberalism underscores the importance of an open market economy and less state intervention. In the light of the above, analyse the main tenets of liberalism and neoliberalism in understanding IPE.

4. A model of complex interdependence has been forwarded by Nye and Keohane. How relevant do you think the theory is in the contemporary IPE?
5. Do you consider hegemonic stability theory to be reflective of a particular period of functioning of IPE or do you think it to be reflective of the current economic order?
6. Dependency is a condition that is created by the dominant core states. Do you agree or not? Give reasons.
7. Examine the dependency theory and modern world systems theory in comprehending the process of working of the IPE. How do these theories portray the underdevelopment of the semi-peripheral and peripheral countries by the advanced core countries?

Bibliography

Baylis, John, Steve Smith, and Patricia Owens. 2005. *Globalization of World Politics: An Introduction to International Relations*. 3rd ed. Oxford: Oxford University Press.

———. 2017. *An Introduction of World Politics: An Introduction to International Relations*. Oxford: Oxford University Press.

Bloomberg. 2020. 'Trump Signs $2 Trillion Virus Bill, Largest Ever U.S. Stimulus.' Available at https://www.bloomberg.com/news/articles/2020-03-27/trump-signs-2-trillion-virus-bill-largest-ever-u-s-stimulus (accessed on 11 May 2020).

Chirico, JoAnn. 2014. *Globalization: Prospects and Problems*. Thousand Oaks, CA: SAGE Publications.

Devtak, Richard, Anthony Burke, and Jim George. 2014. *An Introduction to International Relations*. New York, NY: Cambridge University Press.

Dunne, Tim, Milja Kurki, and Steve Smith. 2015. *International Relations Theory: Discipline and Diversity*. New Delhi: Oxford University Press.

Gilpin, Robert. 1987. *The Political Economy of International Relations*. Princeton, NJ: Princeton University Press.

———. 2001. *Global Political Economy: Understanding the International Economic Order*. Princeton, NJ: Princeton University Press.

Harvey, David. 2007. *A Brief History of Neoliberalism*. New York, NY: Oxford University Press.

Kegley, W. Charles, and R. Eugene Wittkopf. 1997. *World Politics: Trends and Transformation*. New York, NY: St. Martin's Press.

Keohane, Robert. 1984. *After Hegemony: Cooperation and Discord in the World Political Economy*. Princeton, NJ: Princeton University Press.

Peet, Richard. 2010. *Unholy Trinity: The IMF, World Bank and WTO*. New York, NY: Zed Books.

The Statesman. 2020, 14 May. 'FM Decodes Rs.20 Lakh Crore Package.' *The Statesman*, Kolkata.

2 Introduction and Historical Overview: Capitalist Transformation

LEARNING OBJECTIVES

- Acquiring knowledge about the transition from feudalism to capitalism with perspectives from different scholars working on this
- Learning about basic features of capitalism
- Getting to know about evolution of capitalism over time, especially before the Second World War
- Knowing about the 'golden age of capitalism'

Introduction

Maurice Dobb's *Studies in the Development of Capitalism* is an important contribution towards the study of decline of feudalism and the rise of capitalism. He pointed out at the inefficiency of feudalism as a system of production along with the growing needs of the ruling class for revenue which primarily contributed to the decline of feudalism. Overexploitation of the labour force or the serfs led to the end of feudalism. Though the process was not so simple and for a long period of time there was simultaneous existence of feudalism and capitalism. It was through the Industrial Revolution that the final victory of capitalism was achieved. When capitalism reached a monopoly stage through corporations, joint stock companies (JSCs) and cartels there began the quest for markets beyond one's domestic market. This led to imperialism and colonialism. In other words, there was re-division of the world through war and military ventures. Finally, with the end of the Second World War, some kind of stability could be established in IPE through the establishment of the Bretton Woods Conference of 1944. Bretton Woods institutions such as the IMF and the World Bank along with the adoption of dollar as a system of payments. Dollar was itself convertible into gold. Gold exchange standards with gold and convertible currencies were fixed only against the US dollars. The US hegemony was established replacing Britain which was the erstwhile hegemon. This stability in the international economy continued till the beginning of the 1970s. This was the golden age of capitalism. This came to an end with the oil shocks, devaluation of dollar in 1973 and introduction of float exchange rate. There started a neoliberal era based on the Washington Consensus and the mission of exporting free market economy all around the globe followed by debt crisis in developing countries in the 1980s, financial crisis in East Asia and 2008 global meltdown leading to the US subprime crisis. This chapter gives an idea about the emergence of capitalism with the decline of feudalism, characteristics of capitalism, monopoly capitalism, monopoly corporations, imperialism and, of course, the golden age of capitalism.

European Feudalism and Transition to Capitalism

According to Rodney Hilton, Karl Marx while writing about 'feudalism' used the term to refer to a social order whose principal feature was domination of the rest in the society, primarily the peasants, by the military and landowning aristocracy. Marx meant that the domination resulted in the income of the ruling class once the labour of the direct producer met his/her subsistence necessities and the surplus moved into the pockets of the ruling class. The feudal mode of production was characterized by exploitative relationship between the landowners and subordinated peasants. In this system, the surplus beyond the subsistence of the peasants whether through direct labour or in rent in kind or money was transferred under coercive sanction to the ruling landowners. This relationship came to be termed as 'serfdom' grossly.

There have been several debates regarding the transition from feudalism to capitalism. The forerunners have been Maurice Dobb, Paul Sweezy, Rodney Hilton, Christopher Hill, Georges Lefebvre, Kohachiro Takahashi, Giuliano Procacci, John Merrington and Eric Hobsbawm to mention a few.

Starting with Maurice Dobb, who in his *Studies in the Development of Capitalism*, dedicates a whole section to the decline of feudalism and rise of capitalism. According to Dobb, feudalism as a mode of production will be virtually identical to serfdom that comprises an obligation laid on the producer by force and independently of his/her own volition to fulfil certain economic demands of an overlord. These demands take the form of services to be performed or of dues to be paid in money or in kind. Dobb also gave characteristics of European feudalism since this was the region where capitalism emerged and evolved over time. These are as follows:

- A low level of technique in which the instruments of production are simple and generally inexpensive. The act of production is mainly individual and the division of labour at a very primitive level of development.
- Production is for the immediate need of the household or village community and not for a wider market.
- Demesne[1] farming or farming of the lords' estate and often on a considerable scale by compulsory labour services.
- Political decentralization, with the conditional holding of land by lords on some kind of service tenure.
- The possession by a lord of judicial or quasi-judicial functions in relation to the dependent population.

Dobb also comes to explain the factors for the decline of feudalism. The revival of commerce in Western Europe after AD 1100 and its disruptive effect on feudal society is a sufficiently

[1] A piece of land that is attached to a manor and retained by the owner for their own use.

familiar story. How the growth of trade carried in its wake the trader and the trading community, which nourished itself like an alien body within the pores of feudal society; how with exchange came an increasing percolation of money into the self-sufficiency or manorial economy; how the presence of the merchant encouraged a growing inclination to barter surplus products and produce for the market. The consequences for the texture of the old order were radical enough. Money revenue as well as services of bondmen grew to be a lordly ambition; a market in loans developed and also a market in land.

The tendency that developed to commute labour services for a money payment and either to lease out the seigniorial demesne for a money rent or to continue its cultivation with hired labour obviously had the growth of the market and money dealings as their necessary condition. Whether the connection was as simple as direct or whether the widening of the market can be held to have been a sufficient condition for the decline of feudalism is not beyond question. Dobb argues that there are evidences that growth of money economy per se led to the intensification of serfdom and there is evidence that it was also a cause of feudal decline. Some outstanding case was of the 'recrudescence of feudalism' in Eastern Europe at the end of the 15th century in the Baltic states of Poland, Bohemia, Hungary and Russia under the enlightened despots. Therefore, to Dobb, rise of trade alone could not bring a decline to feudalism. There were other factors at work too.

Dobb argues that the evidence may not be plentiful or conclusive, still he feels that the evidence showed the inefficiency of feudalism. Feudalism as a system of production coupled with the growing needs of the ruling class for revenue, which was primarily responsible for its decline. This was because the need for additional revenue promoted an increase in the pressure on the producer to a point where this pressure became literally unendurable. For Dobb, therefore, the essential cause of the breakdown of feudalism was overexploitation of the labour force, serfs deserted the lords' estates *en masse* and those who remained were too few and too overworked to enable the system to maintain itself on the old basis. Dobb emphasizes that such developments rather than the rise of trade forced the feudal ruling class to adopt those expediments like commutation of labour services, leasing demesne lands to tenant farmers and so on which finally led to the transformation of productive relations in the countryside.

The result was economic exhaustion, flight from the land and peasant rebellion. Overexploitation and stagnant productivity resulted in a decline in population after 1300. Subsequent labour shortages, peasant resistance and threat of flight led to widespread commutation of labour to money rent. The manorial system was further weakened by the thinning of the ranks of the nobility through war, the growing practice of leasing demesne, the emergence of a stratum of rich and middling peasants differentiated from the mass of peasant poor and the growing use of wage labour. By the end of the 15th century, the economic basis of the feudal system had disintegrated.

Sweezy agreed with Dobb that serfdom was the dominant relation of production in Western feudalism. But organized around the economically autarchic manor, feudalism was a mode of production for use and as such tended to stagnation. An external force, the growth of trade and increase in production for exchange, was necessary to destabilize the system. Sweezy argued that long-distance trade brought into existence a creative force that created a system of production for exchange alongside the old feudal system of production for use. These two systems acted upon one another and finally influence running from the exchange economy to the use economy. The factors which induced such trends were as follows.

- **Inefficiency of the manorial organization of production:** Manufactured goods could be bought more cheaply than they could be made and this pressure to buy generated a pressure to sell. This pushed feudal estates within the orbit of the exchange economy.
- **Existence of exchange value made possession of wealth possible and change in attitude of producers:** Riches/wealth could be accumulated not in the form of perishables but in more convenient money or claims to money. The old feudal lords assumed business-like attitude and there was a growing need for revenue for them.
- **Change in the development of the tastes of the feudal ruling class:** They wanted more revenue to procure luxury for themselves. As commerce spread, it created the desire for new articles of consumption.
- **Rise of towns which became centres and breeders of exchange economy:** It also opened up to the servile population of the countryside the prospect of a freer and better life. This was the major cause for flight from land which was the main cause of decline in feudalism.

Sweezy contends that the superior efficiency of more highly specialized production, the greater gains to be made by producing for the market rather than for immediate use and the greater attractiveness of town life to the worker were more than enough to end feudalism. Sweezy agrees with Dobb, as discussed above, that this did not mean a complete end to serfdom. Both feudalism and progress of trade went hand in hand as 'recrudescence of feudalism' or second serfdom. When the expansion of trade instils a lust for gain into a ruling class in this position, the result is not the development of new forms of exploitation but the intensification of old forms of exploitation. Sweezy agrees that the decline of Western European feudalism was due to overexploitation by the ruling class of society's labour power.

Eric Hobsbawm points out towards the universality of feudalism, though it varied widely across the world; however, whether there was a universal tendency of feudalism to develop into capitalism is doubtful. In the case of Europe and part Mediterranean area (Italy and Rhine Valley), there was this tendency, whereas the countries of Asia and Africa experienced such a phenomenon only when they came in contact with European colonialism, but with uneven development. The European capitalism marched ahead towards its triumph through conquest or colonial exploitation of America, Asia, Africa and parts of Eastern Europe and primary accumulation of capital finally gained its victory.

Hobsbawm also points out the stages of economic development as follows:

- The period of relapse following the break-up of the West Roman Empire followed by gradual evolution of a feudal economy and most probably a recession in the 10th century AD and moving towards 'the Dark Ages' in Medieval Europe.
- In the period following the 'High Middle Ages' of Medieval Europe, there was widespread rapid economic development from about 1000 AD to the early 14th century. This period was the peak of feudalism. This period witnessed growth in population, agriculture, manufacturing, towns and cities as well as Crusades into the Middle East, emigration, colonization and setting up of trading posts abroad.
- The period of major 'feudal crisis' in the 14th and the 15th centuries followed by the collapse of large-scale feudal agriculture, manufacturers and international trade.
- The period of renewal of expansion from the mid-17th century marked for the first time the break in the base and superstructure of feudal society with the Reformation

movement and bourgeois revolution clearing the field for capitalist development. This was followed by all-out conquest into America and the Indian Ocean countries which Marx had described as the beginning of the capitalist era.
- Presence of fundamental contradiction of the feudal society that drives towards the triumph of capitalism, though this has not been clearly stated by theorists. Still around the 14th century, for example, not only large-scale feudal demesne agriculture collapsed but Italian and Flemish textile industries also collapsed with their capitalist employers and proletarian workers. At best, it can be explained as those tendencies of capitalist development were there but time and again failed to burst out of the feudal integument or shell of feudalism.
- Outside the 'heartland' of capitalist development (West Europe), they were integrated into the world market since the 16th century, for example, Indian textile manufacturing, but the question is 'how'. The European powers establishing colonies and creating dependent economies actually set in motion opposite tendency in these countries. A large part of America was turned into slave economies to serve the needs of European capitalism. So were large parts of Africa pushed into slave trade and also large parts of Eastern Europe were under the neo-feudal economies for the same reason. Deliberately, the European capitalism de-industrialized the colonies and semi-colonies as soon as they looked like competing with home production as in India when it attempted to supply its own market instead of relying on imports from Britain. The total effect was that capitalism created uneven development and divided the world into developed and underdeveloped countries with a relation being one of exploiting and exploited.

Rodney Hilton's observation into the transition from feudalism to capitalism is quite noteworthy. According to Hilton, fluctuating pressure by the ruling class for occupying the peasant surplus labour or surplus product was the root cause of the technical progress and improved feudal organization which led to the enlargement of the disposable surplus. He says that this is the basis for the growth of simple commodity production, seigneurial incomes in cash, international luxury trade and urbanization. The peasants' effort to retain the surplus to subsistence led to resistance movement. This was also crucial to the development of the rural communes, the extension of free tenure and status, and the freeing of peasant and artisan economies for the development of commodity production, ultimately leading to the emergence of the capitalist entrepreneur. The 14th and the 15th centuries have witnessed successful peasant resistance to the lord's pressure, which is the critical turning point in the history of the 'prime mover' towards capitalism.

Hilton says that neither feudalism nor capitalism is easy to understand as phrases in economic history. Society and its movement must be examined in their totality in order to examine and analyse the significance of uneven developments, contradictions between the economic foundations of society and its ideas and institutions. Dobb and Sweezy among others have attempted to give us a picture of transition from feudalism to capitalism; still, an exhaustive explanation may not be available as to what actually happened. Tentative trends could be pointed out by scholars.

Let us conclude with Susan Strange's analysis of the production structure. The European feudal production structure was based primarily on agriculture. The Church factor played an important role in Europe which was the uniting authority running across Europe from Ireland to Bohemia and from Italy to Denmark. In the medieval period, the authority of the Church over the production structure was greater than that of the temporal rulers of states or the local lords and barons. The cultural and social unity provided by the Church created a primitive kind of common market in Europe. This also made possible the accumulation of capital, especially by the great religious orders. As the Church's authority declined due to the Protestant Reformation movement and the Treaty of Westphalia of 1648, the nation states emerged in Europe. They inherited from the earlier regime an economy already pregnant with the growing points of technical change and a commercial structure ready for exploitation by a nascent merchant class.

Capitalism: Basic Features, Accumulation and Crisis, the Modern Corporations, Monopoly Capitalism and Imperialism

Basic Features of Capitalist Mode of Production

To identify the basic features of the capitalist mode of production, a differentiation with pre-capitalist society would make the task easier. The pre-capitalist society and capitalism differ primarily in the method of exploitation. Although all are class societies, there are differences in the mode of exploitation. This will become visible once we illustrate with an example. In a slave society, as Marx had pointed out, 'the slave did not sell his labour power to the master, any more than ox, its service to the peasant. The slave, together with his labour power, has been sold once for all to his owner'. Therefore, there was direct domination of the slave owner over the means of production and thereby direct exploitation. In a capitalist system, the method of exploitation is flexible. Under this system, wage labourers are free to sell their labour to anyone who owns the means of production or the capitalist. One is not tied with the owner of means of production. One is selling one's own labour and not himself/herself like the slave.

Another feature which differentiates the pre-capitalist and capitalist societies is the motive of production in these two societies. If the base of production in a pre-capitalist society is 'need oriented', in a capitalist society, it is 'profit oriented'. 'Capital' is the driving force of a capitalist society. In a pre-capitalist society, 'consumption' was for the dominant class. The pre-capitalist mode of production aimed at their comfortable life and luxurious consumption. The exploitation of the dominated class served the consumption of the dominant class. In a capitalist mode of production, the production process aims to produce more so that greater surplus can be generated. This is not used for self-consumption of the dominant class but more so for sale in the market. So earnings or the surplus earned from the production process in a capitalist system goes partly for consumption of the dominant class but mostly for continuous 'valorization of capital'. This means a relentless pursuit for more and more accumulation. This valorization process involves various production and exchange processes such as bank capital, merchant capital, industrial capital and finance capital.

The other important feature of capitalist mode of production is 'value'. The value of labour for Adam Smith and David Ricardo was the quantity of labour necessary to produce something that comprised its value. For Marx, the quantity of labour that produces the value is 'social necessary labour time'. This means the labour time required to produce any use value under the conditions of production in a given society with average degree of skill and intensity of labour in that society.

Capitalism is also linked with money form of value. The exchange system of human labour as a form of commodity production depends on the money form of value. This money form of value is the driving force of production and exchange transaction under capitalism. This becomes more important when it becomes a real source of surplus value and real vehicle of production.

In the pre-capitalist society, money does not play a primary role. It is just a medium of exchange in a simple economic transaction with simple circulation. In this kind of society, the producer of a simple commodity with a particular use value sells the commodity in the market and earns money. With this money that person buys some other commodities for personal consumption simply because that individual does not produce that commodity. Here, labour power does not assume the form of commodity and labour is not bought and sold at the marketplace. This is just an economy of simple commodity production and thereby no systematic process of accumulation takes place which is the cardinal principle of capitalism. In a capitalist commodity production system, there is 'commodification' or 'commoditization' of labour power. This means that labour can be purchased and sold in the market.

The other feature of capitalism is 'surplus value'. Unlike the simple commodity system where personal consumption is the sole motive in a capitalist system, the motive is profit by generating surplus value. According to Marx, in a capitalist system of production, the only aim of the movement of capital is to increase the sum of the value that is initially invested.

Therefore, in the capitalist system of production, there is presence of a social relationship between a class of property owners and the propertyless. There is exploitation and creation of surplus value that is appropriated by the propertied class.

Capitalism, therefore, assumes the existence of private property, appropriation of surplus, profit-making and accumulation of wealth. This creates inequality and unequal relations as shown in Chapter 7 by Marx and the advocates of Marxist ideology. Price mechanism is also a feature of capitalism as this means free working of the supply and demand forces without any intervention of the state. Only market is important which should work free from interferences. As we will see below, the growing importance of corporations and, at present, MNCs, and growth of finance capital has taken capitalism to a new stage of exploitation. Here, we find exploitation of developing countries by the developed ones with the spread of neocolonialism or neo-imperialism subtly through the international financial institutions and international trade regimes along with working of the MNCs and TNCs.

Contemporary capitalism exhibits a few different characteristics from the above. It is difficult to identify exactly the timeline of the emergence of contemporary capitalism or trace the 'periodization' of capitalist development. Fine and Harris in their *Rereading Capital* (1979) define periodization as the effects of the development of the forces and relations of production on the form of social relations within the mode of production which will reveal itself in the methods of appropriating and controlling surplus value. They further contend that these methods will assume increasingly socialized forms as the socialization of production progresses.

As we will see in Chapter 4, capitalists have to adjust to new organizational forms and competitiveness. While Fordism gave them mass production technologies, post-Fordism saw a shift in production to customized delivery of products/commodities. At the macroeconomic level, there have been changes. From Keynesian interventionist state, there has been a shift to a neoliberal state based on market economy, internationalization of capital, financialization and globalization. From this point, it becomes a task to identify the current developments vis-à-vis the general theory of capitalist mode of production, appropriation and accumulation. Ernest Mandel in his *Marxist Economic Theory* (1968) had referred to this as a 'synthesis of economic history and economic theory'. He identified this new stage of capitalism as 'neo-capitalism' or 'late capitalism'. He argues that the uniqueness of 'late capitalism' is in the third technological revolution which is driving up profit rates, increased military spending, permanent inflation, increased role of state and planning across all organizations. Now, we will discuss the process of accumulation, monopoly capitalism, monopoly corporations and imperialism one after the other.

Accumulation and Crisis

Accumulation of the capitalist is the most important feature of the capitalist mode of production. Surplus extraction and generation of profit lead to accumulation of wealth by the capitalist. Now how is this surplus value created? This is an important question to be pondered upon. Marx had pointed out that the capitalist or who is the owner of production finds a commodity in the market whose use value creates value more than the value of the commodity itself. Marx finds this commodity to be the 'labour power'. Two conditions are also necessary to use labour power as a commodity and generate surplus. On the one hand, there must be people who are legally free and voluntarily ready to sell their labour power and, on the other, they must not be owners of any means of production, that is, propertyless. According to Marx, 'the value of labour power is determined as in case of every other commodity, by labour time[2] necessary for the production and consequently also the reproduction, of this special article'.

The capitalist needs to worry about the subsistence necessary for the maintenance of the production system. Therefore, the capitalist ensures that the labour power should be equal to the cost of its reproduction. This is necessary to generate more surplus. The difference between the money invested or the total value and the value of labour power is the surplus value. The whole process is unequal. The labourers who are the real producers receive lesser value from the capitalist than the value they have produced. This is exploitation and surplus generation for Marx. This can be depicted as follows:

1. Money invested (M) — Labour wages (L) — Price of commodities (P) = Surplus (S)

   (Total money)

2. Money invested (M) — Labour wages (L) — Price of reproduced commodities (RP) = Surplus (S)

   In both (1) and (2), labour time (L) is same.

   Therefore, in the first case, M – L = P, P > M = Surplus (S)

   In the second case of reproduction, RP > M = More surplus (S)

[2] The time required to reproduce the value of the labour power.

Given L is of lesser value than P and RP, there is generation of S.

$P > L$ and $RP > L$, whereas reproduction is done at the same price as production, that is, L is of same value at both stages. Therefore, more surplus is generated and accumulation takes place.

We can describe this, following Marx in his *Capital,* as a circulation of capital. Money capital is what the capitalists invest in production of commodities. The capitalists procure means of production which is constant capital and labour power which is the variable capital. The productive capital is the combination of means of production and labour power. The commodities are created out of these, known as the commodity capital. Selling these commodities in the market will give money capital which is much more than the original money capital invested. Therefore, surplus is generated.

$$\text{Money Capital (M)} = \text{Commodities (C)}$$

$$\text{Commodities Sold (C)} = \text{Money Capital } (M^1)$$

$$M^1 > M = \text{Surplus}$$

However, this is a case which Marx proposed in the case of circulation of industrial capital. This does not include merchant capital or trading capital, insurance capital and the like. They do appropriate surplus but the production of surplus value does not create their capital function. It is only in the capitalist commodity production that capital enters into three stages of money capital, productive capital and commodity capital in order to generate surplus leading to accumulation. This kind of production of surplus value refers to an early phase of capitalism where techniques of production almost remain unchanged.

Surplus can be generated by specialization of production and enhancing efficiency. It can also be done by speeding up labour through mechanization of production process. However, this may bring about technological unemployment and hurt the capitalist in the long run. Marx said that mass production in place of mass of labour power will create the reserve army of labour. Introduction of machines in the production process or in other words labour displacing technology will throw a huge number of labour force into involuntary unemployment. Ricardo in his *On Principles of Political Economy and Taxation* (1817) also pointed out the same as he talked about redundancy of labour from the productive process due to mechanization. Keynes in his 'Economic Possibilities for Our Grand-children' in *Essays in Persuasion* (1963) during the years of Great Depression had also expressed same thinking. He said that all manufacturing, agriculture and so on with high mechanization may not be labour intensive. This will cause technological unemployment.

In the case of financial capital or the interest-bearing capital, it is the interest that is the price that is paid. It is like a profit. The interest-bearing capital moves from the owner to the industrialist and then the person invests in profit-making commodity production. Part of the return goes to the industrial capitalists as profit and from them to the lenders as interests. There is also a credit system for loans, shares stocks and bonds but is always suffering from insecurity. It is of a speculative nature. The speculations in the capital markets lead to financial crisis as it happened in the global meltdown due to sub-prime crisis and bubble burst in the USA (discussed in Chapter 6).

Crisis of capitalism as seen by Marx can be explained only as 'the real movement of capitalistic production, competition and credit'. In a simple commodity production system, a crisis is unlikely as 'Say's Laws of Markets' upholds that commodity against money and money against commodity, that is, C – M – C model goes uninterrupted in a simple commodity production society. There is no overproduction and no crisis, therefore. Ricardo says that one produces with the aim to consume or sell and one sells with the goal to purchase some other commodity useful for that individual. So the C – M – C goes uninterrupted. Productions according to him are always brought by productions or by services. Money is the medium to bring about such exchanges.

Marx was quite critical about the above view. An individual may not be prompted to buy just because one has sold. Money is more than the medium as pointed above, a medium by which exchange is effected. Money is a medium by which exchange is split into two transactions involving sale and purchase. Here lies the root of the crisis. If one sells and fails to buy, then there will be overproduction and, hence, crisis. Even this possibility lies in simple commodity production when there may be mismatch between sale and purchase.

In simple commodity production, as we have seen above, the circulation form is C – M – C where the first C may have none or very little value to the producer but the second C is desired so it will have greater user value. However, in a capitalist production system, the circulation is characterized by $M - C - M^1$. The M at the beginning and M^1 at the end are not the same. M^1 has exchange value and not use value. The capitalist begins one's venture with money (M) which he invests in the form of capital. He puts them into circulation in exchange of means of production and labour power (C) and then transforms this into commodity for sale in market and again gains money (M^1). However, the $M^1 - M = \Delta M$ must be positive or there must be profit. Appropriation of more and more wealth is the motive of the capitalist. On the other hand, for the great majority of the people like the labourers, the circulation type is C – M – C. The labour converts his/her labour power in making the commodity and converts it into money to get the basic necessities of one's life.

The capitalist circulation process is as follows:

$$M - C - M^1$$

$$M^1 - M = \Delta M$$

$$\Delta M > M$$

Accumulation of the worker is different from the accumulation of the capitalist. The labour may have inclination for use values and accumulation may take the form of bank savings account, insurance and the like. For the capitalist, ΔM is very important, and this must be in large quantity and in positive. The proportion of ΔM must emerge bigger than his/her original capital. This is what is identified as profit. Maximization of profit is the ultimate motive of the capitalist. Any interruption in the circulation process will end up in withholding the buying power from the market and there will be contraction in the circulation process. This will lead to overproduction and curtailment of production itself and the capitalist will reconsider his/her option of circulating his/her M or capital in the market.

In one case, if the rate of profit is in the negative, that is, ΔM is less than the M invested, then the capitalist will withdraw the capital and circulation will contract and a crisis followed by overproduction will start. If the rate of profit falls, then also the motivation of the capitalist to further invest might disappear. There are also chances that even if the rate of profit is in the positive, the capitalist might cut on the production and there can be a crisis. Once the profit goes below the usual rate of profit, there can be a curtailment of production by the capitalist. In such a case, the capitalist can shift the capital out of that particular industry and invest in some other. If here also the rate of profit goes below the usual, then the capitalist will not reinvest until conditions become favourable. Such decision of postponement of reinvestment will interrupt the circulation process and a crisis will set in. There can be, therefore, crisis due to falling tendency of the rate of profit. Crises can emerge from disproportionality among the value lines of production and underconsumption of the masses.

The Modern Corporations

Before going into the discussion about corporations, it will be pertinent to look into the cause of rise of corporations. The capitalists accumulate wealth and thereby increase one's capital and invest in large-scale production. This is what Marx called concentration of capital. However, Marx talks about centralization of capital which is different from accumulation and concentration of capital. Regarding centralization of capital, there is a change in the distribution of capital. Capital gets centralized in a few hands as it gets deprived to many hands. Centralization is the result of economies of production. Competition among capitalists cannot be ruled out. The battle is won by cheapening of prices of commodities which again depends upon the productiveness of labour and scales of production. In this process, larger capitals are definitely to emerge as winners.

Centralization can be achieved through credit system as well as through banks and even financial machinery of investment houses, security markets and the like. The credit system at first appears to be a helper but in the process draws the money resources scattered in the society into hands of individuals or associated capitalists through invisible threads. This gradually leads not to expropriation of smaller capitalists by larger but 'the amalgamation of a number of capitals which already exist or are in the process of formation ... by the smoother road of forming stock companies'. This would go on, and ultimately, the end of centralization would leave with one firm and for the society the end will be reached when 'the entire social capital would be united either in the hands of one single capitalist, or in those of one single corporation'. Ultimately, centralization leads to replacement of competition among a large number of producers. This gives rise to monopolistic or semi-monopolistic corporations and their control over markets.

Marx sees this as a social control over production as transformation will take place whereby functioning of the capitalist would be like the role of a manager or an administrator of other people's capital. It will make the owners of the capital into mere owners or mere money capitalists. He was hinting at the emergence of stock companies. Marx points out at the development of a new aristocracy of finance in the form of promoters, speculators, nominal directors and the like. He further goes to emphasize the process as a 'whole system of swindling and cheating by means of corporations juggling, stock jobbing and stock speculation. It is private production without the control of private property'.

According to Rudolf Hilferding in his work *Finance Capital: A Study of the Latest Phase of Capitalist Development* (1910), where he proposed a theory of corporations, in the corporate form of organization there is the 'freeing of the industrial capitalist from the function of industrial entrepreneur'. There is a dissolution of the ownership of capital and the actual direction of production. What becomes important is to get a reliable market for the corporate securities and the fate of the enterprise depends upon the securities market. The shareholder, therefore, is no longer the earlier version of a capitalist operator but more of a moneylender who can regain possession of money on demand. The shareholder becomes a money capitalist receiving interest. However, the shareholder runs a higher risk of loss and therefore higher yield on shares is expected on the interest on money invested by a variable risk premium. If yield is high (suppose 20%) and risk is low (suppose 10%), then 'floating' the enterprise in markets will enable promoters to sell shares to double the amount of capital actually invested. This, according to Hilferding, is 'promoter's profit' which leads to increase in the scale of production as well as the centralization of capital.

Now coming to the operations of such corporations, one corporation can own shares of one or more other corporations. Big capitalists, therefore, can command a large block of shares in more than one corporation and thereby actually control an amount of capital several times more than he/she actually owns. This is the final step towards centralization of capital. Promoter's profit makes available huge amount of wealth in the hands of a few capitalists which can be invested in such a way that it is able to secure control over a far larger aggregate of capital. According to Hilferding, there is a creation of a circle of persons who by their possession of capitals or as representatives of concentrated power over other people's capital like the bank directors can occupy boards of a large number of corporations. In this form, there will be cases of personal union among insiders as they have a community of interests. This closeness will result in more organizational unification in the form of cartels, trusts or mergers aimed at monopolistic control over market. This will, according to Engels, result in the elimination of the 'long cherished freedom of competition' which 'has reached the end of its tether and is compelled to announce its own palpable bankruptcy'.

The banks too play an important role in this process. As Hilferding writes, '[t]herefore the striving of banks to eliminate competition among the firms in which they are interested'. He further stipulates that there will be a situation where the entire money capital would be at the disposal of one bank or groups of banks or rather a central bank. However, this has been criticized because this may be a part of the transitional phase of capitalist development where mergers, acquisitions and so on are taking place, and the banks play an important role in this. The big monopolistic corporations come to acquire such a position that they are able to command profit and vide the possession of internal sources of additional funds (profits not distributed among shareholders and reserve accounts), and achieve greater freedom from reliance on markets for new securities as source of capital and from dependence on banks for source of capital.

Therefore, the rise of corporations leads to centralization of capital, more accumulation and emergence of a small group of capitalists with their control over capital beyond the limits of their ownership. Thus, concentration of control over capital is not restricted by the concentration of the ownership as it can move beyond it as pointed above. Majority of owners of capital lose their control to a small minority of owners. The large corporations are examples of concentration in a small group of property owners and finally elimination of rivals and establishment of monopolistic productive process.

Monopoly Capitalism and Imperialism

From the above discussion, we have a clear idea that centralization of capital led to the growth of monopoly capital, that is, the fusion of many capitals into 'a huge mass in a single hand'—the era of free competition and replacement of individual capitals or firms by corporations. Thorstein Veblem in *Theory of Business Enterprise* (1904) and *Absentee Ownership and Business Enterprise in Modern Times* (1923) showed the growing importance of monopoly capital through the rise of corporate finance, tendency towards monopolistic profit margins at the expense of smaller firms and workers and systematic promotion of excess capacity. In the previous section we saw how Rudolf Hilferding emphasized the importance of growing market securities, role of banks, subsequent concentration and centralization of capitals, and expanding monopolization.

Michael Kalecki in his *Essays in the Theory of Economic Fluctuations* (1939) and *Theory of Economic Dynamics* (1954) analysed the 'degree of monopoly' while forwarding a theory of accumulation under monopoly capitalism. He opines that monopoly is inherent in the very nature of capitalism and free competition may be relevant in the initial stage of capitalist economy but actually it is a myth. Paul Baran and Paul Sweezy in their *Monopoly Capital* (1966) write that free competition and rate of falling profit had been replaced by monopolistic capitalist stage where there is a tendency of the surplus to rise. The surplus was generated through the difference between social output and socially necessary labour costs for producing.

However, such views have been contended by economists like John Week in his *Capital and Exploitation* (1981) where he said that 'the monopolies that stalk the pages and writings of Baran and Sweezy have no existence beyond the work of those authors'. In the 1980s, there was a thinking that the decline of the US hegemony advanced capitalist countries becoming vulnerable to foreign trade and capital movements and overall demolished the structure of monopolistic accumulation.

Many radical Marxist theorists such as Keith Cowling (*Monopoly Capitalism*, 1982), John Bellamy Foster (*The Theory of Monopoly Capitalism*, 1986) and Bellamy with Robert W. McChesney (*The Endless Crisis*, 2012) contended that the reality was different. There is continuing concentration and centralization of capital. In reality, there is internationalization of monopoly capital with very few firms controlling national and international economies. Foster and McChesney even showed in an empirical study that during the 2007–2009 global melt down, the top 200 corporations in the USA accounted for 30 per cent of gross profits in the economy. At the world level, top 500 global corporations received about 40 per cent of total global revenue.

In a later work in 1997, Paul Sweezy in his *More (or Less) on Globalization* argued that monopolization and stagnation had led to the emergence of a new kind of contradiction in capitalism. This was 'the financialization of the capital accumulation process'. Later, theorists of monopoly capital tried to develop theories regarding the advent of monopoly capitalism or monopoly finance in their quest to show that monopolization, stagnation and financialization operated simultaneously as mutually reinforcing trends. Foster and McChesney pointed out that the financial crisis of 2007–2009 resulted in stagnation which will persist for long. Amin in his *The Law of Worldwide Value* (2011) contended that we are living in 'the late capitalism of generalized, financialized, and globalized oiligopolies'.

The ultimate outcome of the monopoly stage of capitalism is imperialism and colonial domination. Classical theories of imperialism show the principal features as territorial expansions in quest for economic spheres of influence ultimately resulting in setting up colonies across the globe. The logic behind such imperial expansion lies in the internal contradiction of capitalism itself. Imperialism is a necessary condition for the sustainability of capitalism and accumulation of wealth. In the 21st century, colonialism is passé, yet the fundamental parameters of imperialism remain valid though the phenomenology of imperialism has changed. Neo-imperialism through political, economic and even cultural means is the new rendition of classical imperialism.

Concentration and centralization of capital replaced the perfect competition-driven price mechanism with monopolistic price set-up which widened the gap between consumption and production. Even capital accumulation and realization of surplus value in a closed economic set-up is difficult to realize because of narrow base of domestic consumption. This cannot be increased even through intensification of domestic market by employing new workers as wages remain low. This will create the predicament of overproduction and underconsumption. If this is one side of the crisis of capitalism, then on the other side, growth of large-scale production units by destruction of smaller units that begun in the initial stages of capitalism leads to growth of monopoly capital in the form of cartels, syndicates, trusts and so on in the national economies. This now leads outlets beyond the domestic markets and there starts a struggle, according to Bukharin, among stupendous opponents in the world market. There is collusion between industrial capital and bank capital to control national and world markets.

Lenin in his seminal work, *Imperialism: The Highest Stage of Capitalism* ([1917] 2010), contends that 'economically, the main thing in this process is the displacement of capitalist free competition by capitalist monopoly'. As the title of his work suggests, imperialism is the highest stage of capitalism. Certain basic features pointed out by Lenin are as follows:

- The concentration of production and capital has developed to such a high degree that it has created monopolies which play a decisive role in economic life.
- The merging of bank capital with industrial capital and the creation on the basis of 'finance capital' of a financial oligarchy.
- The export of capital as distinguished from the export of commodities acquires exceptional importance.
- The formation of international capitalist combines which share the whole world among themselves.
- The territorial division of the whole world among the biggest capitalist powers is completed.

Therefore, to sum up, imperialism is such a stage of monopoly capitalism where the capitalist countries enter into a squabble amongst themselves to re-divide the world in order to get access for their industrial produce and surplus capital.

Lenin further argued that cartels or combined enterprises gained more clout rather than the non-combined ones, and in the 19th century, the latter were crushed between high prices of raw materials and competitive final produce. Cartels for him became powerful transitory phenomenon and nerve centres of economic activities gobbling one industry after the other. Lenin noted down the stages of growth of monopolies which can be summed up as follows:

- 1860–1870 marked the highest stage and the apex of development of free competition but monopoly was barely discernible and still in an embryonic stage.

- After the crisis of 1873, there was a lengthy period of development of cartels, but they were still the exception. They were not yet durable and were still a transitory phenomenon.
- With the boom at the end of the 19th century and the crisis of 1900–1903, cartels became one of the foundations of the whole of economic life. Capitalism was transformed into imperialism.

Cartels came to an agreement on the terms of sale, dates of payment and so on. They divided the markets among themselves. They fixed the quantity of goods to be produced. They fixed prices. They divided the profits among the various enterprises and so on. Rudolf Hilferding contended that combined enterprises or cartels accumulated more competitive strength than the non-combined ones.

The JSCs along with the cartels modified the form of economic control and organization in the field of industrial production. JSCs divorced ownership from control through stock market operations in the form of issuing shares and raising equities in the stock exchange. Bank capitals played a vital role in it. Lenin upheld that the big enterprises and the banks in particular completely absorb the small ones. They 'annex' them and by subordinating them, bring them into their 'own' group or 'concern'. This is done by acquiring 'holding' in capital by means of purchase or exchange of shares in a system of credit. This collusion between banking capital and industrial capital led to the consolidation of monopolization. This stage was identified, as Rudolf Hilferding puts it, as 'finance capital' which was capital controlled by banks and employed by industrialists. Lenin identified this as coalescence of the bank and industry.

What caused imperialism or venturing out is important to consider. The late 19th century economic protectionism in the form of protective tariffs in capitalist countries led to competition among these countries against each other's products that were sure to hurt their domestic industry. Therefore, a scramble for world market ensued, fuelled by nationalism, militarism, war and conquest of colonies. Bourgeois nationalism and international protectionism ultimately led to imperialism, war and colonial domination.

The fusion of political and economic interests is quite striking as we hinted at bourgeois nationalism. As Rosa Luxemburg in her *The Accumulation of Capital* (1913) pointed out, 'political power is nothing but a vehicle for the economic progress. The conditions for the reproduction of capital provide the organic link between two aspects of the accumulation of capital'. For Lenin, 'politics is the most concentrated expression of economics, its generalization and its culmination'. Hobson points out that imperialism actually was driven by private interests and it was imposed by privileged groups on the national policies. The huge accumulation capital in advanced capitalist countries faced difficulties in surplus extraction in domestic market as discussed above due to mismatch between consumption and production. So now imperialism or search for external markets emerged as the most effective policy.

Hobsbawm in his *The Age of Empire* (1994) showed that political rivalries between states and the economic competition between national groups of entrepreneurs got fused or combined. This led to imperialism whose outcome was the First World War. These also led to the growth of industries like armaments in which the role of government was decisive. However, armaments are important attributes of state power but are utilized for militarism when imperialism leads to war. Paul Sweezy in his *The Theory of Capitalist Development* ([1942] 2016) puts this in perspective when he writes, '[i]n advanced countries, nationalism and militarism cease to serve the purpose of realization internal unification and freedom on a capitalist foundation'. He also points out to the objectives of growth of armaments. It was required to create a strong image of the country in the eyes of the country men. Armaments were part of a policy also to grab more non-capitalist territories to ensure at home capitalist accumulation and surplus realization through militarism. Therefore, the rule of finance capital implied the simultaneous rule of imperialism and militarism. Thus, Hobsbawm argued that in a capitalist society, politics and economics cannot be separated from each other. In the 1880s, economic protectionism in Europe and the USA with a trend towards monopolization at home and abroad, the non-capitalist elements and territorial expansion became the war cry of capital. The non-capitalist territories just fell prey to the competing international capitals and turned into their colonies of the victor capital and became the sphere of interest and influence of the metropolitan capital.

Hobsbawm has shown that during 1870, four main industrial states produced 80 per cent of the total world manufacturing output and by 1913, they manufactured 72 per cent of world output which was five times higher. The compulsion to go out for quest for markets on an imperialist mission was not depression in production but it was depression of prices, interest and rate of profit. Therefore, the imperialism of the late 19th and the 20th centuries was set in motion as all advanced capitalist countries were trying to export a larger share of their capital beyond their domestic market. This was only for quest for earning higher profits. Hobson argued that the industrial class which was interested to invest abroad and was not getting profitable opportunities at home influenced the governments to help it to search for profitable and secure investment abroad.

Imperialism's objectives can be summarized in the words of Rosa Luxemberg as 'the imperialist phase of capitalist accumulation which implies universal competition comprises the industrialization and capitalist emancipation of the hinterland where capital formerly realized its surplus value. Characteristics of this phase are: lending abroad, railroad constructions, revolutions and wars'. Hobsbawm argued that the relationship between the metropolis and the colonies or the dependencies was asymmetrical, as pointed out by the dependency theorists (discussed in Chapter 1).

The characteristic feature of this state of capitalist development experiences a re-partition or re-division of the Earth. As Lenin points out, the colonial policy of the capitalist countries completes the seizure of unoccupied land in our planet; for the first time, the world is now divided. He contends that in the future only, re-divisions can be possible only through transfer of one owner to the another and not of unowned territory to an owner. Further, Luxemberg and others also argue that the territories can be classified as a few handful of industrialized countries as well as those which are formally independent but backward countries. The latter group occupies semi-colonial position relative to great powers. These become the focal point of conflict when balance of power is disrupted and major battles are fought for wars of re-division. The first war of re-division was the First World War (1914) ending with the Treaty of Versailles, 1919, which was a major imperialist re-division of Germany. When the balance of power was disturbed again by the revisionist states like Germany, Japan and Italy, the Second World War took place in 1939. The trigger points were the Japanese invasion of Manchuria (1931), Italian absorption of Ethiopia (1935) and final German aggressions into European continent and occupation of Austria (1938). Therefore, because of the increased competition at the international level in the search for newer markets for their products and generating surplus capital, capitalist states engage in imperialism. The above examples show how the colonial division of the globe becomes inevitable through war and militarist policies.

Samir Amin in his *The Implosion of Contemporary Capitalism* (2013) pointing towards the trend in modern capitalism argues that it is not only driven by the monopolistic control over the selected production activities but 'monopolies now tightly control all the systems of production'. Small and medium enterprises of the peripheries are locked into 'a network of control and contracts put in place by the international monopolies. Their degree of autonomy has shrunk to the point that they are nothing more than subcontractors of the monopolies'. There has been a change in the process only. Through neoliberal policies, trade liberalization, international financial institutions and SAPs, the international monopoly capital having its origin in the advanced countries of the Global North still maintains direct and indirect control over the agricultural, industrial, financial and almost all sectors of activities of the Global South. We can conclude with David Harvey and his exposition in *The New Imperialism*, 2003, where he identified new imperialism as a search for a 'spatial fix' to an economic crisis in core countries through 'accumulation by dispossession' in peripheral countries.

Development of Capitalism in the Pre-Second World War Period and the 'Golden Age' of Capitalism

In the first section, we have seen the transition from feudalism to capitalism as analysed by Maurice Dobb and Paul Sweezy, Hobsbawm and Hilton. Here again following Dobb and agreeing, we can trace the rise of capitalism. Following Marx, Dobb cited Marx's emphasis on merchant capital that industrial capital develops in two ways. One of the methods is through 'the really revolutionary way' and the other 'takes possession directly of production'. In the first method, producers accumulated wealth and took to trade and over time started to organize their production along capitalist line free from guilds. In the second method, they took possession of production directly and served as a mode of transition.

Marx takes on the 'really revolutionary way'. The transition from the feudal mode of production takes two roads for him. The producer becomes a merchant and capitalist which was quite different from agricultural natural economy or the guild-encircled handicrafts of medieval town industry. The other way through direct form of production may help in transition but cannot overthrow the old mode of production and rather it preserves it and uses it as its premise. Marx saw the genesis of the industrial capitalist when many small guild masters, independent small artisans or even wage labourers transformed themselves into small capitalists. Gradually, by extending exploitation of wage labour and corresponding accumulation, they became full-blown capitalists. This was such a slow process and would have taken years if this was not supplemented by the new world market through great discoveries at the end of the 15th century.

Dobb, however, sees the process of accumulation as the rise in certain bourgeoisie assets and claims to wealth like the Church lands under Henry VIII. Wealth gets transferred to the hands of the bourgeoisie and gets concentrated in a few hands. These objects of original accumulation were realized and sold fully or partly in order to make possible an actual investment in industrial production, for example, acquiring cotton machinery, factory buildings, iron foundries, raw materials and labour power. Sweezy while analysing Dobbs exposition to the rise of capitalism contends that acquisitions of various types were made like land, debt claims, precious metals or frozen and liquid assets. Assets were also concentrated in a few hands. However, one thing that is to be recognized which Sweezy says Dobb did is that this was the period during which the bourgeoisie developed banking and credit system for turning frozen assets into liquid assets. But only another bourgeoisie belonging to the same class could buy and sell the assets during the period of capitalist development. Later to a critique of Sweezy about the unclear exposition of this realization phase, Dobb stated that maybe the new entrepreneurs were handicapped by the lack of capital and the credit system had not developed adequately yet, the tendency to shift in preference had a large influence on the economic transition to capitalism. Unlike the earlier preference for the bourgeoisie to hold onto real estates or valuable things or bonds, now they preferred to invest in means of production and labour power.

E. P. Thompson in his *The Making of the English Working Class* (1963) shows that in this new condition of economic revolution, industrialists replaced merchants as the key players in the capitalist system. Also were replaced the handicrafts and artisanship, the powers of the urban-based guilds, the traditional networks of masters, apprentices and journeymen. Alongside this development on the political front, the Protestant Reformation movement and the end of the Thirty Years' War vide the Treaty of Westphalia in 1648 established strong states under the European monarchs. This helped the early capitalists enjoy the benefits of the rise of strong states during the mercantilist[3] era. The policies of the state power succeeded in providing certain basic social conditions such as uniform monetary systems and legal codes which were necessary for economic development at that point of time. This ultimately made possible the shift from public to private initiative.

It was the ethic fostered by the Protestant Reformation movement of the 16th century leading to the emergence of the Protestant ethic as contrary to the traditional contempt for acquisitive effort. Protestant ethic gave importance to work, and frugality was given a stronger religious sanction. Max Weber in his *Protestant Ethic and the Spirit of Capitalism* (1905) argues that the modern spirit of capitalism saw profit as an end in itself and pursuing it as being virtuous. Justification of economic inequality was made on the grounds that the wealthy were more virtuous than the poor. The ideology of classical capitalism was best expressed in *An Inquiry into the Nature and Causes of the Wealth of Nations* (1776) by Adam Smith. He recommended leaving the economic decisions to the free play of self-regulating market forces or the invisible hands. Therefore, by the mid-19th century, Britain had fully embraced laissez-faire economics as in the 1840s, the duty on grain imported to Britain was abolished by the repeal of the Corn Laws[4] imposed during 1815–1846. Liberalism and competition in trade with the development of a free market economy now became the central political and economic basis of capitalism during this period.

---

[3] *Mercantilism:* An economic theory and practice common in Europe from the 16th to the 18th centuries, which promoted governmental regulation of a nation's economy for the purpose of augmenting state power at the expense of rival national powers. It was the economic counterpart of political absolutism.

[4] *Corn Laws* were imposed to keep the prices of corn high for domestic producers by keeping import duties high even if there was shortage of corn and availability of cheap corns from outside Britain.

By the early 1770s, the economic and social conditions were ready for the Industrial Revolution to take off towards the direction of becoming world economies. Powered by a number of new inventions such as flying shuttle for easy weaving, the spinning jenny, the Watt steam engine and locomotive revolution, the cotton gin, the telegraph communications, Portland cement, modern road building techniques, Bessemer process for mass production of steel, Volta's electric battery and many others changed the production process. The primitive factory system was transformed with machine power driven productivity to unprecedented levels. The first documented factory was opened by John Lombe in Derby around 1721 for mass production of silk products. With the factories transformed by the new machinery, the cottage industries could not possibly compete and soon collapsed. Between the 1770s and the 1830s, capitalist experienced a boom in factory production with all types of buildings being converted into factories with the majority of waged labour taking place within factory buildings.

After the French Revolution and the Napoleonic Wars, the remnants of feudalism vanished. With the Industrial Revolution, capitalism reached the stage of huge accumulation of wealth by the capitalist class. Laissez-faire became the dominant philosophy of classical capitalism. The assumptions of the 19th-century political liberalism included free trade, the gold standard, balanced budgets and minimum levels of poor relief. The growth of industrial capitalism and the development of the factory system in the 19th century led to creation of classes as Marx had pointed out as the haves and the have-nots, the bourgeoisie and the proletariat. There was an enormous new class of industrial workers or proletariat or the have-nots who worked in the factories and the capitalists or the factory owners or the bourgeoisie class. The exploitation and surplus accumulation made the rich richer and the poor poorer.

Outwardly, in the quest for markets abroad, capitalism grew into its grotesque form of imperialism and conquest of territories. Conquests led to the conversion of captured territories into colonies. Colonies became the supplier of primary goods and cheap labour and accumulation in the homeland of the capitalists increased by leaps and bounds. (Imperialism has been discussed in the earlier section of this chapter). Colonial expeditions led to wars and division of the world/markets. The First and Second World Wars had been a fight to maintain a status quo in the division of global economic power between the Allied and the revisionist alliance, the Axis power.

From the perspective of IPE, the First World War was a significant turning point in the development of capitalism. Post-First World War, international markets shrank, the gold standard was abandoned in favour of independently managed national currencies, banking hegemony passed from Europe to the USA and trade barriers multiplied. The Great Depression of the 1930s brought the policy of laissez-faire (non-interference by the state in economic matters) to an end in most countries and for some time, created heavy state intervention, embracing Keynesian economics to tide over economic crisis.

During the interwar period, as discussed in Chapter 3, especially after the Great Depression of 1929, we have seen how the gold standard was undermined and different exchange rates were adopted by countries. The Great Depression as seen earlier had led to the adoption of protectionist strategies by the states like the US Smoot–Hawley Pact of 1930. Therefore, there was a collapse in global trade which reduced the trade gains of a fixed exchange rate system. It was felt that programmes of fiscal and monetary expansions and competitive devaluations to combat the depression required a degree of flexibility and this cannot be achieved within a fixed system. Thus, we have seen abandonment of the gold exchange system by many countries before the beginning of the Second World War. Britain got back to gold standard system in 1925 itself and abandoned the system in 1931. A breakthrough was achieved through the Bretton Woods Conference of 1944 (detailed discussion in Chapter 3) where the leaders from 44 countries agreed to an international monetary policy world over. Bretton Woods established a system of payments on the basis of dollar. Dollar was itself convertible into gold. Gold exchange standards with gold and convertible currencies were fixed only against the US dollars. It was assumed that dollar was 'as good as gold' for trade purposes. It also created the IMF to keep a watch that all countries followed the agreed set of rules while conducting their international trade and finance. Later on, two other institutions were created—the World Bank (1944) and the GATT (1947)—to solve global economic problems. This was a stepping stone towards rolling the ball of capitalism globally.

The other epoch which helped in the quick recovery of war-torn Europe was the Marshall Plan (1946–1947). The European countries which were reluctant to take the IMF support on grounds of its conditionalities opted for the recovery assistance offered by the USA. The Marshall Plan was officially known as the European Recovery Program and was a US initiative with an objective to assist countries in Western Europe to work towards restoring productive capacity and resolving widespread poverty and hunger issues. According to the UN/DESA Policy Brief #52, the Plan amounted to about 1 per cent of the gross national product (GNP) of the USA in each year from 1948 to 1952. The Marshall Plan was in operation for four years, beginning in 1948. At its peak, the US aid, together with a similar type of aid to Japan, amounted to 40.5 per cent of the US exports in 1946–1949. Through this international support, development of productive capacities in deficit countries could be attained enabling them to gain access to dynamic world markets. The Marshall Plan helped restore production capacity in Western European countries while improved domestic price stability and helped to realign their currencies in the immediate post-war period. The successful implementation of the Marshall Plan in Western Europe is an example of development cooperation till today.

If we examine the post-war recovery of some countries such as Britain, the USA, Germany and Japan, we will have an idea of the overall economic performance catching up to the pre-war levels. In Western Europe, it took only three years for production to return to pre-war levels and four years in the case of exports, compared with six years for both production and exports after the First World War. By the 1950s, economic recovery was accomplished by the USA, Western European countries and Japan. The average annual growth rate of GDP among developed market economies was 5 per cent for the period 1961–1970, while that of developing countries was 5.5 per cent for the same period. Table 2.1 will give us an idea of annual increase in GDP for developed as well as developing countries.

Japan was defeated in the Second World War. The US Occupation of Japan introduced a series of reforms to reconstruct and recover the devastated country and ultimately Japan emerged as a major economic power. The three major reform policies implemented by the USA/Allied Force were breakup of the *zaibatsu*, land reform and labour democratization. These reform policies had a long-lasting impact in democratizing and modernizing Japan and future economic progress. Efforts were made towards the so-called 'economic democratization' reforms. The basic features are as follows:

1. *Zaibatsu* were big conglomerates of major companies and banks which were dissolved in 1945 to eliminate concentration of economic power. The most powerful ones were

Table 2.1 Average Annual GDP 1961–1970

GDP (Constant Price 1960)	
Countries	**Average Annual Rate of Change**
World	5.4
Developed countries	5.0
Centrally planned economies	6.7
Developing countries	5.5
Industrial Production	
World	6.7
Developed countries	5.8
Centrally planned economies	8.3
Developing countries	7.1
Agricultural Production	
World	2.6
Developed countries	2.5
Centrally planned economies	3.0
Developing countries	2.8

Source: United Nations (2017).

Mitsui, Mitsubishi, Sumitomo and Yasuda. The Fair Trade Law and the Economic Power Excessive Concentration Elimination Law were enacted in 1947.

2. Through fair market rules, 1947, American-style market rules were embraced. The most important of them were the Anti-trust Law and the Securities Exchange Law. These were enacted in order to secure market competition and transparency.
3. Agricultural reforms were carried out in 1945. The government purchased land from absentee landlords and all the tenant land in excess of one hectare and then sold them to tenant farmers at nominal prices. The percentage of tenant land dropped from 46 per cent to 10 per cent. Therefore, the number of independent farmers increased.
4. Labour market reforms were carried out in 1945. Through the enactment of the Labour Union Law, 1945; Labour Relations Adjustment Law, 1946; and the Labour Standards Law, 1947, the organization of labour unions was promoted and their labour movements were legalized.
5. Education reform in 1947 extended the compulsory education from 6 years to 9 years.

The recovery of the Japanese economy was achieved through the implementation of the Dodge Plan. Joseph Dodge introduced a plan of recovery in 1949. His stabilization policy included macroeconomic tightening, balanced budget on a consolidated basis, forced rationalization in private business and unification of yen exchange rate to 360JPY/1USD. The international conditions also favoured the recovery. The outbreak of the Korean War had an impact on the Japanese economy. The so-called Korean War boom caused by the high military demand made the economy to experience a rapid increase in production and marked the beginning of the economic miracle. Import of technologies and improved business conditions were some of other factors for growth. Credit must also be given to the ability of the Japanese people to adapt the knowledge and skill learned from the Western countries which made the amazing growth happen.

Germany at the end of the Second World War, according to the agreement reached at Yalta, in February 1945, between Winston Churchill, Franklin D. Roosevelt and Joseph Stalin, was divided. The Allied powers—Britain, the USA, the Soviet Union and France—divided Germany into four zones of occupation. Each of the Allies ran their zone more or less independently for the first two years of the occupation. In 1947, the British and US zones combined economically to form the 'Bizone' but remained separate political entities. In 1949, after the end of the war, the three Western zones formally joined together to form the Federal Republic of (West) Germany, and the Soviet zone became the German Democratic Republic (East Germany).

German recovery is associated with two names. German economist, Walter Eucken, introduced the social market economy which was a concept that promoted free market capitalism while also allowing government involvement in creating social policies. He was in favour of strong regulations that would be introduced to prevent cartels or monopolies from forming. Along with this, a large social welfare system also served as a safety net for those suffering or struggling. The next person whose contribution cannot be ignored is Ludwig Erhard who was the federal minister for economic affairs. He came to be known as the 'father of the German economic miracle' after successfully promoting Germany's social market economy. He introduced a new currency in place of currency issued by the Allied power. His plan reduced the amount of currency available to the public by a staggering 93 per cent. This was intended to reduce the little wealth that German individuals and companies still held. Along with these, large tax cuts were also introduced in an attempt to spur spending and investment. The currency was scheduled to be introduced on 21 June 1948. In October, just weeks after the new currency was introduced and price controls were lifted, the hours of work a week were down to 4.2 hours per week. In June, the nation's industrial production was about half of its level in 1936. By the end of the year, it was close to 80 per cent. The Marshall Plan which was the European Recovery Program helped in German recovery.

The USA played an important role in the post-war recovery of the UK. In the course of the Second World War, Britain and the other Allied powers had taken loans from American banks and the US Treasury for war expenditures. In 1941, President Roosevelt signed the Lend-Lease Act, approving US$1 billion in aid to Britain by virtue of which it had taken some US$30 billion in Lend-Lease aid from the US. As it was towards war effort, it did not permit any export of lend-lease goods, articles made with lend-lease goods or even 'substantially similar' articles. Britain's exports suffered and it desperately needed foreign exchange. However, the Marshall Plan and a huge loan of roughly US$5 billion (which if estimated at today's value will be a huge amount) was given to Britain for its reconstruction. It was only in December 2007 that Britain repaid the loan to the USA after deferring a number of times.

American economy even before the end of the Second World War was experiencing a massive growth due to its wartime production that led to the emergence of a huge Military–Industrial Complex as most of the arms supplies were made to the warring parties by the USA. This heavy production, as shown in Chapter 8, continued even after the war because of the outbreak of the Cold War between the two super powers, the USSR and the USA. Following the

Vietnam War, the Korean War and many other such conflicts as a consequence of the Cold War, calculations kept the munition productions high. This was coupled with the high savings that people were encouraged to make during the wartime. With the war over, people started spending on lifestyle commodities. Therefore, there was massive growth of demand for houses, cars, furniture, appliances and a host of other consumer products. Industries now encouraged mass production with assembly line organizational principles (Chapter 4). To keep the demand growing, the Employment Act of 1946 was passed that stated the government policy to promote maximum employment, production and purchasing power. In the *Outline of the U.S. Economy* by Conte and Karr,[5] they showed that the nation's GNP rose from about $200,000 million in 1940 to $300,000 million in 1950 and to more than $500,000 million in 1960. On the one hand, America ensured that markets for the US goods pumped money to the war-ravaged European economies for their post-war reconstruction. On the other, the USA tried to stabilize the IPE by the establishment of the Bretton Woods system, the IMF and the World Bank to ensure an international open market economy. Post-war America, therefore, replaced Britain as a powerhouse.

Therefore, Bretton Woods institutions, Marshall Plan and European economic recovery ushered in the 'golden age of capitalism'. Gianni Toniolo ('Europe's Golden Age, 1950–1973: Speculation from a Long-run Perspective', 1998) stated, '[t]he achievements of the European economy in the quarter century that followed the Second World War were so impressive that the period has been referred to as the golden age. The word miracle has also been used'. Nicholas Crafts and Gianni Toniolo ('Postwar Growth: An Overview', 1996) also brought up unemployment figures as something that had contributed to the unique character of those decades: 'In most countries, the "triumph of full employment" was a historically distinct feature of the period'.

Hobsbawm (1994) argues that the golden age was a worldwide phenomenon, even though general affluence never came within sight of the majority of the world's population. Hobsbawm contended that the industrial world was, of course, expanding everywhere. It expanded into the capitalist and socialist regions and in the 'Third World'. He opined that in the old West, there were dramatic examples of Industrial Revolution, such as Spain and Finland. In the world of 'really existing socialism' like in the purely agrarian countries such as Bulgaria and Romania, there acquired massive industrial sectors. In the Third World, the most spectacular development of the so-called 'newly industrializing countries' occurred after the golden age, but everywhere the number of countries depending primarily on agriculture diminished sharply. However, Hobsbawm also observed that the 'golden age' was succeeded by a period that was alternatively called the 'landslide', the 'slowdown', or the 'long downturn'.

In the 1960s, the US current account and the oil shock of 1973 ended the Bretton Woods system. Thus, on 14 August 1971, President Nixon did not hesitate and suspended the convertibility of the dollar (or, more precisely, of other countries' current account surpluses in dollars) into gold. The 1971 collapse of the Bretton Woods system was a signal that the golden age was coming to an end. This was paving the way for 'Washington Consensus' and

[5] This volume was prepared for the U.S. Department of State by Christopher Conte, a former editor and reporter for the *Wall Street Journal*, with Albert R. Karr, a former *Wall Street Journal* reporter. It updates several previous editions that had been issued by the U.S. Information Agency beginning in 1981. Available at https://usa.usembassy.de/etexts/oecon/index.htm (accessed on 12 November 2021).

re-emergence of economic liberalism was making its comeback at the expense of the little achievements of post-war developmentalism.

Therefore, the 1950s and the 1960s, the period of unprecedented worldwide economic prosperity, came to be called the 'golden age' of capitalism. The 'golden age of capitalism' is identified with the period following the conclusion of the Second World War. In fact, the trajectory of development of capitalism prior to the golden age and post the golden age can be classified as the Great Depression (1929), the golden age of capitalism, decline of golden age and stagflation, rise of Washington Consensus and subsequent financial crises with the global crisis of 2008. Each of the periods have been followed by stock market crash in 1929, decline in profits and investment in the late 1960s and the early 1970s with intensification of crisis due to oil shocks of 1973 and 1979 and finally the subprime crisis in the USA causing the global financial crisis of 2008.

Conclusion

It is quite interesting to note the development of the capitalist system. As scholars have pointed out the inefficiency of the feudal system, growth of towns and cities and growth of trade have ultimately led to the emergence of capitalism. With the Industrial Revolution and path-breaking inventions, the ultimate victory of capitalism was achieved. It happened over centuries and not in a day. Gradual accumulation of surplus from appropriation of labour power and rise of monopoly capitalism and with it monopoly corporations, there started a scramble for world markets. This gave rise to imperialism and re-division of the world among the colonial powers. The First and the Second World Wars in reality were the conflict between status-quoist power and revisionist power, the Allied and the Axis power as the latter wanted a share of the world market. The two wars were actually for the re-division of the world. The period after the Second World War witnessed a wave of decolonization and emergence of newly independent countries which were erstwhile colonies. They became politically independent but economically they were dependent on the advanced countries or former colonizers for funding, R&D, technology and host of other things. This dependency has created the situation of neo-imperialism or neo colonialism and there can be no escape from it in near future also.

Patnaik and Patnaik have contended that in the age of financialization and free flow of international finance capital, the underlying principle is that there should be no barrier. It might sound that the inter-imperialist rivalry is muted as barriers are removed between rival finance capitals. However, this is not the case. This period is witnessing end of wars caused by inter-imperialist rivalry. A spatial perspective like colonial days is missing now. We now have globalized finance capital of which the finance capitals of individual countries are parts and they do not belong to a particular country. They are reluctant to use the term imperialism even though they acknowledge the exploitative nature of imperialism.

David Harvey in his commentary to this theory said that money is 'butterfly' form of capital and the movement of finance capital since the 1970s has led to the debate between geographical fixity of the state and the fluidity of money flows so much so that the latter exercises much greater control over state policies like the power of proverbial bond holders. Further, a group of states like the EU can use their political powers globally to weld highly mobile capitals as per their particularist agendas. Quasi-imperialist practices are also present like the control of the USA over the IMF and the World Bank. Uneven geographical developments, shifting hegemonies, fluid movement of extractivist practices and accumulation and exploitation still continue in the global economy.

The stability in the IPE during the post-Second World period till the 1970s has been the flourishing period of capitalism. These 30 years have been termed as the 'golden age of capitalism'. It came to an end with the oil shocks, devaluation of dollar and finally the end of the Bretton Woods system in the early 1970s.

Summary

The inefficiency of feudalism as a system of production along with the growing needs of the ruling class for revenue primarily contributed to the decline of feudalism. Overexploitation of the labour force or the serfs led to the end of feudalism. Though the process was not so simple and for a long period of time, there were simultaneous existence of feudalism and capitalism, it was through the Industrial Revolution that the final victory of capitalism was achieved.

In the capitalist system of production, there is presence of a social relationship between a class of property owners and propertyless. There is exploitation and creation of surplus value that is appropriated by the propertied class.

Accumulation of the capitalist is the most important feature of the capitalist mode of production. Surplus extraction and generation of profit lead to accumulation of wealth by the capitalist.

Big capitalists can command a large block of shares in more than one corporation and thereby actually control an amount of capital several times more than they actually own. This is the final step towards centralization of capital and emergence of monopoly corporations, JSCs, cartels and so on. The large corporations are examples of concentration in a small group of property owners and finally elimination of rivals and establishment of monopolistic productive process.

The ultimate outcome of the monopoly stage of capitalism is imperialism and resultant colonial domination. Classical theories of imperialism show the principal features as territorial expansions in quest for economic spheres of influence ultimately resulting in setting up colonies across the globe. The logic behind such imperial expansion lies in the internal contradiction of capitalism itself. Imperialism is a necessary condition for the sustainability of capitalism and accumulation of wealth. In the 21st century, colonialism is a passé, yet the fundamental parameters of imperialism remain valid though the phenomenology of imperialism has changed. Neo-imperialism through political, economic and even cultural means is the new rendition of classical imperialism.

Bretton Woods institutions, Marshall Plan and European economic recovery ushered in the 'golden age of capitalism'. This was characterized by the achievements of the European economy in the quarter century that followed the Second World War. Japan and Germany showed miraculous economic recovery. Britain and the USA also made post-war recovery fast. With the Bretton Woods institutions in place, the US hegemony was established till the 1970s. The stability in the IPE during this period has characterized these almost 30 years as the 'golden age of capitalism'. It came to an end with the oil shocks, devaluation of dollar and finally the end of the Bretton Woods system.

REVIEW AND REFLECTION QUESTIONS

1. Comment on the decline of feudalism and rise of capitalism.
2. Following Dobb and Sweezy, try to trace the emergence of capitalism from fragments of feudalism.
3. Capitalism has some specific features which make it different from other modes of production. Identify the basic features of capitalism.
4. Marshall Plan, Bretton Woods system and European economic recovery paved the way for the golden age of capitalism. Explain.
5. The golden age of capitalism is a post-Second World War development. Comment on the rise and decline of the golden age.

Bibliography

Dobb, Maurice. 1947. *Studies in the Development of Capitalism*. New York, NY: International Publishers.

Chandrasekhar, C. P. 2017. *Karl Marx's Capital and the Present: Four Essays*. New Delhi: Tulika Books.

Hobsbawm, E. 1994. *The Age of Empire*. London: Abacus Publications.

Lenin, V. I. (1917) 2010. *Imperialism, the Highest Stage of Capitalism*. Lucknow: Rahul Foundation.

Patnaik, Utsa, and Prabhat Patnaik. 2016. *A Theory of Imperialism*. New Delhi: Tulika Books.

Sweezy, Paul M. (1942) 2016. *The Theory of Capitalist Development*. Delhi: Aakar Books.

Sweezy, Paul, Maurice Dobb, Christopher Hill, Georges Lefebvre, Kohachiro Takahashi, Giuliano Procacci, John Merrington, and Eric Hobsbawm. 2018. *The Transition from Feudalism to Capitalism*. New Delhi: Aakar Books.

Toniolo, Gianni. 1998. 'Europe's Golden Age, 1950–1973: Speculation from a Long-run Perspective.' *The Economic History Review* 51, no. 2: 252–267.

Upadhyay, V., and Singh Paramjit. 2021. *Global Political Economy: A Critique of Contemporary Capitalism*. New Delhi: Aakar Books.

United Nations. 2017. *World Economic and Social Survey 2017*. New York, NY: United Nations.

3 Developments in IPE: Post-Second World War Developments

LEARNING OBJECTIVES

- Getting acquainted with the Bretton Woods system
- Learning about the IMF and its functioning
- Knowing about the World Bank
- Learning about the multilateral agreements like GATT/WTO and their negotiations in various rounds
- Examining the roles of MNCs and the issues related with global trade and security

Introduction

The 'triad' with their overwhelming presence in the IPE is well known. The triad refers to the IMF, the World Bank and the GATT/WTO. The emergence of this triad is quite interesting. It dates back to the period after the Second World War. The emergence of this triad better known as the Bretton Woods institutions in 1944 was with a prime motive of stabilizing the international monetary system as discussed in this chapter. They were later supplemented by the Washington Consensus which vociferously propagated a free market economy and absence of state intervention. The prime targets were the developing countries which followed protectionism. In the 1980s when majority of the developing countries embraced free market reforms for their economy, they experienced cycles of prosperity and crisis. It is at this crisis moment that they had to approach these international agencies for debt. Debt did not come as free. Strings of conditionalities were attached to it. The conditionalities obviously related to the stabilization measures directed by the IMF and the SAPs by the World Bank. These were reinforced by the GATT/WTO once the countries became a part of it. Mainly all conditionalities revolved round the issues of tariff reduction, trade liberalization, opening up of markets, privatization, removal of restrictions on FDI and a host of other things. Coupled with these under the impact of globalization, there has been free flow of private FDI and the drivers have been the MNCs which operate globally but have their headquarters in some developed countries. The consequent economic challenges for the host countries have been discussed in this chapter. The Bretton Woods system might have collapsed in the 1970s, but the institutions are still existing and have a tremendous control over world economy. However, they have been reinforced by the Washington Consensus which filled up the vacuum after the collapse of the Bretton Woods system. Whatever kind of regime at present exists in the world, there is preponderance of the USA, the EU, China, Japan and Russia with a minimum say for the developing countries. Even the SDRs comprise five currencies, that is, dollar, euro, yuan, yen and pound sterling, which makes the above statement quite obvious. The working of the international economic institutions becomes a challenge for the developing countries, so this chapter is quite significant to know the current trade regimes.

The Bretton Woods System: Evolution and Collapse

The Bretton Woods system is an international economic regime regulating international monetary processes. Economic regimes are those which lay down rules, customs and facilities by creating instruments governing international trade and tariffs, payments and other economic/financial activities. Bretton Woods dates back to 1944 after the end of the Second World War. It led to the establishment of the IMF, the World Bank and beginning of negotiations for GATT. Bretton Woods system for the first time established the supremacy of dollar as an exchange rate. Before the Bretton Woods, there was the gold exchange rate system succeeded by fluctuatory exchange system which was finally replaced by the Bretton Woods system.

The period 1875–1914 was the age of Pax Britannica. This was a period which saw the supremacy of European powers and their economic and political domination over non-industrialized parts of the world, especially Britain. Colonies were established and imperialism became the integrative force politically using economic exchanges through trade, investment and technologies with the colonies for extracting profit from them. Global trade in the first 50 years preceding the First World War rose from $550 million to $19.8 billion (Eckes 1975). The value of trade rose by an average of 34 per cent per decade and the volume rose by 36–37 per cent each decade.

During the period from 1880 to 1914, international monetary exchange was a gold standard rate system. This was a fixed exchange rate system based on the gold exchange rates. This was possible as England's powerful rentier lords wanted the gold standard system which was suspended during Napoleonic wars. This suspension brought about inflation and depreciation. With the end of the Napoleonic wars (Battle of Waterloo, 1815), London emerged as the world financial centre because of political stability of England and its increasing worldwide trading relations. Sterling was attractive as a unit of account and as a medium of international exchange and London became the world's great settling centre for commercial contracts. Sterling balances were built up in a system committed to the gold convertibility of sterling, backed by England's industrialization along with the policy of free trade that generated a huge stock of wealth and savings available for loan and investment abroad. Therefore, on the ground of sterling's position in international financial system, Britain commanded the then international political economy. This generated rent for the banking sector and gave the international system a medium of reserve and payment of unquestioned reliability.

The gold content of the currencies was the standard. The gold content in one unit of each currency was fixed. Therefore, the exchange rate was also a fixed rate system. For example, the gold content of £1 was fixed. The gold content of $1 was also fixed. To fix the exchange rate 1 pound: $1 is worked out. The value that is reached is called *mint parity*. Exchange rates could not fluctuate above and below the mint parity. Therefore, it was a fixed exchange rate system (Figure 3.1).

Figure 3.1 Calculating Mint Parity

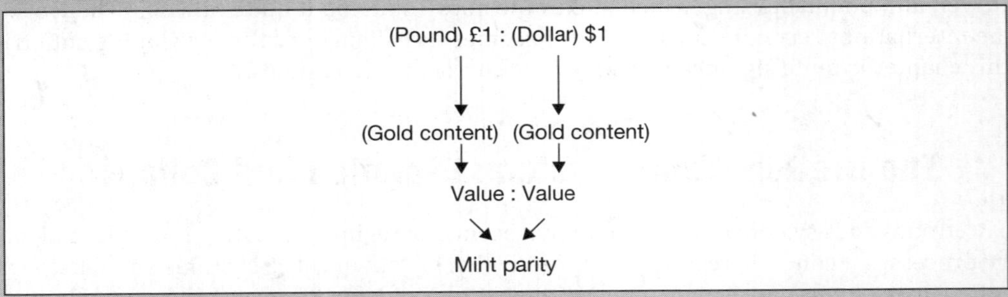

During the interwar period or more precisely between 1919 and 1924, exchange rates fluctuated. Countries faced inflation which they tried to meet up by printing money. Therefore, there was sharp increase in money supplies and consequential price rise. In other words, the countries faced hyperinflation. One example is Germany. Heavy reparation payments that were imposed on Germany forced it to continue having a fiat currency and to print German marks. This created hyperinflation in Germany in the 1920s. Countries tried to get back to gold standard. Britain returned to gold standard in 1925 and re-established the convertibility of the pound to pre-war price and lifted the embargo on gold exports which it had imposed during the First World War. The other countries followed the suit and went back to gold standard. The USA had already returned to gold standard in 1919. However, pre-war parity left the pound grossly overvalued accounting for the balance of payments deficits and deflation in Britain. Therefore, Britain lost its competitiveness to the USA and now as a substantial portion of its foreign investments stood liquidated to pay for the war and settling the pound at pre-war parity.

With end of First World War, England lost its political and military superiority to the USA, France, Germany and Russia. Leaders were more interested in more political environment râther than economic factors. The UK lost the position of the world leader as well as that of a leading financial centre. It faced economic stagnation. France tried to become a leading financial centre replacing Britain as it was enjoying large balance of payments surplus after franc was stabilized at a depreciated level in 1926. It passed an act for settling balance of payments surpluses in gold and not in pound which caused a drain of British gold. However, when France sought to convert its earlier accumulated pounds into gold, Britain had to suspend convertibility of pound into gold which devalued gold and meant the end of gold standard.

Several plans were floated to tackle international monetary system. Many conferences were held under the auspices of League of Nations to work towards establishing some type of a gold regulatory system. Countries like the USA and Soviet Union floated a number of proposals to address issues of trade, cartels and other economic issues plaguing the world economy at that time. As discussed above, Britain abandoned gold standard in 1931, which, in 1925, it had returned to when it pegged pound to gold at the pre-war price. In 1933, a World Economic Conference was held to cope with the international economic problems by restoring gold standard. An appeal made in that direction to US President Franklin D. Roosevelt was refused as he was unwilling to restore gold standard. The USA was not willing to assume the hegemonic power capable of stepping into Britain's shoes to bring about stability in international political and economic environment.

Thus, more instability was created in the international monetary system. The period between 1929–1933 was the period of Great Depression. There was instability in IPE and subsequent devaluations of currencies by countries. The USA devalued its dollar by increasing the dollar price of gold from $20.67 to $35 an ounce. Matters became critical as there was no free flow of trade. Countries imposed high tariffs and import restrictions which hampered international trade. For example, the Smoot–Hawley Tariff Act of 1930[1] imposed high tariffs on imports, which was retaliated by imposition of trade restrictions by other countries. Clearly, therefore, the interwar period was marked by instability of exchange rates system and destabilizing speculations. It is said that the world economy was disintegrated into autarchic (self-sufficient) national units during this period. Curtailing trade links from others made the countries eliminate trade deficit or external imbalance.

This crisis situation became a lesson for the leading countries of the world. The United Nation Monetary and Financial Conference was hosted by the US Treasury Department. Therefore, 44 states met at the United Nations Monetary and Financial Conference, Bretton Woods, New Hampshire, 1 July 1944, to draw a blueprint of international monetary system after the Second World War. However, it was mainly a conference where the British and American earlier agreements were formalized for which the two countries had been holding negotiations for two and a half years and even political agreements between President Franklin Roosevelt and Prime Minister Winston Churchill were formalized.

According to Raymond Mikesell, an economist in the division of Monetary Research, US Treasury Department, 'Bretton Woods was a drafting meeting, with the substance having been largely settled previously by the U.S. and U.K. delegations supported by the Canadians'. Eckes is of the opinion that through successive bilateral agreements, the USA and the UK worked together towards forming a world with expanding trade and easily convertible currencies—a world to match their own economic interests as dominant powers.

Whatever undercurrents had been behind the Bretton Woods Conference, yet at this conference leaders expressed their willingness to establish the IMF. The IMF was created to keep a watch that all countries followed the agreed set of rules while conducting their international trade and finance. The IMF was supposed to provide borrowing facilities to the members in case of temporary balance of payments difficulties. The IMF came into existence in 1945 after the signing of the Articles of Agreement by its first 29 countries. It became operational in 1947. The International Bank for Reconstruction and Development (IBRD), now known as the World Bank Group,[2] was established in 1944. This was responsible for providing financial assistance for the reconstruction after the Second World War and the economic development of less developed countries.

With the Bretton Woods began the hegemony of the US dollar in IPE. It established a system of payments on the basis of dollar. Dollar was itself convertible into gold. Gold

---

[1] *Smoot–Hawley Tariff Act of 1930:* The Smoot–Hawley Tariff Act of 1930 raised US import duties with the goal of imposing protectionist trade policies in the USA. It was sponsored by Senator Reed Smoot and Representative Willis C. Hawley. President Herbert Hoover signed it on 17 June 1930. At least 25 countries responded by increasing their own tariffs on American goods. Global trade plummeted or declined contributing to the worsening of the Great Depression that started in 1929.

[2] https://www.worldbank.org/

exchange standards with gold and convertible currencies were fixed only against the US dollars. It was assumed that dollar was 'as good as gold' for trade purposes. Therefore, the US currency became the world currency which meant that other currencies were pegged against dollar as the global standard. The Bretton Woods regime is a hegemonic monetary order centred on dollar. Thus, the Bretton Woods institutions were created to direct and control IPE that developed over the next two decades which almost became identifiable as an extension of American political-economic power.

However, the Bretton Woods system came under terrible pressure and ultimately collapsed in 1971. The USA being the key player in world economy came under stress which affected the entire Bretton Woods system. The USA faced a huge balance of payments deficit which it could not manage. Dollar had to be devalued. Problems of liquidity regarding official holdings of gold, foreign exchange and so on arose. Since the 1970s, the average annual GNP growth rates in Europe, China, Japan and some newly industrialized countries outstripped that of the USA. The US share of world financial reserves had declined, and the USA became the principal debtor from a principal creditor.

There was no adequate adjustment mechanism to correct the system. The lingering of the US balance of payments deficit led to loss of confidence and trust in dollar. The confidence shifted to stronger currencies such as the German mark, the Japanese yen and the Swiss franc. In 1971, President Nixon had to suspend the convertibility of dollars into gold. The Bretton Woods system almost met its end. Dollar was devalued in February 1973. In March 1973, the major currencies were allowed to fluctuate either independently or jointly. Since March 1973, the world has operated on a managed float system. Floating exchange rates are determined by market forces rather than governmental interventions. Yet countries still need to intervene in foreign exchange rates to handle short-run fluctuations in exchange rates because economies still need international reserves. Such interventions are mostly done in dollars.

International Monetary Fund

The Bretton Woods system comprises the triad, namely the IMF, the World Bank and the GATT/WTO. At the Bretton Woods, there was an agreement for fixed exchange rates against the US dollar. The dollar price was fixed at $35 ounce. This was also a gold exchange rate but this time it was with dollar as the main reserve currency.

The experience of the interwar period with fluctuating currency rates made the countries realize that some sort of monetary discipline was required. This discipline can be brought by a fixed exchange rate system. Therefore, fixing exchange rates to the dollar which was in turn tied to gold was thought to be disciplining monetary system. With this objective, the IMF was formed at the Bretton Woods. It was established in 1944 and became operational in 1947. The other objective was to create financial reserves from the contribution of the members that would enable it to lend to the countries to put their external balance in order. In case of fundamental disequilibrium, the exchange rates against the dollar could be devalued or revalued with the consent of the IMF. Richard Peet (2010) has summarized the objectives of IMF as:

- Facilitating the expansion and balanced growth of international trade and contributing to high levels of employment, real income and development of the productive resources of member countries.

- Promoting exchange stability to maintain orderly exchange arrangements among members while avoiding competitive exchange depreciation.
- Assisting the establishment of a multilateral system of payments for current transactions among members and in the elimination of foreign exchange restrictions which prove to be obstacles to the growth of world trade.

The IMF is placed under the UN and is the central institution of the international monetary system, international payments and exchange rates among national currencies and prevents crises in the payments system. The Board of Governors with representatives appointed by all member countries is the highest authority governing the IMF. They meet twice a year at the joint annual meeting of the IMF and the World Bank. The Executive Board meets thrice a week at the IMF headquarters in Washington DC. The five major shareholders of the IMF are the USA, Japan, Germany, France and the UK along with China, Russia and Saudi Arabia who have their seats in the Board.

The arrangements and facilities under which the IMF provides loans can be in the form of standby agreements to deal with short-term balance of payments problem. There is also extended fund facility to make structural economic changes which the IMF thinks can improve balance of payments. There is also the poverty reduction and growth facility which provides low-interest loans to the lowest-income member countries facing protracted balance of payments crisis (replaced the Enhanced Structural Adjustment Facility, 1999). There is also provision for supplemental reserve facility providing additional short-term loans at higher interest rates to member countries witnessing exceptional balance of payments crisis. Contingent Credit Lines provide precautionary IMF financing on a short-term basis for countries faced by a sudden loss of market confidence. The IMF provides emergency assistance to help countries coping with balance of payments problems arising from sudden and unforeseeable natural disaster or emergency conditions created by military conflicts.

A member while joining the IMF is assigned a quota on the basis of its position in the international trade and finance as well as its economic performance. The voting power of members is related directly to their quotas (the amount of money they contribute to the institution). At the end of 2011, the total subscription of the IMF had grown from $8.8 billion in 1944 to $369.2 billion or 238.0 billion SDRs. The US quota has decreased from 31 per cent to 16.80 per cent. Japan's quota is at 6.25 per cent and Germany's is at 5.83 per cent. France and the UK have a quota of 4.30 per cent and 3.82 per cent, respectively. The total subscription was around SDR 475 billion (US$645 billion) as of September 2017. Initially, the member countries could borrow not more than 25 per cent of its quota in one year and not more than 125 per cent of its quota over a period of five years. Later, this was revised to 50 per cent of their quotas in one year.

Members of the IMF do not have an equal voice and it is on the basis of quota subscription and this quota is the basis for determining voting power. So this can never be equal. Emerging countries and poor countries are almost voiceless in this financial institution. In December 2010, the 14th General Review of Quotas was held for bringing about reforms in the IMF quotas and system of governance to be effective for January 2016. Some important reforms included a major decision to doubling of quotas and a major realignment of quota and voting shares to emerging and developing countries. This was done with more than 6 per cent quota shift to dynamic emerging market and developing and under-represented countries. Protecting the quota and voting share of the poorest countries (defined as those eligible for the low-income Poverty Reduction and Growth Trust and whose per capita income fell below $1,135 in 2008, which has been set up as threshold by the International Development Association [IDA] or twice that amount for small countries) have been an objective. The most important has been a proposal for a new composition and more representative board. The 2010 reforms included an amendment to the Articles of Agreement and established an all-elected Executive Board as seen in the first all-elected Board that has been in place since November 2016. The European members are committed to reduce their number of Board members representing advanced European countries by two in favour of emerging market and developing countries and have made significant progress.

The IMF also negotiated General Arrangements to Borrow (GAB) to the tune of $6 billion with Group of Ten high-performing industrialized countries such as the USA, the UK, West Germany, Japan and France. This was mainly done to help countries with balance of payments difficulties. Later, the amount of GAB was expanded. The IMF also started negotiating swap arrangements for a specific period of time with an exchange rate guarantee. Swapping each other's currency was used to intervene in foreign exchange markets to stabilize hot money flows (flow of capital from one country to another to earn higher interest rate/profit but always under risk of being moving out in times of crisis).

The IMF introduced the provisions for SDRs in 1969. It is an artificial basket currency of additional reserves of gold and foreign exchange. SDRs are referred to as 'paper gold' and were created to ensure the growth of international liquidity. Initially, they were defined as equivalent to 0.888671 grams of fine gold equivalent to USD1 ($35/oz). Currently, the SDR is based on a basket of five currencies. They are US dollar, euro, Chinese renminbi/yuan (from 1 October 2015), Japanese yen and British pound sterling.

SDR is neither a currency nor a claim on the IMF. To participate in the SDR, a country must have official reserves of gold and foreign currencies in the central bank or the government that could be used to buy local currency in foreign exchange markets to stabilize the exchange rate. The member countries that hold SDRs can exchange them for freely usable currencies by voluntary swaps or on the instructions of the IMF directing members who are strong economies or are with larger foreign currency reserves to buy SDRs from less endowed members. This is usually done to adjust their unfavourable balance of payments positions. Members can also borrow from SDRs at favourable interest rates. Every five years the IMF determines which five currencies will enter the basket. SDRs were created to supplement a shortfall of preferred foreign exchange reserves and assets—gold and US dollars. SDR is ISO 4217 and the currency code is XDR (numeric, 960). The current value of SDR is given in Table 3.1.

Table 3.1 SDR (as per 2015 Review by IMF), October 2016–December 2020

Currency	Assigned Weights as per 2015 Review	Values
US dollar	41.73	0.582520
Euro	30.93	0.386710
Chinese yuan	10.92	1.017400
Japanese yen	8.33	11.90000
Pound sterling	8.09	0.085946

Multiple changes have been introduced in the operations of the IMF. The quotas of the IMF members have been raised a number of times. The 25 per cent of increased quota is to be paid in SDRs and rest by currency chosen by the IMF. There has been revision in the GAB and it now extends up to New Arrangement to Borrow, 1992, and by 2011, the IMF could lend up to SDR $564.2 billion. Borrowing rules have been relaxed and swap arrangements have been expanded. These have increased the amount of credit available to member countries from the IMF. Other new credit facilities include the Supplemental Reserve Facility, the Extended Fund Facility, the Compensatory and Contingency Financing Facility, the flexible credit line and other arrangements.

Developed countries hold the largest amount of XDRs and are reluctant to use them for any purpose. Till date, the IMF has allocated SDR 204.2 billion to its member countries. Another SDR mobilization came upon during the global economic crisis of 2008 as it helped to provide liquidity to the international economic functioning and averting the use of member countries' official reserves in the face of this crisis. The SDR played a critical role in supplementing the official reserves in 2008–2009 global economic crisis. Almost SDR 182.6 billion was mobilized to cope with the crisis. Developing countries are in need of credit but nothing comes for free. Besides interests/debt servicing, the developing countries have to accept the IMF conditionalities which come in the form of SAPs.[3] It is due to the debt crisis of the 1980s of the Sub-Saharan countries that the IMF made its lending more flexible and, in some cases, extends loans to overcome problems arising due to the SAPs.

In 1997, a wave of financial crises swept over East Asia as discussed in Chapter 6 that extended from Thailand to Indonesia to Korea and beyond. The IMF forwarded a series of bailouts or rescue packages for the crisis-driven economies to enable them to avoid default, tying the packages to conditionalities of carrying out currency, banking and financial system reforms.

During the Global Economic Crisis of 2008, the IMF undertook major initiatives to introduce surveillance to respond to the working of a more globalized and interconnected world. The IMF worked out initiatives like revamping the legal framework for surveillance to cover spillovers (when economic policies in one country can affect others), deepening analysis of risks and financial systems. It also included stepping up assessments of members' external positions and responding more promptly to concerns of the members.

During the COVID-19 pandemic, beginning from 2020, the IMF pledged to continue to support countries on the path to recovery by providing them policy advice, financial support, emergency financing, capacity development, grant for debt relief, calls for bilateral debt relief; enhancing liquidity and adjusting existing lending arrangements. The most important thing which the IMF wanted to do is a call for a new SDR allocation of $650 billion. In April 2021, the International Monetary and Financial Committee proposed to the IMF to make a comprehensive proposal on a new SDR general allocation of US$650 billion. This is intended to help meet the long-term global need to supplement reserves and, at the same time, enhancing transparency and accountability in the reporting and the use of SDRs.

Currently, the number of IMF members is 189. The headquarters is at Washington, DC. The current IMF chairman is Ms Kristalina Georgieva and she assumed office in October 2019.

---

[3] SAPs are discussed in Chapter 6.

World Bank

Another Bretton Woods' institution is the World Bank. In 1944, the World Bank was the outcome of the Bretton Woods Conference along with the creation of the IMF. It is the world's first multilateral bank. The mission of the World Bank is 'to end extreme poverty: by reducing the share of the global population that lives in extreme poverty to 3 percent by 2030'. It further resolves 'to promote shared prosperity: by increasing the incomes of the poorest 40 percent of people in every country'. The World Bank at present has 189 members in IBRD and 173 in IDA. The members of the IBRD should also be the members of the IMF. The World Bank is headquartered in Washington DC. It works in 170 countries and has offices over 130 locations. Mr David Malpass assumed the role of the World Bank Group president in April 2019.

The voting rights were revised by 2010 Voice Reform to include the voices of the developing countries. The country with the highest voting power is now the USA (15.85%), followed by Japan (6.84%), China (4.42%), Germany (4.00%), the UK (3.75%), France (3.75%), India (2.91%), Russia (2.77%), Saudi Arabia (2.77%) and Italy (2.64%). The Voice Reform (voting power GDP), however, did not change the situation much and the developing countries remained almost voiceless.

The World Bank functions through five institutions—the World Bank Group. They are as follows:

1. The IBRD which provides loans, credit and grants to middle-income but credit-worthy countries.
2. The IDA which provides low or no interest loans to low-income countries.
3. The International Finance Corporation (IFC) provides investment, advice and asset management to companies and governments.
4. The Multilateral Investment Guarantee Agency (MIGA) which insures countries against political risks like war.
5. The International Centre for Settlement of Investment Disputes (ICSID) which looks into investment-related disputes between investors and countries.

Article 1 of the original (Bretton Woods) Articles of Agreement uphold the purposes of the World Bank inter alia as follows:

- Assist in reconstruction development of member countries for restoration of economies disrupted by war, reconversion of productive facilities to peacetime needs and other needs for developing productive resources in less developed countries.
- Promote private foreign investment through private investors and if private investors are not available, then private investment to be supplemented for productive purposes out of its own capital or funds raised by it and its other resources.
- Promote long-range balanced growth of international trade and maintenance of equilibrium in balances of payments.

The World Bank has the Boards of Governors which consists of one governor and one alternate governor appointed by each member country. They serve for a period of five years and can be reappointed. Though the powers are invested in the Boards of Governors, they have delegated their powers to the executive directors. All the institutions of the World Bank are guided by the Articles of Agreement. They pertain to general principles of organization, management and operations. The IBRD is guided by the Articles of Agreement arrived at the United Nations Monetary and Financial Conference at Bretton Woods in July 1944. The IFC Articles of Agreement were chalked out by the World Bank's executive directors in July 1956. The IDA Articles of Agreement were drawn by the executive directors in September 1960. The MIGA Convention came into effect in April 1988. The ICSID was established by a multilateral agreement which came into force in October 1966.

With a vision of bridging the gap between the poor countries and the rich ones, the World Bank provides low-interest or interest-free credit and grants to developing/poor countries. These are targeted to bring about development in education, health and infrastructural sectors of the developing/poor countries. It also aims at helping in the reconstruction of countries emerging from war. The World Bank tries to manage international crisis and promote open trade.

The World Bank provides data of economic indicators of more than 200 countries. It can be accessed on the Bank's website and easily the development indicators could help examine a country's profile. There are almost 298 indicators including poverty, gender and aid effectiveness. Other indicators include business, agriculture and other financial areas, government economic policy and sovereign debt, health (life expectancy), climate change and a host of others.

Since 1947, the World Bank has provided funds for over 12,000 development projects. However, the World Bank has been rigged with controversies. The credit extended to developing countries often creates economic problems for them. The SAPs or the World Bank conditionalities are back breaking and sometimes austerity measures suggested by the World Bank may cause recession. Many a time in the vicious debt cycle, the countries are unable to service the debt. The IMF and the World Bank often work together; however, whereas the IMF extends short-term loans to stabilize trade deficit, the World Bank makes long-term loans to promote economic development. However, the functioning of both the institutions has aroused suspicion in the minds of developing countries, especially their conditionalities.

General Agreement on Tariff and Trade/World Trade Organization

The GATT is the predecessor of the WTO. History of evolution of these trade regimes dates back to the experience of the Great Depression. The USA in 1930 passed the Smoot–Hawley Act which raised the trade tariffs to a very high level. Under this Act, the average import duty in the USA was raised by 59 per cent by 1932. This was retaliated by 60 countries with steep increase in tariff rates amidst the Great Depression. There was a total collapse of the world trade which further affected the US trade. Only with the ascendency of President Roosevelt, the Trade Agreements Act was passed by the US Congress in 1934.

Bilateral arrangements on the basis of quid pro quo that is bilateral tariff reduction could help to some extent after the Second World War. It was mostly on the basis of the principles of most favoured nation (MFN) and non-discrimination with trading partners. However, to get more benefits from trade liberalization, multilateral negotiations began post-Second World War. However, the initial attempts to reach at a multilateral arrangement in the firm of

International Trade Organization could not take root. In 1947, ultimately 23 countries set out to form rules regarding trade regulations which came to be known as the General Agreement on Tariffs and Trade. There were several rounds of GATT negotiations at Geneva (1947), the Kennedy Round (1964–1967), the Tokyo Round (1973–1979), the Uruguay Round (1986–1994) and the Doha Round (2001). Ultimately, in the Uruguay Round, which began in 1986 and came to an end in 1994, the WTO came to existence. The Marrakesh Agreement expressed through the Marrakesh Declaration established the WTO. This was signed in Marrakesh, Morocco, by 123 nations on 15 April 1994. The WTO officially came into being on 1 January 1995. The Doha Round, the latest round of trade negotiations, began in 2001 but by 2014, it seemed to have failed. Subsequent ministerial meetings had taken place in Cancún, Mexico (2003), and Hong Kong (2005). Related negotiations took place in Paris, France (2005), Potsdam, Germany (2007), and Geneva, Switzerland (2004, 2006, 2008), without much breakthrough amidst persisting differences between the developed and the developing countries.

The GATT is based upon three principles. They are the principles of non-discrimination, elimination of non-tariff barriers and consultation for resolving disputes. The first principle of non-discrimination extended to all members who were to treat fellow member countries on the basis of MFN in matters of export and import. Only non-GATT countries were permitted to discriminate. However, GATT makes exceptions for the formation of customs union (CU) and preferential trade agreements (PTA) under the circumstances that they do not work to increase the tariffs and trade barriers against other parties.

The second principle is regarding the prohibitions of quantitative restrictions or non-tariff barriers under the GATT. Trade restrictions were also to be reduced to lesser tariffs. Exceptions to these extended to countries facing balance of payments deficit and also extended to agricultural products. The third principle provided for resolution of disputes among GATT members on the basis of consultation within the GATT framework.

Between the period of formation of GATT and creation of WTO, as pointed out earlier, several rounds of trade negotiations were held to sort out differences on various trade-related issues. The Tokyo Round of negotiations from 1974 to 1979 discussed tariff reductions over an eight-year time span beginning from 1980. This round further worked upon the conduct of countries with regard to non-tariff barriers. It also laid down certain prescriptive code for reducing the effect of non-tariff barriers such as uniformity in application of duties in countervailing and antidumping cases, and a generalized system of preferences.

The Uruguay Round of negotiations was the most critical. It began in 1986 and finally came to an end in December 1993. The main outcomes of this eighth round of negotiations were regarding tariffs, quotas, safeguards, intellectual property, antidumping, subsidies, services, other industry provisions, General Agreement on Trade in Services (GATS), Trade-related Aspects of Intellectual Property Rights (TRIPS), Trade-related Investment Measures (TRIMS) and, most importantly, the WTO.

To sum up the outcome of the Uruguay Round, it will help us see the major breakthroughs in the negotiation. First, regarding GATS, the member countries agreed on a set of specific commitments made to each other with respect to market access, market access limitations and exceptions to national treatment in specified services. Regarding textile, the member countries agreed to eliminate quota of every type of textile traded in the world which they used to enjoy under the Multi-fibre Agreement (MFA) of 1995. In 1995, members had agreed to eliminate 16 per cent of the quotas, three years later, 17 per cent, four years after this, 18 per cent and by 2005, total elimination of quotas on all textiles covered by MFA. Members agreed to reduce tariffs on textiles by about 20 per cent. Regarding TRIPS in the Uruguay Round, one major breakthrough was the inclusion of intellectual property rights (IPR). IPR extends to copyrights, patents and trademarks. Minimum standards of protection were included in the Uruguay Round. It also gave the member countries the obligation to work out procedures and remedies under domestic laws for enforcement of IPR by both national and foreign right holders. TRIMS agreement addressed policies or measures created by member states to govern investment that can distort trade. The agreement prohibits any measure or policy that is inconsistent with Article III of the GATT. This is again a reference to the norm of non-discrimination that means that countries should treat foreign and domestic firms at par.

Regarding agriculture, which was the most disputed of all sectors, some modest agreements could be reached. There were commitments on reduction of internal supports by 20 per cent with no future increase. Three categories of supports were created with red, amber and green. Supports which fell under green were out of the Uruguay Round requirements. Export subsidies were reduced by 36 per cent in value which was to be achieved within six years with 1986–1990 set as the base period for determining reductions. All non-tariff barriers to agricultural trade were to be eliminated. There was a single fixed tariff to be created by WTO members. Overall tariff levels were to be reduced by 36 per cent for developed countries and 24 per cent for developing countries in 10 years from the signing of the agreement.

The GATT regime reduced tariffs by a total of 35 per cent through several rounds of trade negotiations till 1962. By 1993, almost 123 countries had signed the GATT and 24 countries had applied for admission. In 1994, Arthur Dunkel presented a draft agreement which was based on the Uruguay Round of negotiations. It formed the basis of an International Trade Accord which was signed by 125 countries in Marrakesh, Morocco, in April 1994. This became effective from 1995. From this process what emerged was the WTO. This was not an agreement but a formal organization with the headquarters in Geneva, Switzerland.

The WTO was formed with the objectives of tariff reduction by developed countries on manufactures by an average of 40 per cent through a phase of five equal annual reductions in 10 major sectors. Abolition of non-tariff barriers as well as phasing out of MFA imposing restrictions on textile exports was another objective. Agricultural trade was to be progressively liberalized and brought under the WTO. Restrictions of non-tariff barriers on agricultural trade were replaced by tariff and subsidies were reduced. There were also provisions relating to GATS, TRIMS and TRIPS.

TRIMS address issues such as product mandating, export balancing and local content requirement. Further, TRIMS also ensures that no country should adopt any measure which is inconsistent with the treatment of the exporter and domestic producer. Both must be treated on equal terms. There should not be any quantitative restrictions like the quota system. TRIMS also prohibit those measures which are inconsistent with national treatment between exporters and domestic producers pertaining to local content requirement and import balancing. Those measures which are inconsistent with the principle of elimination of quantitative restrictions are also prohibited such as import limitation, export limitation and foreign exchange limits.

As far as TRIPS are concerned, they pertain to patents, trademarks, copyrights, industrial designs, trade secrets and so on. TRIPS provide patent for the products or the processes in various technological innovations. IPR under TRIPS are provided for 50 years for copyright, 20 years for patents, 10 years for industrial designs, 10 years for layout designs and 7 years for trademark. A patent holder's right for 20 years puts the entrepreneurs from developing countries to take up research and development in a product whose patent is with some other entrepreneur and can go on inventing some derived variety and patenting that too. These are detrimental to R&D for innovation in these fields.

However, the WTO has been rigged with criticisms and in each round the developed and the developing countries were at loggerhead with each other. When GATT was conceived in 1947, there was no provision regarding the developing countries. With the decolonization of the developing countries and emergence of newly independent countries, they started to raise concerns and identify special challenges that they might face in international trade due to GATT. The apprehension was that liberal trade policies would hinder the development of infant industries and there will be continued dependence on primary commodity and raw materials exports that would result in volatile export earning and deteriorating terms of trade for developing countries.

In the Kennedy and Tokyo Rounds, developing countries fought for their position for undertaking the rights and obligations of the multilateral trading system and the negotiation of specific concessions and commitments for them. The result was the 'Framework Discussions' of the Tokyo Round on the 'Enabling Clause' of 1979. The Clause established the principle of differential and more favourable treatment, reciprocity and fuller participation of developing countries. It provided for:

- Preferential market access of developing countries to developed country markets on a non-reciprocal, non-discriminatory basis
- 'More favourable' treatment for developing countries in other GATT rules dealing with non-tariff barriers
- The introduction of preferential trade regimes between developing countries
- Special treatment of least developed countries in the context of specific measures for developing countries

Thus, the establishment of the 'Enabling Clause' gave a stronger legal basis for the special and differential treatment of developing countries within the rules of the multilateral trading system.

In the Uruguay Round of talks, agreements of great potential importance to developing countries were taken up.

- Strengthening of dispute settlement mechanism for providing the developing countries judicial system protection against the larger and more powerful developed countries.
- Negotiations regarding market access to developing countries in areas of interest such as agriculture, textiles and clothing, which were of particular interest to developing members.

Doha Round was held in November 2001 with much positive thoughts and is also known as the 'Doha Development Agenda'. It had on its agenda a further liberalization of production and trade in agriculture, services and industrial products. It also wanted more tightening of anti-dumping measures and safeguards, and investment and competition policies. Major disagreement arose between the developed and the developing countries, especially with regard to agriculture and existence of agricultural export and production subsidies in the developed countries.

Due to unequal participation and lack of bargaining power, the developing countries could not strike a fair deal at the WTO. The developed countries are opening up markets, whereas developing countries are increasing protection in many areas, especially agriculture. Joseph E. Stiglitz in his *Globalization and Its Discontent* had observed that developed countries should make WTO work for making globalization work and for the benefit of all and not just industrial countries. Even the IMF observes that small and poor countries have acquired very little say in the decision-making in the WTO and their ability to play the 'reciprocity' game is very limited in scope. Their ability is also limited by their small market size and, therefore, not much lucrative market access.

The COVID-19 crisis is showing the limitations of the TRIPS as it is circumscribing the ability to produce vaccines on a mass scale. Production is now limited to only a few pharmaceutical firms which have taken the patent for the COVID-19 vaccines. India and South Africa and other developing countries (G-60) demand waiver on TRIPS for COVID-19 vaccine, drugs and medical tools. The US trade representative, Katherine Tai, however, indicated the US support for talks only on patent flexibility for vaccines under the aegis of the WTO.

At present, the number of members of the WTO is 164. China became the 144th member in 2001 and Russia became the 156th member in 2012. The headquarter is at Geneva, Switzerland.

Globalization and MNCs: Issues Related with Global Trade and Security

It is a very common way of defining globalization as a process through which the world is becoming one 'global village'. This has several aspects which must be taken into consideration. The most important is obviously the economic factor other than the social, political or cultural factors. For our discussion, we will focus on the economic factors primarily. The process of globalization hints at economic interdependence and deepening of economic integration among the economies of the world. There is the emergence of new international division of labour, new migratory movements, internationalization of production and a new form of interplay between economics and politics.

Plainly looking at globalization, it would give us a picture as stated above. But the question is whether the reality is the same. The driver behind globalization is capitalism and market economy. It can be said that global capitalism rules the roost. It is fuelled by the ideology of neoliberalism based on free trade, market economy and lesser state interventions. The tools for imposing the neoliberal agenda are the same Bretton Woods institutions—the IMF, the World Bank and the GATT/WTO. The emerging of 'Washington Consensus' after the collapse of the Bretton Woods system further reinforced the capitalist quest for world market. This also prescribed for the developing countries that the only road towards economic development is by allowing competitive free markets to play their role. These regimes have defined the terms of international trade. They have vouched for a liberalized trade order. The developed countries had brought down their tariff barriers under the regulations of GATT/WTO and the developing countries by the 1980s began embracing liberal economic reforms. The package of market-oriented reforms including trade liberalization by the developing countries continued to feed the aspirations and economic motives of the developed world. These have been reinforced by the international trade regimes—the IMF, the World Bank and the GATT/WTO.

These institutions have extended loans to the poor countries of the world or troubled economies of the developing world on the basis of conditionalities of trade policy reforms. In the 1980s, the developing countries had to accept the trade policy recommendations of the World Bank and went on to introduce SAPs. It is also not unknown that the Sub-Saharan countries in the 1980s were caught in the vicious cycle of debt and it became a lost decade for the poor African countries. These institutions have always taken advantage of the economic crisis of the less developed and developing countries and leave no stone unturned to ensure that the liberalization process is not reversed.

With more openness of economies, there is an environment of free trade and from material acquisition to production, the process is now globally dispersed. There is now a global market for goods, services and labour. The main non-state actors in the entire process are the MNCs. These MNCs move around the world, acquire resources, produce goods, sell goods, create jobs, move jobs from one part of the world to another (outsourcing) and indulge in many other global activities. They are the flag bearers of global capitalism. The largest MNCs in the world include Toyota, General Motors, Volkswagen, Samsung, Hitachi, Daimler, General Electric, Ford Motor, Hewlett Packard, Nissan Motor, IBM, Apple and so on. These MNCs have their origin in developed countries and they go out into the world for capturing global market. In their quest, they not only influence domestic decision-making but also policy-making of host countries.

If one looks into the Middle East where the most precious resource is oil and then tries to enquire into the companies engaged at the rigs, the story becomes clear. The top oil companies involved in oil exploration, production and shipping in joint venture or as major concession holders are Harken Oil, Texas, of Grand Prairie and Texas in Bahrain, Gazprom, Petronas and shell in Iran. Shell and British Petroleum (BP), Chevron and Coastal are vying to buy Iraqi crude. Others like BP, Chevron, Getty Oil Co., Mobil Corporation, Royal Dutch Shell, Texaco, Shell International Petroleum Co. Ltd function in Kuwait, Shell Petroleum Co. Ltd in Oman, Royal Dutch Shell, Enron, Chevron and many others in Qatar, Mobil and Shell among host of others in Saudi Arabia and BP and Caltex Petroleum Corporation, Pennzoil, Shell Gas BV and others in UAE. This makes it quite clear that Middle East politics is just not politics but it is oil politics and the players are these MNCs. However, these corporations have a tremendous influence upon domestic government which shapes the foreign policy orientations of the domestic government towards the Middle East.

In Venezuela, which is again an oil-rich country and given its current state of economic crisis, the ruling regime has started underhand liberalization. Underhand privatization is leading the country to lose control of the largest state-controlled oil company, PDVSA, as it is passing into the hands of foreign companies/partners. It seems whoever is able to steer clear of US sanctions imposed in 2019 is welcome to be a partner of PDVSA. Chevron (an US-based oil giant) has become the largest foreign producer of oil in Venezuela for which the Trump administration has waived the 2019 sanctions. Others in line are Rosneft of Russia and Eni of Italy. A host of other foreign companies may have an eye on Venezuelan oil and the future would see another scramble around oil-involving states and their MNCs.

An example from not so old a history is that of the Banana Republic (e.g., Honduras and Guatemala) and the US-based MNCs. The United Fruit Company, the Standard Fruit Company and the Cuyamel Fruit Company dominated the orchards of the Central American countries, especially Honduras and Guatemala, in the late 19th century. Their prime motive was exploitation and profit earning through cultivation of bananas. Many a time, the MNCs have led coup against a government to install a friendly government who will give them the ease of doing business. In the 1950s, the United Fruit Company wanted to topple the Árbenz government of Guatemala for nationalizing the orchards. A coup d'état by the US Central Intelligence Agency toppled the Árbenz government and installed the Armas government who was pro MNCs. Therefore, the MNCs also interfere with the political functioning of their host countries and what can be a better example of the installation of a puppet government in the Banana Republic of Guatemala.

What are then these MNCs? These are companies which conduct and control their production and resource collection not only in the parent country/home country but also in other countries of the world. They are quite significant drivers in international trade and finance and international markets. The above examples explain how powerful MNCs are in influencing domestic and international relations of parent country and the host country. It is often said that MNCs are the major vehicles of FDIs in host countries. They also bring with them technological expertise, skill and transfer of modern machinery and equipment to host countries which are mostly developing countries. MNCs, therefore, increase investment level and thereby generate income and employment in host countries. In many cases, MNCs can enable the host countries to increase their exports and decrease their import requirements. MNCs help to integrate national economies with world economies. Domestic suppliers of host countries also may be boosted by the MNCs and their operations. Sometimes the managerial efficiency is infused into the work culture of host countries as MNCs bring their professional management and the employment of sophisticated management techniques.

Susan Strange in her *States and Markets*, 2015, bases her analysis on Raymond Vernon's *Sovereignty at Bay*, 1971, and his product cycle to be the beginning of the internationalization of business. Additionally, to this, she points out that Ricardian notions of rent to the spread of business abroad. The company could extract a rent which is of a higher price than warranted by its cost of production, including interest on capital and normal profit under competitive conditions. This they do by exploiting its monopoly of a new product. As back at home competition rose, the companies first exported the product and then produced it abroad with extracting at each point of the cycle another kind of rent. The cycle was completed when the accumulated rents invested in innovative R&D produced another new product to start all over again. This is not the complete story. A necessary condition for so rapid a spread of international production was the political acquiescence of industrialized countries with the open world economy objective to be actively pursued and promoted by the USA. The underlying assumption is that political liberalism and economic liberalism go together so that freer trade and freer movement of capital are not just an end in themselves but also means to building a free world. Susan Strange opines that the nature of the global production structure has become increasingly dominated by international business but this cannot be adequately explained by any single factor. She observes that it is the combination of state policies, market trends, management strategies and changing technology. Therefore, entry of MNCs is the result of political preference and acceptance of multilateral agreements on trade and money by countries on their part which resulted in the increasingly opening up of world economy.

MNCs are in an advantageous position than any national firm. A combination of factors makes this possible. They enjoy economies of scale in production, financing, R&D and even access to the current market information. By exploiting the conditions in the low-wage countries, they can create product components and assemble in another country. By their sheer size, they can, thus, manoeuvre the production process and enjoy economies of scale in production. MNCs have greater access to international capital markets than smaller firms and purely national firms. On the basis of market information, MNCs can adapt their products to local choices and conditions. Modes of firm investments by the MNCs can be in the form of horizontal FDI and vertical FDI. When an MNC carries out production process similar to the pattern followed in their home country in a foreign country located near to a large customer base, it is known as horizontal FDI. A substitute to horizontal FDI is that a parent company can license an independent firm to produce and sell its products in a foreign country. Sometimes a MNC might break up their production chain and carry out parts of that chain in their foreign facilities and this constitutes vertical FDI. Sometimes an alternative to this vertical FDI can be entering into a contract with a local firm to perform certain parts of production process in the foreign locale, keeping in mind the cost advantage. This is known as foreign outsourcing. Offshoring has also become common with relocating parts of production chain in foreign countries and groups with foreign outsourcing and vertical FDI.

However, arguments are well placed against the activities of the MNCs also. MNCs working on increasing their profit indulge in practices which harm the indigenous production fabric of a host country. For example, resource collection in the form of intermediate products instead of depending on local supplies, the MNCs might procure those from other countries where they have affiliates or subsidiaries. Therefore, the indigenous industry cannot survive this stiff competition and is sure to die. The MNCs by eliminating any sort of competition might capture the domestic market of developing countries by reducing the competitiveness of the national firms of the host country.

It is often alleged that though MNCs bring in technology with them, most often, the developing countries become the dumping grounds of redundant technology for the MNCs. Besides, MNCs bringing capital-intensive technology into developing countries might cause unemployment. Replacing human-intensive technology by capital-intensive technology might not be appropriate for the economy of the developing economies. Initially, though the MNCs might bring in foreign exchanges, this might create volatility in the foreign exchange rate system of the host country as well as foreign exchange earnings of that country. The inflows and outflows of capitals by the MNCs have created a volatile situation for the host countries many times. Outflow of capital in the form of repatriation of profit, royalty, technical fess and so on results in a disadvantage for the host countries like the developing countries and might add to their foreign exchange problems.

MNCs also give rise to inessential consumption of goods which might not match the economic condition of the developing countries. However, a consumer culture is encouraged and a whole array of electronic goods, expensive cars, cosmetics, apparels and so on is encouraged through glitzy advertisements. Most often, MNCs evade environmental control measures and set up polluting units in developing countries rather than their parent country. The Bhopal gas tragedy in 1984 was caused by leaking of methyl isocyanate from the Union Carbide India Limited plant killing thousands and creating health hazards for the residents of Bhopal in Madhya Pradesh, India. It has been one of the worst industrial disasters in the world.

MNCs indulge in transfer pricing and evasion of local taxes which hurts the revenue earning of the host countries. By transfer pricing, the MNCs charge higher prices for its component product used for the entire production process and show lower profit and thus evade taxes. In the host countries also, MNCs might create problem as they may outsource jobs and result in loss of domestic jobs. Thus, when President Donald Trump fought the US presidential elections, his agenda was job creation for the US citizens and he vowed to punish those companies which moved jobs out of America. However, more than the home country, the host countries, mostly the developing countries, face the challenging task of balancing the needs of development of its own country vis-à-vis the MNC functioning.

Since 1991 post-economic reforms in India, there has been rise in the FDI in India. MNCs are the main drivers of FDI and their entry has brought in investments, technology and opportunity of jobs. India offers to the MNCs, among many, the ease of doing business, huge workforce with potential and a dynamic consumer-oriented market. The top MNCs in India, to mention a few, are the Hindustan Lever Limited (Anglo-Dutch company), Samsung (South Korean MNC), Adidas (German MNC), Lotte Confectionery (South Korean MNC), Mercedes-Benz India (Daimler AG), Toyota (Japanese MNC), Garnier (French MNC), Panasonic (Japanese MNC), LG (South Korean MNC), Microsoft (Bill Gates, Washington-based MNC), International Business Machines Corporation, IBM (New York based MNC), Nestlé (Swiss MNC), Procter & Gamble (Ohio-based MNC), Coca-Cola (Atlanta, US-based MNC) and PepsiCo (US-based MNC).

The World Investment Report 2021 of the UN Conference on Trade and Development (UNCTAD), June 2021, highlighted that the global FDI flows have been severely hit by the pandemic. FDI flows have dropped by 35 per cent in 2020, to $1 trillion from $1.5 trillion the previous year. However, the report pointed out that as for India, FDI increased by 27 per cent, to $64 billion in 2020 from $51 billion in 2019. These have been pushed by acquisitions in the information and communication technology (ICT) industry. Therefore, India became the fifth largest FDI recipient in the world even in the pandemic year 2020.

The pandemic boosted demand for digital infrastructure and services globally. This led to higher values of greenfield FDI project announcements targeting the ICT industry, rising by more than 22 per cent to $81 billion.

Conclusion

COVID-19 has set before us a challenge unprecedented in history. How far should the states go for a free market and privatization? How much will the people be left at the mercy of the invisible hands? The SAPs have been back breaking for the developing countries. Added to it is the COVID-19 crisis. A virus has made the humanity think of what next if unbridled globalization is pursued. Now as islands cut off from the rest of the world, each country is bringing back the state in a larger way to meet the crisis. The states are mobilizing their resources, personnel and infrastructure to fight against the coronavirus. It is to be seen how much they revert to non-intervention by states after the pandemic is over.

MNCs are to be watched out carefully as they might move in to buy holdings and shares in countries facing terrible economic distress. Overall, this COVID-19 pandemic has forced the states to rethink about their neoliberal agenda of public welfare. In 2020, India, in apprehension that there might be predatory acquisitions of sensitive sectors during the COVID-19 economic crisis, amended the FDI policy to put a blanket ban on investments through automatic routes by entities from countries sharing borders with India (Pakistan, Bangladesh and China). The sensitive sectors which might be overtaken are pharma, e-comm, digital infrastructure and so on which by the ban will be able to avert acquisitions by foreign firms. This is a balance between economic openness and national security.

It is to be watched how the IMF, the World Bank and the WTO respond to the crisis and after the crisis. As usual, though they have predicted an economic depression or global recession in the period following the pandemic, they are showing concern about increasing trade barriers that countries are indulging in. They have urged to keep the trade lines open. COVID-19 has shown that what is needed is a balance between the requirements of a market economy and public interest. COVID-19 definitely will accentuate new trends in IPE.

Summary

At the Bretton Woods Conference, leaders expressed their willingness to establish the IMF. The IMF was created to keep a watch that all countries followed the agreed set of rules while conducting their international trade and finance. The IBRD, now known as the World Bank Group, was also established in 1944. This was responsible for providing financial assistance for the reconstruction after the Second World War and the economic development of less developed countries.

The **IMF** was established to facilitate the expansion and balanced growth of international trade and to contribute to high levels of employment and real income and also development of the productive resources of member countries. Promoting exchange stability to maintain orderly exchange arrangements among members while avoiding competitive exchange depreciation was also another important objective. The IMF conditionalities which come in the form of SAPs for the debtor countries have been criticized over the years. The IMF has helped many countries to come out of economic crisis but in some cases have been criticized (read also Chapter 6 for SAPs).

The **World Bank** was the outcome of the Bretton Woods Conference in 1944 along with the creation of the IMF. It is the world's first multilateral bank. The mission of the World Bank is 'to end extreme poverty: by reducing the share of the global population that lives in extreme poverty to 3 percent by 2030'. The SAPs or the World Bank conditionalities are back breaking and sometimes austerity measures suggested by the World Bank may cause recession. Many a time in the vicious debt cycle, the countries are unable to service the debt.

The **GATT/WTO** is a multilateral trade and tariff agreement. The **Uruguay Round** of negotiations was the most critical, beginning in 1986 and finally coming to an end in December 1993. The main outcomes of this eighth round of negotiations were regarding tariffs, quotas, safeguards, intellectual property, antidumping, subsidies, services, other industry provisions, GATS, TRIPS, TRIMS and, most importantly, the WTO. The WTO was established by the Marrakesh Agreement and was signed in Marrakesh, Morocco, by 123 nations on 15 April 1994.

From the time GATT was conceived in 1947, there was no provisions regarding the developing countries. In the Kennedy and Tokyo Rounds, developing countries fought for their position for undertaking the rights and obligations of the multilateral trading system and on the negotiation of specific concessions and commitments for them and the 'Framework Discussions' were worked out.

The main non-state actors in the entire process of globalization are the **MNCs**. These MNCs move around the world, acquire resources, produce goods, sell goods, create jobs, move jobs from one part of the world to another (outsourcing) and many other global activities.

REVIEW AND REFLECTION QUESTIONS

1. Post-Second World War, there was a necessity to stabilize the global economy and draw a blueprint of the functioning of the international economic order. How do you think that was managed by the Bretton Woods system?
2. The IMF was a creation of the Bretton Woods Conference. Comment on its functioning with reference to its conditionalities.
3. Write a brief note on the functioning of the World Bank by focusing on its lending to the developing and poor countries.
4. The WTO is the ruling economic regime in contemporary IPE. Hinting at the various negotiation rounds of GATT/WTO, bring out the significance of the WTO in the current world economic order. Also point out the developing countries' perspectives on the WTO.
5. MNCs are movers of foreign capital in the form of FDI. Bring out in your discussion the positive and negative aspects of the role of MNCs in the host countries.

Bibliography

Cavusgil, S. Tamer, Knight Gary, and Riesenberger John. 2018. *International Business: The New Realities*. London: Pearson.

Cherunilam, Francis. 2011. *International Economics*. New Delhi: Tata McGraw Hill Education Private Limited.

Chirico, JoAnn. 2014. *Globalization: Prospects and Problems*. Thousand Oaks, CA: SAGE Publications.

Eckes, A. E., Jr. 1975. *A Search for Solvency: Bretton Woods and the International Monetary System (1941–1971)*. Austin, TX: University of Texas Press.

IMF. 2021. How the IMF Makes Decisions. Available at https://www.imf.org/en/About/Factsheets/Sheets/2016/07/27/15/24/How-the-IMF-Makes-Decisions (accessed on 23 September 2021).

Kegley, W. Charles, and R. Eugene Wittkopf. 1997. *World Politics: Trends and Transformation*. New York, NY: St. Martin's Press.

Krugman, Paul, Maurice Obstfeld, and Marc Melitz. 2018. *International Economics: Theory and Practice*. London: Pearson.

Lake, David A., and Jeffry A. Frieden. 2000. *International Political Economy: Perspectives on Global Power and Wealth*. New York, NY: Routledge.

Mukherjee, Aparajita, and Saumya Chakrabarti. 2016. *Development Economics: A Critical Perspective*. Delhi: PHI Learning Pvt. Ltd.

NDTV Profit. 2021. 'India Received $64 Billion FDI in 2020, Fifth Largest in World: UN.' Available at https://www.ndtv.com/business/india-fdi-news-india-receives-64-billion-fdi-in-2020-fifth-largest-inflows-in-world-un-2468655 (accessed on 23 September 2021).

Peet, Richard. 2010. *Unholy Trinity: The IMF, World Bank and WTO*. New York, NY: Zed Books.

Salvatore, Dominick. 2018. *International Economics: Trade and Finance*. New Delhi: Wiley.

Strange, Susan. 2015. *States and Markets*. New York, NY: Bloomsbury Academic.

The Times of India. 2021. 'Not Just Vaccine, India Seeks Patent Waiver for Covid Meds Too.' Available at https://timesofindia.indiatimes.com/business/india-business/not-just-vax-india-seeks-patent-waiver-for-covid-meds-too/articleshow/82471616.cms (accessed on 23 September 2021).

4 Changing Dynamics of Capitalist Production

LEARNING OBJECTIVES

- Getting to know organizational theories
- Learning about Taylorism and Fordism and gaining knowledge about scientific management theory and assembly line production
- Examining the changing nature of organization and emergence of post-Fordism with customized production in place of mass production
- Learning about the changing nature of job and changing stances of employer–employee bargaining, unionism and labour rights

Introduction

Production system is an ongoing process. As science and technology make progress, production system also undergoes change. We have seen in Chapter 2 how the Industrial Revolution caused a massive change in the production process as well as relations of production, and how capitalist mode of production led to industrial mode of production. The labour force involved in the production process put in their labour and produced commodities for market consumption. There was a level of people/hierarchy above them who gave directions. The entire system was based on a certain kind of organization.

The various interdependent parts are conjoined through coordination to give an orderly structure to the industrial production process. The basic aim of organization was an attempt to create a structure which was to be maintained for achievement of specific objectives and in the case of industrial production, it was commodities for market consumption. The industrial production not only involves machines but also human beings to operate them. Therefore, as we discussed in the beginning, it involved a certain division of labour and followed/s a hierarchical authority structure. The main component is role and not the person. So the work/role continues even if the person changes. Organization involves a set of relationship of jobs to jobs, of processes to processes and persons to persons with a common objective to achieve the goal.

In order to achieve maximum productivity, several organizational theories came to the fore. Industrial production had not evolved to a point of sophistication and uniformity soon after the Industrial Revolution. Productivity was low, so was profit. Workers were also not trained and their roles in production were not specified. It was in the 1930s that certain organization theories started to make inroads into the industrial production process. The forerunner, in this discourse, was the classical theory of organization. The chief proponent was Frederick Winslow Taylor with his scientific management theory. The next in line during the 1930s and the 1940s was the human relations theory propounded by Elton Mayo and his colleagues as a counter to scientific management theory that had put sole emphasis on efficiency and economy and not on the human beings involved. They carried out experiments on the workers in the Western Electric Company during 1927–1932. These came to be identified as the Hawthorne experiments, which highlighted the social and psychological influences on organizational behaviour. There was emphasis on inter-personal relations, communications, leadership and motivation.

In the 1950s and the 1960s, post-Second World War period, there was, on the one hand, emergence of neo-human relations theory and, on the other, impact of behavioural revolution in social sciences on organizational theories. The neo-human relations approach was a further improvement upon the human relations theory. This was popularized by Abraham Maslow, Rensis Likert, McGregor, Herzberg and others. While talking about a self-actualizing[1] man, they also emphasized on the importance of intrinsically rewarding work. Their theory of self-actualization pinned on individual dignity, personal growth along with innovations and creativity. Systems theory of organization which was an offshoot of behavioural revolution in social science laid importance on several variables such as economic, social, psychological, structural and technological which though independent are also interdependent.

Out of these theories, the scientific management theory came to influence industrial production for a long time and even became the path bearer of Fordist modes of production. With Fordism, assembly line of production became the key mover in industrial production which led to huge increase in production and reduction in cost of goods. However, it reduced workers to almost machine-like existence who were doing repetitive jobs throughout the entire line of production process without scope of creativity or innovation. They had no control over decision-making as this job was to be done by their managers. This system of production continued for long almost till the 1970s when there was a change in production process with the emergence of service sector.

Thus emerged post-Fordist form of organization, which is quite flexible and creative without much control over the end product which in a post-Fordist era needs to be customized according to the demand. Mass production is passé and customized products are in. The taste and demand of the customer/client have to be addressed without compromising the quality in a competitive market.

Capitalist mode of production puts an emphasis on markets and in this, labour becomes a commodity of sale and purchase. Market processes have evolved over time with changes and complexities of production processes. Labour, wage and collective bargaining through trade unions have always been critical phenomena. Especially, globalization has changed the nature of work and side by side industrial production and trade union activities have undergone changes and, in many cases, are losing their previous position. The changes in the nature of work in the Fordist and post-Fordist times have also changed the labour relations. This chapter discusses organizational forms, both Fordist and post-Fordist modes of production and changing nature of job and labour rights.

[1] *Self-actualization:* The desire for self-fulfilment or a person's tendency to be actualized in what he or she is potentially or complete one's realization of complete potential.

Organizational Forms: Fordist and Post-Fordist Modes of Production

The scientific management theory can be said to be a precursor to Fordism. Frederick Winslow Taylor as seen above forwarded this theory to replace the 'rule of thumb' (doing according to one's own wish) through proper scientific management guidelines in order to increase efficiency in factory production. Taylor did not coin the term scientific management. It was first used by Louis Brandeis in 1910. Taylor had forwarded the theory because he pointed out that management is a true science and that management principles can be applied in all types of organizations even in the management of homes, farms, businesses, philanthropic institutions, governmental departments and the like. Taylor said that scientific management is 'no single element, both rather this whole combination, which included—Science, not rule of thumb, Harmony, not discord, Cooperation, not individualism, Maximum Output in replace of restricted output. The development of each man to his greatest efficiency and prosperity'.

In his *The Principles of Scientific Management*, a speech delivered in 1911, he talked about this principle of scientific management. His exposition was based upon the study of the science of shovelling at the Bethlehem Steel Company at the Midvale Steel Works. Here, he started to introduce scientific management to handle pig iron on task work. Task work idea was quite path breaking. The entire task to be handled by the workmen was to be designed and planned in advance. Every task would have to be explained by a joint initiative of the workmen and the management. This included what and how of the task as well as the time limit. If the task could be completed within a time limit, there would have been an addition of some percentage to the workmen's ordinary wages.

Overcoming the existing mindset with a mental revolution, both management and workers must work towards embracing scientific management in a congenial atmosphere. The four principles of scientific management are as follows:

1. Developing a true science of management replacing the rule of thumb.
2. Scientific skill enhancement of workers through teaching and training, replacing the old method of worker's selection of method of learning and training himself/herself in the way he/she produced which he/she thought to be the best.
3. Cooperate and ensure that all work is done in accordance with the principles of management.
4. Equal division of work between management and the workmen. In other words, there should be friendly cooperation between management and the labour.

In the words of Taylor, scientific management's principal objective was maximization of prosperity of the employer as well as that of each employee. To achieve this, again Taylor forwarded three principles of reorganization. They included greater division of labour along with greater specialization, full managerial control of workplace and cost accounting based organization based on time and motion study that includes analysis, and measurement of the separate steps in the performance of a specific job for the purpose of establishing a standard time for each performance ultimately aiming at improving procedures and increasing productivity. However, Taylorism was criticized for being primarily concerned with organizational efficiency and was, therefore, highly mechanistic. Humans were considered to be adjunct of the machine and work like a machine which is a highly mechanical view of a human being. Motivational factors of the employees were disregarded. Only that part of human activity which was related to production was to be focused upon. Therefore, it was quite narrow in its view but nevertheless provided insights into introduction of science of management into organization. The overall view of the Taylorist model, therefore, shows that there is no control of the 'operatives' on the production ideas and designs on the part of the labour. The organizers of production would be totally in control of that. The 'operatives' need not think but do.

If Taylor gave the industries the scientific management theory, it was Henry Ford who held the key to mass production with his model popularly known as Fordism. Henry Ford, the founder of the American Ford Motor Company, gave an opportunity to the Americans to buy automobiles at an affordable price as he developed the organizational principles based on assembly line and mass production providing commodities at low cost. The Ford *Model T* was the first such automobile which was made available to the middle-class Americans. Using the assembly line of production made production easier and saved time. What is then this assembly line production? In an assembly line of production, every worker is assigned his part of the task, which is then moved to the next worker. Each worker is stationed at a particular position along the assembly line and performs his/her bit of task which involves several motions or one motion and for which it requires no skill at all or very less skill and training. Initially, in place of conveyor belts, the auto parts were put on skids and moved to the next worker. Later, with the introduction of more technological innovation, rope and pulley powered conveyor belts were used. These saved time and increased production.

The Fordist model underlined several features which are enumerated as follows:

1. Assembly line was the basis of Fordism. It operated on a semi-skilled labour support. It meant movement of the parts/components of the products and not that of the workers. It was, therefore, a mass force, and it also worked towards mass production.
2. Standardization of products and components as well as the manual labour and the task involved.
3. Use of semi-skilled labour doing repetitive jobs organized by the principles of scientific management.
4. A Fordist model worked on accumulation through the process of mass production on the basis of economies of scale which kept prices low and, therefore, addressed mass demands. This indirectly led to profit and wealth accumulation.
5. Underscored that increased profits leads to increased investment in improved mass production equipment and techniques.
6. Like Taylorism, Fordism also suggested multi-divisional decentralized organization under centralized control.
7. The most important feature was standardization of production involving mass consumption.
8. The intrinsic features of Fordism include monopoly pricing, union activity and collective bargaining, and connection of wages to productivity.

Fordist mode of production enabled firms to produce large volumes of the same goods by using production standards. Therefore, firms could ensure low prices for the customer but with a limited range of choice. The work method was monotonous. Overall, Fordism was based on a strategy of 'intensive' capital accumulation and for this, the emphasis was on Taylorist reorganization of the labour process.

Fordism as an organizational principle was prevalent till the 1970s. It was found to be robotic, highly mechanical, repetitive and devoid of motivation to the workforce. Though there were attempts for 'humanization' of labour, under the emerging economic scenario, Fordism failed to address the growing needs of changing nature of jobs.

From the 1970s onwards, there was an increasing emphasis on service industries, information technologies and need-based production and consumption. In other words, from an industrial society, there was a shift towards post-industrial knowledge and information society. The rise of computer technology and improved international telecommunications required redesigning of mass production to customized production. Things will become clearer if we take up the views put forward by the American sociologist, Daniel Bell (1999), in his popular work, *The Coming of Post-industrial Society*. He projected major changes in the post-industrial society. He predicted, though agrarian and industrial sectors of the economy would remain, there would be a huge surge in 'human services'. There would be new principles of innovation, new modes of social organization and emergence of new classes in the *post-industrial society.* He maps the major shifts in his book as well as in his 1999 foreword to the new edition of his *Post-industrial Society*. According to Bell, the major shifts or changes would be as follows:

- A shift from manufacturing to services. Bell citing the American case in the 1990s showed how only 15 per cent of the American labour force is engaged in manufacturing as against 25 per cent, 25 years ago.
- Ringing in occupational changes. Bell predicted an extraordinary surge in the professional and technical employment with a relative decline of skilled and semi-skilled workers.
- A shift from property to education. He predicted that gone are the days when property would be the identity of a person in a society. Education is the basis of social mobility. The expansion of professional and technical jobs has expanded the scope of recruiting people with higher education background.
- Capital is central to any economic activity in a society. Strictly, in economic sense, capital meant financial capital. Bell also predicted that in a post-industrial society, human capital will come to play an important role in the society. He talked about social capital too which meant access to opportunities and basic needs of human beings.
- Technology will be revolutionized and intellectual technology will be in use. Intellectual technology will run the new 'high technology' with the use of linguistics, mathematics, algorithms, software and simulations. This is just a break from the use of cumbersome machine technologies in the industrial societies.
- Communication is the infrastructure of post-industrial society as against transportation which was the basic infrastructure of industrial societies.
- Bell proposes a knowledge theory of value as opposed to labour theory of value in the industrial society. The latter invested upon the idea of increasing industrial proceeds through labour-saving devices and going in for more capital-intensive and not labour-intensive production mode. For Bell, knowledge is central to innovation and inventions and often can be capital saving.

Further, John Naisbitt (1988) in his path-breaking work, which caught the attention of the academia, his book *Megatrends*, analysed 10 megatrends of the future society and economy. He forecasted shifts in various forms which are summarized as follows:

1. A shift from an industrial to a communication-based economy. Connectivity through communication in all aspects of economy replaced industrial blue-collar society to a white-collar information society.
2. A manufacturing-intensive labour force to a high-tech labour force, balanced with an emphasis on human values, motivation and may be religion also.
3. A short-term to a long-term social and economic philosophy. There will be a shift in business planning from short-term perspective to long-term planning.
4. Economic isolation to global economic interdependence. No economy, even the giant economies like the US economy, can be expected to be the industrial leader but must accommodate world production and world trade.
5. Centralization to decentralization in business, politics and culture. A shift from the unions, presidency and the Congress towards states and regions.
6. From reliance on institutional help provided by governments, medical institutions, school system and corporations to self-help at grassroots. This means self-help through natural childbirth, parental involvement in education, alternative cancer treatment programmes, religious revivalism, venture capitalism, survivalism and other various self-help groups.
7. Representative democracy to participatory democracy.
8. Dependence on hierarchical institutional structures to informal social/economic networks. Development of networks which would transform and increase access of people to goods, services and data on a global scale. What he predicted is the revolution in information technology (IT) and the internet—the lifeblood of communication system.
9. From the Northeast to the Southwest and Florida, leaving behind the old industrial cities and emergence of new cities of rapidly expanding possibilities such as California, Texas, Florida and others.
10. A society with limited options to one with multiple social, cultural and economic options. This will provide more roles for women, specialty foods, cable television with multiple channels and flexitime in the workplace to cite a few examples of the options.

Writing in the 1980s, however, Naisbitt's observations were based on his study of American society, yet they were pointers to future trends in a post-industrial society too. Naisbitt's main focus was a shift from industrial society to information society. Therefore, from the above discussion it becomes clear that Fordism is inapt to address the changes in the economic sectors as they have become quite expansive and not restrictive to industrial sector only.

As pointed out above, economy becomes more and more communication based with the IT revolution, use of web services and the internet. Industry now did not mean only heavy industries with high investments. Investments in global markets can also be done either through portfolio investments or FDI as discussed in Chapter 6. Investments through e-facilities have changed the face of financial movements across the globe. World trade system is like a web now, connected through various means of communication.

Production under such a system cannot be guided by Fordist principles of production. Mass production is no longer the rule of the day. It is not a homogenous market that exists whether in the domestic front or globally. Needs are different of the clientele. Production no longer requires to be centralized in a few key manufacturing centres. Globalization and movement of capital have made it possible that production could be dispersed all over the world. Large-scale production now has to be replaced by computer-controlled tools along with specialized manufacturing techniques that would customize products. The post-Fordist production process is not producer driven but production has become more and more consumer oriented. New designs are important for products to exist and survive. A 'customization' of products is what a post-industrial society look for. Therefore, post-Fordism caters to what the customers want and how and in what form they want. Demands as well as quality are the factors of post-Fordism. Mass consumption is also replaced by mass customization.

Skilled workers working in pairs or in teams with comparative freedom to take decisions in the production process breaks the form of hierarchy present in Fordism. As we have seen in Fordism, workers would work and in no way they would be involved in planning and designing the task. In post-Fordism, managers or supervisors and the employees can have a space to use their skill and expertise to produce a customized product or provide a customized service. Thus, innovation becomes handy to have a competitive advantage in the market. Workers, unlike industrial workers, are not glued to the job for a long term. Even geographical limits are surpassed through outsourcing (next section).

Regarding employment, there is also a flexibility factor as much as there is in production. There can be part-time as well as fixed-term workers. There can be temporary workers hired for their expertise only in providing some kind of a service or produce a customized product or just sharing their technical knowledge. Skilled labour is needed for flexible production which has replaced the Fordist model of unskilled labour performing repetitive and monotonous tasks. The features of post-Fordism are enumerated as follows:

- Highly skilled work
- Customized production
- Customer's choice, a priority
- Continuous training and upgradation
- Complex supply chains and sub-contracting
- Flexible production and decentralized forms of labour process and organizational set-up
- Spread beyond territories and MNCs spearheading the flexible production probes globally
- Emergence of white-collar professional, highly technical and managerial jobs
- Decline of blue-collar unionized labour force
- Expansion of service sector

Still, we must not conclude that Fordism is passé. It is not. In major industrial production units like automobile sectors, assembly line production still exists. However, the production process has become highly automated and is not human intensive. Work once done by humans has now been replaced by highly automized machines and robots. So if Fordism caters to industrial sector, then post-Fordism is the current trend in the era of expanding service sector.

Markets and Labour Process: Changing Nature of Job Security and Labour Rights

Markets and labour process have changed over time. Demand and supply of labour are what constitute the labour market and real wages of the labour. Wages are determined by interaction between demand and supply and sometimes mediation by government and trade unions. High wages are often substituted by firms by capital-intensive technologies or getting cheaper labour. Firms tend to determine their labour supply as well as their wages depending upon the demand of their products. Productivity of a labour is determined by skill levels, education and training, and the use of technology. However, during the Fordist era, mainly the industrial labour was in demand in the market. Skilled, semi-skilled and unskilled labour were supposed to do a particular job for which they had been employed as discussed above. Mass production was the goal for mass consumption. The best example is automobile production at the Ford factory.

However, we have taken into cognition that there have been changes in the nature of jobs in the post-Fordist era. Skilled and even expert manual labour are hired to satisfy customized product demands. Labour can be permanent, semi-permanent, contractual, temporary or even job specific. Firms in a globalized world go for an international staffing policy where recruitment, selection and developing talents are prime motives. Inculcating global mindsets is also necessary. Firms have a huge task of human resource management as well as management of international labour relations. Global outsourcing and offshoring are also now the trends of the international economic order.

Global sourcing is now common which means procurement of products or services from suppliers or company-owned subsidiaries in host countries for consumption in the home country or elsewhere. Business process outsourcing (BPO) is a growing sector. These refer to outsourcing of business functions like finance, accounting or even human resource. Some top companies that outsource are Google, WhatsApp, Alibaba, Skype, Basecamp, Apple, Slack, GitHub and Opera to mention a few. India has the fastest-growing BPO of the IT-enabled services industry. The BPO in India provides various services such as customer support, technical support, insurance processing, telemarketing, forms processing, data processing, bookkeeping and online research among others. In India, Bengaluru is the hub of BPO/ICT sector. India holds 65 per cent of the international offshore BPO market, making it the leading country in providing inbound call centre outsourcing services. Companies outsource for a number of reasons, which are given as follows:

- Reduce cost
- Solve capacity issues
- Enhance service quality
- Access to intellectual capital
- Address critical business needs
- Manage business environment
- Adjust to transformation and changes in business

Offshoring is relocation of a business process and even an entire production unit in a host country. This may involve procurement of products or services from suppliers or company-owned subsidiaries in host countries. A company relocates its in-house jobs to be performed in another country. The top US companies who offshore to India are Ford Motor Company, Cisco, American Express, General Electric and Microsoft. India, over the years, has gained the confidence of the global business community for stability, quality, developed technological infrastructure and the largest professional and technical talent pool in the world, making it a destination for offshoring. The prime motives for offshoring can be summed up as follows:

- Potentiality to offer services and products at lower rates yet probability to earn huge profits as the cost of production gets cheaper.
- Non-availability of resources in the internal market can be accessed easily in the international market through offshoring.
- Involving expert services for the jobs that are offshored such as customer service, IT and software development, which will bridge the gap of talent shortage and expertise for specific jobs.

Therefore, 'standard employment relationship' is now substituted by 'non-standard' flexible forms of employment as discussed above. Such flexible labour relations help firms to adapt to market-related fluctuations. This makes jobs in a globalized market highly risky, insecure and unpredictable for the worker with often no protection of the social benefits. The other factors associated with flexibilization are lower pay, firing and creation of unemployment. Some scholars prefer to call such job insecurity indicative of 'precarious work'. Thus, flexibilization is advantageous for the employer as this helps them to keep a large labour force at a low wage. Firms create jobs and keep them flexible, adaptive and competitive. As quite a contrast to the International Labour Organization (ILO; discussed below), such 'precarious work' induces the employers to shrug off their responsibilities to create situations and work conditions providing rights and security including fixed wages and opportunities for skill development.

In unorganized sectors, especially in the developing countries, such flexible relations had persisted for long. However, in organized sectors, whether industrial or service sector, jobs now tend to be insecure. The motive which works behind this is avoiding tax and dismissal cost liabilities by clinging to hiring flexibility in comparison to permanent work managements.

Newer job opportunities are created and a kind of growth of 'gig economy' is noticeable. App-based services which are geared towards social and community needs are glaring examples of digital online services which are on the move. Concept of 'gig economy' is much larger than online services. Here, a person may be engaged in many services like trading on a part-time or full-time basis. The person might be working from one place or many places. 'Gig-style' employment may, thus, relate to multiple job holding, work from home, self-employment, freelancing and fewer permanent employee jobs. Flexibility in job markets has replaced and re-casted full-time employees into vendors, temporary workers, contractual workers or just service providers for a particular job.

Way back in 2006 in France, student groups and labour unions had protested against the First Employment Contract which was supposed to allow hiring workers under the age of 26 on a trial basis for a two-year period, who could be fired or laid off easily under the country's so-called inflexible labour laws. There have been several protests and millions have taken to the streets to protest against the negative impact of globalization on job security. Virtual migration of labour from developed to developing countries threatens job security. This had helped Donald Trump to whip off the campaign that jobs should be brought back to America. Knowledge cannot be stopped by borders. It will flow using faster internet speeds and hit the jobs of destination countries where there exists supply of skilled low-cost labour. Firms are always looking for low cost in their production/services and labour being an essential input, they like to make minimum investment in it. If in domestic front wages and salaries are high they will divert to destinations where wages are low.

COVID-19 has pulled out of gear a large number of employed people. In May 2020, it was reported that in the USA, 20.6 million jobs had been lost since mid-March, resulting in an unemployment rate of 14.7 per cent, a level not seen since the Great Depression in the 1930s. It has been reported that the number of jobs lost is double the number seen in the 2007–2009 Great Recession, when 8.7 million Americans lost their jobs. The US economy lost 140,000 jobs in December 2020 as unemployment held at 6.7 per cent amid COVID-19 spike as per the data released by the US Labor Department in January 2021.

In India, after the second wave of pandemic overtook the country, 73.5 lakh jobs were lost in April 2021. Data from the Centre of Monitoring Indian Economy (CMIE) showed that the number of employees, both salaried and non-salaried, fell from 39.81 crore in March to 39.08 crore in April 2021. In January 2021, the number of people employed in India was 40.07 crore, according to the CMIE data. Labour economists are of the opinion that the demand in the market has fallen and reverse migration has picked up like 2020 when the first wave had hit India. The next few months will be crucial and the job market stability will depend on how well India can manage the crisis.

There are apprehensions that there will be more use of robots and automation. This means millions will lose their jobs amidst the pandemic post-COVID-19. This brings us to the discussion of labour rights present internationally. They are standards which provide the yardstick for domestic laws. The ILO has played a pivotal role in identifying the basic standards of decent work ensuring productivity as well as equity.

Before going into the discussion about ILO standards, let us look at the significance of 1 May. It is not just a holiday but a commemoration of workers' struggle for their rights. May Day was associated with the demand for eight hours a day of working hours. Unfixed and long working hours had been prevalent in the industries for years. Haymarket was the place chosen for staging the protests which took place on 4 May 1886. The Haymarket affair or the Chicago protests are now commemorated as Labour Day on 1 May. After its proclamation by the First International Congress of Socialist Parties in Europe on 14 July 1889, in Paris, France, 1 May is celebrated every year as the 'Workers Day of International Unity and Solidarity' since 1890. The ILO celebrates 1 May every year as May Day. A theme is chosen every year for the commemoration of workers' movement for their demands pertaining to their working and living standards across the globe through marches, rallies and sensitization programmes. The theme for International Labour Day, 2019, was 'Uniting Workers for Social and Economic Advancement'.

May Day 2020 had to be observed amidst the COVID-19 pandemic when millions of people had come to the verge of losing their jobs or they had lost their jobs due to lockdown and subsequent economic downturn. World Day for Safety and Health at Work 2020 was celebrated on 28 April by the ILO. Addressing the outbreak of infectious diseases at work, the focus was mainly on COVID-19 pandemic. The year 2020 being a challenging one due to the pandemic outbreak across the world, the theme for International Labour Day 2020 was 'maintaining safety and security at the workplace'.

Here, one should not forget about the children too. Hence, 12 June is observed as World Day against Child Labour every year. The day is observed to raise the concern for child labour across the globe who work in deplorable conditions and sometimes hazardous too at minimum wages. The exploitation of a child by snatching away the basic rights to education, food, security and childhood is of increasing concern among the NGOs as well as human rights and child rights activists globally. Therefore, each year, to highlight the plight of child labour across the globe, this day is celebrated on 12 June. The theme for the year 2020, the year of the pandemic was, 'COVID-19—protect children from child labour now, more than ever'. According to figures available from the 'Global Estimates of Child Labour: Results and Trends, 2012–2016', published by the ILO in 2017, approximately 152 million children have been pushed into child labour. Out of the 152 million, around 72 million are involved in hazardous work. Further, the data also reveals that around 48 per cent victims of child labour are aged between 5 years and 11 years, 28 per cent are aged between 12 years and 14 years and the remaining 24 per cent fall in the 15–17 years bracket. So when we discuss about the labour market, we need to focus on child labour as well. In 2021, the ILO, in collaboration with Alliance 8.7, global partnership, launched the International Year for the Elimination of Child Labour. This aims to encourage legislative and practical actions with the objective of eradication of child labour worldwide.

Working class and their problems related to their work conditions are to be borne in mind when we discuss about labour rights. The ILO provides for international standards for guaranteeing workplace conditions, hours of work and other rights. These are envisioned to help in obtaining decent and productive work under conditions of freedom, equity, security and dignity. The essence of the ILO labour standards is enumerated as follows:

- Development of individuals as human beings
- Labour is not a commodity
- Work is integral part of a dignified and decent life
- Economic development encompassing creation of jobs and working conditions so that people can work with freedom, safety and dignity
- Decent work will help in achieving targets of sustainable development (Sustainable Development Agenda 2030)

International conventions that address labour standards have been identified by the ILO. They are considered to be fundamental because they emphasize the rights at work, freedom of association, collective bargaining, elimination of forced or compulsory labour, abolition of child labour, elimination of discrimination in workplace and employment opportunities. The major convention regarding these principles is the **Declaration on Fundamental Principles and Rights at Work, 1998.**

The other conventions are as follows:

1. Freedom of Association and Protection of the Right to Organise Convention, 1948
2. Right to Organise and Collective Bargaining Convention, 1949
3. Forced Labour Convention, 1930 (No. 29, and its 2014 Protocol)
4. Abolition of Forced Labour Convention, 1957 (No. 105)
5. Minimum Age Convention, 1973

6. Worst Forms of Child Labour Convention, 1999
7. Equal Remuneration Convention, 1951
8. Discrimination (Employment and Occupation) Convention, 1958

As the pressure of globalization was creating insecurity and instability in the job market, the ILO in 2008 adopted a path-breaking convention—the ILO Declaration on Social Justice for a Fair Globalization. The Declaration is reaffirmation of the basic principles of the ILO. The International Labour Conference in 2008 upheld through this Declaration the aim to create decent work through a coordinated approach to achieve four strategic objectives. The objectives identified were employment, social protection, social dialogue, and fundamental principles and rights at work.

In India, we have a plethora of labour laws. However, to consolidate the labour laws, the present government has plans to put them into four codes that would merge 44 labour laws under four categories—wages, social security, industrial safety and welfare, and industrial relations. The Code on Wages, 2019, would be replacing the extant Minimum Wages Act, 1936; the Payment of Bonus Act, 1965; and the Equal Remuneration Act, 1976. The Occupational Safety, Health and Working Conditions Code, 2019, will replace 13 labour laws pertaining to safety, health and working conditions. The laws include among many, the Factories Act, 1948; the Dock Workers (Safety, Health and Welfare) Act, 1986; the Contract Labour (Regulation & Abolition) Act, 1970; and the Inter-State Migrant Workmen (Regulation of Employment and Conditions of Service) Act, 1979. The third code proposed is the Industrial Relations Code, 2019, which seeks to replace the extant Industrial Disputes Act, the Trade Unions Act and the Industrial Employment (Standing Orders) Act, 1946. The Code of Social Security, 2019, the fourth code, will replace the existing labour laws on social security in India including the Employees' Provident Funds and Miscellaneous Provisions Act, 1952; the Maternity Benefit Act, 1961; and the Unorganized Workers' Social Security Act, 2008. Except the first one, the other three have been referred to the Standing Committee for its observations.

The prominent trade unions in India are the All India Trade Union Congress (AITUC), the Bharatiya Mazdoor Sangh, the Indian National Trade Union Congress, the Centre for Indian Trade Unions, the All India Trade Union Centre, the Self Employed Women's Association and the Hind Mazdoor Sangh, among others. AITUC is the first trade union of India that was established on 31 October 1920 and completed 100 years in 2020.

Trade unions in India are facing a fast-changing employment scenario. Instead of industry job, there is a continuous growth of services sector where unionism is almost negligible. There is also lack of permanent jobs, and often industries plan to outsource and this poses threats to the existence of the trade unions. Even the new Labour Codes discourage their involvement in workspace. Trade unions now feel that from physical fight on streets to launching of digital mass movements will be needed if they have to survive and put up a collective bargaining strategy.

Globalization has eased the flow of goods, services and capital beyond territories. FDI provides with necessary capital without the host country investing capital directly. Therefore, international trade and FDI have become the main determinants of employment and labour conditions both for the country of origin of FDI or industrialized countries and for host countries or the developing countries. Whenever FDI makes inroads into a host country, labour conditions get affected. When we talk about labour conditions, trade unions and collective bargaining have to be taken into consideration. However, labour in both industrialized and developing countries is under threat. Therefore, there is a widespread fear of jobs being outsourced or firms 'delocalizing' or offshoring through penetration into low-wage countries, which has adverse labour market consequences for domestic workers of the country of origin. Liberalization of trade, rising wage inequality and persistence of high unemployment in advanced economies serve to highlight various labour market 'trends' in advanced economies. There is a concern in industrialized countries that globalization can lead to deterioration of labour conditions. The belief is that rich countries when they open their borders to trade with and provide FDI to poor countries, the poor countries are forced to reduce their labour standards in order to keep up with the increased competition.

A pertinent issue is how unions might respond to the possibility of outsourcing production and employment by firms. If FDI, outsourcing production facilities overseas and offshoring by firms are characteristics of the new global business environment, then these are going to pose challenges to unions and workers and the entire process of collective bargaining. The increased importance of multinational firms and the greater exposure to international competition have brought with them many changes. The most significant change has been the gradual diminution of centralized wage bargaining.

According to Katz (1993), '...increasing prevalence of multinational trade and multinational firms may ... help to explain the declines in multi-employer bargaining that have occurred in a number of countries'. Standing (1997) also argued that international trends towards increased labour market flexibility and deunionization have been propelled by globalization. In fact, the 'erosion' of labour security has been 'fuelled by the international division of labour'.

Therefore, Bhagwati says (1995), '...the bargaining power of employers has increased vis-à-vis that of employees because employers can increasingly say in a global economy that they will pack their bags and leave'.

There is also another view according to Bluestone and Harrison (1982), '...large corporations ... can build, expand, or acquire facilities outside the [USA] altogether. In fact, all the strategic innovations devised by multiplant companies for playing off one group of workers against another ... have become standard operating procedure in the global economy'.

Conclusion

Fordism to post-Fordism, from mass production to flexible customized production, the process and organization of production have come a long way. Firms being located domestically have now spread globally. MNCs are prominent features of contemporary global economy. They are the drivers of FDI. They can bring economic growth to the host economy as well as pose challenges for them. The capital-intensive technologies that the MNCs bring in displace the labour-intensive technologies and create dislocation of job forces. This is quite a challenge in the age of globalization. However, trade unions and collective bargaining can, to some extent, put things into perspective, but they have also weakened. On the one hand, post-Fordism employs flexible labour force and hiring and firing can be done when the requirement ends. On the other, FDI will move into those countries where there is ease of doing business and minimum disturbances from unionism. The collective bargaining power has waned in the face of tough competitions between capitals and productive processes, giving minimum power to the labour. While the wage/salary can be high, the permanency of the job is lost. Creativity, merit, technological expertise and maximum customer satisfaction are requirements to survive in a global economy which requires everything to be customized.

Summary

Organization involves a set of relationship of jobs to jobs, of processes to processes and persons to persons with a common objective to achieve the goal. In order to achieve maximum productivity several organizational theories came to the fore.

The scientific management theory came to influence industrial production for a long time and even became the path bearer of **Fordist modes of production.** With Fordism, assembly line of production became the key mover in industrial production which led to huge increase in production and reduction in cost of goods. Fordist production reduced workers to almost machine-like existence, who were doing repetitive jobs throughout the entire line of production process without scope of creativity or innovation. They had no control over decision-making as this job was to be done by their managers. This system of production continued for long almost till the 1970s, when there was a change in production process with the emergence of service sector giving rise to post-Fordism.

The **post-Fordist form of organization** is quite flexible and creative without much control of over the end product which in a post-Fordist era needs to be customized according to the demand. Mass production is passé and customized products are in. The taste and demand of the customer/client has to be addressed without compromising the quality in a competitive market.

Changes in the nature of jobs in the post-Fordist era witness hiring of skilled and even expert manual labour to satisfy customized product demands. Labour can be permanent, semi-permanent, contractual, temporary or even job specific. Firms have a huge task of human resource management and management of international labour relations as well. Global outsourcing and offshoring are also now the trends of the international economic order. This is obviously related to labour rights.

Working class and their problems related to their work conditions are to be borne in mind when we discuss labour rights. The ILO provides for international standards for guaranteeing workplace conditions, hours of work and other rights. If FDI, outsourcing production facilities overseas, offshoring by firms are characteristics of the new global business environment, then these are going to pose challenges to unions and workers and the entire process of collective bargaining. The most significant challenge has been the gradual diminution of centralized wage bargaining.

REVIEW AND REFLECTION QUESTIONS

1. Assembly line production was the feature of Fordist model of organization. Comment on the features of Fordism. Also, bring out the earlier attempts to organize factory production.
2. Customized products and client satisfaction are the tag lines of the post-Fordist model. Examine the characteristics of the post-Fordist model of organization.
3. Analyse the change in the labour market requirement for skilled workers and flexible labour relations. How this has affected the labour relations and collective bargaining capability of the labour/workers.
4. Give an idea of international labour laws following ILO.
5. Labour has been the backbone of Fordsim, whereas service is the prevalent form of the post-Fordist model. Analyse the changes in the nature of job in the post-Fordist era. Also, analyse whether collective bargaining or trade unionism is on the decline.

Bibliography

Bell, Daniel. 1999. *The Coming of Post-industrial Society*. New York, NY: Basic Books.

Bhagwati, J. 1995. 'Trade and Wages: Choosing among Alternative Explanations.' *Economic Policy Review* 1, no. 1: 42–47.

Blau, F. D., and L. M. Kahn. 1996. 'International Differences in Male Wage Inequality: Institutions versus Market Forces.' *Journal of Political Economy* 104, no. 4: 791–837.

Bluestone, B., and B. Harrison. 1982. *The Deindustrialization of America: Plant Closings, Community Abandonment, and the Dismantling of Industry*. New York, NY: Basic Books.

Business Today. 2021. 'US Reports 140,000 Job Loss in December, First Time since April.' Available at https://www.businesstoday.in/sectors/jobs/breaking-us-reports-140000-job-loss-in-december-first-time-since-april/story/427420.html (accessed on 11 October 2021).

CIDRAP. 2020. 'US Job Losses due to COVID-19 Highest since Great Depression.' Available at https://www.cidrap.umn.edu/news-perspective/2020/05/us-job-losses-due-covid-19-highest-great-depression (accessed on 11 October 2021).

Cooke, W. N. 1997. 'The Influence of Industrial Relations Factors on U.S. Foreign Direct Investment Abroad.' *Industrial and Labor Relations Review* 51, no. 1: 13–17.

Hindustan Times. 2021. 'Covid-19 Second Wave Left 73.5 Lakh Jobless in April.' Available at https://www.hindustantimes.com/business/covid19-second-wave-left-73-5-lakh-jobless-inapr-101620069475883.html (accessed on 11 October 2021).

History.com. 2009. 'Ford's Assembly Line Starts Rolling.' Available at https://www.history.com/this-day-in-history/fords-assembly-line-starts-rolling (accessed on 11 October 2021).

Katz, H. C. 'The Decentralization of Collective Bargaining: A Literature Review and Comparative Analysis.' *Industrial and Labor Relations Review* 47, no. 1: 3–22.

Maheshwari, Shriram. 2003. *Administrative Theory: An Introduction*. New Delhi: Macmillan.

Naisbitt, John. 1988. *Megatrends: Ten New Directions Transforming Our Lives*. New York, NY: Grand Central Publishing.

Pugh, D. S. 1997. *Organization Theory: Selected Readings*. 4th ed. London: Penguin Books.

Standing, G. 1997. 'Globalization, Labour Flexibility and Insecurity: The Era of Market Regulation.' *European Journal of Industrial Relations* 3: 7–37.

5 The State in the Era of Globalization

LEARNING OBJECTIVES

- Gaining knowledge about globalization
- Learning about the main tenets and theories of globalization
- Knowing about the impact of globalization and neoliberal policies on the activities of the welfare state/s
- Comprehending the complexities of relation between development and state autonomy
- Bringing out the importance of development–democracy debate

Introduction

This chapter is quite important as it tries to look into the aspects of globalization, on the one hand, and tries to ponder over the role of state in an age of globalization, on the other. The state as we know is a political unit in international relations with a definite territorial boundary, population, government and, most importantly, sovereignty. The states in contemporary world are subjected to both domestic and international environments. In its domestic front, a democratic state has to abide by the constitution and public opinion. Externally, it is subjected to many international forces such as the IMF, the World Bank and the WTO. It may also be a part of international organizations like the UN and, therefore, has to abide by international law and will of the international comity. However, the picture is not so simple because in the age of globalization, the external forces, especially the economic forces, have an impact on the domestic policies of a state, whether democratic or authoritarian. (The debates on state sovereignty and globalization have been dealt with in Chapter 8 of this book.)

Once a state has gone for economic reforms and has embraced liberalization, the drivers of globalization quickly come to work. The governments might have aimed to allow greater economic integration of their economy through the adoption of market-oriented policies but this, to a great extent, limits the traditional roles of the states. These reforms include various policies such as the removal of controls over foreign exchange, the progressive elimination of capital controls, entry of FDI, the removal of controls over interest rates and the lifting of barriers to entry to banking and financial services, ease of doing business and creation of environment for working of the MNCs. Borrowing from the IMF or the World Bank and working on the guidelines of the WTO means that the states have to remove barriers to facilitate trade in goods, liberalize services and capital flows. This involves introducing SAPs or conditionalities attached with loans from international financial institutions.

Therefore, once a state walks on the path of liberalization and market economy, there arise questions about the limits of its welfare activities. According to Stiglitz (2003) and Bertucci and Alberti (2003), since its inception from the days of the Treaty of Westphalia in 1648, the state has guaranteed internal and external security, looked after law and order, funded national social welfare, provided the structures of democracy, established public accountability and provided the framework for economic and social pursuits. The role of the state has become quite expansive and includes the need to supply collective public goods and provide for minority groups. This chapter will look into whether these welfare activities of the states have been limited by globalization or not. Whether or not a democratic state has difficulty in carrying out reforms and development programmes than an authoritarian state. The debates between democracy and development have long been doing their rounds in the academic circle. So it will be pertinent to take up the issue of democracy and development debate. Most importantly, we will see how autonomous is the state in making its decision in the domestic front or at the international level. These questions are of utmost importance as globalization overtakes the world and the belief is that it universalizes and creates a global village. First, this chapter will address the concept and theories of globalization and then will go into the challenges that states face in the age of globalization.

Globalization: Concept and Theories

A single word which has been used and overused is 'globalization'. From Apple computers to *iPhones,* to pizzas, burgers and other food items, to garments, cosmetics and so on, all the international brands have their presence around the globe. These are only a few examples. Hundreds and thousands of commodities, brands and online service providers with global reach have now become part of our daily life. Amazon, Flipkart, Ola and Uber services, none are indigenous brands. Only a few decades ago, life was content with the things that were produced in the local markets without much intrusion from the global brands. However, life began to change with the opening up of markets since the 1980s, and a phase of liberalization was set rolling around the globe, especially in the developing countries.

Alongside the opening up of markets, there has been a revolution in IT, which has given greater interconnectedness across the globe. Open markets backed by IT and developments in transport and communication system as well as rapid industrialization accelerated the process of integration of the world economy with the national economies. Financial flows in the form of FDI, international trade, flow of goods and services, job outsourcing, global reach of MNCs and host of other activities have increased with liberalization of economies. The growing interconnectedness, therefore, seems to have made the world a web of national economies, resulting in the world becoming a 'single place'. This is what globalization is all about.

The UN also acknowledges the difficulty to define globalization and refers to it as 'increasing and intensified flows between countries of goods, services, capital, ideas, information and people, which produce national cross-border integration of a number of economic, social and cultural activities' (United Nations Department of Economic and Social Affairs 2001).

Further, the United Nations Development Programme (UNDP; 1991) defines *globalization* as the growing 'interdependence of the world's people ... integrating not just the economy but culture, technology and governance. People everywhere are becoming connected – affected by events in far corners of the world'.

Robertson and Chirico define globalization as a set of processes (precisely mentioned above) through which the world is becoming 'a single place'. This definition hints at the growing pace of globalization. The parts that are the states, which comprise the world as so interconnected that events in one part send ripples in others. If we look back at the global financial crisis of 2008 that began in the USA, it sent tremors in all the markets around the globe. Even manufacturing, services, management, technology, raw materials, labour and capital keep on moving around the world. The MNCs and transnational corporations (TNCs) come along with capital and technology and invest in countries where there is an ease of doing business. Media, entertainment, books, education, students, medicines and medical services are all connected in a globalized world. Social media platforms such as Facebook, Instagram, WhatsApp, Signal and Twitter are a growing example of person-to-person contact sans boundaries. The mobile phones, computers and laptops have made the world a small place almost like 'a single place' of interconnectivity and a web of interactions among the parts—the states and the people.

Robert Cox looks at globalization as a process of internationalizing production with new international division of labour. This also involves new migratory movements from the South to the North. He further says that the new competitive environment accelerates these processes and increases internationalizing of state and makes states into agencies of the globalizing world. According to Deepak Nayyar, globalization is 'a process associated with increasing economic openness, growing economic independence and deepening economic integration between countries of world economy'. Therefore, what was being discussed in the preceding portions has been summarized well in these definitions.

Globalization is not a new phenomenon but is a continuous process which started may be with the age of exploration for trade and commerce activities via the Silk Route connecting the East with the West in the 1400s, marking the exchange of products, culture and knowledge through the intermingling of the people. Globalization dates back to Roman, Hellenistic and Persian empires when trade and exchange of products with Asia took place. The ancient trade routes which had shaped history of the world besides the Silk Route are the Spice Routes, the Incense Route, the Amber Road, the Tea Horse Road, the Salt Route, the Trans-Saharan Trade Route and the Tin Route. Lack of or scarcity of commodities which could be only available in certain locations were the main driver behind the operations of such trade networks. It became a bit different with the Industrial Revolution and technological inventions of the 18th century which took place in Europe. This led to unprecedented growth in trade and travel across the globe. Railroads, maritime transport and emergence of manufacturing and trading firms led to movements beyond national boundaries and establishment of colonies in Asia and Africa.

The British East India Company is an example of an early MNC establishing its foothold in Asia and India came under its domination for 100 years till 1858. The Charters provided by Britain to the East India Company formally accessed India as a colony of the British Empire. By the Queen's Proclamation of 1858, after the Sepoy Mutiny, Queen Victoria took direct control over administration of India. So started the direct colonial domination of the British Empire over India which continued till India got her independence in 1947. Similarly, this was the scenario in Africa and other countries of Asia. The entire world became protectorates/

colonies or dependencies of the European colonial powers. Some examples of colonization can be illustrated here. In the 17th century, there were British American colonies in New England, Maryland and Virginia including settlements in the Bermudas, Antigua, Honduras, Nova Scotia and Barbados. Jamaica became a British colony in 1655. The East India Company began establishing foothold in India around 1600. The Straits Settlements on the Strait of Malacca comprised of four trade centres of Malacca, Penang, Labuan and Singapore, established by the British East India Company around this time. In 1661, the first permanent British settlement in the African continent was made at James Island in the Gambia River. Later, Sierra Leone and the Cape of Good Hope were acquired by the Britishers.

This was the Age of Imperialism. Lenin views imperialism as the stage of capitalist development created by certain features of monopolist capitalist stage. Along with exportation of finance capital, there is an economic division of world by multinational enterprises through international cartels. Over and above, the flow of finance capitals is facilitated by the political division of the world by great powers of the day into their colonies wherein there is continued exploitation and continued investment. Eric Hobsbawm in his *Age of Empire* (1994) has shown that during the period between 1880 and 1914, most of the world outside Europe and the Americas was formally partitioned into territories under the formal rule or informal political domination of one or the other handful of states. These dominant states were Great Britain, France, Germany, Italy, the Netherlands, Belgium, the USA and Japan. The process of exploitation of the colonies was later given a newer outlook with the development of the modern world system theory and the dependency theory in the 1970s (Chapter 1).

The process of globalization of the colonial period took a different turn in the period after the conclusion of the Second World War. The Great Depression of the 1930s and a worldwide economic downturn compelled the states to pursue inward economic policies and different exchange rate systems. The whole system underwent a change with the end of the Second World War. In 1944, the Bretton Woods institutions were established to bring about stability in the world economy. The IMF, the World Bank (1947) and the GATT (1947) were established to open up trade and remove tariff barriers. On the other hand, with the establishment of the Bretton Woods institutions, the US hegemony was established with the introduction of a fixed exchange rate system where currencies were pegged to the US dollar (details in Chapter 3). Dollar could be exchanged for gold. It was as good as gold.

The Bretton Woods institutions became the main engines of globalization as they made every endeavour towards spreading liberalization worldwide. Following the phase of decolonization which started in the aftermath of the Second World War, the newly independent countries pursued their individual models of economy. Mostly, they followed not-so-liberal economic policies. In fact, they were sceptical about opening their markets. There were huge trade and tariff barriers for imports and mostly public enterprises were encouraged. State intervention at all levels was present in these newly independent countries. India followed a mixed economic model where there was a heavy presence of state in every sphere of economy with emphasis on welfare of the people and an import substitution industrialization model. Following the economic hardships of the developing countries including India in the 1980s, there was an unprecedented spree for liberalization and opening up of economies. These gave a spurt to globalization. The drivers obviously were the IMF, the World Bank and the WTO (erstwhile GATT) which bailed out the economies in lieu of SAPs or conditions which were dictated by them to the economies to move towards more liberalization and privatization.

This phase of globalization was markedly different from the earlier phases. There were movements of capitals, FDI, goods and services, labour, transfer of technologies and exchange of information with great speed as world experienced unparalleled growth in trade and finance. Rapid growth in cross-border trade of products, services and capital with the rise in international firms and increased potential of the emerging markets took globalization to new heights. The contemporary phase of globalization was further boosted by IT revolution, improvement in transportation and technologies, worldwide reduction in barriers to trade and investment, market liberalization and adoption of free markets, industrialization, economic development and modernization and integration of world financial markets.

However, there are different perspectives on globalization. The scholars fall into three categories as they put forward three different perspectives/waves of globalization. They are the hyperglobalists, the sceptics and the transformationalists. The **hyperglobalists** are the proponents of the 'first wave' in the theory of globalization. They are the enthusiasts about globalization. The key points that they hinge upon are decreasing relevance of national economies and emergence of a global economy. This is set in motion by the opening up of national markets and their integration into the global market through transnational networks of production, capital mobility, transborder movement of trade and finance brought about by increased activities of the MNCs. A single global market is created where MNCs become active carriers of global capital movement. The international economic and political institutions also make the states constraint their activities. The internet, technological innovations and more connectivity through improved transport and communication system and social media mark globalization of the contemporary times. The global economy is characterized by openness and the parts of the world are integrated through a globalized international market. In other words, the spirit of globalization is neoliberal capitalism. The hyperglobalists, therefore, propound economic interdependence in a globalized world with transborder movement of capital, labour, services, technology and information.

The **sceptics** have doubts about the even distribution of the effects of globalization. For them, global economy is not inclusive. The rich and poor divide becomes blatant. The Sub-Saharan countries cannot match up to the economies of the Global North. For that matter, the less developed countries and the developing countries are at a disadvantageous position compared to the developed North. The North–South global divide is quite well known. The sceptics also point out that politically the effects are also uneven. In the global scenario, there are powerful states, middle-range states and weak states. The international bodies like the UN Security Council, international negotiations on global warming, agreements of nuclear non-proliferation and even international financial institutions are driven by the interests of the powerful and dominant states of the world. While the dominant states try to impose liberalization and free trade on others, they may themselves follow protectionism for several sectors of their economy. The glaring example is the US subsidies for agriculture even if the USA is under the WTO stipulations. The USA has used the 'green box' and 'blue box' model of subsidies. These are subsidies which are direct payment to farmers made by the governments. These protect the interest of farmers whereby the WTO guidelines can be bypassed as these are not linked with production and, therefore, are not market distorting in nature. However, these subsidies increase the competitiveness of the farmers of developed countries such as the USA, Europe and Japan and put the farmers of the developing countries in a challenging position.

The sceptics have pointed out that states of Europe, North America and East Asia are dominant players in international political economy rather than the states of most part of Asia, Africa and Latin America. States, for the sceptics, do exist and do not become insignificant as per the hyperglobalists, but they retain their sovereignty and autonomy unevenly in the global order.

P. Hirst and G. Thompson (2009) have outlined their take on globalization although they kept their focus on economic globalization. They use the word 'internationalization' rather than globalization. They see internationalization of technology, financial markets, manufacturing and services. Their logic is globalization is happening within existing global economic structures and among states. So it is international rather than what has extended globally. In reality, world economy is concentrated in the triad—Europe, Japan and North America—and they exert influence over financial markets. So internationalization is limited to the triad only and not global or something that goes beyond national or international structures. Thus, globalization should be demystified as a process that develops in an uneven way.

The **third wavers** or the **transformationalists** like Held opine that globalization brings about transformative changes in all aspects. Domestic and international in economic, social and political spheres cannot be clearly demarcated. The international influences the domestic. National gets transformed under the influence of the international in all spheres of life. Economies under the spell of globalization become more deterritorialized, transnational and global. Still sovereign states exist though their functions are restrained by multiple factors such as international organization, global transport and communication, MNCs and global governance. National societies do exist but are enmeshed in interregional networks. There is no global convergence like a single world society. Stratification is reconstituted. Apart from core–periphery or North–South model, the middle-range economies of Latin America and Asia are recognized as getting more integrated into the world economy. On the other hand, African countries get more debilitated. Therefore, globalization has an uneven effect and creates exclusion. Governments try to handle the challenges of globalization by adopting neoliberal strategies, economic liberalism and levels of state intervention vis-à-vis global economy.

Scholte gives a view of qualified globalism. For him, globalization involves supraterritorial relations hinting at the intensification of global connectivity which goes beyond units but retains territory which is transcended. There is no pure globality that exists beyond independent territorial spaces. There is an intersection of global, regional, national and the local levels. This is the most encompassing definition that can be given for globalization.

It is unquestionable that despite such variations in the thinking about the perspectives of globalization, there is an immense interconnectedness among the states of the world, among the people and revolution in technology, transport and communication and, of course, the internet along with greater movement of capital, labour, technology, products and services. Whether such activities limit the autonomy of states and their welfare activities is an important point of argument which must be a matter of predilection for academic discussion.

Globalization and the Limits of Welfare State

State as we know is a sovereign territorial political entity with a government and a population called citizens. The relationship between the government and its citizens is the basis which determines the political rule as democratic, semi-democratic or authoritarian. The other way in which the relation between the government and its citizens can be examined is how responsive is the government to the basic needs of the citizens. Whether it has some welfare schemes for its citizens or not?

The 19th century witnessed the emergence of welfare states in Britain, the USA, Germany and France, those countries that constructed developmental states during this time. Welfare state grossly means the different ways in which states aim to provide social justice through the practice of redistribution of taxes, which constitutes the main way of financing the welfare state (Chapter 7). In the 21st century, it is criticized as an obstacle for the self-regulating forces of the free market within a state as well as globally from the neoliberal perspective.

Although the typical 19th- or 20th-century welfare states with heavy spending on social security schemes may not currently exist in a globalized world, the question can very well be raised whether a state addresses the welfare of the people or simply play in the hands of market economy. The COVID-19 crisis of 2020 has forced us to rethink about the role of the state in the lives of the citizens in the face of terrible economic crisis.

Social security programmes might include schemes such as agricultural price support, housing policies, cash benefits to households, subsidies on various government services, access to education (primary and secondary), healthcare benefits, pension schemes and old age care to mention a few. In India, there are several schemes of social funding such as Atal Pension Yojana, Employees' Provident Fund Organisation, Mahatma Gandhi Pravasi Suraksha Yojana, Pradhan Mantri Kisan Samman Nidhi, Ayushman Bharat and many others. In the USA, there are social security schemes which were started by President Franklin Roosevelt in 1935 vide the Social Security Act. The schemes include Old-Age, Survivors, and Disability Insurance; health insurance for aged and disabled; temporary assistance for needy families; State Children's Health Insurance Program for low-income citizens; and Supplemental Security Income. From the period 2017–2019, in the Organisation for Economic Co-operation and Development (OECD) countries, on average, public spending on old age and survivor pension payments was 7.8 per cent of GDP and on health was 5.6 per cent of GDP. These are the largest spending amongst all sectors although there are variations across the OECD countries. According to the OECD Social Expenditure update (2020), public pension spending is highest in Italy and Greece, almost at over 15 per cent of GDP and lowest in Chile, Korea and Mexico, around 3 per cent of GDP. In France and Germany, public expenditure on health is over 8 per cent of GDP, while it is less than 3 per cent of GDP in Mexico and the Netherlands. Therefore, it can be said that states currently pursue a policy of public spending even if they follow a neoliberal model of economies.

Whenever we talk about welfare of people or social or public spending for ensuring basic amenities to the people, we have to mention about John Rawls' *A Theory of Justice* (1971), where he has provided a case for distributive justice. Rawls assumed that principles of justice are chosen in the 'original position' behind a 'veil of ignorance'. This would ensure that the principles are chosen under a fair condition. 'Original position' is such a state of affairs in which the individuals can enter any time by following certain procedure. It is a contract but not in the sense of the contract arrived in the state of nature as propounded by the social contract theorists. As individuals enter into the 'original position' through the 'veil of ignorance', the choices made are rational and objective. 'Veil of ignorance' in the original position makes everyone forget about one's status, class or position in the society. Rawls' two principles of justice are as follows:

1. Each person should have an equal right to the most extensive basic liberty compatible with a similar liberty for others.
2. Social and economic inequalities are to be arranged so that they are both, first, reasonably expected to be to everyone's advantage and, second, attached to positions and offices open to all.

From the second principle, he deduces that 'difference principle' is better than other choices in dealing with inequalities in society. He argues that social and economic inequalities are to be arranged so that they are both to the greatest benefit of the worst off and attached to offices and positions open to all under the conditions of fair and equal opportunity. This is a reformulation of his own second principle as his conviction was that difference principle is the basis of the general conception of justice applicable to liberty opportunity as well other than primary goods. Rawls argues that such a society is a well-ordered society which ensures the welfare of its members and is regulated by a public sense of justice. If seen from this angle of distributional justification and human development (Chapter 8), social security and welfare schemes help to fight several negative factors detrimental to human progress and increase in human productivity. Eradication of poverty, providing access to education, fighting gender discrimination, robust healthcare system and improving human rights system are among many such objectives behind the welfare schemes. Nevertheless, there is also a linkage between such schemes and politically generated redistribution for voting and electoral benefits.

Many scholars have linked the early 19th- and 20th-century public spending in most of the Western countries to the emergence of franchise and suffrage. Urbanization, industrialization and its fall out creating groups of new voters which required new social arrangements had geared up social welfare mechanisms. Welfarism needs huge public spending. Neoliberal thinking goes in the way that public spending would be a burden for the government and would bring down growth. As COVID-19 has put us in a difficult situation, it is high time to question the precept of neoliberal state which is based on market economy and downsizing public spending.

Joseph E. Stiglitz in his 'The Welfare State in the Twenty-first Century' (2017) opines that the main principle of neoliberal states is market-driven economy with limited governmental control. Governmental intervention is only a welcome to ensure macroeconomic stability. Many neoliberals argue that welfare states creates a kind of culture of dependency and welfare schemes are burden on the state. On the other hand, advocates of welfare states believe that market failures are pervasive and they create hardships for individuals. Government is needed to play a more active role and help individuals from being exploited by market forces. Therefore, a certain kind of depravation induces the advocacy of a welfare state or welfare-oriented state.

Chapter 8 deals with the concept of human development which is a paradigm shift from the conventional concept of development defined strictly in an economic sense. GDP does not ensure an inclusive development. Human development in all aspects will increase the potentials of individuals, secure an inclusive development and contribute to higher GDP. To ensure this kind of human development, thinking beyond the market is, therefore, necessary. The Universal Declaration of Human Rights adopted by the General Assembly in 1948 recognized access to basic amenities as primary human rights. For example, food, shelter, education, health and economic opportunities are some of the basic rights which can ensure human development. Left to the market forces, these will be deprived to the masses. Such depravations which are deep and pervasive necessitate the intervention of the state to ensure welfare of the masses. Depravations may be looked at from the perspective of the deprived as social injustice. Thus, as Stiglitz points out, the creation of the welfare state was conditioned by the failures in the economy and the society which have created socially unacceptable outcomes in the form of depravations. The 21st-century welfare state may not exist per se but countries, even the most developed ones as well as the developing ones, have retained the social security schemes or social protection in order to achieve societal well-being.

The current concern is that in the face of globalization and free market economy, how far welfare state is viable. In other words, how does globalization set the limits of the welfare state? As pointed out earlier, the conventional thinking is that welfare states and economic globalization cannot be compatible. Redistributive taxation is a source of welfare schemes. However, in the domestic arena as well as at global level, this constrains, on the one hand, the competitiveness of domestic firms and, on the other, lessens the lucrative attraction of global investments and financial flows. There has been rapid integration of international markets for capital, services and goods. Financial capital flow usually is against all government policies that distort markets and welfare programmes are among the most prominent targets creating obstructions.

Factors of production and market, therefore, constrain the limits of the welfare state. Globalization with its homogenizing agenda seeks to create uniform kind of market functioning around the globe. Since the current brand of globalization is based on free market economy on the principles of neoliberalism, it has pushed for similar kind of free economy and free trade regime globally. As seen in Chapter 3, the Bretton Woods system with its triad, the IMF, the World Bank and the GATT/WTO, has been set on the mission of homogenizing market production around the globe. Thus, liberalization has led to disinvestment in public sector, privatization, opening up of all sectors of economy, allowing entry of FII, FDI and MNCs and so on. A simple example will explain how the states are throttled by the agenda of free economy. MNCs look out for economies of scale and invest in those countries where they get tax benefit and concessions than their home countries (Chapter 3). If they face a high taxation regime in a host country, they would not move in and, therefore, FDI would be low.

Globalization creates new pressures and challenges, such as shocks and market failures, the latest being the 2008 financial crisis, to the sustainability of the welfare state. Nevertheless, it also hinges upon the importance of the fact that income redistribution and social insurance programmes can help welfare-oriented states. These will be means to reduce the risk and inequalities created by the working of the market. Scholars like Rodrik (1997, 1998) put forward **compensation hypothesis** which can be viewed as attempts by welfare states to address the rising demands of social security because of external risks and economic dislocations caused by open market economy. Here, the state with its political institutions has to mediate between the market and the masses.

Social protection helps in fighting if not eliminating poverty, deprivation and inequality. In times of crisis like the COVID-19 with deep social and economic impact leading to loss of jobs, lives, stresses, in short existential problems, such social protection expenditure not only mitigates greater hardships and poverty but also plays an important counter cyclical role. Social protection can then ensure the basic human rights also.

Even though India from 1991 to the current time is walking on the path of liberalization, there has been an increasing rise of revenue expenditure on social security since 1991. In India, by October 2020, the budget estimates of revenue expenditure on social security and welfare of central and state governments amounted to more than ₹1.6 trillion. This value saw an exponential increase since fiscal year 1991. The COVID-19 crisis has once again made it a necessity to rethink about the social security expenditure. The Economic Survey 2019–2020 revealed that the expenditure on social services by the centre and states increased from ₹7.68 lakh crore in 2014–2015 to ₹15.79 lakh crore in 2019–2020. COVID-19 crisis showed that India is among the countries with the lowest public healthcare budget in the world. When compared to the OECD expenditure on social security, it revealed that the public healthcare system in India, both at the state and central levels, is close to 1.3 per cent of GDP, whereas in the OECD countries, the average is at 7.6 per cent and other BRICS countries have an average of 3.6 per cent. In the Union Budget 2021–2022, the finance minister, Nirmala Sitharaman, proposed an outlay of ₹2.23 lakh crore towards health and well-being. This is seen to be a 137 per cent increase over the ₹94,452 crore budgeted expenditure on healthcare in the ongoing fiscal year. The health scheme is an addition to the existing National Health Mission that is focusing on three areas: preventive, curative and well-being.

Joseph E. Stiglitz in his 'The Welfare State in the Twenty-first Century' again asks a pertinent question which is very relevant to conclude the discussion on the limits of welfare state. The question he asks is, 'Is a welfare state viable today?' He answers that too. Stiglitz is of the opinion that although there is a need of a welfare state, the fiscal capacity of the states has been reduced and is insufficient due to tax competition. He sees taxing the MNCs and redesigning the tax structure money can be used for providing basic social protection. The other point that Stiglitz provides is that a welfare state can increase the overall economic performance by creating situations for equitable distribution of resources and social justice. There can also be other arguments like social stability and support for the open international economy are dependent on providing collective good that governments can help maintain through large welfare state effort, especially in the short-term market where volatility is high, especially with respect to financial markets.

Thomas Piketty in his book, *Capital in the Twenty-first Century* (2017), talked about the 'social state'. Pointing out first to the fact that after the global economic crisis of 2008, a crisis/crash of capitalism since the Great Depression of 1929, the central banks came to the rescue and played the role of the lender of last resort. The state too played a greater role than ever during this crisis. In the European countries, during the Great Depression, the Second World War and their post-War reconstruction had heavy public spending and expanding role of the state. This was also thought to be the capitalist design to cope with the crisis by increasing social spending. Piketty says that the increase in government tax revenues was used for the construction of a 'social state'. However, the question is that if total taxes and social spending taken in the case of European countries remain the same in proportion to the national income, then how can the states cope with that huge rising expenditure. When trying to figure out social state in the poor and emerging countries, it can be seen that a meagre percentage of national income goes for social spending. Therefore, Piketty suggests that a continuous assessment of situation is needed in order to adapt the social services to the public's needs because at the end, the consensus support high level of taxation and, thus, the social state may not last forever.

When asked in an interview in *The Guardian* in May 2020 about if there is a possibility that the COVID-19 pandemic is tipping us towards the kind of participatory socialism that Piketty had recommended, he said that it is too early to say. Nevertheless, it will reinforce the legitimacy of public investment in healthcare. He further opined that building a welfare state within a nation state was already a huge challenge. Doing it at a transnational level is possible but it will probably have to be done in a small number of countries first. Others can join later if they believe in the ideology. From an EU perspective, he hoped that it can be done without breaking the current EU, and also hoped that Britain will rejoin the EU eventually. On the talk about de-globalization after this crisis, Piketty opines that it will happen in some strategic areas, such as medical supplies, just because we need to be better prepared for the next pandemic. However, more work needs to be done like getting out of this zero-tariff mindset, if only to pay for global threats such as climate change and pandemics. This means inventing a new narrative about where we stop with tariffs. He ends by saying that history has shown us, there is never just one solution. This is, therefore, an ongoing debate about the limits of the welfare state.

Development and State Autonomy

Whenever autonomy of state comes up for discussion, the starting point is the concept of relative autonomy as expounded by Karl Marx in his *The Eighteenth Brumaire of Louis Bonaparte* (1852). Here, he had forwarded the concept of relative autonomy as state being absolutely or relatively autonomous from the ruling class. Early writings of Marx treated state as a product of the class divisions of a given economic stage of development. For example, in a capitalist society, the state reflected the capitalist interest. The ruling class controlled the state and the state was the instrument of oppression and exploitation of the have-nots by the haves. It was in *The Eighteenth Brumaire of Louis Bonaparte* (1852) that Marx talked about relative autonomy of Bonapartisim. Marx said, 'Bonaparte is the executive authority which has attained power in its own right, and as such it feels it feels to be its mission to safeguard the "bourgeois" order ... by creating its [the bourgeoisie's] material power, it recreates its political power'. This kind of observation actually points out that the state has separated itself from the society and that the state is the political form of class domination in a bourgeois society which enjoys relative autonomy. There is an apparent separation between state and society and ultimately there are mechanisms that link the state and the dominant class/es.

Relative autonomy model has also been forwarded by Ralph Miliband in his famous work *The State in Capitalist Society* (1969). While distinguishing between ruling class of civil society and the governing class holding positions in the institutions of the state, he pointed out the relative autonomy of the state. However, the private ownership of the capital and ideological processes created popular consent to the class-based rule of the capital. Therefore, the institutions of the state met the instrumental needs of the capital even though the state was relatively autonomous from the capitalist class.

Another great work on the concept of relative autonomy was that of Nicos Poulantzas. In his *Political Power and Social Class* (1968), he pointed out that the relative autonomy of the state was due to a spatial separation of the juridico-political level which ran the state and the economic level or the owners of the capital and means of production. The state in historical trajectories has enjoyed autonomy from the political interests of the capitalist classes. However, due to the structure of the state, it compromises with the interests of the dominant classes for the purpose of their political interests and hegemonic domination. To him, the state was not an isolated set of institutions but a platform for class struggles and political compromises which in turn shaped the structure of the economy.

The social democratic welfare policies of European countries can be tracked to the idea of development by Keynes, especially in Sweden, Norway and France, in response to unemployment during the *Great Depression*. Therefore, accordingly, they included three main features following Keynesian ideas: (a) the state operates those activities which are unprofitable for private firms but necessary for the economy as a whole; (b) the state regulates, particularly by pursuing anti-cyclical policies, the operation of the private sector and (c) the state mitigates, through welfare measures, the distributional effects of the operation of the market.

Social democratic regimes allowed that the capital and labour influence public policies in accordance to their interests while the state was caught in between class struggles. In Europe, such regimes enjoyed autonomy while they combined elements that comprise the sociopolitical and institutional production of the autonomy of the state including interests, struggles and power resources of the classes (partisan and associative organizations), class balance, neo-corporatist institutional arrangement of interest intermediation, class compromise and state capacities. As a result of these elements of state power and public policies, Keynesianism and welfare became popular. Post-Second World War, Keynesian economic policies had a great impact but began to be counteracted by neoliberalism since the 1980s.

From the 1990s, there was the wave of globalization and economic reforms with emphasis on less state interventions and privatization across the globe. On the other hand, in Latin American countries since the late 1990s, there have been countervailing movements that rearranged relations of forces, produced greater balance in class relations and constructed new political coalitions. In the early 2000s, Venezuela, Brazil, Bolivia, Ecuador, Argentina, among other countries, pursued counter-neoliberal policies on a new national feeling as key point to development. The execution of counter-neoliberal policies was intended to broad social bases addressing the poor people and the productive capitalism aiming at more inclusion. In these countries, in the period of the 1990s, the state was less captured by rentiers and financial institutions and more accountable to the nation as a whole enjoying greater relative autonomy.

Thus, absolute autonomy and even relative autonomy of states vary in degree depending upon their nature of political system and capacity to make policy decisions and bring in development. Now the question arises, if there is relative autonomy, then what is this autonomy from classes or the economy or the international system or organized interests. Development and state autonomy, a subject too complex to understand must be examined from these angles also. Development involves stakeholders and state is a part of it. Without the consent and permission of the state, especially in a democracy, it is difficult to carry out development. The question is how far this consent or permission is autonomous and how far it is conditioned. Whether all the stakeholders are brought into the structure of planning, designing and execution of the development projects?

Planning and execution of development projects depend upon factors like state capacity. What is state capacity? First, state has a capacity unparalleled to other and that is power. State is the repository of power or capacity to get members of the society to do things which they might not do otherwise. The state exerts this power through policy instruments and its institutions of execution. The outcome of the policy depends upon the other capacity of the state. Second, resources at disposal of the state are another important capacity of the state. How much the state can deploy its assets in order to increase the efficacy of policy instruments is very important. The most effective state will have the capacity to select a broad range of policies as it is confident that it can implement them well. Therefore, it can target to achieve a broad range of outcomes. Resources may range from financial assets to natural resources to human capital to economic growth to size of population and it might even include in the contemporary times access to information and better communication facilities.

As we started our discussion with democracy, let us now examine the relationship between capacity and autonomy first before we go into totalitarian states. This can be analysed from the point of how far the state is controlled by external forces and its capacity to control the outcomes in a democratic set-up. A constitutional government prevents illegitimate interventions of social and economic power. In other words, the privileged interests are not given a primacy over common interests. Democracy as it is associated with the rule of the people, it is assumed that minimal control over the state would be exercised by different factors in the society. In a representative democracy, however, control over the political elites who are elected by the people is more indirect. Elections and exercise of adult suffrage are the means of exercising control but that control does not extend to control over their policy decisions yet restrains the state's aversive behaviour. Here comes the interplay between politico-socio-economic factors in democracy which constrain the relative autonomy of the state.

On the other hand, in totalitarian regimes, there is absence of factors that are present in democracies. Thus, whatever despotic power of the state will wish to achieve through policy decisions would be achieved in connivance with or without conforming to organized interests or even going against the common interests. A despotic state is, thus, more autonomous than a democratic state. According to the Democracy Index, published by Economic Intelligence Unit (EIU), 2020, Russia, China, North Korea, Cuba, Vietnam, Venezuela, Afghanistan and most Middle East countries and most African countries are examples of authoritarian states. The North American countries, especially the USA, and the European countries are examples of democracies ranging from full democracies to flawed democracies. Countries such as India and Sri Lanka are flawed democracies, whereas Pakistan, Bangladesh, Bhutan and Nepal are hybrid regimes.

Figure 5.1 Autonomy of State: Democratic and Totalitarian Set-ups

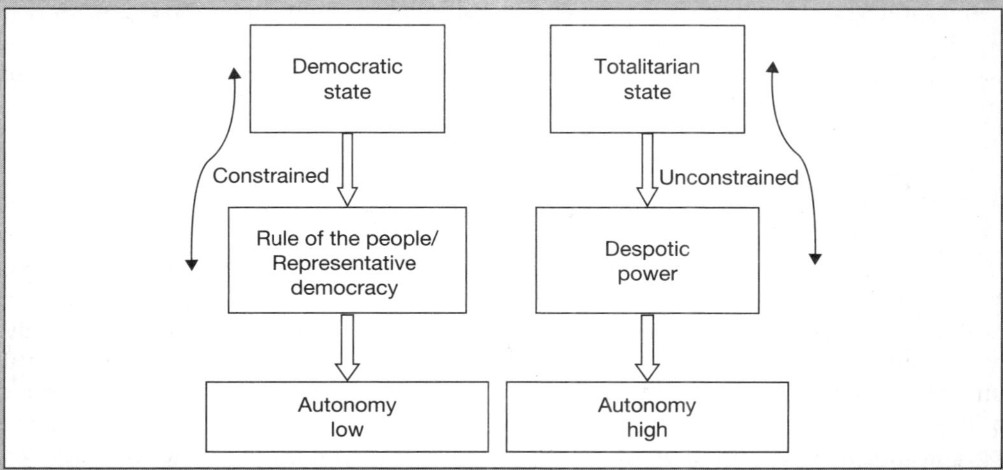

As pointed out in the previous section on globalization and welfare state, here also the same thing comes into the discussion as the scope of the governments gets narrowed by international factors. Free trade and capital movements across the globe impact domestic decision-making in countries in all spheres. Further, through integration with the world economy, the countries become vulnerable to external shocks as happened in 2007–2009, known as the global melt down or global economic crisis (Chapter 8). This vulnerability results in income volatility or aggravated inequality. These then lead to domestic conflicts as well as increasing demand for public services. As Sheve and Slaughter (2004) put it, economic integration exposes national economies to the turbulences in the world economy which generate more uncertainty and volatility in the domestic economy. In the face of such crisis and greater insecurity, the state would be forced to provide more social protection and insurance. This, in the words of Rodrik, is known as 'compensation hypothesis'. How much the state will deliver to its people again depends upon the nature of the regime. If it is democratic, then the 'compensation hypothesis' to some extent can work under public pressure or voting and electorate. Under a totalitarian set-up, which is quite autonomous, the 'compensation hypothesis' is difficult to work.

To conclude this discussion on relative autonomy, one has to bring in the views of Theda Skocpol (1985). She is of the view that all states perform exclusively certain political tasks that include administrative, legal, extractive and coercive. To a certain extent, the state competes with the dominant class in the appropriation of economic resources. During certain crisis moments, such as the economic and international crisis, the state can assume more power and a greater autonomy. Examples can be cited as the New Deal in the USA which in general follows a neoliberal policy. The COVID-19 crisis that has grappled the world has again proved her point. The states have assumed more strength and are making efforts to mitigate the sufferings of the people through aid, welfare schemes and vaccinations. US President Donald Trump signed a $2 trillion bailout package, the largest after President Barack Obama signed a $800 billion bailout package during the 2008 economic crisis. India declared a ₹20 lakh crore package for all segments of the economy in 2020.

However, it should not be forgotten, as discussed in Chapter 2, that monopolistic firms, cartels and currently MNCs and TNCs have a great influence on the domestic as well as foreign policies of states. If not colonial domination, but neo-colonialism or neo-imperialism is still exists through the coalescence of political and economic factors. Therefore, relative or absolute autonomy had been a debatable issue and it will still remain a contentious issue in IPE.

Development–Democracy Debate

The relationship matrix between democracy and development remains a very highly contested issue. Development studies have long pondered over the debate between democracy and development. The prime question that comes to our mind is the compatibility factor between democracy and development. Is democracy conducive to development? Or does democracy bring in economic and human development at the same pace? Are the authoritarian regimes more autonomous than democracies in the case of development also? Couple of these questions haunt our minds. The answers to these are not simple and cannot be put into a straightjacket.

Let us look at what democracy has to offer to its people. Democracies are related to presence of a number of factors which distinguish them from authoritarian regimes. What are then the conditions of democracy? Free and fair elections and civil liberties are necessary conditions for democracy, but they are unlikely to be sufficient for a full and consolidated democracy if unaccompanied by transparent and at least minimally efficient government, sufficient political participation and a supportive democratic political culture. It is not easy to build a sturdy democracy. Even in long-established ones, if not nurtured and protected, democracy can corrode.

In a democratic state, what one usually finds is that the political power is organized and institutionalized in a particular way. Gianfranco Poggi in *The State: Its Nature and Development* (1990) puts forward certain conditions of democracies at large. He has used the term **democratic legitimation** by which he meant the state's acknowledgement of the fact that it regards the citizens as the foundation of its rule and the 'ultimate seat of all powers that it exercises'. He also claimed that a bond that links the populace to the state through the notion of citizenship is a set of general and equal entitlements and obligations vested in individuals with respect to the state, as well as the content of society's activity and outputs. Further, he stated that democracies are marked by the existence of the **rule of law.** There is the presence of Weberian legal-rational domination in the organization of political power expressed through laws. The most vital point about democracies is the presence of or allowance of opposition to the state, debates and contestation over policies, critical orientations and expressions which are legitimized and institutionalized and may be regarded as productive. Therefore, democracies acknowledge the public sphere and give recognition to the rights of assembly, association and petition to the masses. Needless to say, in democracies, there is the established institution of **representative government** based on periodic elections.

The noteworthy thing about the democratic institution of power is the position of powerholders and officials or, in other words, the incumbents to power. In a democratic set-up, one thing is sure that the powerholders are temporary tenants of power and after a certain period of their tenure, they have to seek people's mandate in elections. This makes the representatives of the people subject to **removal by political-legal means** if they abuse their power. Administrative officials exercise power on behalf of the public and are public servants. The state is not the 'creature' of rulers and officials but the state is 'separated', conceptually and institutionally, from officials and holders of power. In other words, the office is more important than the office-holder.

Poggi points out that political power in a democracy is 'tamed' and 'depersonalized'. This means that the use of arbitrary power can be restrained by legal safeguards ensured through rule of law. Political participation is a vanguard against state control or excesses. The state can be made to respond to popular demands if it goes against them. Thus, to Poggi, the state–society interrelationship is monitored and moderated by the legal sphere and legal-rational procedures which are binding on both rulers and ruled. Power is institutionalized in such a way that state power—and state autonomy—is moderated by countervailing forces in the public sphere.

Theoretically speaking, these are the broad parameters which distinguish democratic systems from autocratic or authoritarian ones. However, the functioning of established democracies or transitional democracies has put many of these parameters under scanner. If the guise of democracy is used by a person/group of persons, at the helm of powers, to tighten their grip on political power, then revolution or changing of status quo may become inevitable. Such deviations make situations prone to conflict. The situation may be said to be one where there is **democracy deficit.** When there is a democracy deficit, the regime can be classified as transitional democracy, flawed democracies, authoritarian regimes or even dictatorship.

The basic features of democracies can be enumerated as follows:

1. Presence of universal adult franchise or voting right.
2. Periodic elections which must be free and fair.
3. Representative democracies to have people's representatives elected through elections.
4. Freedom of speech and expression for all.
5. Rights and liberties to be ensured to the citizens.
6. Popular sovereignty to be a cardinal principle.
7. Subject to the rule of law.
8. Laws to be enacted through institutions of democracies (the legislatures) and not personal whims of leaders. Laws should be reflection of common interest and not personal preference.

In sum, it can be said that a democratic state is a complex system which is characterized by multiple features such as electoral institutions, political parties, pressure groups/interest groups and constitutional safeguards. Democracies ensure individual rights and liberty, effective legislation and reflection of popular sovereignty.

Now coming to the discussion on development, it is pertinent to analyse the problematic nature of development. What are the considerations for development? Development does not necessarily mean solely economic development. As discussed in Chapter 8, concept of development now has come to include the aspect of human development. Economic development is usually understood as growth in different sectors of the economy—agriculture, industry and services. Growth in GDP is an indicator of economic development. There is also development in terms of infrastructural development such as bridges, roads, dams, townships and other facilities linked with the development of the core sectors of economy. However, as discussed in Chapter 8, economic development does not ensure the well-being of citizens. Only a few countries with high GDP rank high on Human Development Index (HDI).

Human development points out to the fact that inclusive and sustainable development can be ensured only with the improvement of lives of the people. There should be distribution of wealth and economic assets among population. Human development should hit hard at poverty, illiteracy and poor health. Human development should aim high at achieving improvement of quality of life by providing access to healthcare, education, gender equity, and sustainable and clean environment. This also includes fighting against poverty, poor economic opportunities, illiteracy, lack of access to resources and other kinds of depravations hindering human development.

Now let us look into the relationship between democracy and development. As in the previous section, we have discussed about state and autonomy and we have found out that authoritarian regimes are much freer to embark upon development programmes than democratic regimes. Democracies have to keep common interest in mind and electoral dynamics constrain taking up of challenges of development. No one takes the chance to jeopardize voting blocs. Therefore, development choices are very difficult in democracies. Nevertheless, economic growth is the cornerstone of political stability of democracies. This involves, therefore, decisive policy choices and effective policy implementation of developmental programmes.

In democracies if we go by pluralist theory, there are multiple organizations present within the states which not only compete amongst themselves but bargain with the states to fulfil their agenda for which they have emerged. They may be parochial in their approach and engaged in giving voice to their own demands. They may also be taking up a public cause which they find is being affected by a governmental policy. The point of reference here is the pressure groups and political parties which are quite active in democracies. If we take up the case of the powerful Zionist or Jewish lobby in the USA, then we will see that the pro-Israel foreign policy leaning of the USA is behind this. It is known that Israel is a part of the US containment and strategic posture since the Cold War days. Notwithstanding which American president is in power, Israel has been used for containing the Soviet influence during the Cold War days and currently strategic control over Middle East politics. Added to this, no one can deny the influence of the Zionist lobby such as American Israel Public Affairs Committee and Conference of Presidents of Major American Jewish Organizations. New social movements such as the Chipko movement, Narmada Bachao Andolan and various other anti-dam movements (discussed in Chapter 8) are known to be outstanding environment movements which had put a lot of pressure on the government to uphold rights of indigenous people and protect the environment. Trade unions, working class movements, business groups, peasants and farmers movements and even mass media have powerful influence on the governments as pressure groups.

Robert Dahl in his book, *Polyarchy: Participation and Opposition* (1971), pointed out that in democracies, there is a tendency to fragment, diffuse and divide power among different stakeholders as discussed above, both within the state and among societal actors. This makes implementation of policies sometimes difficult and may hinder development in the end. On the other hand, in authoritarian regimes, it is argued, as decision-making is centralized and highly autonomous, developmental decisions can be taken quickly and time consumed is minimum. In a similar tone, Pranab Bardhan (n.d.) opines that democracy does not ensure that developmental decisions are implemented in a conducive way. The reason behind may be that the decision-making process is participatory to a large extent and this makes the process cumbersome. He says democracies might be susceptible to populist pressure and, therefore, hamper long-term investment.

Examples to prove the point have been provided from the success of developmental programmes in the East Asian economies of Korea, Taiwan, Hongkong and Singapore. Authoritarian regimes in these countries led the path of socio-economic transformation in the 1960s–1990s. Even China followed the neoliberal path. David Harvey has shown the emergence of neoliberalism with 'Chinese characteristics' in the post-Mao era under the leadership of Deng Xiaoping. China could not remain isolated as the other East Asian states and Southeast Asian states had already started walking on the path of liberalization and market economy. To integrate itself with the world economy, China joined the WTO in 2001. Thereafter, till today, the world has seen the rise of an emerging power, both economically and politically, so much so that it can challenge the hegemonic power like the USA. Vietnam also followed the same path of economic transformation on neoliberal path and saw success. Peter Evans (1995) points out that the secret of these East Asian developmental states lies in their 'embedded autonomy'. According to Peter Evans, their institutional capacity/autonomy to promote developmental goals without being 'captured' by particularistic interests while remaining 'embedded' in society through a concrete set of social ties binding the state to society provides institutionalized channels for the continual negotiation and renegotiation of goals and policies with the society. However, Rocha Menocal (2004) observes that this embedded autonomy is exclusionary in nature where the state is actually linked with dominant groups like the industrial classes.

This will become evident when we will examine the countries with democracies and high GDP and countries with authoritarianism and high GDP. As we have pointed out earlier, GDP is no measure of all-round development. So HDI will also be considered to supplement the debate between democracy and development. The is based on five categories: electoral process and pluralism, civil liberties, the functioning of government, political participation and political culture. Countries are placed within one of the four types of regimes: full democracies, flawed democracies, hybrid regimes and authoritarian regimes.

Taking into account first the GDP ranking according to the IMF 2020 estimates of top 20 countries, we will find a few authoritarian regimes. The countries by ranking are the USA, China, Japan, Germany, the UK, India, France, Italy, Canada, South Korea, Russia, Brazil, Australia, Spain, Mexico, Indonesia, the Netherlands, Switzerland, Saudi Arabia and Turkey. Among these, China, Russia, Saudi Arabia and Turkey are authoritarian regimes. The rest are democracies ranging from full democracies to flawed democracies. If we take up the HDI and try to find out the top 20 countries again, it will be the European, Scandinavian countries and, of course, the USA, which will top the list. Only a few authoritarian regimes can make up to the top 20. It is to be noted that among the list of top 20 countries in UNDP's HDI, only Hong Kong is a hybrid regime according to the EIU democracy index. This list comprises almost all the rich Western countries. Even we will find among the top 50 countries that achieved the highest level of human development in 2021, there are only few authoritarian and hybrid regimes. While Saudi Arabia, Qatar and Baharain are authoritarian regimes, Hong Kong and Malta are hybrid regimes, and they find a place among top 50 of the HDI report, 2020. The rest of the 50 countries with the highest human development score are considered full democracies, while some are flawed democracies.

As now development encompasses economic as well as social aspects, in democracies, therefore, the core issues are conflict of interests of the stakeholders, and how to organize cooperation and negotiations which will influence decisions. In the words of David Easton, 'who gets what, when and how?' Central to democracies are resources that are to be made accessible, distributed and used. This in turn depends on the distribution of power and citizen–state relationships, as well as those institutions which mediate conflicts over competing interests. This entire mosaic of relationship is absent in authoritarian regimes. In China or North Korea or for that matter Middle Eastern countries, the citizen–state relationship is absent. Development takes place in the direction in whatever way the ruling elites decide.

Coming to the countries which are underdeveloped and poor economies and how they cope with the process of democratization and economic development, inadequate state capacity obstructs them from providing basic minimum social welfare services to the people and, therefore, they have low human development apart from low economic development. Besides that, they succumb to external pressures from international funding agencies. To be eligible for receiving funds from the IMF and the World Bank, they have to open up their economy and abide by the WTO regulations. Therefore, they suffer internally from incapacity and externally from pressures from funding agencies. Neither they can transform themselves successfully into democracies nor they can carry out economic and human development properly. Moreover, corruption and patronage system may further impair the process for democratization and democratic consolidation. It also affects the state capacity towards service delivery, and other dimensions of governance are compromised by vices like corruption.

However, democracy cannot be all that negative, and incompatibility towards development must be judged from the perspective of the citizens also. If development is exclusive, then protests are inevitable. Inclusive sustainable development involving stakeholders will not invoke protests in a democratic set-up. So it can be concluded that participatory democracies may be cumbersome and a lot of bargaining among stakeholders may take place, but they are not without worth. Democracies make the political elite accountable and check the political power-holders and make them undertake policies serving general interests. Democracy deficit can really endanger human development, let alone economic development.

Conclusion

The above discussion on the role of state in the age of globalization involves, as we have seen, several issues which have intrigued the academic community for long. As globalization is all pervasive and it enters into every aspect of life, it has also altered the role of the state. Once heavy spending on public welfare has taken a back seat and market functions and processes are prioritized. Still, this does not make the state 'wither away'. The state is very much needed to help to ameliorate the sufferings of its people from market shocks and economic crisis. More during the COVID-19 pandemic, beginning in 2020, the need of increased state role and social security schemes is being felt. One the one hand, there is the pandemic itself affecting the people of a country and, on the other, economic recession following the lockdowns is causing existential hardships for the people. Here, there is the necessity of the state. How much the state does for its people and how much less it intervenes depend upon the nature of the political system as well as the question of relative autonomy of state as discussed above. Nevertheless, though there may be debates regarding the efficiency of regimes to address development issues/projects and democracy may look clumsy because of accommodating public opinion and interests, democratic states have made to the top 50 countries in the HDI, 2020.

Summary

The UN definition of globalization hints at the process that it assumes to proliferate even the remotest part of the world. The UN defines globalization as 'increasing and intensified flows between countries of goods, services, capital, ideas, information and people, which produce national cross-border integration of a number of economic, social and cultural activities'.

The proponents of the three waves of globalization theory fall under the following categories: hyperglobalists, sceptics and transformationalists. The **hyperglobalists** are the proponents of the 'first wave' in the theory of globalization. They are the enthusiasts about globalization. The **sceptics** have doubts about the even distribution of the effects of globalization. For them, global economy is not inclusive. The 'third wavers' or the **transformationalists** like Held opine that globalization brings about transformative changes in all aspects.

Globalization with its homogenizing agenda seeks to create uniform kind of market functioning around the globe. Since the current brand of globalization is based on free market economy and on the principles of neoliberalism, it has pushed for similar kind of free economy and free trade regime globally. Globalization creates new pressures and challenges to the sustainability of the welfare state, such as shocks and market failures, the latest being the

2008 financial crisis. Nevertheless, it also hinges upon the importance of the fact that income redistribution and social insurance programmes can help the welfare-oriented states.

Relative or absolute autonomy had been a debatable issue and it will remain a contentious issue in IPE. In a representative democracy, however, elections and exercise of adult suffrage are the means of exercising control but that control does not extend to control over the policy decisions. What happens is interplay between politico-socio-economic factors in a democracy, which constrains the relative autonomy of the state. An authoritarian state is, thus, more autonomous than a democratic state.

All states perform exclusively certain political tasks that include administrative, legal, extractive and coercive tasks. To a certain extent, the state competes with the dominant class in the appropriation of economic resources. During certain crisis moments, such as the economic and international crisis, the state can assume more power and a greater autonomy; for example, the COVID-19 crisis has increased the role of states.

Coming down to the democracy–development debate, most scholars opine that in democracies, there is a tendency to fragment, diffuse and divide power among different stakeholders as discussed above, both within the state and among societal actors. This makes implementation of policies sometimes difficult and may hinder development in the end. However, when we take into account the GDP ranking, according to the IMF 2020 estimates, among the top 20 countries, we will find a few authoritarian regimes. The countries by ranking are the USA, China, Japan, Germany, the UK, India, France, Italy, Canada, South Korea, Russia, Brazil, Australia, Spain, Mexico, Indonesia, the Netherlands, Switzerland, Saudi Arabia and Turkey. Among these, China, Russia, Saudi Arabia and Turkey are authoritarian regimes. When we take into consideration the HDI, only a few authoritarian regimes can make up to the top 20. Therefore, we can say that participatory democracies may be cumbersome and a lot of bargaining among stakeholders may take place, but they are not without worth.

REVIEW AND REFLECTION QUESTIONS

1. There are three waves or principal lines of thinking in the theories of globalization. The hyperglobalists, the sceptics and the transformationalists. Try to figure out their main ideas regarding globalization.
2. Neoliberalism puts a cap on heavy governmental spending on public welfare. Do you think that states are reluctant to carry out welfare functions today? Do you think states need to perform welfare activities to cushion the shocks emitted by the market forces?
3. Examine the debate between development and autonomy bringing up cases of democracies and authoritarian regimes. Which one do you favour of the two—authoritarianism or democracy—in carrying out development works?
4. Do you think democracy due to its participatory nature with the presence of pluralist organizations can neither take on development projects with autonomy nor embark on development projects? Argue your case from the above discussion from the point of view of development–autonomy and development–democracy debate.
5. Bring out the development–democracy debate and highlight the case of authoritarian regimes as compared to democracies.

Bibliography

Bardhan, P. n.d. 'Democracy and Development: A Complex Relationship.' Berkeley, CA: University of California.

Bertucci, G., and A. Alberti. 2003. 'Globalization and the Role of the State: Challenges and Perspectives.' Available at https://pdf4pro.com/amp/view/globalization-and-the-role-of-the-state-challenges-and-5ad29b.html (accessed on 6 October 2021).

Chen, Yu-Fu, Holger Görg, Dennis Görlich, Hassan Molana, Catia Montagna, and Yama Temouri. 2014. 'Globalization and the Future of the Welfare State.' IZA Policy Paper No.81, IZA, Bonn.

Dahl, R. A. 1971. *Polyarchy: Participation and Opposition*. New Haven, CT: Yale University Press.

Dube, M. P. 2017. *Social Justice: Distributive Principles and Beyond*. New Delhi: Rawat Publications.

Evans, Peter. 1995. *Embedded Autonomy: States and Industrial Transformation*. Cambridge: Cambridge University Press.

Held, D., and A. McGrew. 2021. *Globalization and Global Politics*. Cambridge: Cambridge University Press.

Hirst, Paul, and Grahame Thompson. 2009. *Globalization in Question*. Cambridge: Polity Press.

International Monetary Fund. 2021. 'World Economic Outlook Database, April 2021.' Available at https://www.imf.org/en/Publications/WEO/weo-database/2021/April (accessed on 6 October 2021).

Mann, Michael. 1984. 'The Autonomous Power of the State: Its Origins, Mechanisms and Results.' *European Journal of Sociology* 25, no. 2: 185–213.

Menocal, Rocha A. 2004. 'And If There Was No State? Critical Reflections on Bates, Polanyi and Evans on the Role of the State in Promoting Development.' *Third World Quarterly* 25, no. 4: 765–777.

OECD. 2020. 'Social Spending Makes Up 20% of OECD GDP.' Available at https://img.lalr.co/cms/2020/11/27201231/OECD2020-Social-Expenditure-SOCX-Update-1.pdf (accessed on 6 October 2021).

Piketty, Thomas. 2017. *Capital in the Twenty-first Century*. London: The Belknap Press of Harvard University Press.

Poggi, Gianfranco. 1978. *The Development of the Modern State: A Sociological Introduction*. Stanford, CA: Stanford University Press.

———. 1990. *The State: Its Nature and Development*. Stanford, CA: Stanford University.

Poulantzas, Nicos. 1968. *Political Power and Social Class*. Available at https://www.ssc.wisc.edu/~wright/Soc924-2011/Poulantzas.pdf (accessed on 12 November 2021).

Przeworski, A. 1985. *Capitalism and Social Democracy*. Cambridge: Cambridge University Press.

Ralph, Miliband. 1969. *The State in Capitalist Society*. Available at https://legalform.files.wordpress.com/2019/04/miliband-state-in-capitalist-society.pdf (accessed on 12 November 2021).

Rodrik, D. 1996. 'Why Do More Open Economies Have Bigger Governments?' NBER Working Paper Series 5537, NBER, Cambridge, MA.

———. 1997. *Has Globalization Gone too Far?* Washington, DC: Institute for International Economics.

———. 1998. 'Why Do More Open Economies Have Bigger Governments.' *Journal of Political Economy* 106: 997–1032.

Scholte, Jan Art. 2005. *Globalization: A Critical Introduction*. London: Palgrave.

Sheve, Kenneth, and Matthew Slaughter. 2004. 'Economic Insecurity and the Globalization of Production.' *American Journal of Political Science* 48, no. 4: 662–674.

Skocpol, Theda. 1985. 'Bringing the State Back In: Strategies for Analysis in Current Research.' In *Bringing the State Back In*, edited by Peter B. Evans, Dietrich Rueschemeyer, and Theda Skocpol. Cambridge: Cambridge University Press.

Spinney, Laura. 2020. 'Will Coronavirus Lead to Fairer Societies? Thomas Piketty Explores the Prospect.' *The Guardian*. Available at https://www.theguardian.com/world/2020/may/12/will-coronavirus-lead-to-fairer-societies-thomas-piketty-explores-the-prospect (accessed on 6 October 2021).

Stiglitz, Joseph. 2003. *Globalization and Its Discontents*. New Delhi: Penguin Books India.

———. 2017. *The Welfare State in the Twenty-first Century*. Available at http://policydialogue.org/files/publications/The_Welfare_State_in_the_Twenty-First_Century.pdf (accessed on 12 November 2021).

Statista. 2021. 'Revenue Expenditure on Social Security and Welfare of India's Central and State Governments from Financial Year 1991 to 2018 in Billion Indian Rupees.' Available at https://www.statista.com/statistics/626351/social-security-and-welfare-expenditure-india/#:~:text=Social%20security%20and%20welfare%20government%20revenue%20expenditure%20India%201990%2D2018&text=The%20budget%20estimates%20of%20revenue,than%201.6%20trillion%20Indian%20rupees (accessed on 6 October 2021).

United Nations Department of Economic and Social Affairs. 2001. *2001 Report on the World Social Situation*. Available at https://www.un.org/development/desa/dspd/world-social-report/2001-report-on-the-world-social-situation.html (accessed on 24 November 2021).

United Nations Development Programme. 1999. *Human Development Report 1999: Globalization With a Human Face*. Available at http://hdr.undp.org/en/content/human-development-report-1999 (accessed on 24 November 2021).

6 Globalization of Finance

LEARNING OBJECTIVES

- ❐ Familiarizing with the concept of financial liberalization, theoretical precepts and explanations
- ❐ Figuring out the movement of capital across globe under the impact of globalization and free market economy
- ❐ Knowing about FDI
- ❐ Gaining critical knowledge about SAPs
- ❐ Trying to understand the new structure of corporate organizational mechanisms due to their global activities
- ❐ Examining financial crisis with the help of examples

Introduction

We have seen in Chapter 3 how liberal reforms have opened up the economies, especially of the developing countries. The international economic regimes perpetuated by the IMF, the World Bank and the WTO ensure the non-reversal of the liberal reforms in the developing countries. The opening of markets has expedited the movement of capital across the globe. The financial liberalization has set the opportunities for global investors. The international capital market sets goals and challenges for the investors. There is not only sale and purchase of assets but there are also direct investments in foreign countries. FDI has seen an upward trend post the liberalization set in motion in developing countries. However, the political regime, ease of doing business, risk factors and market conditions determine the outflow or inflow of FDIs. The MNCs are usually the most important vehicles of moving in FDIs. However, there are arguments both in favour and against such foreign investments which will be dealt in this chapter. One thing which seems to be certain is that the openness of the market and the absence of global vigilance over the activities of firms and corporations make the world economy susceptible to crisis. There are booms as well as bust cycles. As of now, the COVID-19 pandemic has pushed the world into recession and each of the domestic economies is on the verge of collapse. The states/governments are coming in a big way to rescue the economy.

Globalization and Financialization: Financial Liberalization

In Chapter 5, we have at length discussed about globalization. We have come to know that globalization is a process which integrates economies of the world through a homogenous process of financial and trading activities. In this chapter, we will in particular concentrate on the financial globalization and liberalization. There have been debates regarding whether there would be financial repression or financial liberalization.

Following Keynes and Tobin, in the 1970s, there was a concept, which was quite popular, concentrated around financial repression. Most of the countries adopted policies to generate growth and revenue through artificially low interest rates and inflationary monetary policies. Keynes and Tobin had advocated such governmental interference in the credit market. However, in 1973, both Ronald McKinnon and Edward Shaw contradicted the dominant theoretical schools of financial repression. Negating Keynes and Tobin, they argued in the favour of liberalization of interest rate and abolition of other repressive policies of the governments.

McKinnon (1973) and Shaw (1973) argued the importance of financial liberalization in relation to economic growth. McKinnon upheld that financial liberalization is an important component in the generation of high saving rates and investment. They observed that the subsequent real growth in the financial institutions gives incentive to domestic investors to borrow and save. This enables them to accumulate more equity by lowering the cost of borrowing. However, financial liberalization is usually introduced along with other macroeconomic reforms aimed at developing the domestic financial market. Now, what do people arguing for financial liberalization say in favour of it? According to this group of scholars, financial liberalization leads to integration of domestic markets with the global equity markets. They further emphasize that the financial sector can play an active role in increasing the volume of savings with the creation of appropriate incentives. In order to reach higher savings and investment rates, it is recommended to governments to abolish interest rate ceilings and give up raising seigniorage through inflationary monetary policies.

Harvey and Lumsdaine suggest removal of restrictions for cross-country capital mobility which will result in increase in capital inflows. As investors rebalance their portfolios, they observe that net capital inflows increase sharply in the initial years following financial liberalization. These capital inflows level off thereafter. However, some say that there is not so much significant effect of portfolio investment on firm's financing constraints. They argue that this is because portfolio flows are short term and volatile and are speculative or 'hot money'. Thus, we find Joseph Stiglitz (1989) criticizing financial liberalization on the theoretical ground of market failures in financial markets.

However, economic liberalization gained momentum in the 1980s around the globe. The economic crises in several developing countries forced them to approach international financial institutions, such as the IMF and the World Bank, and accept SAPs, which are conditionalities for borrowing from these financial institutions. These conditionalities obviously make economic reforms compulsory, mostly making the economy open. Among other things, creating situations for flow of international capital is also asked for. Among other policies of economic liberalization such as withdrawal of governmental intervention from all kinds of economic activities in production of goods and services, allocation of resources and marketing, trade and commerce distribution, except defence, and some specialized services of the state, there is also liberalization of the financial sector along with other sectors, followed by complete abolition or partial abolition of private FDI, private foreign portfolio investment (FPI), FII and inflow of international capital. There is also removal of restrictions on entry and activities of MNCs operating globally. Further, to ease the flow of finance capital into domestic markets of the countries, the governmental control on the movement of exchange rates has been lessened. This has been left to be determined by the demand–supply interaction of foreign exchanges in the market. Even the institutions to oversee the discipline of security market functioning like SEBI in India should be free from governmental control. In the following sections, we will discuss movement of capital, both FDI and portfolio investments, in detail.

Let us take up the example of liberalization of the Indian economy. The late 1990s Gulf crisis and rise in oil price put the economy under stress. With a huge balance of payment deficit and foreign reserves to last for about a fortnight, India was in a deep economic crisis. Therefore, India had to approach the IMF for a large fund. However, SAPs were attached to it, which were nothing short of establishing an open economy with necessary reforms. There were also reforms in the financial sector in India. Stock market deregulation was initiated in 1992 with the abolition of a central regulating authority, namely Controller of Capital Issues. Liberalization of the financial sector was carried out by the Indian government under the recommendation of the Narasimham Committee. The reforms that were introduced included reduction in reserve ratio, de-controlling interest rate and lesser governmental interventions in banking operations. Stock market reforms were introduced like statutory regulator, guidelines for different types of investors in the capital market, elimination of inside trading and takeover bids and replacing them by electronic trading. This facilitated FDI movement into India and it increased to $21 billion in 1993. There was a sudden boom in the Indian stock market following the liberalization of stock market and a huge capital inflow.

Even the East Asian economies of Southeast Asian countries of Thailand, Singapore, Malaysia, Indonesia, the Philippines and Japan had made great strides in economic development by introducing liberal reforms in the economy in the 1980s. However, in 1997, they were caught in a severe economic crisis, discussed in this chapter under the heading 'Financial Crisis'. Hot money or speculative money started to be pulled out of these countries in late 1990s, which culminated into a severe crisis. These countries were bailed out of the crisis by the IMF in return of conditionalities or SAPs. Therefore, financial liberalization has two sides. It can bring in economic growth as well as it can carry with it the probability of economic crisis.

Globalization and Movement of Capital

The opening up of the markets has not only created free trade by bringing down tariffs, but it has also created international capital market. There has been movement of resources from a resource-surplus country to a resource-scarce country. However, a calculation of the amount of returns is always a motive behind such movements. This movement of resources can be of capital itself or capital-intensive commodities to foreign destinations. Both somehow supplement each other.

Let us now examine the US capital movements in other countries and things will become clear. Over the period of 1950–2010, the US private holdings of foreign securities and foreign private holdings have shown an upward trend. The US international investment by the end of the year 2018 was $9.55 trillion and by the end of the year 2019, it was $10.99 trillion. The US FDIs rose from $1.46 trillion in 2001 to $2.24 trillion in 2005, to $3.74 trillion in 2010, to $5.29 trillion in 2015 and to $5.95 trillion in 2018. In 2019, according to the US Bureau of Economic Analysis (BEA), the US foreign financial assets totalled to $29.32 trillion and liabilities were $40.31 trillion. Therefore, at the end of 2019, the net investment was (–)$10.98 trillion (in the negative). The US assets increased which included portfolio investments and direct investment assets. Portfolio investments increased to $471.5 trillion and direct investment assets to $8.84 trillion. Table 6.1 will show the US investment position for the year 2019, fourth quarter. The US assets showed an increase of $1.04 trillion, resulting in a total of $29.32 trillion during this quarter. This was mostly because of increases in portfolio investment and direct investment assets. Portfolio investment assets showed an increase of $874.6 billion, resulting in $13.51 trillion. Direct investment assets increased by $471.5 billion to $8.84 trillion. The reasons for these increases were mainly increase in foreign stock price along with the appreciation of foreign currencies against the US dollar and this raised the value of these assets in dollar terms.

There was also increase in US liabilities by $1.05 trillion, leading to a total of $40.31 trillion during this quarter, which was mainly due to increases in direct investment and portfolio investment liabilities. There was an increase in direct investment liabilities by $641.3 billion, resulting in a total of $10.58 trillion and increase in portfolio investment liabilities by $614.4 billion, leading to $21.48 trillion. The increases were driven mainly by US increased stock price that raised the value of these liabilities.

Table 6.2 will give us a picture of the highest receiver of US direct investments destination wise in the year 2018.

Table 6.1 US Investment Position in Billion Dollars (Year 2019, Fourth Quarter)

US net investment	(–)10,991.4
US assets (excluding financial derivatives and financial derivatives other than reserves)	29,317.5
US liabilities (excluding financial derivatives and financial derivatives other than reserves	40,308.8

Source: https://www.bea.gov/news/2020/us-international-investment-position-fourth-quarter-and-year-2019 (accessed on 12 November 2021).

Table 6.2 US Direct Investments in Billion US Dollars (Year 2018)

S. No.	Countries Receiving Highest Direct Investments	Direct Investments in Billion US Dollars
1.	Netherlands	866.33
2.	UK	757.78
3.	Luxembourg	713.83

S. No.	Countries Receiving Highest Direct Investments	Direct Investments in Billion US Dollars
4.	Ireland	442.17
5.	Canada	401.87
6.	Switzerland	278.04
7.	Bermuda	249.39
8.	Singapore	218.84
9.	Australia	162.98
10.	Germany	140.33
11.	Japan	125.49
12.	China	116.52
13.	Mexico	114.88
14.	France	86.86
15.	Hong Kong	82.55
16.	Brazil	70.88
17.	Belgium	64.05
18.	India	45.98
19.	Republic of Korea	41.53
20.	Sweden	39.31

Source: https://www.statista.com/statistics/188806/top-15-countries-for-united-states-direct-investments/ (accessed on 12 November 2021).

FDIs into the USA also show an upward trend. If we analyse these trends as shown in Table 6.3 over the period of 2001–2019, it will help us to grasp the FDI scenario in the USA itself.

To map the FDI outflows globally, Table 6.4 gives an idea about the leading countries in FDI outflows in the years 2018 and 2019.

From the above discussion, we have gained an idea of capital inflows and outflows that take place globally. Such capital movements can take place in international capital market or they can move to a foreign destination as FDIs. We will first consider the case of international capital market in this section and FDIs in the next section. The international capital market signifies a network or a web of markets which are connected with each other. This obviously happens at an international level and has been increased multiple times by greater financial activity. It is in this international market that assets are sold and purchased. The assets that are traded are stocks, bonds and deposits denominated in different currencies as well as foreign exchanges. The most known international capital markets are New York Stock Exchange (NYSE), American Stock Exchange, Nasdaq, Hong Kong Stock Exchange, London Stock Exchange, and to mention here, Bombay Stock Exchange and National Stock Exchange of India also.

International capital market sees participation by governments, companies and people, and they borrow and invest across national boundaries. On the one hand, the investors can

Table 6.3 FDIs in Billion US Dollars in the USA (Year 2001–2019)

(Year 2001–2010)	
Year	**FDI in Trillion US Dollars**
2001	1.34
2002	1.33
2003	1.40
2004	1.52
2005	1.63
2006	1.84
2007	1.99
2008	2.05
2009	2.07
2010	2.28
(Year 2011–2019)	
Year	**FDI in Trillion US Dollars**
2011	2.43
2012	2.58
2013	2.73
2014	2.95
2015	3.35
2016	3.77
2017	3.79
2018	4.13
2019	4.46

Source: https://www.statista.com/statistics/188870/foreign-direct-investment-in-the-united-states-since-1990/ (accessed on 12 November 2021).

Table 6.4 Leading Countries in FDI Outflows in Billion US Dollars

(Year 2018)		
S. No.	**Countries Leading in FDI Outflows**	**FDI Outflows in Billion US Dollars**
1.	Cayman Islands	40.38
2.	UK	49.88
3.	Canada	50.46
4.	British Virgin Islands	506.02

S. No.	Countries Leading in FDI Outflows	FDI Outflows in Billion US Dollars
	(Year 2018)	
5.	Netherlands	58.98
6.	Germany	77.08
7.	Hong Kong	85.16
8.	France	102.42
9.	China	129.83
10.	Japan	143.16

S. No.	Countries Leading in FDI Outflows	FDI Outflows in Billion US Dollars
	(Year 2019)	
1.	Japan	226.65
2.	Netherlands	124.65
3.	China	117.12
4.	Germany	98.70
5.	Canada	76.60
6.	Hong Kong	59.28
7.	British Virgin Islands	41.01
8.	France	38.66
9.	UK	31.48
10.	Cayman Islands	7.33

Source: https://www.statista.com/statistics/273931/largest-direct-investors-worldwide/ (accessed on 12 November 2021).

diversify risk and, on the other, they aim to get higher returns and cheaper borrowing costs. International capital markets provide a window of opportunities to companies, governments and even individuals for borrowing or investing in other countries in order to earn higher rates of return or lower their borrowing costs.

The international capital market comprises primary market and secondary market as shown in Figure 6.1. In the **primary market,** new securities like stocks and bonds are issued. If a corporation or government agency needs funds, it can sell securities to purchasers in the primary market. Here, the investment banks assist in this issuing process by playing the role of intermediaries (Figure 6.2).

A vast majority of capital transactions take place in the **secondary market.** The secondary market includes venues that include stock exchanges such as the NYSE, the London Stock Exchange and the Tokyo Nikkei and various bond markets among others. The secondary markets deal chiefly in the trade of securities. Securities include financial instruments such as stocks and bonds. Investors have options for two kinds of securities available to them like the equity securities and debt securities. Equity securities represent ownership of a part of a company, whereas debt securities refer to a loan from the investor to a company or

Figure 6.1 The Structure of Capital Markets

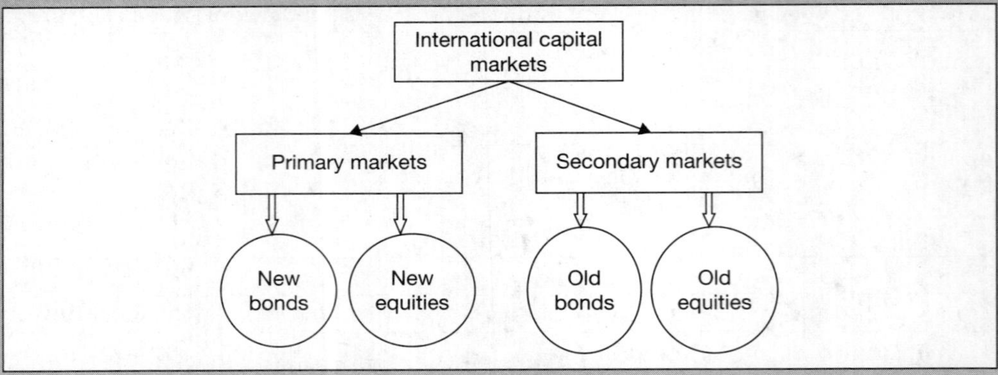

Figure 6.2 Investments in International Capital Markets

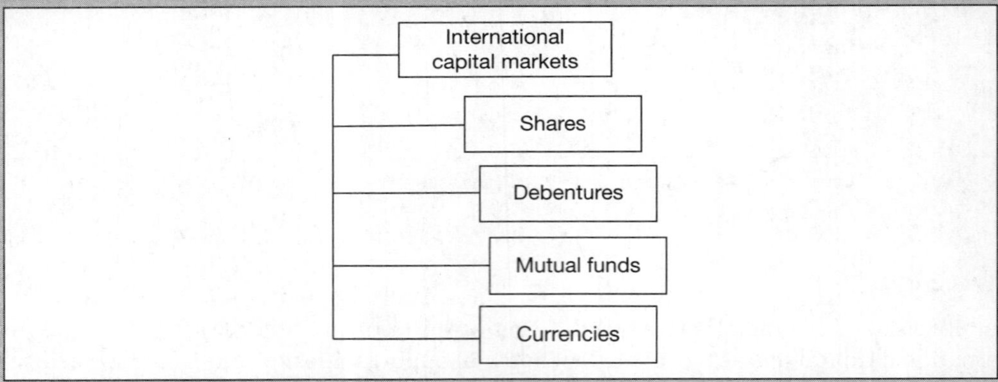

government entity. Stocks are kinds of equity securities where investors buy stock and become owners of a share of a company's assets and earnings. One common example of a debt instrument is the bond.

These supplement the international commodity trade. Stocks and bonds are purely financial assets and the purchase and sale are carried out through banks and investment funds. There are also direct investments in the form of capital goods, land, inventories and industries which involve both capital and management. Such FDI activities, as we have seen in Chapter 3, are carried out by MNCs. Here, the entire control of the invested capital is with the MNCs/investors.[1]

[1] Pension funds are investment pools that pay for workers' retirements.

The primary actors in the international markets are commercial banks, large corporations, non-bank financial institutions, central banks and other governmental agencies. The non-bank financial institutions include insurance companies, money market funds, hedge funds[2] and pension funds.[3] However, banks are the nerve centre of the international capital market. In a globalized world, the banks may be engaged in offshore banking as well as offshore currency trading. Banks being so central to the international capital market help in expanding trade gains by providing worldwide payment system and, therefore, lowering the cost. The role of banks in international trade is to provide financing products such as letters of credit. This diminishes risks and allows smooth transactions for buyers and sellers in the international market. Trade gains can be obtained from trade of goods and services for goods or services, trade of goods or services for assets or trade of assets for assets.

Now to map the international capital flows, an assessment is needed of how the capital flows from one country to another. The capital may assume the structure of international portfolio investments as well as direct investments, to be discussed later in this chapter. International portfolio investments are passive ownership of securities such as stocks and bonds in foreign countries to make financial gains. We came across portfolio investments in the beginning of the discussion and how it has increased for the USA. To earn higher returns abroad becomes an alluring factor in such investments. Here, assessing the market situation and risk involved in the asset's return become important. Risk aversion, therefore, prompts people to consider collection or portfolio of assets not only on the basis of expected returns but also by calculating the risk involved. Minimum fluctuations in returns on a year-to-year basis in portfolio investments are always desirable. From the element of risk, there arises the concept of portfolio diversification. This means diversifying investments in wide spectrum of assets, thus reducing risk in each asset.

On the other hand, countries can manage home and foreign portfolios so that the risk is divided and the return is on the whole average on an annual basis. This motivates investors to follow diversification of their asset portfolios globally. Thus, yield maximization and risk diversification are primary motives of portfolio investments. In sum, an investor with interest in investing capital in buying bonds, equities or securities in other countries is classified as portfolio investment. FPI is investment in capital markets in financial instruments such as stocks and government bonds by individuals, firms or public bodies like governments or government organizations.

Let us now classify the types of international capital flow.

- Portfolio investment in international capital market.
- Establishing new firms in foreign markets that are also known as greenfield investment.
- Merger and acquisition (M&A) of existing firms in foreign country. MNCs are drives of such FDI movement.

The first of these three has been discussed in this section. The other two will be discussed in the subsequent sections. Portfolio investment can be liquidated more easily and has

[2] A hedge fund is basically an investment pool contributed by a limited number of partners (investors) and operated by a professional manager with specific goals in mind, mainly to maximize returns and minimize risk.

[3] Funds are paid by either employees, employers or both.

short-term gains and no direct responsibility like management of enterprises. Portfolio investment can take the following forms:

- Government, institutional and private capital
- Short-term and long-term capital
- Home and foreign capital
- Foreign aid

Foreign capital investment has both positive and negative impact on domestic economy. It is argued that often the developing economies cannot generate domestic capital formation which can give their economy a 'take-off' stage or a 'big push'. Therefore, foreign capital investment may supplement the gap and help the domestic economy to arrive at the 'critical minimum' investment which will help it to break the vicious cycle of low income, low savings, low investment and low growth. There can also be increase in higher real wages from the resultant increase in productivity. There can be spillover effect from capital inflows in the form of technology, skills, new products, higher efficiency of domestic financial markets, managed resource allocation and effective financial intermediation by domestic institutions. There can be realization of external economies through inflow of foreign capital. In other words, foreign capital investment in infrastructural development may encourage domestic investment in industrial and other sectors. FDI inflow can also rectify the balance of payment position and better the foreign exchange reserves position of developing countries. FDI has an overall advantage over official development assistance (ODA) taken from international financial institutions like the World Bank or the IMF. FDI helps to manage risks by shifting the burden of risk from domestic to foreign investors. Debt servicing can be avoided under ODA. FDI inflow can help achieve higher GDP.

The economic liberalization wave which engulfed the developing countries in the late 1980s and the 1990s led to massive flow of international capital. The economic crisis in the developing countries and their borrowing from the IMF, the World Bank and the GATT/WTO created situations for international financial flows.

However, there are certain disadvantages of foreign capital. Lack of proper management, infrastructural facilities, markets along with inefficiency and inadequacy of implementing administrative machinery affect the proper utilization of foreign capital which is known as absorptive capacity. Often SAPs are attached to official assistance which affects domestic economy of a recipient country which might change the nature and character of the economy. Private capital inflows are speculative in nature and are volatile, especially the short-term capital movements, often identified as *hot money,* which might take a flight if the capital markets become unfavourable. Debt servicing of foreign debt capital, both public and private, can cause balance of payments situations. There can also be drain of foreign exchange through payments towards royalty, dividend, repatriation of profit and the like. FDI through MNCs and its disadvantages have been discussed in the next section.

Foreign Direct Investments

In the earlier part of this chapter, portfolio investments in international capital markets have been discussed. These include stocks, bonds and notes in the international credit and equity markets. There can be other kinds of direct investment which can be an addition or expansion of FPIs. Movement of world capital in the form FDI is quite a phenomenon in contemporary world economy. Initially, the flow of FDI was primarily within developed countries. The USA was the biggest investor abroad. There has been a sea change since the 1990s with liberalization of economies of the developing countries. Thereafter, developing countries became the destination of FDI. As far as the UNCTAD trade statistics between the period 1980 and 2009 show, the FDI inflows into developing countries increased from 12 per cent to 42 per cent during this period. Destination was mostly Asian countries. However, the UNCTAD gave a bleak picture of FDI flows as uncertainty looms over the world due to the COVID-19 pandemic. It says that this will go on affecting the global investment policy environment as well as FDI flows in 2021, especially for developing countries, the prospects for 2021 are a major concern. UNCTAD (2021) observes that global FDI collapsed in 2020, falling 42 per cent from $1.5 trillion in 2019 to an estimated $859 billion. This is following UNCTAD Investment Trends Monitor published on 24 January 2020. FDI has been a major non-debt financial resource for the economic development.

As we have discussed in the previous section, international capital flow can be in the form of portfolio investment as well as acquisitions, mergers or setting up of new enterprises in a host country or FDIs. As we have discussed in detail about portfolio investments in this section, we take up FDI as a part of internationalization strategy undertaken by firms based in a particular country to establish its physical presence in other countries. This may range from direct ownership of capital, labour, technology, plant, equipment and land. Companies use various strategies to enter into foreign markets. These include acquisitions and even joint collaborative ventures. Acquisitions and mergers happen when a foreign firm acquires or merges with a company in the host countries. Joint venture is a kind of collaboration between two or more firms with an aim to create a new jointly owned enterprise. There can be international collaborative venture which is most likely in the nature of a cross-border business partnership but here no new entity is formed.

MNCs are the main drivers of FDI. There can be joint ventures between a local firm and a foreign company. On many occasions, there are takeovers, mergers and acquisitions through FDI. Operating through subsidiaries in host countries is often a choice of MNCs. Cost calculations are behind the choice of producing goods through subsidiaries. Cheap labour in host countries, escaping high transportation cost of finished goods to the host countries and, above all, avoiding the high tariffs and non-tariff barriers in host countries make choice for subsidiaries obvious. Subsidiaries become easy options for MNCs investing in a particular country and producing as per local market demands too. Further fragmentation of technology and production means intermediate goods produced in a host country are again exported to the home country or country of origin of the MNC and final goods are produced. Transport cost calculation is vital in this regard. If the transport cost is manageable, then through fragmentation of technology and outsourcing, MNCs can be in a better position to compete in the world market.

MNCs obviously take into consideration trade policies of the host government and work on the motive of tariff jumping and outsourcing of production. By setting up subsidiaries in the host countries, they can avoid paying tariffs which they would have otherwise paid if they had exported the product from their country of origin. Benefit of tax by the host country will also help the MNCs to get encouraged to invest in host country market and increase its market share and profit. However, given the process of liberalization which has overtaken almost the entire globe and has led to the slashing down of tariff barriers, tariff jumping may not be an incentive any more to attract FDI. Fragmentation and outsourcing of production are rather more viable incentives behind foreign capital inflow.

The classification of FDI is given as follows:

- Flows of capital (directly or through other related enterprises) by a foreign direct investor to a FDI enterprise
- M&A of an existing firm in the host country through FDI
- Establishing a new unit in a host country (greenfield investment)
- Establishing subsidiaries

In short, there can be greenfield investment which involves establishing new units of production. There can be acquisition of existing facilities from another firm. There can be vertical and horizontal integration. In vertical integration, the firm owns multiple stages of its value chain. Horizontal integration involves owning activities involved in a single stage of its value chain. Merger of firms is acquisition of two companies which join and form one large firm. Now, if we try to identify the factors leading to FDI flow, we can identify them as follows:

- Ease of doing business.
- Trade policies of host government such as openness to FDI, regulations on FDI and technology transfer, intellectual property rights, extent of trade and other tariff barriers.
- Industrial prospects such as level of taxes, tax rates for profit repatriation, complexity of tax system and rate of inflation.
- Business environment including cost of land and facilities, condition of local economy, stability of currency and extent of free trade.
- Human resource factors involving cost and productivity of skilled labour, involvement of trade union, availability and quality of managerial workplace and employment regulations.
- Market condition involving market factors such as size and growth of host country market, regional market and proximity to key export markets.
- Stability of economic and political system, level of red tapism and transparency and corruption.
- Infrastructural factors such as availability and quality of local manufacturing, efficiency of physical distribution, cost, availability and quality of utilities and finance and quality of marketing and distribution.

FDI requires substantial commitment of resources, local presence and operations in target countries after accessing comparative advantage. MNCs as seen above are main drivers of FDIs. The reasons behind FDI by foreign companies are their motives of seeking markets and resources/assets such as access to raw materials, knowledge and technical know-how, and increasing value-added activities of firms resulting in enhanced efficiency. They seek to reduce sourcing and production cost, locate production near client base/customers, take advantage of government incentives and avoid trade barriers.

As pointed out in the above section on capital flow, FDIs do play a significant role for the host economy. They may lead to growth and improvement in GDP as well as a favourable balance of payment among others. Yet there are dangers from FDI. First and foremost, FDI can lead to weakening or even destruction of small and indigenous enterprises. FDI can result in situations of monopolistic or oligopolistic structures by minimizing or eliminating competition due to their sheer size and volume of capital. Often technologies are brought by the firms bringing in FDI which may not be conducive to the size of domestic market, consumption needs, resource availabilities and labour market. An example is MNCs replacing labour-intensive technologies with capital-intensive technologies, which may not be conducive to labour market requirements.

Considering the case of FDI in India will give us an idea of investment prospects in India. Foreign investment in India was to the tune of US$51 billion in 2019 and India was the ninth largest recipient of FDI in 2019 according to the World Investment Report by UNCTAD. This was an increase from 42 billion dollars of FDI received during 2018 and India ranked 12th among the 20 host economies in the world and 5th in the 'developing Asia' region. Amid the pandemic, India received FDI as a result of what experts think that it may be the government's effort to improve ease of doing business and relaxing FDI norms. According to Department for Promotion of Industry and Internal Trade (DPIIT), FDI equity inflow in India stood at US$500.12 billion between April 2000 and September 2020. FDI equity inflows in India stood at US$30.0 billion in 2020–2021 (between April 2020 and September 2020). In 2020–2021 (between April 2020 and September 2020), India received the maximum FDI equity inflows from Singapore (US$8.30 billion), followed by the USA (US$7.12 billion), Cayman Islands (US$2.10 billion), Mauritius (US$2.0 billion), the Netherlands (US$1.49 billion) and the UK (US$1.35 billion). DPIIT report said that India attracted a total FDI inflow of $72.12 billion during April–January (2020–2021), the highest ever for the first 10 months of a financial year.

Structural Adjustment Programmes

Before going into the details of SAPs, it would be pertinent to look into the history of emergence of SAPs. The Bretton Woods institutions were created in the aftermath of Second World War. The triad, the World Bank, the IMF and the GATT, had the objective, among others, to move the developing and underdeveloped economies towards the path of development. For this, the international organizations made available economic aid, loans, economic assistance and the like to the developing and underdeveloped countries. However, the newly independent countries following the wave of decolonization and freedom from colonial rule mostly wanted to achieve self-reliance. They tried to pursue a kind of planned economy to achieve high growth rate and a self-sustained economy. Most developing economies followed a mixed economy model with the presence of both private and public sector ownership. As it is known, a mixed economy model has quite a substantive direct government ownership of productive enterprises and a control over crucial aspects of economy that are absent in non-interventionist market economies. The reality was that planned economy in most cases failed to deliver the much-needed economic growth. Unemployment, poverty and inequality prevailed and there was very little progress towards industrialization. In many countries, a balance between agricultural growth and industrialization could not be balanced and there was a tendency towards more industrialization and less incentive for agriculture. Many scholars have pointed out that such an imbalanced growth has led to creation of rural migrants, urban unemployment, poor agricultural growth, increase of informal sector, deplorable living standards, poverty and inequality. Subsidization of social sectors often led to high government expenditure. Most notably, the private sectors were restricted through government control in the form of licensing, quotas and permits and host of government policies discouraged newer entrepreneurship or expansion. An import-substitution model was mostly followed with quantitative control on imports of commodities which to a meagre extent led to growth of self-enhancing capacities of domestic industries. It only led to high-cost industrial production in the absence of imports of vital intermediate goods, raw materials, machinery and other necessities. Overall, no path-breaking achievement could be made through mixed economy or planned economic growth.

Though initially there was a spree for industrial growth with a huge public sector growing up, by the 1970s and 1980s, the industrial growth rate showed a decline in most developing countries. Huge losses were incurred by public sector enterprises. The World Bank's observation was that policies of government subsidies, price control and import substitution had a negative impact on GDP growth rates. To cope with these situations, governments in various countries tried out new economic policies of encouraging consumer goods producing industries and creation of demands through increasing income level of a section of the population. The result was huge government expenditure and budget deficit as revenue earned was low and public sector enterprises incurred huge losses. There was a huge balance of payment [illegible] cit as in the case of India in the 1990s. Increase of imports in capital goods for dom[illegible] sumer industries led to huge balance of payments deficit. India had to go for m[illegible] from international market in the 1990s as its foreign exchange was on the [illegible] This was almost the case of most of the developing countries. Under su[illegible] ndia as well as many other developing countries took a huge volume of ass[illegible] IMF in the 1990s. These loans came with strings attached with them. The [illegible] conditionalities or SAPs.

As we will discuss in Chapter 7, under the section on neol[illegible] of 'Washington Consensus' around the 1970s which were later on solidifie[illegible] ch as US President Ronald Reagan and British Prime Minister Margaret Th[illegible] in favour of diminished role of the state and a complete rejection of Key[illegible] s. This was acclaimed as 'neoclassical counter revolution'. This was the begi[illegible] beral economic policies which came to govern the IPE till the present time[illegible] 010) points out that this was expressed in President Reagan's phrase, 'the r[illegible] ketplace', with the internal neoclassical 'scientific' economic culture of the I[illegible] e of neoliberalism. As these leaders were key figures in the international ag[illegible] the World Bank and the IMF, these came to be d[illegible] new thinkir[illegible] ned that economic growth and efficiency ca[illegible] et econ[illegible] here is competition and free mar[illegible] ets. T[illegible] riv[illegible] public enterprises, removal of trade [illegible] ations on stock markets, removal of [illegible] king p[illegible] ralization on the whole. In short, with[illegible] sorts of governme[illegible] interventions. There should be free play of market forces in absence of governmental restraints. These were part of the IMF and World Bank conditionalities that were imposed on those countries borrowing from these international agencies. These constituted SAPs. At the annual meetings of the Boards of Governors of the IMF and the World Bank in 1989, the then managing director of the IMF, Camdessus, said that the countries were finally taking 'painful decision' to 'strengthen' their economic policies and implement growth-oriented adjustment programmes with the financial support coming from the IMF.

The countries of Asia, Africa ar ... e 1980s and the 1990s faced acute
economic crisis with fiscal defic ... of foreign reserves and balance of pay-
ment crisis to mention a fe ... option but to approach the international
lending agencies to resc ... IMF rescue package imposed SAPs as condi-
tionalities to becom ... oans. SAPs were nothing but economic reforms of
one's economy to ... blishing free market economy and financial liberaliza-
tion. The con ... stabilization measures to settle the balance of payments
crisis and ... so aimed at curbing government expenditure, rationalization
of tax ... olicy of central bank, interest rate and credit control policies and
m ... c reforms were to take place almost in every sector of the economy
... or, FDI, public sector, trade regime, financial sector and all other sectors
... e IMF and the World Bank. In short, an open economy was to be established
... ed flow of international capital and technology, creating conditions for public
... nvestment and privatization, banking sector reforms, unregulated domestic capital
... s, removal of protection to domestic industry and many such reforms touching upon
... sectors of economy.

Why were SAPs introduced in the IMF lending procedure—a viable question that can be raised at this point. Initially, the IMF used to handle debt crisis by 'rescheduling'. The Third World countries' debt crisis from 1982 to 1985 was handled by new loans organized by commercial banks, the IMF and other lenders. The countries in debt crisis were supposed to follow the IMF-sponsored adjustment measures. These included raising taxes, raising tariffs, devaluing currencies and reducing government expenditure. Therefore, debt relief took the form of payment rescheduling sometimes on low interest rates and sometimes coupled with new loans. It was felt that such 'rescheduling' must be replaced by some new process of restructuring the economy of the indebted countries. The SAPs can be seen as a combination of strategies summed up as follows:

- To get loans from the IMF, the debtor countries have to make structural adjustments in order to invigorate their economies so that their economies can 'grow their way out of debt'.
- The SAPs included market-oriented reforms than the previous ones under 'rescheduling' as mentioned above. These involved tax reduction, privatization of state-owned enterprises, reduction of trade barriers and liberalization of investments and included unrestricted access for foreign investors.
- IMF would be supervising the macroeconomic changes in the debtor countries. The World Bank was to also get involved in 'modernizing' the economies of the debtor countries.

This led to the Baker Plan which was accepted by the IMF. In 1985, James A. Baker III, secretary of Treasury of the Reagan administration, came up with a plan which was later identified with the entire idea of SAPs or conditionalities attached to the IMF lending.

SAPs have been put under scanner as they produced different consequences for different economies. Withdrawal of restrictions on foreign investment most likely made the economies vulnerable with respect to short-term institutional finance or speculative money. Therefore, capital markets of developing countries suffer from risk from the movement of speculative money, often leading to financial and economic crisis. MNCs' entry into domestic market may bring in opportunities for growth, but they often replace the domestic firms in the competitive market which lead to liquidation or merger of the domestic firms with the MNCs. Capital intensive manufacturing also does not create employment facilities. Examples of Asia and Africa show that liberalization has brought in jobless growth. There has been an increase in capital intensity and fall in employment. Simultaneously, there is a high growth rate accompanied by reduced employment rate. There has been increase in the proportion of informal sector which is engaged in low-paid jobs and unfavourable quality of employment. India also experiences jobless growth since the introduction of economic reforms in the 1990s. Growth in manufacturing became more capital intensive and labour displacing. Opening of domestic market to MNCs has changed the consumption pattern and production process too. Since the economic reforms, there has been fall of real wage rate in organized manufacturing. Fall in public investment and disinvestment in public sector have also added to rising unemployment in India as well as other developing countries.

The case of Sub-Saharan Africa is beyond words. The debacle that Sub-Saharan Africa faced due to SAPs has gone down in history as the lost decade for the Sub-Saharan economy. Gaining independence in the 1960s, the African countries followed a heavy state-controlled economy and huge public expenditure, which failed to bring in desired economic growth. The World Bank's Berg Report (1981), *Towards Accelerated Development in Sub-Saharan Africa*, attributed the causes of the failure to mismanagement of resources, faulty exchange rate policies, heavy state intervention, subsidization of urban consumers, extraction of high rents from rural producers and corruption in different spheres. The report as a solution recommended opening up of the economy and withdrawal of state intervention by bringing in SAPs. SAPs were a precondition for getting structural adjustment loans and sectoral adjustment loans from the international lending agencies.

The SAPs were introduced across Africa in the 1980s and continued to operate throughout the 1990s. The IMF stressed on the macroeconomic development and policy agenda in the countries of Africa. The World Bank conditioned its lending on the introduction of structural adjustment of the economies. As followed elsewhere, the international financial institutions emphasized on anti-inflationary macroeconomic stabilization policies and were bent on private sector and free market development, controlling budget deficits, privatization of public sector companies and services, eliminating subsidies and lessening or curtailing of public support for social services. Those sceptical about the World Bank and the IMF have argued that policies implemented by African countries, which were intended to control inflation and generate foreign exchange to help pay off the IMF debts, often resulted in increased unemployment, poverty and economic polarization, thereby impeding sustainable development. These countries were caught in a debt trap and the 1980s was known as the 'lost decade' for the Sub-Saharan economies.

The handling of some of the economic crises will show us how the IMF had bailed out the economies in exchange of SAPs, or conditionalities. Here, let us take up the case of Argentina, a Latin American country which sank in a deep crisis in the 1990s till 2000. Argentina had an exchange rate system that fixed/pegged peso to the dollar followed by overpricing exports and undercutting international competitiveness. The economy began to shrink in 1998 with a debt burden of $128 billion. Exports became unsustainable and decreased. Apprehending a financial collapse, there was flight of assets out of the country. Argentina, however, received $13.7 billion as the IMF loan almost at the fag end of Bill Clinton's presidency. Coming of President George W. Bush saw a reluctance to allow repeated bailouts of failing economies.

After two weeks of negotiations, the IMF declared emergency aid of $8 billion to Argentina to stabilize its economy. Out of this $8 billion, $5 billion were lent immediately and the other $3 billion were delayed depending upon the rescheduling of debt payments, fiscal discipline and reduction in central and provincial government spending This must be read at tandem with the US Treasury Secretary Pau O'Neil and his rigorous attempts to ensure that Argentina would demonstrate that the money lent to it would last beyond the usual terms of three years. Argentina following the loan received froze its bank accounts, pension funds to gather hard currency to repay IMF loans. In 2002, Argentina refused to repay the IMF from its diminishing reserves, and in 2003, it announced a temporary default to the IMF. However, the economy walked on the path of recovery. The Argentine debt crisis had damaged the reputation of the IMF; it was alleged of prescribing inappropriate policies and its future projection of Argentina's economic growth was underestimated.

Next, let us look at Brazil, another Latin American 'poster' country of free market orthodoxy during the regime of Fernando Henrique Cardoso who was also a dependency theory protagonist. Brazil followed an import-substitution model which gave it a growth of about 10 per cent annually between 1968 and 1973. However, investing in heavy infrastructural projects in power, steel and transport needed huge money. Therefore, Brazil became dependent on world economy and financial markets. In 1982, Brazil was unable to procure additional loans as prices of its exports dropped. It declared a moratorium on repayment of foreign debts in 1982. Brazil made an urgent request for an IMF loan of $30 billion. The IMF tried to impose conditionalities and Brazil had to depreciate currency, lower real wages and cut in governmental subsidies. The conditionality in Brazilian case was that most of the loan, $24 billion, will be delivered if these conditionalities were met within three years by whichever government is in power. The IMF conditionalities resulted in economic instability. There had been widescale criticism against the IMF funding. George Soros, a well-known American billionaire investor, said, 'In ancient Rome, only Romans voted. In modern global capitalism, only US financial agents vote, not Brazilians'. A report in the *New York Times* said that the IMF involvement in the voting process in Brazil was an act of subversion of democracy by an autocratic institution confident that it knows what is best, and it was quite critical of George W. Bush administration and its policies towards Latin America.

The East Asian financial crisis discussed below was resolved by the IMF which provided the loans necessary to stabilize the troubled Asian economies. In late 1997, the IMF had committed more than $110 billion in short-term loans to Thailand, Indonesia and South Korea to help stabilize the economies. This was more than double of IMF's largest loan ever. However, in exchange for the loans, the IMF required the countries to adhere to strict conditions or in other words, conditionalities. These included higher taxes, reduced public spending, privatization of state-owned businesses and higher interest rates designed to stabilize economies. Other restrictions required the countries to close illiquid financial institutions without even a concern for jobs lost.

We can conclude with L. Rohter (2002), who wrote in *The New York Times*, that the people in these countries suffered from debt crisis and SAPs imposed by the IMF, as these countries were given the standard advice by the IMF which this institution gives to clients facing crisis. These were insistence on increased austerity as IMF argued that fiscal discipline is a necessary precondition to prosperity which created hardships for the people in these countries. However, Rohter says that translates into enormous suffering for millions of people, strengthening the critics of free market economies arising out of Washington Consensus.

Globalization and Corporate Structure

Globalizations has given incentives to firms to become international and operate from different countries. MNCs are the main agents in internationalization of business. The necessary question is why do firms/business internationalize. Globalization provides opportunities to the firms to make entry into worldwide markets. Opening up of economies and ease of capital movement have made it easier for firms to establish subsidiaries abroad or even merge or acquire existing firms. Firms can also go into joint venture or international collaboration to make their operation international.

There are several incentives which lead to the internationalization of firms. The first and foremost reason is increasing sales and profit, followed by others such as access to lower cost of factors of production, optimize sourcing activities, utilize economies of scale and, most obvious, outplay competitors. Foreign markets provide potential to marketable life of products of services that have saturated in the domestic market. Competition in domestic market may reduce the margin of profit. However, in markets abroad, usually in developing economies or even high-growth emerging markets, there is less intense competition, strong market demand, ease of doing business and lower cost of factors of production. Overall, firms can increase their margin of profit by spreading their activities worldwide. Expanding themselves globally, firms tend to increase their customer base and production. Additionally, on a per unit of output basis, the greater the volume of production, the lower will be the cost of production. Economies of scale in sourcing, production, marketing and R&D can be developed in foreign markets with the help of key value-adding activities which reduce the costs of R&D and result in production gain and closer access to clients.

For such global activities, the international business needs to strategize its international activities in a planned way. This will enable the firms to utilize their resources and competence and acquire competitive advantage. For best strategy, first, an assessment of a firm's strengths and weaknesses has to be made. This will move the management to the next level of planning by assessing the target customers, demand of products and presence of competitors in the market and coordinating global activity of the firm. To become globally competitive, the firms must strategize to achieve efficiency, flexibility and learning. Most importantly, businesses to go international must learn international organizational culture encompassing global teams and global information system.

These firms must also strike a balance between global integration towards achieving worldwide standards and efficiency and local responsiveness which involves coordinating firm's value chain activities and opportunities and risks in host countries. The most important part is the coordination of activities between headquarters and subsidiaries and types of international staffing. Next comes what would be the strategy for production process. For this, there are many alternatives. There can an approach where the expansion in foreign markets is seen as an additional opportunity for increase in sales for domestic products. In such cases, the international business is treated as secondary to the domestic business. Firms which operate in markets where demand for products is similar to the home markets can undertake such strategy. The other approach can be multidomestic strategy. Here, the headquarters delegates a considerable amount of autonomy to the subsidiaries so that they can function along the lines of local responsiveness. A global strategy, on the other hand, creates a central coordination and control from the headquarters over the subsidiaries in host countries. It is in quest of achieving efficiency, minimizing redundancy and global integration that some firms adopt global strategy. Transnational strategy is often adopted which is a mix of strategies where local responsiveness is balanced with retaining central control of operations.

Market entry in a foreign country is vital for any firm which undertakes international endeavours. There are also strategies for that too. First and foremost, global sourcing through which there is global procurement of products or services from suppliers other than the subsidiaries or from the company-owned subsidiaries located in the home country. Exporting is also a strategy in foreign markets whereby services and produced products in home country are sold and distributed to the customers in host countries. Countertrade is also a strategy in international business where payments can be made in kind or cash like other products and commodities. FDI, joint and collaborative ventures are other strategies for entry into international business. Obviously, choice of strategies is determined by resources available, inherent risks, conditions in target country, nature of product and service to be offered in the target market and competitors in the foreign market.

The internationalization of business activities of firms is currently supplemented by outsourcing, offshoring and global sourcing. Realizing the strengths and weaknesses of firms, they can outsource value chain activities. This may involve some types of value-adding activities, production of intermediate goods or even finished products from independent suppliers. Through BPOs, firms procure services such as IT services, technical support, accounting and human resource functions from external suppliers. Back-office activities like internal business functions and front-office activities like customer-related services, marketing or providing technical support are also included in the list. Global sourcing is procurement of products and services from subsidiaries or independent suppliers for home market consumption or for a target third country. Offshoring is like relocation of a business process or the whole manufacturing unit to a host country abroad. It is up to the firms to make sourcing decisions by taking into consideration cost cutting, risks involved, firm's competitive advantages and accessing cost of doing business and achieve strategic goals.

Human resource management is core in global corporate structure. Human resources are vital for firms going global in both domestic and subsidiaries in foreign countries to carry out their functions efficiently. There can be a parent-country national as employee in the home country where the firm is headquartered. There can be a host-country national as employee working in the subsidiaries of the firm in host countries. Third-country national can be working either in the home country unit or in the subsidiaries. Coordinating their activities is vital to the efficient and cost-effective functioning of the global firm. This involves international human resource management that includes international staffing policy, selection and training of staffs/international employees, labour relations including labour wages and labour unions, performance appraisal and compensation packages, and management of workplace environment, especially gender-friendly environment. Figure 6.3 gives us an idea of evolving corporate structure.

Financial Crisis

The Great Depression as it is called shook the economic bases of the world economy. The NYSE bubble burst violently and the US stocks crashed on 24 October 1929, which is often called 'Black Thursday'. The following week, there was a Black Monday, 28 October, and a

Figure 6.3 Global Corporate Structure

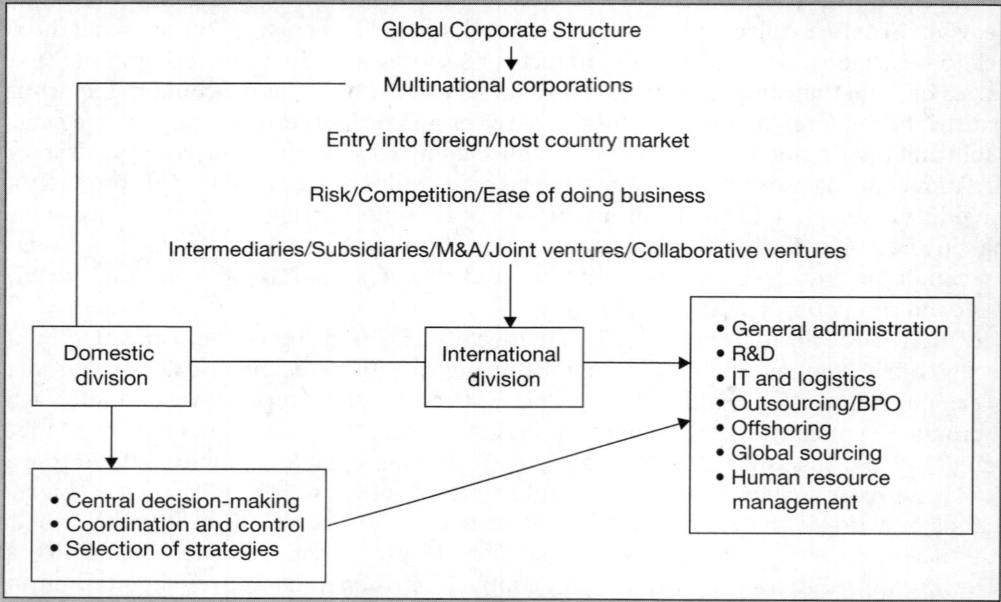

Black Tuesday, 29 October, as the Dow Jones Industrial Average index fell more than 20 per cent in these two days. Eventually, the stock market fell almost 90 per cent from its 1929 peak.

The stock market crash ran a panic among the investors. There was decline in consumer demands, panic in financial sector and improper government policies to stabilize the economy. Further, a fall in the USA spread to the rest of the world because of the gold standard which linked nearly all the countries of the world in a network of fixed currency exchange rates. The recovery from the Great Depression was boosted by the abandonment of the gold standard and the monetary expansion.

Franklin D. Roosevelt initiated the New Deal in early 1933 to cope with the crisis. This was a programme aimed at government spending. This included many new federal programmes that aimed at generating recovery, such as the Works Progress Administration and the Tennessee Valley Authority. The former hired the unemployed to work on government building projects and the latter constructed dams and power plants in a particularly depressed area.

The Great Depression of 1929 or the global meltdown of 2008 make us wake up to the reality of the shocks and fluctuations of a capitalist system. To begin a discussion on financial crisis, a point of reference needs to be made regarding Marx's views on financial crisis. We have discussed this in Chapter 2, still a reference can be made here in this context. There is an internal contradiction of capitalism which propels the capitalist system of production towards crisis. The process of accumulation working through the process of increasing the value by extraction of surplus value while directing this to expanded production creates its own contradiction. The reason is that, on the one hand, there is competition between capitals, which prevents wages from rising at the expense of the profit. On the other hand, there are investments in newer and improved means of production that lead to the rise of productivity and this is sustained by employing the reserve army of labour at a low wage. This results in more accumulation and as wages and employment do not keep pace with it, overproduction is mired by underconsumption. Therefore, surplus cannot be realized as profits and affects the process of expanded reproduction and disrupts the production.

As we have seen in Chapter 2, due to the falling rate of profit and overproduction disabling the capitalists to realize the surplus value, they move outwards for conquests of markets. Militarism, war and imperialism are fall out of the monopoly stage of capitalism. This leads to turning the underdeveloped parts of the world into satellites or colonies of the metropolitan countries. There was creation of dependence and domination over these colonies as well as extraction which sustained the capitalist mode of production. Even the period following the end of the Second World War, which witnessed the phase of decolonization, did not bring an end to such an exploitative system or relation. As the dependency theorists put it, the core countries representing the Global North through the means of neocolonialism exploit the Global South and siphon profit which makes capitalism so resilient. However, capitalism is bound to experience crisis due to its internal contradictions.

However, it should be remembered that when Marx was writing his *Das Kapital*, it was an age of industry and now we live in an age of finance. Financial capital has spread globally and the direction is obviously from the metropolitan centres to underdeveloped countries. The age of industry and capitalist growth were based on credit assets as being main financial assets and banking was the significant financial activity. Contemporary capitalism, after the regulations of the Great Depression era were lifted, is characterized by massive financial activity involving movement of capital, expansion of capital markets and role of stock exchanges, FDI as well as MNCs and TNCs playing greater roles in world market. Globalization which sustains capitalism has widely led to the process of integration and has increased the probability of instability of capitalism. Capital movements from the metropolitan have been globalized with the spread of neoliberalism and liberalization of economies across the globe, especially to the developing countries or emerging markets. This has resulted in free market access for goods, services, labour and finance across the globe. However, this reordering of the global production has its own share of problem in the form of global trade imbalances. Some countries became exporters and some importers and this created differential levels of surpluses and deficits. However, all developing countries may not be at a disadvantageous position. Some may benefit from the restructuring of the production system, offshoring, outsourcing, utilizing the reserve army of labour abroad, FDI, MNC activities and so on. These countries may earn surplus also, but these mostly end up being diverted from productive accumulation to the global financial system under the control of the metropolitan countries.

Contemporary capitalism in the search for capital gains that is the appreciation of values of financial assets spearheads the economic activities even outside the financial sector but they are very much influenced by finance. This is done with the aim of transforming financial wealth into real wealth. Even technology has improvised the ways of capital accumulation by a combination of software and hardware parts of the capital for undertaking production of specific goods; for example, search engines like Google; social media platforms such as Facebook, Twitter, Instagram and WhatsApp; e-commerce services such as Amazon and Flipkart and aggregator services like Ola, Uber or other cab services apps. New technologies, newer designs and new products are what finance puts its bets on to earn more profit.

Ultimately, in the race, few remain and others become obsolete either through shutdowns, merger or amalgamation. Those who survive, they become the leading firms and the richest of the rich globally. The end result is huge accumulation of financial wealth waiting to be transformed into real wealth. However, wealth is in very few hands resulting in inequality. As globalization has taken production system to a global scale, this inequality is seen globally too. The regime of accumulation reproduced globally shows the similar tendencies of overproduction and underconsumption. This not only rocks world economy through periodic crisis but marks it with slump and deflation. The fact that accumulation of wealth in the financial sector raised through financial assets in other modes of capital accumulation is in parts is illusionary. This part of the wealth is paper wealth and illusionary and when the bubble bursts, the capital gets vanished.

This brings us to the bubble crisis of 2007–2009. It is also known as home loan bubble burst. The 2000s experienced a housing boom globally. Till the mid-2000s, the interest rates on home prices were low in the USA. Many borrowers with shaky credits took loans with an aim of selling off the homes after holding them for a brief period of time and make profit. As interest was low, many people took the loan but they did not have the capability to meet the mortgage requirements when interest rates would rise. As the interest rates started rising in the mid-2000s, the housing prices started to fall. This was the 'subprime' crisis. The subprime borrowers could not repay the payments around 2007. Panic grappled the credit market. Borrowing costs increased and participants in financial markets, most of them, had to sell assets to get cash. Credit markets saw rising interbank interest rates rising above central banks' target rates around the world. Banks faced terrible crisis. The European Central Bank became the lender of last resort to the European interbank market; the Fed in the USA did the same and it announced that it would accept mortgage-backed securities as collateral for loans to banks. Stock markets crashed globally. The US economy slipped into recession in late 2007 and the tremors of the crisis shook the world markets. The Fed bought $30 billion of Bear Stearns' 'toxic' assets. The aim was to persuade J. P. Morgan to buy Bear at a fire sale price. Even bailout packages could not become a saviour for the market. Mortgages were mounting, home prices declining, banks hoarded toxic assets difficult to value or sell and the US government took control of Fannie Mae and Freddie Mac (government-sponsored mortgage intermediaries). Lehman Brothers filed for bankruptcy in 2008. Lehman fall out despite several efforts to find a bail out could not be avoided. American International Group was bailed out when Fed stepped in with $85 billion loan and later was loaned more billions by the US government. Goldman Sachs and Morgan Stanley became bank-holding companies subject to Fed supervision. After much debate, the US Congress passed a bill through which it allocated $700 billion to buy troubled bank assets from banks with a hope that this would regularize normal lending. Europe tried to bail out the banks by issuing blanket deposit guarantees. Many countries guaranteed interbank loans. However, the crisis had gone global and the global economic meltdown became a reality. (The Eurozone crisis is discussed in Chapter 10 under the heading 'European Union'.)

The other notable economic crisis but not on a global scale like the Great Depression or the 2007–2009 crisis was limited either to a region or a country. The East Asian crisis and the Mexican crisis need mention over here. In the 1980s, the Southeast Asian countries of Thailand, Singapore, Malaysia, Indonesia and the Philippines were making great strides towards economic development. They had followed capitalist principles of low wages and liberal economic policies that opened up domestic financial and capital markets to foreign investors. However, by 1997, these countries were grappled by economic crises. Once 'tiger economies' or 'Asian Tigers', experienced their stock markets and currencies lose about 70 per cent of their value.

The IMF had summarized the causes for the crises in these countries. This financial crisis started off with a series of asset bubbles. High growth in the export of the region's economies attracted high levels of FDI. This led to booming real estate values, bolder corporate spending and investments in large public infrastructure projects. Heavy borrowing from banks was the source of funding behind these activities. Therefore, finance capital led to investment in other sectors of non-financial character, as discussed above, with the aim of accumulation. High economic growth rate led international investors underestimate the risks. Their motive was for higher yields as at this time, investment opportunities appeared to be less profitable in Europe and Japan because they were experiencing sluggish economic growth and low interest rates.

Several exchange rates in East Asia were pegged to the US dollar, therefore, fluctuation in the dollar/yen exchange rate. The US Federal Reserve began to raise its interest rates around this time in order to counteract inflation. This led to less attractive exports (for those with currencies pegged to the dollar) and less FDI. The devaluation had dire consequences on Asian currencies—the Thai baht, the Malaysian ringgit, the Indonesian rupiah and the Singapore dollar—and their value sharply decreased. These devaluations led to high inflation and a host of problems that spread as wide as South Korea and Japan. Unsustainable competitiveness due to the appreciation of the US dollar from mid-1995, particularly against the yen, and with that the associated losses of competitiveness in countries with dollar-pegged currencies, contributed to the export slowdowns in 1996–1997 and wider external imbalances. This led to the flight of foreign capitals from the countries and led to the crisis. Ultimately, the IMF came to bail out the countries out of the crisis. In late 1997, the IMF committed more than $110 billion in short-term loans to Thailand, Indonesia and South Korea to help stabilize the economies, as pointed out above, through certain conditions.

The Mexican Crisis of 1994–1995 is also known as 'The Tequila Crisis' overtook the economy. Mexico undertook large-scale reform and deregulation of its economy in the second half of the 1980s. The then president, Miguel de la Madrid (1982–1988), liberalized trade and international capital flows. These steps were necessary to foster Mexico's integration with the developed world. Import tariffs were reduced rapidly as part of the Uruguay Round of trade negotiations under the GATT. The Mexican government pursued a series of reforms that facilitated the inflow of portfolio capital and FDI into the Mexican economy which led to the expansion of its domestic financial system.

Political violence in Mexico and, therefore, instability coupled with changes in monetary policy in the USA led to radical changes in investor perceptions of the future of Mexico to a balance of payments and banking crisis. The crisis started with the devaluation of the Mexican peso in December 1994. This was the largest depreciation of the currency in a year. It fell from about 5.3 pesos per dollar to over 10 pesos per dollar between December 1994 and November 1995. This was the most severe recession in over a decade and the GDP fell over 6 per cent in 1995. Mexico was exposed to a sudden change in investor destination to invest as investment in Mexico became less lucrative. This fleet of investors led to increase in interest rates in Mexico which pushed many consumers and businesses to default their loans who had borrowed funds from commercial banks or from foreigners. There were apprehensions that the contagion of the Mexican crisis may spread to other emerging markets in 1995 and it was dubbed as the 'tequila effect'. Robert Rubin, the then Treasury Secretary of the USA, warned that a further collapse of the peso and of the Mexican economy would bring down the economies around the world. In 1995, President Bill Clinton and a Treasury Department team including Rubin and Under Secretary Lawrence Summers infused a large-scale standby loan for Mexico to ward off the crisis.

Conclusion

Contemporary world economy is characterized by liberalization and free market economy working in line with the neoliberal approach to IPE. There has been a transformation of power structure under the free market economy. The locus of power has shifted from the state-controlled authority to the liberalized markets situated in powerful positions in different sectors of the economies. This is the age of finance capital and as capital moves across the globe sharing markets, there are chances of capital becoming susceptible to crisis or frequent fluctuations. In the case of hot money or speculative money, there is always a chance of flight of these capitals from countries which no longer provide them lucrative interest rates or are on the verge of a crisis. As shown above, there is a steady decline in wage share of output, whereas increase in income such as interest, corporate profits, bonuses earned by managers and other capital gains in unregulated markets. At the same time, the developing countries are forced to dismantle their old pattern of economy in order to integrate with the world economies and reform all sectors of economies following the path of liberalization. Sometimes restructuring of the economies of the developing countries is done under the IMF and the World Bank's guidelines or strategies of SAPs if they want to borrow from these financial institutions to tide over any ebbing economic crisis. This will continue as financialization and liberalization go on and there will be cycles of boom and bust causing financial crisis.

Summary

Financial liberalization includes withdrawal of governmental intervention from all kinds of economic activities in production of goods and services, allocation of resources and marketing, trade and commerce distribution except defence and some specialized services of the state. There is also liberalization of the financial sector along with other sectors followed by complete abolition or partial abolition of private FDI, private FPI, FII and inflow of international capital.

The opening up of the markets has not only created free trade by bringing down tariffs, but it has also created international capital market. The **international capital market** signifies a network or a web of markets which are connected with each other. This obviously happens at the international level and has been increased multiple times by greater financial activity. It is in this international market that assets are sold and purchased. The assets that are traded are stocks, bonds and deposits denominated in different currencies as well as foreign exchanges.

FDI is a part of internationalization strategy undertaken by firms based in a particular country to establish their physical presence in other countries. This may range from direct ownership of capital, labour, technology, plant, equipment and land. Companies use various strategies to enter into foreign markets. These include acquisitions and even joint collaborative ventures. Acquisitions and mergers happen when a foreign firm acquires or merges with a company in the host countries. Joint venture is a kind of collaboration between two or more firms with an aim to create a new jointly owned enterprise. There can be international collaborative venture which is most likely in the nature of a cross-border business partnership but here no new entity is formed.

The IMF and the World Bank conditionalities that were imposed on those countries borrowing from these international agencies constituted the **SAPs.** These included withdrawal of all sorts of governmental regulations and interventions. There should be free play of market forces in absence of governmental restraints. In the 1980s and the 1990s, the countries of Asia, Africa and Latin America faced acute economic crisis with fiscal deficit on the rise, depletion of foreign reserves and balance of payments crisis to mention a few. They had to concede to these conditionalities but some countries of Africa and Latin America faced such hardships and acute economic crisis that they became defaulters and could not service their debts. The IMF and the World Bank have been questioned time and again for these conditionalities of SAPs.

Global corporate structure has to be developed if the firms go global. For undertaking global activities, the international business needs to strategize its international activities in a planned way. To become globally competitive, the firms must strategize to achieve efficiency, flexibility and learning. Most importantly, businesses to go international must learn international organizational culture encompassing global teams and global information system.

The regime of accumulation reproduced globally shows the tendencies of overproduction and underconsumption. This not only rocks world economy through periodic crisis but marks it with slump and deflation. There have been several financial crises such as the East Asian Crisis, the Mexican Crisis and the bubble crisis of 2007–2009, among others.

REVIEW AND REFLECTION QUESTIONS

1. We have discussed arguments for and against financial liberalization. What do you think about financial liberalization in the contemporary times?
2. Globalization has eased movement of capital beyond borders. Briefly note the movement of capital and the activities of the international capital market.
3. FDIs move into a host country in various forms. Hinting on that, comment on the flow of FDI across globe.
4. Corporates going global have to revamp their organizational structure. Examine the evolving nature of organization of corporate structure.
5. Global financial crisis hit the world economies hard. Explain the causes of global economic crisis through a few examples.

Bibliography

Acharyya, Rajat. 2014. *International Economics: An Introduction to Theory and Policy*. New Delhi: Oxford University Press.

Bekaert, G., C. R. Harvey, and R. L. Lumsdaine. 2002. 'The Dynamics of Emerging Market Equity Flows.' *Journal of International Money and Finance* 21, no. 3: 295–350. Available at https://ideas.repec.org/a/eee/jimfin/v21y2002i3p295-350.html (accessed on 6 October 2021).

Cavusgil, S. Tamer, Gary Knight, and John Riesenberger. 2018. *International Business: The New Realities*. London: Pearson.

Cherunilam, Francis. 2011. *International Economics*. New Delhi: Tata McGraw Hill Education Private Limited.

Chirico, JoAnn. 2014. *Globalization: Prospects and Problems*. Thousand Oaks, CA: SAGE Publications.

Keynes, John Maynard. 1936. *The General Theory of Employment Interest and Money*. London: Macmillan.

Krugman, Paul, Maurice Obstfeld, and Marc Melitz. 2018. *International Economics: Theory and Practice*. London: Pearson.

McKinnon, Ronald I. 1973. *Money and Capital in Economic Development*. Washington, DC: Brookings Institution.

Mukherjee, Aparajita, and Saumya Chakrabarti. 2016. *Development Economics: A Critical Perspective*. Delhi: PHI Learning Pvt. Ltd.

Peet, Richard. 2010. *Unholy Trinity: The IMF, World Bank and WTO*. New York, NY: Zed Books.

Salvatore, Dominick. 2018. *International Economics: Trade and Finance*. New Delhi: Wiley.

Sen, Sunanda. 2013. *Globalization and Development: With an Afterword*. New Delhi: National Book Trust.

Shaw, Edward S. 1973. *Financial Deepening in Economic Development*. New York, NY: Oxford University Press.

Stiglitz, Joseph E. 1989. 'Financial Markets and Development.' *Oxford Review of Economic Policy* 5, no. 4: 55–68.

Tobin, James. 1965. 'Money and Economic Growth.' *Econometrica* 33, no. 4: 671–684.

UNCTAD. 2021, 24 January. 'Global Foreign Direct Investment Fell by 42% in 2020, Outlook Remains Weak.' Available at https://unctad.org/news/global-foreign-direct-investment-fell-42-2020-outlook-remains-weak#:~:text=Although%20FDI%20flows%20to%20developing,in%20developing%20countries%20in%20Asia (accessed on 6 October 2021).

7 Development: Theories and Context

LEARNING OBJECTIVES

- ❒ Familiarizing with the discourse on development and knowing various perspectives of development
- ❒ Learning about classical liberalism and neoliberalism in addition to what has been discussed in Chapter 1
- ❒ Knowing more about the Marxist and Neo-Marxist approaches to development
- ❒ Gaining knowledge about welfarism and market mechanisms and the complexities
- ❒ Learning about non-Western models of development through the lens of the post-development paradigm

Introduction

Development has been linked with the industrial revolution of the 18th century in Europe. Since then, it has evolved around a Western concept of development, which was seen to be universal and correct. If a country failed to match up to the yardstick of the Western concept of development, then it would be considered as underdeveloped. With the USA coming to play a major role in global politics since the post-Second World War era, it has not bulged from the universal concept of development, which is associated with economic development.

Modernization was supposed to be associated with the technological revolution followed by the scientific innovations of the Industrial Revolution. Pathbreaking inventions changed the course of industrial production. If we mention a few noteworthy inventions, it would clearly give us an idea of the jump in technology which changed the very idea of the traditional, cumbersome production process. The spinning jenny, steam engine, power loom, sewing machine, the telegraph, hot blast and Bessemer's converter, dynamite, incandescent light bulbs and internal combustion engines are a few among many such innovations. Questions may arise about how such things contributed to revolutionizing the production process. If the first two transformed human power into machine power, then the power loom led to large-scale cloth production, and the sewing machine created mass production of clothing. Hot blasting led to low-cost steel production, and dynamite made mining economic. Incandescent lights improved productivity and lessened working hours. The revolution in the automobile sector was brought about by the internal combustion engine. Undoubtedly, the telegraph system revolutionized communication systems. Overall, steam power, electricity, textile technology, communication and transportation changed the entire facade of the production process.

Modernization of the manufacturing process led to the Industrial Revolution, which gave rise to a new kind of economic system, replacing the traditional feudal order with the capitalist system of economic production. It was a shift from merchant capital to a capitalist form of production in which wealth came from the ownership and control of the means of production. Rapid industrial growth was marked by urbanization and growth of cities. Jobs were created through the setting up of industries. These came to signify modernity and modernization. The 16th century Renaissance had already lifted Europe from the dark Middle Ages and directed it towards a secular scientific emancipation. Enlightenment as a process hit the religious dogmas, leading to an elevated search for *sapere aude* (dare to know things) (Immanuel Kant). Succeeding this was the unprecedented technological revolution which set the stage for the evolution of industrial capitalism, first in Europe and then expanding to North America. Therefore, the conceptualization of modernity linked with development necessarily means development in the production process and wealth creation. This almost became a universal phenomenon. According to Richard Peet and Elaine Hartwick in their *Theories of Development* (2009), 'development is the founding belief of modernity'. It was not only liberation from the wrath of nature by harnessing its resources and controlling them through technological inventions but also self-emancipation through the application of reason and democratic control of human personality.

Development studies picked up interest in the academia due to the massive all-round destruction of human beings and resources in the post-Second World War. In the 1950s and 1960s, development studies gathered momentum as the process of decolonization started, and newly independent states emerged. These states looked at the Western model of development to catch up with the economic growth of the industrialized world. There was a political and economic background to it. In the post-Second World War, global politics was engulfed in the Cold War between the two superpowers: the USA and the USSR. Each one tried to maintain their spheres of influence. Not only this, in order to 'contain' the spread of Communism, the USA pumped money into the reconstruction of Eastern Europe in the form of the Truman Doctrine and the Marshall Plan. The ultimate aim was to trigger economic progress in the line of industrialized economies, which would work as a bulwark against communist expansion.

According to David Moore and Gerald J. Schmitz in their book *Debating Development Discourse: Institutional and Popular Perspectives* (1995), there have been two phases of development discourse. The first one is state-mediated capitalism, almost modelled around Keynesian economics. The second is the development of neoliberal and deregulated capitalism in the 1970s. In between, there has been the domination of the Bretton Woods institutions as drivers of capitalism induced development around the globe in the post-Second World War era till the beginning of the 1970s.

The modernist theorists of the 1940s, 1950s and 1960s, along with their allied branches of theories of growth and development, made an impact on the very idea of development as growth. Growth, in strictly economic terms, is measured by GDP or the aggregate output of an economy. However, GDP cannot be a wholesome parameter to measure development. It can only point out economic progression or regression but not the development of people per se. There are various dimensions of development, such as the level of literacy, standard of living, life expectancy and extent of political freedom. GDP cannot measure the extent of such social and political phenomena. Growth in terms of GDP may not amount to human development. Therefore, the neoliberal theory of 'trickle down' cannot hold good if growth fails to bring in human development. The mainstream liberal and neoliberal approaches to development came under scanner with the arrival of the 1970s and rise of critique of mainstream development theories modelled around Western capitalist economies.

This line of thinking first came under attack from the branch of scholars identified as dependency theorists as well as modern world system theorists in the 1970s. In the 1990s, the post-development scholarship, especially Escobar (1994), brought out a critique of the development discourse where he showed development as a unitized, homogeneous power play with the 'poor' as the victim.

Post-development emerged as a result of both post-modern trends in social sciences and a development impasse dividing the world into the global rich and the global poor. The North–South divide obviously questions the basic premises of development as homogeneous criteria. Further, the concept of human development gave a new dimension to the entire discourse of development. This chapter will explain the various perspectives on development, encompassing classical liberalism and neoliberalism, Marxist and neo-Marxist approaches, welfarism, Gandhian approach and post-development paradigm.

Classical Liberalism and Neoliberalism

The roots of liberal thinking have been discussed in Chapter 1. Here, we will go into more details about how they have shaped the idea of development over time and how liberalism has transcended its original concept and assumed the avatar of neoliberalism. To begin with the concept of liberal thinking, Francois Quesnay needs to be mentioned first. He is supposed to be the pioneer of modern economics. He belonged to the group of *physiocrats* ('physio' means nature and 'kratos' means power). In his *Tableau économique* (1758), he advanced the economic theory of growth. Identifying agriculture as the primary sector, he identified three classes who were the landowners, the farmers and the 'sterile' classes who only consumed everything that they produced. Industry and manufacturing fell into the category of 'sterile' sectors. According to the *physiocrats*, economic development meant agricultural development, the rest being sterile. They recommended laissez-faire in the agricultural sector.

In their *laissez faire la naturale* (natural order of things) in the agriculture sector or in the natural order of things, everything else was sterile, and as the agricultural sector created a surplus, it induced growth. Governments should be there only to enforce the natural order of things. The main recommendations of the *physiocrats* were deregulation and reduction of taxes on French agriculture on the pattern of British economic measures with more laissez-faire policy. The recommendations were for Louis XV (1715–1774) in order to develop a prosperous France. It was Quesnay who coined the terms 'laissez-faire' and '*laissez-passer*' (permit).

Adam Smith later picked up the term laissez-faire and harped on the policy of free trade. Most scholars agree on the fact that Adam Smith's celebrated work, *Wealth of Nations* (1776), was to put forward a theory of economic development. Adam Smith was intent on the removal of restrictions on free market forces. His idea was to show how the operation of his system of natural liberty would lead to an increase in the total product of the economy. This would then lead to rapid economic growth. This will also improve the conditions of the labouring classes.

In the process of laissez-faire, a division of labour and investment would increase productivity and growth which is explained as follows. The option on 'betterment' to 'get on' is the prime motive behind the activity of savings rather than consumption. This induces individuals to produce their greatest value, which adds up to the annual revenue of society. The individual is unaware of the public interest and only thinks of their own gain. In this way, the individual, through the force of the 'invisible hand', comes to contribute to the public good, an end to which they were never a part. For this, Smith talks about natural liberty to pursue one's own interest which will lead to the promotion of economic progress. Smith is opposed to state regulation which he thinks would hinder the pursuit of natural liberty. There should be free movement of labour and capital, and in a way, free competition in the product markets will protect the public interest. Only interventions to create conditions for generating public interest through the pursuit of individual self-interest may be allowed. He is aware of the conflict between social and private interest, which may just neglect the interests of the community at large. So he reaffirms that the state can retrain the unfettered pursuit of self-interest at the cost of others. Smith supports state activity of welfare nature and demands state action to prevent the undesirable social effects which may be associated with economic progress. Therefore, Smith, side by side, the 'invisible hands' also pinned on state intervention of a limited nature.

John Stuart Mill was another proponent of classical liberalism. His *Principles of Political Economy with Some of Their Applications to Social Philosophy* (1848) contains his analysis of the economic processes present in society. He shows how such economic processes such as production, distribution of goods and exchange, social progress and its impact on production and distribution happen and, above all, the role of government in economic affairs.

In his **Book V**, Mill examines the role of government in this economic process and social progress. Mill divides the functions of government into the necessary and the optional. The necessary functions are those which are crucial to the existence of the state, and therefore, the government has to be involved in security, protection, and taxation. Optional functions of the government are all other functions. The most important question is how much government's interference will be there with individual liberty. Here, Mill is quite clear about his exposition and he clearly restricts the functions of government to doing only what is necessary. A government should only prohibit and punish those individual behaviours that harm other people, like use of force, fraud or negligence. A government should refrain from harming another nation. Destructive behaviour should be transformed by government into improving human faculties, transforming the powers of nature so they serve the greatest physical and moral good. The most important exposition by Mill is his advice to governments to adopt a laissez-faire policy. In sum, Mill suggested that states should abstain from interfering with individual choice and grant unconstrained freedom to people so that they can pursue their happiness without restrictions.

Another classical liberal thinker, Karl Polanyi, opined that *contra von Mises*, which means a self-regulating economic system, is nothing but imagination and can never exist. In his book, *The Great Transformation* (1944), he is quite critical of market forces, and for him, the global self-regulating market system of the market liberals is a utopian fantasy. A stateless autonomous system run on free-market competition has no real existence. Therefore, government intervention or interference cannot be ruled out. Not only public goods but also the major inputs of an economy such as labour, land and finance can be put into proper perspectives of sustenance only through government action. Polanyi puts government and politics at the focal point of any discussion of market economies. Polanyi contends that politics can redefine the meaning of ownership by reconstituting the rights that property holders exercise. Political decisions can also alter the relative bargaining power between owners and non-owners. Polanyi sees politics and government as components of his larger concept of *the social*, which also includes civil society, cultural practices and social relations. Economic order is also constituted through political decisions.

For Polanyi, two types of freedoms are present: one that is good and the other that is bad. The bad ones include the freedom to exploit others and make gains without providing commensurable services to the community. The good ones, such as freedom of speech, association, meeting and choice of jobs, for one's own sake are again produced by the market economies under which the bad freedoms also thrive. He, while citing Friedrich Hayek, opines that planning and control are denials of freedom. Free enterprise and private ownership are declared to be essentials of freedom. However, such liberal utopian freedom can be possible only through power and compulsion and, according to Polanyi, is doomed. The good freedoms are lost and are taken over by the bad ones. As Polanyi contends, neoliberalism confers rights and freedoms on those 'whose income, leisure and security need no enhancing', leaving a pittance for the rest of the people.

John Maynard Keynes's name is more attached to a brand of economics identified as Keynesianism. In his book, *The General Theory of Employment, Interest, and Money* (1936), and other works, he has propounded his idea of macroeconomics. His ideas reigned in economic circle for a long time, until the advent of neoliberalism. Refuting some premises of classical liberalism and pointed out the way the invisible hand functioned resulted in the catastrophe of the Great Depression. Keynes argued that the invisible hand does not always ensure that there will be social good. The market as a self-correcting institution is quite illusive. The market cannot always set things into corrective measures, which suffered from the outside shock. Keynes contended that it is possible for individuals, at the same time, to act rationally and in their individual self-interest, as well as irrationally and destructively in a collective sense. This shows a clear failure of the market or the invisible hand.

Keynes argued that a 'paradox of thrift' in the face of uncertainty about the future makes one bend upon spending less and saving more in order to build a cushion of funds to tide over a financial crunch in the future. However, less spending will lead to fewer purchases, less production and lower incomes, followed by a retrenchment of labour. This will lead to recession and unemployment. Keynes said that speculation in the international economy would make financial markets fragile and prone to financial crisis. According to Keynes, the main driving force in the economy is aggregate demand, which is measured as the sum of spending by households, businesses and the government. Keynes further asserted that free markets have no self-balancing mechanisms that lead to full employment. Keynesian economics assumes that government intervention through public policies should aim to achieve full employment and price stability. Here, Keynes argued that constructive state action enhances economic stability. He proposed that the state should regulate 'many of the inner intricacies of private business' but, at the same time, 'leave private initiative and enterprise unhindered'.

Keynes contended that once an economic downturn sets in, there will be a fear and gloom of uncertainty that will prevent businesses and investors from investing, and this will lead to a sustained period of depressed economic activity and unemployment. In response to such a downturn, Keynes advocated a countercyclical fiscal policy in which, during periods of economic crisis, the government was advised by him to undertake deficit spending. This, for him, will make up for the decline in investment and boost consumer spending in order to stabilize aggregate demand. This can only be done by increasing output under governmental intervention. According to Keynesian economics, state intervention is necessary to moderate the booms and busts in economic activity or the business cycle.

The Keynesian model of economic functioning went on for a long time. As David Harvey points out, some sort of 'class compromise' between capital and labour was sought to maintain peace. Alongside state intervention in industrial policies, there were social welfare schemes in various sectors such as health, wealth and education, to mention a few. In other words, as we discussed in Chapter 1, some sort of embedded liberalism emerged. Keynes had opined that government action was necessary to deal with the complexities of the invisible hand. He also advocated, at the same time, for a free trade regime and an open international system. John Ruggie, the chief exponent of embedded liberalism, explains the concept as striking a balance between strong international markets and domestic priorities through state action and restrictions and regulations.

The principles of embedded liberalism have started to be practised at an international level to stabilize IPE. In the post-Second World War period, several international institutions were established to regulate the functioning of the international economic process as well as international relations. The IMF, the World Bank and the Bank of International Settlements in general were established to bring some stability to the workings of the IPE. Specifically, the Bretton Woods system, as discussed in Chapter 3, was designed to regulate international financial transactions. Currencies were pegged to the dollar and the hegemony of the dollar was established in the international exchange rate system. Since the dollar became the dominant currency, the hegemony of the USA in guise was established, and in the entire period from the establishment of the Bretton Woods system till the beginning of the 1970s, a kind of stability could be noticed in the international economic and political arena. Such conditions in global affairs led scholar Charles P. Kindleberger to propound the hegemonic stability theory, which upholds that for the world economy to be stabilized, a stabilizer is needed who would be a hegemon and who would fulfil the requirements of a liberal economic order (explained in Chapter 1).

Free trade was encouraged as fixed exchange rates were introduced by pegging currencies to the dollar, and it continued under the US umbrella of expansion of its sphere of influence and containment of Communism by the USSR. Embedded liberalism worked well between the 1950s and 1960s. However, with the dollar facing a crisis in 1972–1973, its continued devaluation gave the Bretton Woods institutions a heavy blow and it crumbled. Therefore, there was a revival of liberalism and a **neoliberal** turn in IPE.

Keynesian economics failed to work out as desired around the beginning of the 1970s. Globally, what came to be known as 'stagflation' caught countries badly. The Bretton Woods fixed rate system was hard hit and replaced by the floating exchange rate system. Gold could no longer be the metallic base of international money. Simultaneously, in 1973, the wake of Arab–Israeli conflict and the OPEC imposing an oil embargo on those countries backing Israel put the industrialized countries economies into disarray. The entire world economy was experiencing a recession. The USA is no longer the unchallenged hegemon. The countries of Western Europe, Japan, Taiwan and South Korea became its competitors. Keynesian policies had no solution to such a recession, which accounted for stagflation. Low growth and high inflation engulfed the leading economies, and there was a search for alternatives to deal with the crisis.

A group of scholars, including economists, historians and philosophers, garnered around the notion of neoliberal ideas and limited state intervention. The most prominent of them was an Austrian philosopher, Friedrich von Hayek. Polanyi had little success during his time. Half a century later, his student, Friedrich von Hayek, and his works inspired Margaret Thatcher and Ronald Reagan as market fundamentalism and neoliberalism became the ruling ideas of the day. In his work, *The Road to Serfdom*, he shows the limits to individual liberty due to excessive state regulations. For him, the only way to gain security and freedom is to do away with the role of the government and let the market provide opportunities for individuals. He was quite critical of the way the British and American economies were working and dubbed them as being 'collectivist' and showing centralizing tendencies. Too much government spending and printing money can actually increase inflation. Therefore, the state should give more space to private decisions and stop spending more than it can afford. Hayek's ideas got an affirmation in the writings of Milton Friedman in his book *Capitalism and Freedom* (1962). Here, he out and out slammed state intervention and called it 'Frankenstein' which will destroy the very basis of freedom as concentration of too much power in government hands is a threat to freedom. By the end of the 1970s, neoliberal ideas had caught the interest of politicians, and their induction into economic functioning was just a matter of political decision. The leaders of advanced economies at that point of time all embraced neoliberal ideas and bent on manufacturing 'consent' in the Gramscian sense in order to establish the hegemony of neoliberalism.

In 1979, Margaret Thatcher became the Prime Minister of Britain. As pointed out by David Harvey Thatcher, coming under the influence of Keith Joseph, a strong neoliberal, she accepted that Keynesian economics had to be abandoned. It was felt that the 1970s stagflation of the British economy could be tided over if there was a reform of fiscal and social policies and a doing away with the political ways of the 1945 social democratic state. Thus began the liberalization of the British economy. She upheld that all forms of social solidarity should be abandoned in favour of individualism, private property, personal responsibility and family values. Margaret Thatcher propounded TINA—'there is no alternative'—to neoliberal economic policies. On the other hand, in 1979, US President Carter with Paul Volcker, Chairman of the US Federal Reserve Bank, prepared a draft for US monetary policy. The New Deal, which was based on Keynesian fiscal and monetary policies, was abandoned in favour of reform and deregulation to tide over the stagflation of the US economy. President Ronald Reagan, who came to power in 1980 after Carter, accepted Volcker's monetarist prescription for the stagnant economy. Volcker was reappointed as the chairman of the Federal Reserve. There started deregulation, deindustrialization at home and taking production abroad, reduction of corporate tax and budget cuts, followed by attacks on trade union and professional power. There was a huge uprising of trade union activities against the government, but there was no looking back in the USA.

The neoliberal revolution created a reconfiguration of class power in many cases. In Britain, the nouveau riche were encouraged in place of the aristocratic traditional power constellation. In the USA, the CEOs of large corporations and rising sectors such as computers, the internet, media and retailing. In Russia, there was the rise of a few oligarchs. The Southeast Asian states which also walked on the path of liberalization saw the rise of a few ethnic minority Chinese.

After the decline of the Bretton Woods system, neoliberalism was revived through the Washington Consensus developed in the late 1980s and the early 1990s. This focused on a set of free-market economic policies supported by international financial institutions such as the IMF and the World Bank. The line of thinking is that if markets are allowed to operate freely, there will be development, and any sort of state intervention is distortionary and counterproductive. The core principles are fiscal discipline, redirection of public expenditure priorities towards health, education and infrastructure, tax reforms, unified and competitive exchange rates, reregulation, trade liberalization, privatization, elimination of barriers to FDI and financial liberalization.

Now, the important point to ponder upon is the features of a neoliberal state. The cardinal principals can be summarized as follows.

1. Individual private property rights, the rule of law and freely functioning markets and free trade.
2. The state to use its power to preserve these freedoms at all costs.
3. Private enterprises and entrepreneurial initiatives are the drivers of innovation and wealth creation.
4. An increase in productivity should deliver higher living standards for everyone.
5. There is a 'trickle down' effect that will lift every section of society.
6. An elimination of poverty can be secured through free markets and free trade.
7. Privatization of assets is sought in a neoliberal state.
8. Competition between individuals, between firms and between territorial entities is a key feature of a neoliberal state.
9. Elimination of red tape through privatization and deregulation, along with competition, increases efficiency and productivity.
10. The international institutions, such as the IMF, World Bank and the WTO, define the rules of world trade.

Since the 1990s, the developed industrialized states have spread the neoliberal principles across the globe. Globalization has become the carrier of neoliberal principles, augmenting economic reforms and creating free trade and free markets globally. Thomas Friedman, in his book, *The Lexus and the Olive Tree* (2012), contends that globalization requires a 'golden straightjacket' which includes a set of sovereignty-limiting, economic liberal policies which are to be implemented if states want to realize globalization's benefits. However, the enthusiasm for neoliberal principles aroused criticisms and anti-globalization movements as neoliberal-inspired globalization created unintended consequences in the 1990s. They pointed out unequal distribution of income, environmental damage, labour retrenchment and economic recessions as they happened in Mexico in 1994, Russia in 1998 and in Southeast and East Asia in 1997 and 1998. The policies of the WTO, the IMF and the World Bank were denounced by the protestors as blindly obsessed with neoliberal policies in a series of demonstrations and protests from Seattle, 1999, to Genoa, 2001. There is a long history of struggle against globalization and neoliberal policies.

In his book, *Globalization and Discontent* (2002), Joseph Stiglitz insists that globalization should have a human face, and there is a need to initiate reforms in the international public institutions, particularly the system of governance of the IMF, the WTO and the World Bank. These would make globalization based on neoliberal ideology fairer and more effective in raising living standards, especially of the poor.

Thomas Friedman, in his observation, said that neoliberalism would further invite opposition if it did not widen the rich–poor gap. In his book, *Hot, Flat and Crowded* (2008), he showed the long-lasting effect of globalization on the environment, affecting biodiversity, climate change, energy shortages and many more. Many other scholars, like David Colander, point out that trade and outsourcing may benefit countries, like the USA, in the short run, but may, in the long run, lead to a loss of good jobs. Whatever the arguments and counterarguments may be, the reality is that the free market will lead to an increase in the monopoly power of corporates. Some kind of state intervention is still required. The COVID-19 crisis again proved beyond doubt that the state should come forward to mitigate the sufferings of people facing a socio-economic crisis due to the outbreak of the pandemic since 2020 (discussed in Chapter 5 under the heading Globalization and Limits of the Welfare State).

Marxist and Neo-Marxist Approaches

If Karl Marx and his concept of development have to be put into perspective, then it must be said that Marx reflected the influence of historical contexts in the developments in political economy. While discussing the historical progress of the forces of production and the resultant relations of production, Marx has applied the method of historical materialism. He shows how primitive accumulation had created conditions for abstraction or extraction of surplus value and, gradually through the work of dialectics, transformed or entered into the next stage of the productive system. In his book, *A Contribution to the Critique of Political Economy* (1859), Marx opines that historical developments with transitions through different modes of production have taken place because 'at a certain stage of development the material productive forces of society come into conflict with the existing relations of production or ... with the property relations within which they have operated hitherto.' This, to him, leads to social revolution and changes in the economic foundations lead to the transformation of the whole superstructure. Marx observes that the Asiatic, ancient, feudal and modern bourgeoisie modes of production are just epochs marking the progress of the economic development of society.

For Marx, all societies comprised two significant parts. One being the **foundation or base** and the other being the **superstructure**. As his theory was based upon economic determinism, he was of the opinion that the prevalent economic system formed the basis of society. This again included two components, that is, the *means of production* and the *relations of production*. The material resources at the disposal of society for carrying out production comprise the factors of production, whereas the affiliations of individuals vis-à-vis the factors of production refer to the relations of production. In other words, who is the owner and who puts labour and earns wages from it in the process of production? The basis determines whether society will be feudalistic or capitalist, and what classes will be the owners and which classes will toil. The superstructure is an apparatus to keep the system of exploitation of the dominant class or the ruling class intact. For him, political power is merely the organized power of one class oppressing the other. Thus, the opening words of *The Communist Manifesto* (1848) are 'The history of all hitherto existing society is the history of class struggle.'

While answering the questions of social development, historical materialism puts the 'conditions of material life of society' as the determining cause of social development. Alongside the geographical environment and the growth of the population, the chief force which induces the development of society from one system to another is the method of procuring the means of life necessary for human existence and the mode of production of material values. In the production of material values, people enter into mutual relations of one kind or another within production and also into relations of production. These relations can be of cooperation, domination and subordination or may be transitional from one form of relations of production to another. The production process is always in a state of change and development with changes in the mode of production, which bring about changes in the social system, social ideas, political views and political institutions. The main point of contention is who owns the means of production, such as the land, material resources and instruments of production, and who commands the means of production, like the whole society or individuals, groups or classes, which utilize them for the exploitation of other individuals, groups or classes. In *The Communist Manifesto*, it is upheld that the economic production and the structure of society of every historical epoch constitute the political and intellectual foundation of that epoch. Therefore, as we pointed out earlier, all history has been a history of class struggles or struggles between dominated and dominating classes at various stages of social evolution. The changes in relations of production and transition from old relations of production to new relations therefore proceed through conflicts and struggles. New productive forces come into being and the existing relations of production and their holders who are the old ruling class collide and new classes take over the old ones and introduce new social ideas of new political institutions, new political power.

Through the process of dialectics and the play of thesis and antithesis, every stage of history enters into a new one. To start with primitive communism, it was characterized by no division of labour and private property was absent. However, as specialization of production grew, followed by the division of labour, the antithesis of this system grew, and the impetus was provided by the emergence of private property. Gradually, class structure emerged, and class struggle began with a group of people overpowering others and subjecting them to servitude. Therefore, slavery became the basis of the economic system. Next came the feudal order, where land became private property, and feudal lords exploited the serfs or peasants and reaped profit. An increase in demand for luxury goods, however, could not be fulfilled by the feudal order. Soon, a new class of traders or bourgeoisie entered into the scene. The Industrial Revolution gave them an impetus, as well as the English Revolution of 1642–1651 (between the Parliamentarians and the Royalists), along with the American War of Independence (1783) and French Revolutions (1789) of the late 18th century, in which the feudal order took a back seat.

The new economic order was capitalism and the dominant classes were the bourgeoisie and the proletariat or the working class. The political order was what Marx called a bourgeois democracy. This meant that, behind the camouflage of a popular government, there was a capitalist-controlled superstructure. The antithesis Marx believed would come from the proletariat, and the final dialectic struggle between the bourgeois and the proletariat would be the final one. This would establish the dictatorship of the proletariat, and there would be an end to all exploitation. There will be no class, the state will wither, and everyone will get according to their needs.

Lenin gave an exposition of international capitalism. In his book, *Imperialism: The Highest Stage of Capitalism* (1917), he propounds that advanced capitalist states, which he identified as core states, expanded their control over the backward colonial countries of the world. This is done through the process of imperialism through which the industrialized countries conquer and establish colonies globally. Monopoly capitalism needs an outlet to sustain its profit, and imperialism provides that necessary outlet. However, this made the poor colonial states poorer through exploitation and siphoning of their wealth and resources. For Lenin, imperialism was 'the transition from capitalism to a higher system' from the monopoly phase of capitalism. Imperialism, through its process of exploitation and extortion, converted the poor colonial countries into the new 'proletariat' of the international capitalist system. According to Lenin, 'Monopolist capitalist combines—cartels, syndicates, trusts—divide among themselves, first of all, the whole internal market of a country and impose their control, more or less completely, upon the industry of that country', generating a world market (see Chapter 2).

This idea was revived in the 1970s, as seen in Chapter 1 in the dependency theory and modern world systems theory. A structuralist perspective of IPE in which the Global North dominates the Global South and engages them in a relationship of domination and subordination. Andre Gunder Frank argues that the Global South has become 'underdeveloped' as a result of the colonialization of the Western industrialized countries. Another dependency theorist include Raul Prebisch who has the ECLAC, 1948. Examining the underdevelopment of Latin American countries, this group opined that the wealthy West European countries and the USA have created dependency vis-à-vis resource extraction from these countries.

Another perspective of this structuralist theory is the modern world system theory, which was popularized by Immanuel Wallerstein. He divided the world system into three functional segments, the core, semi-periphery and periphery. The core states constituting the developed industrialized states dominate the semi-peripheral and peripheral states through unequal exchange for the purpose of extracting cheap raw materials and exploit them for the purpose of profit. It is through such exploitation that the Global South is poor and underdeveloped.

It was because of such an unequal world economic structure that there was a demand for NIEO in order to establish a world order where there would be an equitable distribution of wealth and resources and no exploitation. However, there has been a continuation of such exploitation in a more subtler way in the form of neo-imperialism. In his book, *The Age of Imperialism: The Economics of U.S. Foreign Policy* (1969), Harry Magdoff argues that the economic liberal policies of the GATT, the IMF and the World Bank were furthered by the USA because its security interests were also involved in that. US hegemony, though since the Bretton Woods had declined in the 1970s, still remained as a sole superpower after the disintegration of the Soviet Union has held sway in global politics. The US meddling in Middle Eastern politics in the 1970s, 1980s, 1990s and even the 2001 War on Terror were actually nothing but economic interest garbed in perception of security threats. The current emergence of the transnational capitalist class, the owners of MNCs or TNCs, are the influential class in IPE. In his work, 'Global Capitalism: Reflection on a Brave New World' (2017), William I. Robinson argues that the transnational capitalist class not only has structural power over national governments but also is an important player in the IMF, the WTO, the OECD and even bodies like the EU. They try to promote the 'culture ideology of consumerism'. Therefore, the process of globalization, if seen through the lens of Marxism or its other variants, may seem to be the continuation of the international division of labour and exploitation between the Global North and the Global South.

Welfarism

The welfare state came into being in the 19th century. Otto von Bismarck, the Chancellor of Prussia and the German Empire, was the first architect of a near welfare state. Bismark passed the first 'social' legislation in 1883 and 1884 that insured employees against sickness and accidents. Later, other countries, such as Denmark, Sweden, Portugal, Spain, France, South Africa, Japan, South Korea, New Zealand and Argentina, have implemented the 'social' content of legislation. They consciously implemented legislation for the organization of adequate income, housing, education, health care and employment for the citizens of their respective countries. A pathbreaking 1942 report by Sir William Beveridge to the British government identified five 'giant evils' present in society, and those are squalor, ignorance, want, idleness and disease. This report formed the basis of the National Insurance Act, the National Health Act and the National Assistance Act from 1948, and thus began the British welfare state after the Second World War. The degree of welfare obviously differed from one state to another state, depending on the degree to which the state had 'penetrated' the welfare institutions, that is, the *stateness* of the welfare state.

The 19th century witnessed the emergence of welfare states in Britain, the USA, Germany and France that constructed developmental states during this time, although the concept varied from one country and time period to the next. Gøsta Esping-Andersen's (1990) made an effort to provide ideal-type regime classifications. Esping-Andersen identified three variants of the welfare state: (a) social democracy that is proactive and consciously cares for all of its citizens from the day they are born to the day they die, as in the Scandinavian countries; (b) conservatism/Christian democracy which reacts to market failures and helps those who are unemployed or unable to work, as in many continental European countries and (c) liberalism or liberal welfare state which sees the state as a mere provider of security when citizens are not capable of supporting themselves any longer, as in the USA, the UK and Ireland. Another author, Holliday, suggested a fourth regime type which is the East Asian 'productivist welfare capitalism', which was characterized by a narrow focus on welfare for core workers in the service of economic growth objectives, while leaving other welfare provisions to the family as the residual unit.

Why is it that welfare has become an important topic to be discussed when neoliberal ideology is ruling the IPE in the 21st century? As we have discussed above as well as in Chapter 1, liberals speak less and less of intervention by the state. The lessening of state intervention in all sectors of the economy, including financial deregulation, easing of FDI entry, multilateral trade liberalization under the WTO, disinvestment in the public sector and privatization, to mention a few, are prime focuses of neoliberalism. Promotion of neoliberal policies and market principles obviously discourages heavy public spending. Herein lies the debate: How far can the state put its hands off of social welfare?

Such neoliberal policies towards development are underscored by the international financial institutions such as the World Bank and the IMF. While extending loans to the developing countries, as we have seen in Chapter 6, they have insisted on clear adherence to the SAPs or conditionalities to carry out market reforms. The belief that runs through such a perspective is that growth in the long run will be shared by an increasing number of citizens, and there will be a trickle down which ultimately benefits the poor.

The above thinking has opened up debates from both the sides. Mainstream economists have upheld the above theory, whereas alternative development theorists have stressed the importance of state agency and state capabilities in the process of development. This line of scholars emphasize the role of the state in playing a significant role in the transition of the economy to an industry- and information-based economy. The structural needs of the economic transition can be met by developmental states with expanded state agencies and activity. An important feature of a developmental state is to provide social protection to help society significantly deal with the social costs of transition and to avoid a breakdown in public order. Polanyi has described this as 'protective counter movement' and as an effort to combine economic and social progress.

For a long time, economists regarded welfare economics as the branch of the discipline that underlined what a governing body ought to do in terms of maximizing welfare. Each individual interacts with other individuals solely in terms of the contribution that others make to the realization of an individual's goals. The reasons for choice do not matter, but what becomes important is the extent to which individuals' preferences are satisfied. In classic utilitarianism, as developed by Bentham and Mill, utility is taken to be happiness or pleasure. Modem economists regard utility as an index of preferences. This was a reflection of the philosophical theory of utilitarianism. A little reference to Bentham and Mill's utilitarianism can be made over here.

In 1776, Jeremy Bentham, in his book, *A Fragment on Government*, invoked his 'fundamental axiom', which was, 'the greatest happiness of the greatest number that is the measure of right and wrong.' In his book, *Introduction to the Principles of Morals and Legislation* (1789), Bentham writes that humans are ruled by two sovereign masters, which are pleasure and pain. We seek pleasure and avoid the pain. Bentham promulgated the principle of utility as the standard of right action on the part of governments and individuals. Actions are approved when they promote happiness or pleasure and disapproved of when they have a tendency to cause unhappiness or pain.

John Stuart Mill's book, *Utilitarianism,* originally published in *Fraser's Magazine* (1861), contains that,

> Utility, or the Greatest Happiness Principle, holds that actions are right in proportion as they tend to promote happiness, wrong as they tend to produce the reverse of happiness. By happiness is intended pleasure, and the absence of pain; by unhappiness, pain, and the privation of pleasure.

The goal of utilitarianism is trying to **maximize** utility and thereby creating the greatest good for the greatest number of people. General happiness is 'a good to the aggregate of all persons.'

Economics is not the domain of ethics as in philosophical thinking. Economics is concerned with the working of economies and how particular policies change/affects the economy. This comes down to the question of whether or not the policy should be accepted and not from the point of ethics per se. Economists provide value-free technical information or an economic point of view. According to Sen and Arrow, there are also reasons why economists should be concerned with moral, ethical and distributional questions because the morality of agents influences economic outcomes. In fact, economic efficiency depends upon ethical values which can themselves be undermined by the development of market economies (Arrow 1974; Sen 1977).

Economists in general try to separate their analysis into efficiency effects and distributive effects and proceed on that basis to find out whether there is a trade-off between these objectives or not. The interesting bias in this analysis, however, is that taxes which reduce efficiency are described as distortionary taxes, whereas no such derogatory term is attached to policy changes that reduce equity, as pointed out by O'Shea and Kennelly (1993). O'Donnell (1992) also argues that economists can adopt the concepts and language employed by non-economists who are engaged in the policymaking process. Concepts of fairness, opportunity, freedom and rights are more significant in policymaking than the concerns about moving individuals up in their given preference rankings. The reason that Sen and Williams (1982, 13) argue that basing choice (or preference) on valuation is cogent in a way that basing valuation on choice (or preference) is not. An example they give is what people prefer may not always be good for them. Sometimes, people can make mistakes based on false beliefs. An example is that if somebody believes that a glass of poison is water, then one can hardly make that person better off by giving that individual the poison. They argue that it is difficult to envisage how one person's interpretation of another person's position in life can fail to be influenced by self-formulated individual values.

Neoclassical economics looks at economic conditions in terms of utility. The simple logic is that if every member of society maximizes their own individual utility, then the sum total of utilities of all persons is maximized and society reaches an optimal state. This optimal state of a society claims to fulfil the requirement of equality since maximization of aggregate utility, through different distributions of a given aggregate income, is obtained, and here, the marginal utilities from income of all individual members of society are equal. This is the crux of the utilitarian approach to equality. Equal marginal utilities mean equal total utilities of all individuals.

However, there have been criticisms around the concept of equality of marginal utilities. Equal marginal utilities do not mean that equal total utility can be ensured when different individuals have different utility functions. However, in real life, people are not equal with regard to their capacity to convert income into utility. Utility functions are different for different people. This is because of differences in socio-economic, cultural and other conditions in which they live. The reasons are not difficult to figure out. Tastes, habits, preferences, choices and needs are different, and they do not generate same level of utility for all persons under the same level of income. Professor Amartya Sen contends that people may well have unequal utility functions. This means unequal capacity to convert income into utility depending upon the various socio-economic conditions under which individuals live. Therefore, in general, Professor Sen opines that the utilitarian approach to equality may produce inequality in the distribution of income and well-being.

The welfarist approach builds on the utilitarian approach. It also judges the well-being of an individual or a society in terms of utility. Under welfarist approach, basic requirements for equality are attained when the total utility of individuals or societies is the same. However, the difference between the welfarist approach and the utilitarian approach is that the utilitarian approach requires equality of marginal utilities, whereas welfarist approach requires equality of total equality. Professor Sen suggests that the welfarist approach would not help much under such situations unless this concept of total utility equality with some more criterion like Rawls' difference principle. The goodness of a state is judged by the level of utility in that state and different social states are ranked according to the utility levels of the worst-off person in each. However, this approach cannot always be quite helpful. There can be cases where two social states are such that in one state, the worst-off person is in better condition, but a large number of other relatively better-off persons are in worse condition. Under such a situation, judging goodness solely on the basis of the condition of the worst-off person would appear to violate the requirements of justice.

As a critique of the welfarist approach to equality, Professor Sen forwarded his capability approach. In the perspective of human development, the capability approach has been discussed in Chapter 8. For Professor Sen, commodities are not important. In this approach, what is more important is people's relationship with commodities. There must be enough provision for basic characteristics such as nutrition, longevity, mobility and freedom of choice, freedom from hunger, freedom of expression and freedom of participation in everyone's social lives. These basic characteristics and freedom of accessing these basic characteristics are more important than commodities (goods and services).

Professor Sen also contends that people should have adequate entitlement to access to these characteristics based on their purchasing power unless provided by the welfare state or derived from nature directly. Depending on physical and other conditions, people should have the capability to achieve those characteristics such as being able to live long and healthy lives, being educated and the like. The provision of and extent of people's entitlement to different sets of functioning determine the level of development. Professor Sen concludes that what is required is basic capability equality. Equality should be judged on the basis of the extent of the ability of people to meet the requirements of nutrition, the ability to move about, to exercise one's freedom of choice and so on. Professor Sen calls this 'basic capability equality'. His capability approach has been quite influential in the development of HDI (see Chapter 8).

Thus, we can conclude with Joseph E. Stiglitz, as he has put forward his view in his work, 'The Welfare State in the Twenty-first Century' (2015), that the main principles of neoliberal states are market-driven economies with limited governmental control. Governmental intervention is only welcome to ensure macroeconomic stability. There are strong arguments from neoliberals who argue that welfare states create a kind of culture of dependency and that welfare schemes are a burden on the state. However, welfarists believe that market failures are pervasive, and they create hardships for individuals. Thus, the government needs to play a more active role and help individuals from being exploited by market forces. Therefore, a certain kind of depravation induces the advocacy of a welfare state or welfare-oriented state.

Gandhian Approach

Mohandas Karamchand Gandhi, who is known as the 'Father of the Nation', is a figure of such stature in the Indian freedom movement that words become less when we try to describe him. Lawyer, activist, freedom fighter, philosopher, mass leader and a humanist combining everything into one person is such a unique thing. A person who can say 'my life is my message' will leave behind a legacy of innovative philosophy is not doubtful. 'Mahatma', a title given by Rabindranath Tagore, has contributed to India's struggle for independence. He was born in Porbandar, Gujarat, and went to London to become a lawyer. He went to South Africa, and there also started civil rights movements. He founded the Natal Indian Congress (1894) and also the Tolstoy Farm (1910). After coming back to India, he soon devoted himself to the freedom struggle. He founded the Satyagraha Ashram in Ahmedabad in 1915 but later moved it to Sabarmati, Ahmedabad. He led the non-cooperation movement (1920), the civil disobedience movement and the Dandi March (1930) and the Quit India Movement. Here, we will look into his economic thoughts and model of development juxtaposed with the Western model of development.

Sabarmati Ashram, Gujarat

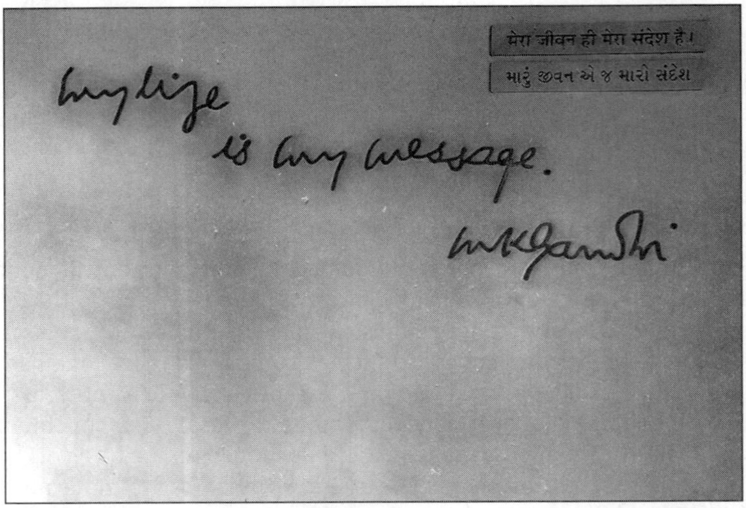

Gandhi's idea about development has to be understood from the perspective of his thinking about civilization, his idea about the Western concept of development and his vision of non-violence, *satyagraha*, *gram swaraj* and sarvodaya. He was not an economist per se, yet his vision of rural development was exemplary. His impact on the Indian constitution can be seen in the form of adoption of Gandhian principles under the rubric of the Directive Principles of State Policy. Panchayati Raj, being a cornerstone of Gandhi's gram swaraj, not just remained a principle but became a reality with the adoption of the 73rd Amendment to the Indian Constitution in 1992, introducing a third tier to the levels of government in India. The panchayats comprise the third tier of the local self-government in India.

Needless to say that Gandhi was influenced by the thoughts of the American activist and writer Henry David Thoreau and also by the Russian writer Leo Tolstoy. Teachings of *Unto this last* of John Ruskin and *What Then Must We Do* of Leo Tolstoy inspired him. Gandhi developed his understanding by taking cues from them about non-violence as well as what should be the chosen way of life. His ideas about simplicity of needs, focus on the means and techniques used to achieve the ends, the fundamental requirement for a sharing of wealth among all people and a focus on grassroots self-organization of decentralized and democratic communities were all influenced by the teachings of the abovementioned thinkers.

Identifying the phases in which he developed his economic thoughts of Gandhi would now be relevant for our discussion. During his earlier life up to 1919, it can be ascribed to a negative phase. During this time, he criticized the Western pattern of economic development and adopted a non-materialistic attitude that is contained in his book *Hind Swaraj* (1909). Next was the positive phase between 1919 and 1934. In this phase, Gandhi presented an alternative to Western civilization in the ideal of *swadeshi*. The constructive phase between 1934 and 1948 was the last phase in which he gave a constructive programme for village regeneration and put forward the ideal of *sarvodaya.*

Let us start with Gandhi's revocation of the Western concept of civilization in his *Hind Swaraj* written in 1909. He says that this booklet is a severe condemnation of 'modern civilization which implies that the whole design of his socioeconomic philosophy is based on a critique of modern civilization.' He adds to it that, 'It is my deliberate opinion that India is being ground down not under the English heel but under that of modern civilization'. For him, materialism was the main characteristic of modern civilization, and in this scheme, spirituality seemed to be undervalued. Gandhi (1957) made a clear difference between 'economic progress' and 'real progress'. He said that, by economic progress, he meant material advancement without limit, whereas by real progress, he meant moral progress. He upheld that economic progress, in his sense, is antagonistic to real progress. 'Civilization, in the real sense of the term, consists not in the multiplication, but in the deliberate and voluntary reduction of wants'. For Gandhi, 'material advancement without limit' was a product of 'industrialism' founded chiefly upon 'machinery' in modern civilization.

According to Gandhi, as a result of industrialism, there has been a series of imperialist dominations by the Western powers which have led to the destruction of the organic structure of non-Western societies since the late 18th century. Therefore, he was against the idea of industrializing India like Western societies. For Gandhi,

> To make India like England and America is to find some other races and places of the earth for exploitation. So far it appears that the western nations have divided all the known races outside Europe for exploitation and that there are no new worlds to discover. (Gandhi 1957)

Gandhi's economic philosophy has always been based on the concept of the man at the centre. Gandhi's economic thought is centred on man and not material prosperity or scarcity. His main aim was the development, enrichment and upliftment of human life rather than the pursuit of a higher standard of living with little respect for human and social values. Elevation of modern economic philosophy from its materialistic base to a higher spiritual plane was his objective. This would, in turn, motivate human actions by the force of social objectives and development from other developments. He gave due importance to the economic activities of an individual because, to him, the main purpose of studying economics should be their whole happiness. For him, if we take the entire scheme of human happiness, material advancement is only one of the ingredients in this. There are also other elements, such as moral, spiritual and psychological, that should also be taken into consideration. It is then and only then, according to Gandhi, that a person can be truly happy, which can lead to the perfect development of their personality.

Gandhi's path of ahimsa and non-violence is a means to attain the end. Non-violence is non-violence of the strong and not of the weak. According to Gandhi, non-violence presupposes the ability to strike. It is a conscious and deliberate restraint put upon an individual's desire for vengeance. It is also not 'passive resistance' because, in the case of non-cooperation, we find that it is not a passive state but an intensely active state. Further, for him, passive resistance involved an amount of violence, and it has been critiqued for being the weapon of the weak. Truth and non-violence go hand in hand. The truth, rather than the insistence on truth, that is, *satyagraha*, is a unique contribution of Gandhi.

The civil disobedience movement saw the active implementation of *satyagraha.* Gandhi believed that 'nothing is or exists in reality except Truth.' Therefore, Gandhi said 'it is more correct to say that Truth is God, than to say that God is Truth' (Gandhi 1931). To achieve one's own personal goal as well as social or political goals, Gandhi insisted that *satyagraha* could only take one nearer to the goals. To Gandhi, the ultimate goal in life was the realization of the truth. To achieve social and political changes, *satyagraha* was a means to that end.

Emphasizing on the inseparableness of truth and non-violence in *satyagraha*, Gandhi describes satyagraha as follows: 'It is a movement intended to replace methods of violence and it is a movement based entirely upon truth....' In his *satyagraha* movement, Gandhi considers truth and non-violence as the two sides of the same coin. For Gandhi, without ahimsa or non-violence, it is not possible to seek and find the truth. According to Gandhi, ahimsa and truth are so intertwined that it is not possible to disentangle and separate them. For him, ahimsa is the means, and truth is the end. 'Means to be means must always be within our reach, and so ahimsa is our supreme duty. If we take care of the means, we are bound to reach the end sooner or later.' Therefore, in the *satyagraha* movement, for Gandhi, it is the truth that is the ultimate goal, and non-violence is the means to it.

Now coming to the *sarvodaya,* it is another important concept which stands for the upliftment and elevation of all. The word sarvodaya is Sanskrit in origin. It is a compound of two words: '*sarva*', which means 'all' and '*udaya*', which means 'welfare' or 'upliftment'. Thus, the etymological meaning of Sarvodaya is the welfare of all. In the words of Gandhi, 'the welfare of all should be the aim of all human activities'.

Gandhi was influenced by Ruskin's book *Unto This Last*, Tolstoy's *The Kingdom of God Is within You*, Thoreau's civil disobedience, the Bhagvad Gita, Isavasyopanisad, Buddhism, Jainism and Islam. The central teachings of *Unto This Last*, according to Gandhi, are as follows.

- The good of the individual is contained in the good of all.
- A lawyer's work has the same value as a barber's insofar as they all have the same right to earn their livelihood from their work.
- The life of a labourer, that is, the life of the tiller of the soil and the handicraftsman, is a life worth living.

Like Ruskin, Gandhi also believed that 'political economy consists simply in the production, preservation and distribution, at fittest time and place, of useful and pleasurable things'.

According to him, a person, if they are allowed to do whatever they enjoys doing, is likely to contribute to the well-being of the nation to which they belong. Integral to his political economy is

> The farmer who cuts his hay at the right time; the builder who lays good bricks in well-tempered mortar; the house-wife who takes care of her furniture in the parlour and guards against all waste in her kitchen are all political economists in the true and final sense, adding continually to the riches and well-being of the nation to which they belong. (Gandhi 1968a)

The sarvodaya social order, therefore, emphasizes equality at all levels. Gandhi had proposed structural arrangements to prevent the possibility of stratification, segregation or exploitation of any kind in the social organization which he envisioned. He visualized a social order where there would be an inbuilt system of moral checks and balances and where everyone would hold one another's talents and wealth in trust and use them for the welfare of all, especially towards the needy and the downtrodden.

He was quite critical of mainstream economic theories. While being quite opposed towards the concept of civilization, he wrote that 'Those who are intoxicated by modern civilization are not likely to write against it' (Gandhi 1909/2019). 'The economics that permits one country to prey upon another is immoral' (Gandhi 1968b). He contends that the mainstream economic theories in Britain were developed to justify the occupation of a territory by a foreign power or, in other words, imperialism. In 1934, he commented, '[In the economics of khadi] human selfishness, Adam Smith's pure economic motive, constitutes the 'disturbing factor' that has got to be overcome'. Going beyond self-interest is moral, and other way around is immoral. Therefore, Gandhi questioned the Smithian-style idea of pre-established harmony and the idea that, if self-interest of everybody is fully accomplished under the name of the laissez-faire, it will benefit society as a whole. He said, 'I have come to the conclusion that immorality is often taught in the name of morality.'

Gandhian ideology and economic thought, therefore, focus on the welfare and dignity of the individual. This provides us with a broad framework for the philosophy of economic development of Gandhi. Gandhi was against India replicating the West and its urban-centric civilization and provided an alternative to it by means of his idea of *gram swaraj* or village swaraj. He firmly affirmed village swaraj and criticized the capitalist system as it was based on ownership of the means of production and other assets. His argument was that unlimited wants, greed, fear and other desires arise from capitalist property relations. As an alternative to it, Gandhi forwarded a theory of trusteeship as an organizational structure under which production could be organized. In large industrial houses, economic power was concentrated in the hands of a few and, therefore, was inherently exploitative and these were to be replaced by *gram swaraj*.

Gandhi's alternative models of trusteeship and *gram swaraj* have been quite contrary to the Western model of development and the capitalist system of production. Trusteeship was Gandhi's critique of the Western model of unbridled capitalism that had always given primacy to competition against cooperation, and this idea of his was more or less in the line of thinking that Ruskin pursued. The underlying proposition of trusteeship was that 'take what you require for your legitimate needs and use the remainder for society [and] it the moneyed classes do not even act on [this principle] in these times of stress'. Gandhi further stressed that 'they will remain slaves of their riches and passions and consequently of those who overpower them'. He added to that 'who ever appropriates more than the minimum that is really not necessary for him is guilty of theft [since] God never creates more than what is strictly needed at the moment'.

Gandhi's primary aim was to achieve economic equality, which, according to him, was 'the master key to non-violent independence' and trusteeship was a means to achieve that end. According to Gandhi,

> Working for economic equality means abolishing the eternal conflict between capital and labour [which meant] leveling down of the few rich in whose hands is concentrated the bulk of the nation's wealth, on the one hand, and the leveling up of the semi-naked millions, on the other. (Gandhi 1960)

Trusteeship thus means 'the leveling down of the few rich in whose hands in concentrated the bulk of nation's wealth on the one hand and the leveling up of the semi-naked millions on the other'. A non-violent system of government remained. Gandhi further argued that a distant goal so long as 'the gulf between the rich and the hungry millions persists'. Bidyut Chakrabarty is of the opinion that Gandhi knew that violent methods of 'dispossession' were likely to alienate the rich. Therefore, he was careful in his response to Nehru who did not seem to appreciate trusteeship as an economic design by saying that 'we do not seek to coerce any; we seek to convert them. This method may appear to be long, perhaps too long, but I am convinced that it is the shortest.'

Gandhi simultaneously proclaimed his profound belief in the rightness of economic equality. He did not visualize a world where there would be no property, but he would restrict the right of private property to what was necessary to yield an honourable livelihood, while for the excess, he prescribed the principle of trusteeship. He asked those who own money to behave like trustees holding their riches on behalf of the poor.

Gandhi believed that the socio-economic construction of India towards *swaraj* or political independence or self-government could be achieved by freeing itself from modern civilization. Gandhi's socio-economic construction was based on *swadeshi* or self-reliance of which village manufacturing industries like charkha and khadi had prime places in this scheme of development. 'When India becomes self-supporting, self-reliant, and proof against temptations and exploitation, she will cease to be the object of greedy attraction for any power in the West or the East.... Her internal economy will be India's strongest bulwark against aggression.' Bidyut Chakrabarty is of the opinion that trusteeship is a three-dimensional concept. First, according to him, Gandhi's trusteeship is a moral attack on those with disproportionate wealth which is possible only when one 'thieves it from somebody else'. The second dimension is Gandhi's view that with equal distribution of what nature produces, there would be 'no pauperism' in this world. The third dimension includes Gandhi's opposition to 'dispossessing' those who have more than is required, since it would be a departure from the creed of non-violence.

Gandhi also advocated plans for reconstructing the Indian economy by building indigenous industries, even at the cost of sacrificing themselves in order to stimulate production of indigenous articles before importing foreign products. Gandhi said that

> India cannot be free so long as India voluntarily encourages or tolerates the economic drain which has been going on for the past century and a half. Boycott of foreign goods means no more and no

> less than boycott of foreign cloth. Foreign cloth constitutes the largest drain voluntarily permitted by us. (Gandhi 1957)

The boycott of foreign clothing was resolved much earlier, even before Gandhi came back to India from South Africa at a convention of the Indian National Congress in 1915. The Calcutta session in 1906 produced resolutions: (a) *swaraj*, (b) boycott of British products (mainly cotton products), (c) *swadeshi* (use of Indian products) and (d) national education. Indian national capitalists tried to explore their domestic market for their own products during the *swadeshi* and boycott movement. Once people started boycotting foreign goods, demand for Indian goods, like Indian textiles, went up. Cotton mills were set up in Bombay (Mumbai), Bengal, Ahmedabad and Kanpur and a spinning and weaving mill in Madras (Chennai). The early entrepreneurs were Jamsetji Nusserwanji Tata, Dwarkanath Tagore and Acharya Prafulla Chandra Roy (Bengal Chemicals & Pharmaceuticals Works/Bengal Chemicals & Pharmaceuticals), to mention a few.

However, Gandhi's thoughts and practices of swadeshi were quite different from those of the Indian National Congress. Gandhi wanted to revive the charkha and the khadi in order to restore the identity of largely impoverished Indian peasants so that they could locate themselves within their own indigenous culture. Sakamoto (1969, p. 163, cited in Ishii 2001) states that the Charkha, depicted at the centre of the flag of the independence movement, was the symbol of 'unity and non-violence' of the Indian people that Gandhi thought as ideal, but it was also another expression of his faith that 'the real India is in villages'. The theory of trusteeship was financially supported by the use of the charkha and khadi movements, and the ideal image of villages that he tried to reconstruct.

From the idea of trusteeship and *swadeshi*, we can now look at the construction of the village economy or self-sustained villages from Gandhi's perception. Trusteeship and the *swadeshi* movement were aimed at achieving a society in which, for Gandhi, instead of half a dozen cities in India and Great Britain living on the exploitation and the ruin of the 700,000 villages of India, the latter will be largely self-contained. Khadi was to be 'the sun of the whole industrial solar system' along with other products, too, like cotton, sugar, rice and wheat, to be produced under cooperative organizations.

With regard to land possession, he stated that 'land and all property is his who will work for it' (Gandhi 1947), but he did not think in principle of any kind of land reform like the ones implemented in China after the Second World War. After the emergence of the People's Republic of China in 1949, the Chinese Communist Party introduced the Land Reform Law on 30 June 1950. By this law, the government abrogated ownership of land by landlords and introduced peasant landownership. For Gandhi, who was a believer of non-violence, it was actually against the spirit in 'non-violence' to confiscate land from landlords. Therefore, as discussed above, he persuaded the propertied to behave as 'trustees'. As far as preventing exploitation of tenants by landlords, Gandhi stated in 1944 that, for this, 'closest co-operation amongst the peasants is absolutely necessary'.

Gandhi envisioned the panchayat as not only a self-governing organization consisting of democratically selected villagers in a narrow sense but also the village itself in a broader sense. Gandhi thought of the decentralization of power in such a way that every village became a fundamental unit of politics. 'Independence must begin at the bottom. Thus, every village will be a republic or Panchayat having full powers. It follows, therefore, that every village has to be self-sustained and capable of managing its affairs even to the extent of defending itself against the whole world'. 'Panchayati Raj' meant by Gandhi to be 'true democracy' which was not to be endowed by the state from the top downward to the people, but to be gained by the people from the bottom. Thus, Gandhi wrote, 'Ultimately, it is the individual who is the unit'.

Gandhi set as the final goal of the theory of trusteeship and the *swadeshi* movement to construct such cooperative villages 'within the means of the villagers including the zamindar or zamindars, without government assistance'. He considered as ideal a simple society staying in nature that is based on its people's spirits of *brahmacharya*[1] and service, replacing a society supported by urban and large-scale industries driven by material development and self-interest of its people. Gandhi sought reconstruction of the Indian economy on a basis which was totally different from what Adam Smith and Karl Marx considered to be social progress.

To conclude, Schumacher in his *Small Is Beautiful: A Study of Economics as if People Mattered* (1973) suggested that 'it [the cultivation and expansion of needs] is also the antithesis of freedom and peace' and that 'only by a reduction of needs can one promote a genuine reduction in those tensions which are the ultimate causes of strife and war' (Gandhi 1947). Schumacher quoted Gandhi's words when he wrote, 'Earth provides enough to satisfy every man's need, but not for every man's greed' (Gandhi 1947). Schumacher emphasizes methods and equipment which are cheap enough so that they are accessible to virtually everyone, suitable for small scale application and compatible with man's need for creativity. This actually echoes Gandhi's belief that production by masses and not mass production can only help the poor.

Gandhi's concept of Panchayati Raj was incorporated in the Directive Principles of the State Policy under Part IV of the Constitution of India. Local self-governments were introduced in India in the 73rd Amendment of 1992. At village level, the Panchayati Raj institutions were established as a part of decentralization efforts towards local governance. The idea of trusteeship has translated itself into corporate social responsibility, working on the Gandhian principle, grossly though, the principle that the wealthy have a social responsibility in corporate social responsibility as in Gandhian trusteeship.

Post-development Paradigm

As discussed at the outset, the very concept of development is modelled out on Western perspectives. Therefore, with the emergence of newly independent countries freeing themselves up from colonial domination, the concept of development drew critical ire. A number of scholars have become quite critical about the way the Western model of development is being universalized. Truman, the then President of the United States, in 1949, at one stroke in his speech on 20 January 1949 made an entire section of the countries of Asia, Africa and Latin America as representing 'underdevelopment'.

On the basis of the economic parameters, these countries were labelled as underdeveloped. Much later, Willy Brandt had forwarded in the Brandt report, *North-South: A Programme for Survival,* the division of the globe into the Global North and the Global South. The developed Western countries of the USA and Europe are represented by the Global North. The entire

[1] *Brahmacharya* means control in thought, word and action, of all the senses at all times and in all places.

'Third-World' countries, comprising Asia, Africa and Latin America, are represented by the Global South. The inequality in the international economic order drew the attention of a group of scholars identified as dependency theorists, as discussed in Chapter 1 in detail, in their quest to find out the cause of the underdevelopment of the Global South.

Raul Prebisch, the Executive Director of the ECLA, popularized the dependency theory. The line of thinking was that economic growth in industrialized countries did not necessarily lead to growth in underdeveloped countries. On the contrary, the underdeveloped countries might be at peril trying to match up to the rate of development of the advanced countries. This was quite contrary to the neoclassical theory of liberalism and its assumption of development bringing development to all. By dividing the world into industrial centres, on the one hand, and raw material-producing peripheries, on the other hand, dependency theorists showed that the cause of the underdevelopment of the periphery was due to the extraction and exploitation of the periphery. According to Theotônio dos Santos, the historical dimension of dependency relationships is that there is a kind of structure in the world that favours some at the cost of others. This creates conditions in which the underdevelopment of certain economies is conditioned by the development of others.

Andre Gunder Frank, in his projection of the underdevelopment of the South, argues that contemporary underdevelopment is the result of the relationship between the metropolitan countries that were the colonizers and their satellites or colonies. The satellites served as the source of raw materials, cheap labour and abundant profit from the exploitation and siphoning of the wealth of the colonies. This legacy of underdevelopment in the colonies left them totally peripheralized even after their independence. They could not catch up to the level of economic development of the advanced economies. Therefore, they could neither make progress economically nor cater to the well-being of their people, which later came to be identified as human development.

In the 1990s, there was the emergence of the concept of human development, as discussed in detail in Chapter 8. It took into consideration social parameters and not economic criteria while measuring the level of human development such as the level of literacy, decent living standards and life expectancy as parameters to measure HDI (Chapter 8).

In the 1990s, another trend came into the fore, being quite a critique of the concept of development, and this line of thinking came to be identified as 'post-development paradigm'. The paradigm shift became visible from labelling countries as underdeveloped to why these countries of Asia, Africa and Latin America came to be labelled as 'underdeveloped' and in dire need of development as pointed out by Harry Truman. How the tag 'Third World' was stuck to the Global South also became a point of query with this brand of thinking. It was a post-structuralist critique of development which had sway over the entire globe by creating a frenzy of economic development to foster the growth of a country. It did not propose another model but provided a critique of the modernist concept of development.

In his book, *Encountering Development,* Escobar provides, in the Foucauldian sense, that forms of knowledge and creation of subjectivity related to power have set in motion the whole discursive of development. Post-development paradigm stresses the need for a critique of scientific discourses in defence of the promotion of localized and pluralistic grassroots activities. Rahnema in *The Post-development Reader* points out that development as a concept was born in the North that was indeed a tool for the economic and geographical expansion of the dominant powers. Rahnema also suggests that every development project carried out on target populations at the grassroots has hurt their traditional modes of living, thinking and doing, which have been doomed. They have been reduced to a subhuman condition. The post-development scholars emphasize grassroots movements, urban and rural local communities and informal sectors while putting forward their 'alternatives to development'.

Escobar has tried to identify certain features of post-development studies. These can be summarized as follows.

- After the Second World War, the frenzy of development emerged in the West and began to be exported to countries in Asia, Africa and Latin America.
- The emergence of Bretton Woods system comprising the triad—World Bank, IMF and GATT/WTO—and even the UN development project were implemented.
- The exclusionary nature of the Western concept of development. Local voices, culture, knowledge and the poor of Asia, Africa and Latin America stood excluded.
- Post-development studies emphasized the re-valorization of vernacular cultures and attempted to construct humane and culturally and ecologically sustainable worlds.
- Social movements and grassroots mobilization for moving towards a more inclusive world.
- Changing practices of contemporary 'political economy of truth' defining development regime.
- Highlighting alternative strategies produced by social movements as they encounter development projects.

In this context, a radical and quite striking claim has been made by Wolfgang Sachs in *The Development Dictionary* 1992 that was quite a controversial claim. He said that the age of development is coming to an end. 'The last forty years can be called the age of development. This epoch is coming to an end. The time is ripe to write its **obituary**'. It was after this that post-development studies took off. Thereafter, Rahnema and Bawtree in 1997 came up with their *The Post-development Reader,* which tried to portray the content and meaning of the concept of post-development. As pointed out earlier, post-development sought to address the absentee voices in the project of development, what Santos calls 'sociology of absence'. S. L. Maiava (2001) forwards five principles which arouse indigenous responses to development interventions. The first of these principles are (a) the need to feel good about oneself, (b) the need to belong to a social security network, assuring a kind of identity and belonging through family and kinship as well as a feeling of security, (c) the need to feel in control of one's life, (d) the need to be free, active and independent and (e) the need to support one's family. Scholars of post-development highlight that such responses are often not recognized by the dominant development paradigm. They opine that there is a need to conceptualize development in a new way, ensuring inclusion rather than exclusionary paradigms, leaving aside indigenous voices.

However, the post-development discourse has not been free from criticisms. The most vocal criticism launched against post-development is that it stands in total rejection of modernity and development and upholds an uncritical stance towards local communities. However, some post-development scholars like Escobar have not over enthusiastically championed 'local alternatives and traditions' unequivocally. Escobar suggests that there is a need to avoid adopting extreme stances. He says that 'to embrace them uncritically as alternatives or to dismiss them as romantic expositions' are both unacceptable. Even examples are cited of societal norms which undermine the dignity of women and children in many societies. Rahnema says a return to the state of nature is not desirable and feasible.

Complete rejection of modernity and development is untenable. Escobar and others have said that the Bretton Woods institutions and their SAPs have endangered millions of lives and have led to a debt crisis in sub-Saharan countries. Even poverty and famine have been vehemently present in underdeveloped countries, but there are other reasons for these too. They have been there even in pre-modern times, only that the development agenda since the post-Second World War has not been able to eradicate them at all. Escobar and others also remind readers that the 'traditional' is also a construct derived from actual practices of the people. So it also becomes a potential for oppression. Therefore, while rejecting universalism as popularized by the Western model of development, one should not oversee oppressions legitimized by societal norms and celebrate cultural differences uncritically. There should be respect towards culturally different world views in which Western paradigms may not be generalized yet not thrown out completely. Post-development is sometimes seen to be neo-populist and even reactionary populism. Therefore, scholars caution that one has to be aware of the reactionary populism and, at the same time, value the emancipator potential of the discourse on post-development. As J. Nederveen Pieterse (2000) has pointed out that, after post-development, development theory has undergone profound changes and encouraging in thinking about alternatives while critiquing the mainstream development theories.

Conclusion

Any discussion on development has look back to the times when there was a revolution in the production process through the ushering in of pathbreaking scientific discoveries. This period can be identified as the 18th century Industrial Revolution. Since then, we have come a long way, but the concept of development is still linked with technological progress and economic performance, among other parameters. From a Western perspective, the concept of development has been predominantly a notion. The liberal line of thinking favours less intervention by states and more inclination towards market economies and economic reforms to usher in liberalization of economic sectors. An example given above is that of TINA, propounded by Margaret Thatcher, which was nothing but a reassertion of liberal thinking in a neoliberal way. Marxism on the other hand, viewed the concept of social progress through the operations of the dialectics in interpreting history—historical materialism. While Karl Marx and Friedrich Engels advanced their views on class and class struggle in *The Communist Manifesto* dependency theorists such as Andre Gunder Frank, Raul Prebisch and the modern world system theorist Immanuel Wallerstein adopted the Marxist idea of exploitation and extraction in the 1970s. The concept of welfarism and the welfare state hinges upon the human aspect of development, but it also involves huge expenditure to carry out such welfare schemes for the people at large. Therefore, as previously discussed, Professor Amartya Sen advocates a capability approach rather than a utilitarian approach which is to build capabilities to achieve characteristics such as being able to live long and healthy lives, being educated and several other essentials in life. Quite contrary to the Western concept, Gandhi forwarded his idea of development through the practice of non-violence (ahimsa), *satyagraha*, sarvodaya and trusteeship. His thoughts on *gram swaraj* and the Panchayati Raj systems based on trusteeship and sarvodaya could usher in development in India. Post-development critiques are of the opinion that economic growth in industrialized countries may not necessarily lead to growth in underdeveloped countries. On the contrary, the underdeveloped countries might be at peril trying to match up to the rate of development of the advanced countries. Post-development scholars, therefore, stress the necessity to look at development beyond the Western perspective, taking into account the realities of underdevelopment in developing countries. There has been a broadening of the scope of looking into development through the lens of the developing world also. This paradigm shift is quite a welcome to broaden the outlook on development studies.

Summary

From Adam Smith to Karl Polanyi to Friedrich von Hayek, all advocated an open market economy with less state intervention. This line of thinking was a reflection of **liberalism,** which got a spurt with the rejection of Keynesian economics, and there was a neoliberal turn to classical liberalism. Margaret Thatcher and Ronald Reagan became the main advocates of **neoliberalism,** with privatization, liberalization and deregulation as its prime mottoes, which was reinvigorated by the Washington Consensus. This is the underlying principle of contemporary globalization and the international financial institutions such as the IMF and the World Bank.

Marxism, with its theory of historical materialism for tracing the trajectory of social progress, develops the theory of class and class struggle with the ultimate dictatorship of the proletariat and the withering away of the state. In *The Communist Manifesto,* Karl Marx and Friedrich Engels expressed their views on class and class struggle. Later in the 1970s, the Marxist idea of exploitation and extraction was adopted by dependency theorists such as Andre Gunder Frank, Raul Prebisch and the modern world system theorist Immanuel Wallerstein. They examined the dependency of the Third-World countries as the creation of the exploitation of the core or advanced countries of the world.

The debate around the **welfare state** is on in contemporary discourse. Some think it is an extra burden on state expenditure and must be done away with, whereas another group of scholars thinks that market failures are pervasive, and they create hardships for individuals. Thus, the government needs to play a more active role and help individuals from being exploited by market forces. Professor Amartya Sen advances a capability approach rather than a utilitarian approach. Depending on physical and other conditions, people should have the capability to achieve those characteristics, such as being able to live long and healthy lives, being educated and the like.

Gandhi's idea about development has to be understood from the perspective of his thinking about civilization, his idea about the Western concept of development and his vision of non-violence, *satyagraha*, *gram swaraj* and sarvodaya. Beginning with Gandhi's revocation of the Western concept of civilization (Gandhi 1909/2019), this chapter explains how through non-violence (ahimsa), *satyagraha*, sarvodaya and trusteeship, India can move towards development. *Gram swaraj* and the Panchayati Raj systems based on trusteeship and sarvodaya will be the main drivers of development in India.

Post-development paradigm was advocated by a group of scholars who became quite critical of the way the Western model of development was being universalized. The line of thinking was that economic growth in industrialized countries does not necessarily lead to growth in underdeveloped countries. Quite the opposite to this, the underdeveloped countries might be at peril in trying to match the rate of development of the advanced countries.

Wolfgang Sachs summarizes the entire line of thinking about development as that time is ripe to write its **obituary**.

These theories of development help us to identify not only the mainstream thinking around this concept but also the paradigmatic shift in the entire development studies.

REVIEW AND REFLECTION QUESTIONS

1. Development is differently viewed. It has different perspectives. Do you think classical liberalism and its new form, neoliberalism, are the dominant paradigms in contemporary times?
2. Marxism and its theory of class and class struggle and social progress have a place in development discourse altogether. Examine the Marxist point of view of development.
3. The Neo-Marxist approach has predominantly taken the form of dependency theory and modern world systems theory. Discuss the basic tenets of both (refer to Chapter 1 for more elaborate study).
4. Welfare or no welfare. Neoliberalism has put a question mark on public spending. Do you think that welfarism is still valid today? How did Professor Amartya Sen suggest an alternative through his capability approach?
5. Gandhi had put forward a critique of the Western model of development. Following Gandhi, illuminate on his basic ideas about *sarvodaya, trusteeship* and *gram swaraj*.
6. Is it the time to write the 'obituary' of development? Comment, following the post-development paradigm discursive.

Bibliography

Arrow, K. 1974. *The Limits of Organization*. New York, NY: Norton.

Balaam, David N., and Bradford Dilman. 2019. *Introduction to International Political Economy*. New York, NY: Routledge.

Bondurant, Joan V. 1971. *Conquest of Violence: The Gandhian Philosophy of Conflict*. Berkeley, CA: University of California Press.

Chakrabarty, Bidyut. 2017. 'Gandhi's Doctrine of Trusteeship: Spiritualizing Interpersonal Relationship.' Working Paper No. 67, Nabakrushna Choudhury Centre for Development Studies, Bhubaneswar. Available at https://ncds.nic.in/sites/default/files/WorkingandOccasionalPapers/WP67NCDS.pdf (accessed on 4 October 2021).

Chandrasekhar, C. P. 2017. *Karl Marx's Capital and the Present*. New Delhi: Tulika Books.

Engels, Frederick, and Karl Marx. 1991. *Manifesto of the Communist Party*. Kolkata: Manisha.

Escobar, Arturo. 1994. *Encountering Development: The Making and Unmaking of the Third World*. Princeton, NJ: Princeton University Press.

Frieden, Jeffry A., and David A. Lake. 2000. *International Political Economy: Perspectives on Global Power and Wealth*. New York, NY: Routledge.

Gandhi, M. K. 1909/2019. *Hind Swaraj or Indian Home Rule*. Mumbai: Indus Source Book.

———. 1931. *Young India*. July 30, 1931.

———. 1947. *India of My Dream*. Ahmedabad: Navajivan Publishing House.

———. 1957. *Economic and Industrial Life and Relations* (Vol. 6). Edited by V. B. Kher. Ahmedabad: Navajivan Publishing House.

———. 1960. *Trusteeship*. Ahmedabad: Navajivan Publishing House.

———. 1968a. 'The Veins of Wealth.' In *The Selected Works of Mahatma Gandhi* (Vol. IV). Ahmedabad: Navajivan Publishing House.

———. 1968b. *The Selected Works of Mahatma Gandhi* (Vol. 6). Edited by S. Narayan. Ahmedabad: Navajivan Publishing House.

Harvey, David. 2007. *A Brief History of Neoliberalism*. Oxford: Oxford University Press.

Ishii, K. 2001. 'The Socioeconomic Thoughts of Mahatma Gandhi: As an Origin of Alternative Development'. *Review of Social Economy* 59, no. 3: 297–312.

Maiava, S. L. 2001. *A Clash of Paradigms: Intervention, Response and Development in the South Pacific*. London: Routledge.

Mathai, M. P. 2000. *Mahatma Gandhi's World View*. New Delhi: Gandhi Peace Foundation.

Mathur, B. P. 2011. 'Gandhian Alternative to Economic Development: Relevance for India.' *Mainstream* XLIX, no. 41.

Mill, John Stuart. 1848/2004. *Principles of Political Economy with Some of Their Applications to Social Philosophy*. Cambridge: Hackett Publishing Company. Available at http://www.untag-smd.ac.id/files/Perpustakaan_Digital_2/POLITICAL%20ECONOMY%20John%20Stuart%20Mill%20%20principles%20of%20political%20economy%20with%20applications%20to%20social%20p.pdf (accessed on 4 October 2021).

O'Donnell, R. 1992. 'Economics and Policy: Beyond Science and Ideology.' *Economic and Social Review* 24, no. 1: 75–98.

O'Shea, E., and B. Kennelly. 1993. 'Poverty, Values and Public Policy.' In *New Frontiers for Full Citizenship*, edited by B. Reynolds and S. Healy. Dublin: CMRS.

Peet, Richard. 2010. *The Unholy Trinity: The IMF, World Bank and WTO*. New York, NY: Zed Books.

Pieterse, J. Nederveen. 2000. 'My Paradigm or Yours? Alternative Development, Post Development, Reflexive Development.' *Development and Change* 29, no. 2: 343–373.

Polanyi, K. 1944/1967. *The Great Transformation: The Political and Economic Origins of Our Time*. Boston, MA: Beacon Press.

Riesco, M., and S. Draibe. 2009. 'Is Global Welfare and a Global New Deal Possible?' Available at http://www.unrisd.org/unrisd/website/events.nsf/ee1a3b60f271933180256b64003a0d88/f6b7601e756cead1c12576a20057505c/$FILE/RiescoDraibe.pdf (accessed on 04 October 2021).

Sakamoto, T. 1969. *Gandhi*. Tokyo: Shimizu Shoin.

Savitha, N. 2015. 'Gandhian Economic Thought and Its Relevance to New Economic Policy.' *International Journal of Management and Development Studies* 4, no. 2: 138–145.

Sen, A., and B. Williams, eds. 1982. 'Introduction: Utilitarianism and Beyond.' In *Utilitarianism and Beyond*. Cambridge: Cambridge University Press.

Sen, A. 1977. 'Rational Fools.' *Philosophy and Public Affairs* 6, no. 4: 317–344.

———. 1982. *Choice, Welfare and Measurement*. Cambridge, MA: MIT Press.

Smith, Adams. 1776/2005. *An Inquiry into the Nature and Causes of the Wealth of Nations*. Pennsylvania, PA: Pennsylvania State University. Available at https://www.rrojasdatabank.info/Wealth-Nations.pdf (accessed on 04 October 2021).

Stalin, J. V. 1950/2004. *Dialectical and Historical Materialism: History of CPSU*. Moscow: Bolsheviks Foreign Language Publishing House.

Ziai, Aram. 2007. *Exploring Post-development: Theory and Practice, Problems and Perspectives*. New York, NY: Routledge.

8 Issues in Development: Social Dimensions

LEARNING OBJECTIVES

- ❐ Knowing about growth inequality and exclusion under the impact of globalization leading to uneven development
- ❐ Learning about the concept of human development
- ❐ Getting to know about UN Millennium Development Goals
- ❐ Familiarizing with non-governmental organizations (NGOs) and their role in development
- ❐ Understanding the role of culture media and TV
- ❐ Identifying big dams and environmental concerns
- ❐ Comprehending the working of global arms industry and arms trade
- ❐ Coming to know about the knowledge systems

Introduction

Chapter 7 gives us an idea of the concept of development from various perspectives. Liberals and neoliberals advocated for less intervention of states in the economy as rest would be taken care of by invisible hands or market forces. Marxist and Neo-Marxist pointed out the unequal relationship between advanced economies (or the core countries) and the backward or developing economies (or the peripheral or semi-peripheral economies). This relation was one of domination and subordination, as well as of exploitation and extraction. The post-development paradigm, in the same way, questions the Western model of development that created underdevelopment in the Global South. The welfare model of the state, with its function of delivering utilities to the maximum number, provides a model of development that keeps welfare first as an agenda. Gandhi provided his own indigenous model of development in *Hind Swaraj,* which was also contrary to the Western concept of development based on less interference and a market economy.

Development, strictly in economic terms, however, does not give the total picture of the well-being of the people living within a state. It gives the picture of the economy, for example, in terms of GDP. Human development since the 1990s has been much discussed around the world. GDP does not measure access to education, health or even life expectancy. Human development in the face of globalization is a challenge given the risk of leaving everything to the market. Some of the challenges are discussed in Chapter 9. Therefore, the international comity of states adopted the UN Millennium Development Goals (MDGs), 2000, and Sustainable Development Goals (SDGs), 2015, with the objectives of making development more inclusive.

Debates regarding inclusive sustainable development have come to the fore because many development projects, some even funded by international financial institutions, cause damage to the environment and displace people from habitat and cause loss of livelihood. Big dams are projects which are required to control floods or generate hydroelectric power, yet they damage, in many cases, the ecology and habitats of indigenous people living there for years. Here, the dialogue with stakeholders is important, as was highlighted by the Rio+20 Earth Summit. Non-governmental organizations (NGOs) can become facilitators in the dialogue process. National and international NGOs play a dominant role in such negotiations or anti-development project protests like the Narmada Bachao Andolan. Globalization has increased their interconnectedness across the globe through the IT revolution.

Globalization also has other challenges too. Globalization, with its homogenizing tendencies, tends to expand its ideas and beliefs through cultural imperialism vis-à-vis the developing countries through the media industry. Indigenous cultures become more and more invisible under the overwhelming influence of the dominant culture, and obviously, that is of the West. Globalization has also not written off war. Even if wars, like the First World War, the Second World War or even the Cold War, may not take place, that does not mean global arms transfers and sales are off. There is an ever-increasing global arms transfer, which has been discussed in this chapter. This chapter therefore rakes up various issues of globalization and their challenges which might lead to inequality, exclusion and unsustainable growth.

Globalization and Uneven Development: Growth, Inequality and Exclusion

Chapter 5 gives us an idea of the concept and theory of globalization. Briefly, it means a process of increasing and intensifying flows between countries of goods, services, capital, ideas, information and people, which produce national cross-border integration of a number of economic, social and cultural activities (United Nations Department of Economic and Social Affairs 2001). The underlying force is neoliberalism, professing a free market economy and liberalization with the free movement of goods, services and capital.

The 1990s saw a massive wave of globalization undertake the world. The developing countries got swept by the tide of globalization. The economic hardships of developing countries due to the international economic situations forced them to approach international financial institutions, such as the IMF and World Bank, for financial support. Therefore, they came under the obligation to adhere to WTO regulations if they were to receive IMF and World Bank loans. These made the developing countries accept SAPs (discussed in Chapter 6) and open up their economies, making the entry of foreign capital, firms, commodities and services easy. The belief in IMF, World Bank or neoliberal thinking was that unnecessary state intervention would hamper economic growth. Therefore, opening up will help in levelling up the economic development of these countries at par more or less with the advanced countries.

The 'oil shocks' of the 1970s following the Arab–Israeli conflict or the Yom Kippur War (1973–1974) and the oil embargo of the OPEC countries and again in 1979 following the

Figure 8.1 Oil Dollar Cycling

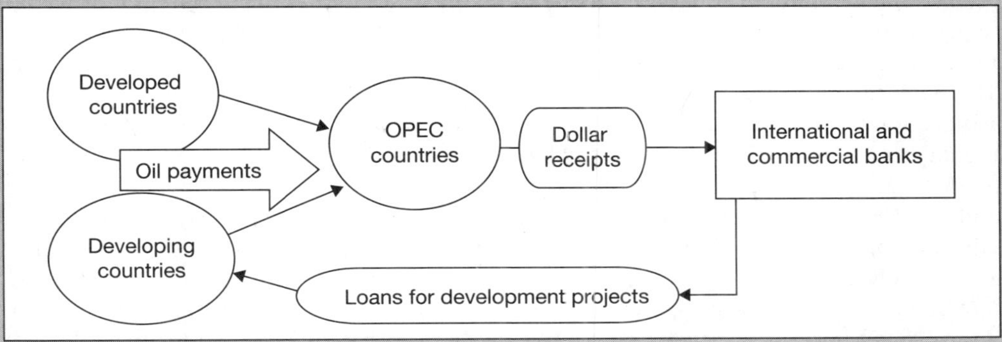

Iranian revolution, oil prices skyrocketed, causing hardships for developing countries. Thus, non-oil-producing developing countries suffered from ballooning trade deficits. OPEC had a huge accumulation of 'petrodollars' which they deposited in big international commercial banks (oil receipts not in US dollars). This was also called 'euro' dollar deposits. These were then reinvested by these banks in developing countries in the form of loans. This was known as 'oil dollar recycling' (Figure 8.1). Latin American countries, such as Mexico and Brazil, and East Asian countries, such as Indonesia and Korea, were the destination of such bank investments for prospects of higher interest and market stability. Continuous borrowing on the part of developing countries has made them heavily dependent on foreign bank loans. However, these countries were not able to manage their foreign debts as well as their domestic economies and were suffering from stagflation, meaning inflation and stagnant output.

At this juncture in 1979, with Mr Paul Volcker being appointed as the new chairman of the US Federal Reserve Board, he initiated an anti-inflation campaign. From 1979 to 1980, the Fed tightened the money supply. This caused a serious economic slowdown in the USA and the rest of the world and hardships for highly indebted developing countries. The USA was successful in taming the global recession of the 1970s, but it drowned the developing countries into indebtedness and default. There emerged the crisis of 'oil dollar recycling' or 'petrodollar recycling'.

What was this dollar recycling problem? As American monetary policy tightened, developing countries faced a back-bending reality. An increase in dollar interest rates has made debt servicing a real problem. Due to global recession, on the other hand, demand for exports fell. Commodity prices fell and developing countries faced lower terms of trade. They started defaulting, like Mexico in 1982 declared itself as a defaulter. A global crisis spiralled. One after another, countries started defaulting on their debts. Chile, Argentina and Brazil all sank into a deep crisis. With the debtor countries failing one by one, the commercial banks stopped lending. The oil dollar recycling loan moved into crisis and finally was terminated. The IMF came to the rescue of these countries. They extended loans to fill the 'financing gap' on the condition that the governments of the defaulter countries take up adjustment policies following the guidelines of the IMF and World Bank, which later in 1985 became SAPs as per the *Baker Plan* (discussed in Chapter 6). Ultimately, these official loans were financed by developed countries through capital contributions and loans. The SAPs involved budget cuts and low credit growth to reduce expenditure. They were supposed to introduce deregulation, privatization, trade liberalization and ease capital markets and so on. The underlying theory of neoliberalism and neoclassical development economics made them understand that the private sector will grow strongly once macroeconomic instability and government interventions are removed, and the economy will regain strength.

This was the centre of the debate about whether globalization and integration with the world economy through such structural adjustments brought development and equality or if it happened the other way round. This debate can be analysed from the angle of the theories of modernization and dependency theories. The mainstream theory of development as propounded by Walt Rostow. In his book, *The Stage of Economic Growth* (1960), he suggested that the developing countries which are poor are just passing through stages of development and will ultimately get to the final stage of development. In the 1960s, developing countries were in a similar stage of poverty to Britain's in the 1780s. Therefore, development was to help them to transit into more developed countries. He said that this is good for both developed countries and developing countries, as development of the poor countries would make them 'richer' as well as help developed countries security-wise, as 'richer' countries would not be attracted to communism. In other words, this meant that contact with the West would be favourable for the development of the 'Third World'. As seen in Chapter 7, in Truman's speech, the term 'Third World' labelled the developing countries, at one time, as the underdeveloped countries of the world.

This was contested by another group of scholars who argued that contact with other countries was a problem for developing countries. Colonialism was the cause of their underdevelopment as these countries specialized in producing primary products, and this led to their excessive dependence on the world price movements. This was because they produced one or two primary goods and the world price movements and this accounted for most of their foreign exchange earnings. However, the developed countries were free from the price movements of these products as they could diversify products as they were far more industrialized than the poorer countries. Raul Prebisch, a dependency theorist, pointed out that primary producers faced a problem because the terms of trade could decline for primary goods as against industrial goods, for example, cocoa against fridge. A larger amount of cocoa has to be produced to buy similar amounts of industrial products. If the price of primary products falls, so will the income of primary producers. Of course, there may be a fall in the prices of industrial products, but not in the way prices of primary goods fall. Therefore, colonies would remain poor, whereas manufacturers of industrial goods would benefit. Prebisch, in his 'Commercial Policy in the Underdeveloped Countries', 1959, published in the *American Economic Review,* and H. Singer, in his 'The Distribution of Gains from Trade between Investing and Borrowing Countries' also published in the *American Economic Review,* have cited the case of Latin American landowners who accrued wealth, and with this, they import manufactured goods rather than develop domestic manufacturing units and production. Therefore, in the post-colonial period, the developing countries carried the burden of colonialism, which accounted for their underdevelopment and created inequality in IPE.

The World Bank has classified countries on the basis of income into low-income groups, lower-middle-income groups, upper-middle-income groups and high-income groups. The 2021 classification of economies on the basis of income parameters is given in Table 8.1.

The tables are proof of the glaring reality of uneven growth and inequality between developed and developing countries. The neoliberal theory of economic growth, therefore, has not given equal growth to the developing countries. The **convergence** theory, therefore, seems to

Table 8.1 World Bank Classification of Economies 2020

Classification by Income	Measure of Income
Low-income	A GNI per capita of $1,035 or less in 2019
Lower-middle-income	A GNI per capita of between $1,036 and $4,045
Upper-middle-income	A GNI per capita of between $4,046 and $12,535
High-income	A GNI per capita of $12,536 or more

Source: World Bank (n.d.).

be simplistic. The basic assumption is that a free market or open economy allows the free flow of capital globally and knowledge across borders, allowing access to cutting-edge production technologies for countries. Therefore, international income gaps tend to converge. Despite such claims by convergence theory, in reality, there is no indication of the convergence of per capita incomes from Tables 8.2, 8.3 and 8.4. In long-term growth rates, there are regional

Table 8.2 World Bank List of Countries in Different Income Groups 2020–2021

Income Group	Countries
High-income	Andorra, Greece, Palau, Antigua and Barbuda, Greenland, Panama, Aruba, Guam, Poland, Australia, Hong Kong, SAR, China, Portugal, Austria, Hungary, Puerto Rico, the Bahamas, Iceland, Romania, Bahrain, Ireland, Qatar, Barbados, Isle of Man, San Marino, Belgium, Israel, Saudi Arabia, Bermuda, Italy, Seychelles, the British Virgin Islands, Japan, Singapore, Brunei Darussalam, Republic of Korea, Sint Maarten (Dutch part), Canada, Kuwait, Slovak Republic, Cayman Islands, Latvia, Slovenia, Channel Islands, Liechtenstein, Spain, Chile, Lithuania, Saint Kitts and Nevis, Croatia, Luxembourg, Saint Martin (French part), Curaçao, Macao, special administrative regions of China, Sweden, Cyprus, Malta, Switzerland, Czech Republic, Mauritius, Taiwan, China, Denmark, Monaco, Trinidad and Tobago, Estonia, Nauru, Turks and Caicos Islands, Faroe Islands, Netherlands, United Arab Emirates, Finland, New Caledonia, the UK, France, New Zealand, the USA, French Polynesia, Northern Mariana Islands, Uruguay, Germany, Norway, Virgin Islands (the USA), Gibraltar and Oman
Upper-middle-income	Albania, Fiji, Montenegro, American Samoa, Gabon, Namibia, Argentina, Georgia, North Macedonia, Armenia, Grenada, Paraguay, Azerbaijan, Guatemala, Peru, Belarus, Guyana, Russian Federation, Belize, Indonesia, Samoa, Bosnia and Herzegovina, Islamic Republic of Iran, Serbia, Botswana, Iraq, South Africa, Brazil, Jamaica, Saint Lucia, Bulgaria, Jordan, Saint Vincent and the Grenadines, China, Kazakhstan, Suriname, Colombia, Kosovo, Thailand, Costa Rica, Lebanon, Tonga, Cuba, Libya, Turkey, Dominica, Malaysia, Turkmenistan, Dominican Republic, Maldives, Tuvalu, Equatorial Guinea, Marshall Islands, Venezuela, RB, Ecuador and Mexico

(Continued)

(Continued)

Income Group	Countries
Lower-middle-income	Angola, Honduras, Papua New Guinea, Algeria, India, Philippines, Bangladesh, Kenya, São Tomé and Principe, Benin, Kiribati, Senegal, Bhutan, Kyrgyz Republic, Solomon Islands, Bolivia, Lao PDR, Sri Lanka, Cabo Verde, Lesotho, Tanzania, Cambodia, Mauritania, Timor-Leste, Cameroon, Federated States of Micronesia, Tunisia, Comoros, Moldova, Ukraine, the Republic of Congo, Mongolia, Uzbekistan, Côte d'Ivoire, Morocco, Vanuatu, Djibouti, Myanmar, Vietnam, Arab Republic of Egypt, Nepal, West Bank and Gaza, El Salvador, Nicaragua, Zambia, Eswatini, Nigeria, Zimbabwe, Ghana and Pakistan
Low-income	Afghanistan, Guinea-Bissau, Sierra Leone, Burkina Faso, Haiti, Somalia, Burundi, Democratic People's Republic of Korea, South Sudan, Central African Republic Liberia, Sudan, Chad, Madagascar, the Syrian Arab Republic, the Democratic Republic of the Congo, Malawi, Tajikistan, Eritrea, Mali, Togo, Ethiopia, Mozambique, Uganda, Gambia, the Niger, the Republic of Yemen, Guinea and Rwanda

Source: https://datahelpdesk.worldbank.org/knowledgebase/articles/906519-world-bank-country-and-lending-groups (accessed on 24 November 2021).

Table 8.3 HDI Ranking of Countries 2020

HDI Sl No.	Countries	HDI Points
1.	Norway	0.957
2.	Ireland	0.955
2.	Switzerland	0.955
4.	Hong Kong	0.949
4.	Iceland	0.949
6.	Germany	0.947
7.	Sweden	0.945
8.	Australia	0.944
8.	Netherlands	0.944
10.	Denmark	0.940
11.	Finland	0.938
11.	Singapore	0.938
13.	United Kingdom	0.932
14.	Belgium	0.931
14.	New Zealand	0.931
16.	Canada	0.929
17.	United States	0.926
18.	Austria	0.922
19.	Israel	0.919
19.	Japan	0.919
19.	Liechtenstein	0.919

Source: UNDP (2020a).

Table 8.4 Annual Average Growth Rate 1961, 2010 and 2019 (% per Year)

Names of Countries	1961	2010	2019
Industrialized countries			
The USA	2.3	2.5	2.1
The UK	2.6	1.9	1.4
Canada	3.1	3.0	1.6
France	4.9	1.9	1.5
Ireland	3.47	1.8	5.5
Italy	8.2	1.7	0.3
Japan	12.0	4.1	0.6
Spain	11.8	0.1	1.95
Africa			
Kenya	−7.7	8.41	5.4
Nigeria	0.192	8.0	2.2
Senegal	2.9	3.56	5.2
Zimbabwe	6.3	19.6	−8.1
Latin America			
Argentina	5.4	10.1	−2.1
Brazil	10.2	7.5	1.1
Chile	5.2	5.8	1.1
Colombia	5.0	4.5	3.2
Mexico	5	5.1	−0.1
Paraguay	6.9	11.1	−0.03
Peru	7.3	8.3	2.15
Venezuela	3.1	−1.4	−3.8
Asia			
China	−27.27	10.6	5.9
Hong Kong	14.2	6.7	−1.2
India	3.7	8.5	4.2
Malaysia	7.5	7.4	4.3
Singapore	8.1	14.5	0.7
South Korea	6.9	6.8	2.0
Taiwan	2.9	3.0	1.2
Thailand	5.3	7.5	2.4

Source: World Bank GDP Growth Annual (%; 1961–2019).

disparities also. Sub-Saharan African countries are at the bottom of the world income scale. East Asian countries show some growth, such as the ASEAN countries and East Asia such as Japan, Hong Kong, South Korea and Taiwan. South Asian countries, such as India, Bangladesh, Sri Lanka and the Maldives, show increasing growth rates. Eastern European countries previously under the Soviet influence during the Cold War also show higher income. Setting aside the economic content of development, let us now see the HDI ranking of developing countries. China, GDP wise, is among the top 10 countries; however, China's HDI ranking is 85. The other HDI rankings like that of Maldives is 95, Tunisia is 95, Suriname 97, Indonesia 107, the Philippines 107, Venezuela 113, South Africa 114, Vietnam 117, Gabon 119, Guatemala 127, Nicaragua 128, Bhutan 129, Namibia 130, India 131, Bangladesh 133, Ghana 138, East Timor 141, Nepal 142, Cambodia 144, Myanmar 147, Zimbabwe 150, Syria 151, Cameroon 153, Pakistan 154, Uganda 159, Rwanda 160, Nigeria 161, Tanzania 163, Afghanistan 169, Sudan 170, Yemen 179, Sierra Leone 182, Mali 184, Burundi 185, South Sudan 185, Chad 187, Central African Republic 188 and the last one in the list is Niger 189. Therefore, if we take development not just as economic growth but also at human development, then it is evident that the high-income countries rank higher in the HDI ranking. Top 50 positions are occupied greatly by the high-income countries. So in the case of human development, the disparity, inequality and uneven development becomes visible between the developed and the developing world.

However, the developing countries have certain structural weaknesses. Paul Krugman et al. (2018) have given an idea of the structural features of developing countries which prevent them from attaining a high degree of growth. These countries before they liberalized had a history of heavy governmental involvement in the economy along with huge public spending in GNP. They also faced inflation as the government failed to pay for its heavy expenditure and the huge losses it encountered from state-owned enterprises. This could not be paid with tax alone. Then the government went to print money or *seigniorage*.[1] As Krugman shows, there is a strong long-run link between national money supplies and national price levels. A doubling of the money supply, as in the case of Latin America in the 1980s, 1990s and 2000s, had the long-run effect of a currency reform in which each unit of currency is replaced by two units of 'new currency'.

Continuous expanding money supplies through seigniorage led to inflation and hyperinflation. Coupled with this were ineffective tax collections, underdeveloped capital markets, weak credit institutions, government control of exchange rates to limit exchange rate flexibility to keep inflation and volatility in markets under control. Added to these was control of capital movements by limiting foreign exchange transactions connected with trade assets. A heavy reliance on primary commodity export, as shown in the beginning of discussion, also impaired their growth. Developing countries have a history of borrowing and suffer from the problem of default. Latin American countries' uncontrolled borrowing led to a generalized debt crisis. The same was the case with sub-Saharan countries. For the countries of both these continents, it was a 'lost decade'.

Oil shocks (1973 and 1979) and rising dollar exchange rates in response to the high US interest rates of the early 1980s, known as the Volcker shock, made it difficult for Latin American countries to meet their debt commitments. The bulk of their debt was placed in dollars; therefore, the burden of servicing dollar debt became increasingly more difficult

[1] *Seigniorage* is the difference between the value of money and the cost to produce and distribute it.

during the 1980s. Capital flight was also taking place as overvalued exchange rates for some of the Latin American countries, like Mexico, generated fears of devaluation and added to liquidity problems. Capital flights occurred throughout Latin America, especially in Argentina, Mexico and Venezuela. The World Bank estimated that, between 1979 and 1982, capital flight from Argentina, Mexico and Venezuela was almost $70 billion or 67 per cent of gross capital inflows (*World Development Report* 1985). This did not deter Latin American countries from continuing their borrowing.

From the period following 1979 till the end of 1982, total Latin American debt more than doubled, increasing from $159 billion to $327 billion. The global recession set off by the record high interest rates of the early 1980s, caused by the Federal Reserve's efforts to curb the oil-based inflation of the 1970s, triggered the debt crisis. In August 1982, Mexico declared itself a defaulter country. By the end of 1982, approximately 40 countries globally were in arrears in their interest payments. In 1983, 27 countries, including the four major Latin American countries of Mexico, Brazil, Venezuela and Argentina, were trying to work out negotiations to restructure their existing loans.

Coming to the African continent, according to the IMF annual report, 1988, there was an increase in external debt. From an estimated $8 billion in 1970, the total external debt of the African countries (excluding arrears) had risen immensely to an estimated $174 billion at the end of 1987, including short-term debt, which was estimated at $12 billion (Greene and Khan 1990). Total African debt (measured in constant [1980]) US dollars at the end of 1987 was a colossal amount, and it was nearly seven and a half times more than its level in 1970. Taking into account the total debt service payments by African countries, it was again enormous. It was estimated to have grown from less than $1 billion in 1970 to nearly $18 billion in 1987, net of arrears and debt relief. The debt and output trends for Sub-Saharan African countries are even more witness to a preposterous increase in external debt burdens. Aggregate debt (excluding arrears) was estimated to have risen from $6 billion in 1970 to $126 billion at the end of 1987, including short-term debt of $7 billion, which in constant (1980) US dollar terms was an increase of about 620 per cent.

Even the East Asian countries, despite their steady growth in the 1980s, were hit by the economic crisis and devastating currency depreciation (discussed in Chapter 6). The IMF came to the rescue of the economies but with conditions. In late 1997, the IMF had committed more than $110 billion in short-term loans to Thailand, Indonesia, and South Korea to help stabilize the economies, which were given with SAPs attached.

The East Asian countries started their economic reform gradually in the 1980s and faced a crisis in 1997–1998. In the 1980s, heavy borrowing from the IMF and World Bank forced the Latin American and African countries to go for liberal reforms in their economies. Their heavy state-led industrialization model of development was rigged by inefficiency and heavy losses because of high tariffs, quantitative import restrictions and too much state intervention. Overall, it was said to be lacking macroeconomic discipline. The SAPs of international financial institutions forced them to move on the path of economic reforms and liberalization.

The question is where these countries stand after liberalization and the open economy came to work in these countries. Table 8.3 gave us the idea of the human development levels in these countries. Table 8.4 provides us with the rate of GDP growth in these countries. So 'exclusion' is visible. The question is exclusion of whom. The answer will be given by the data provided by Our World in Data report (Oxford Martin School 2017) that the excluded human beings who are subject to abject poverty still belong to the developing world.

According to Our World in Data report, 2017 (Oxford Martin School 2017), certain parameters when considered reveal the actual gap between the rich and poor countries and the glaring inequality. When living conditions are considered, the report takes into account the parameters of mortality rate of children under the age of five years, life expectancy at birth, mean years of schooling and average income. The report shows that, in the case of under-five child mortality, in a number of African countries, more than 1 out of 10 children born today die even before attaining five years of age. In Europe and East Asia, which are put in the bracket of the healthiest countries, only 1 in 250 children die before they are five years old. In Europe and North America, where people have the best access to education, children of school-entrance age today are expected to have 15–20 years of formal education. In Australia, school life expectancy is 22.9 years. Children entering school with the poorest access to education can only expect five years and huge dropouts. Income wise, this report makes a comparison between Qatar with a GDP per capita of approximately $117,000 to the poorest country in the world like the Central African Republic with the GDP per capita of $661. The report shows the difference to be 177 fold/times. According to the 2017 GDP per capita, the USA had a GDP per capita of $54,225 and Switzerland of $57,410. This means the Swiss can spend in one month what people in the Central African Republic can spend in seven years. This is a huge disparity, and this also results in low human development and hence the exclusion of the bulk of the population from accessing the mortality rate of children under the age of five years, life expectancy at birth, mean years of schooling and average income.

Global poverty or exclusion of people according to the Human Poverty Index (HPI) includes survival, knowledge and decent living. When people are deprived of these, then they are said to be in poverty. The *World Bank Annual Report 2019: Ending Poverty, Investing in Opportunity* shows that 15 countries were able to lift 800 million people out of extreme poverty, of which seven were Sub-Saharan countries. The 15 countries are Tanzania, Tajikistan, Chad, Congo, the Kyrgyz Republic, China, India, Moldova, Burkina Faso, Democratic Republic of the Congo, Indonesia, Vietnam, Ethiopia, Pakistan and Namibia. Half of the world's poor live in five countries—India, Bangladesh, Nigeria, Democratic Republic of the Congo and Ethiopia. About 33.25 per cent of the poor live in Sub-Saharan African countries. According to the 'learning poverty' indicator, 53 per cent of children in low-income and middle-income countries and 89 per cent of children in poor countries suffer from learning poverty. If the literacy level does not improve, then 43 per cent of children in low- and middle-income countries will still be learning poor by 2030.

Over the last decade, the number of people living without electricity has fallen from 1.2 billion in 2010 to 840 million in 2017, with Bangladesh, Myanmar and Kenya making most of the progress among the 20 countries in the world with the biggest electricity-access deficits. Coming to the facts about displacement and refugees, the 2019 report shows that the number of displaced people in the world rose to 70.8 million in 2018, including a record 25.9 million refugees, 41.3 million internally displaced people and 3.5 million asylum seekers. Developing countries host about 85 per cent of refugees. In 2018, 67 per cent of refugees came from five countries: the Syrian Arab Republic, Afghanistan, South Sudan, Myanmar and Somalia. More than 4.6 million people left Venezuela between 2016 and November 2019, destination wise, towards Colombia, Peru and Ecuador. Overall, the 2019 report concludes that the last two decades have seen significant progress in many of the world's poorest countries. The extreme poverty rate fell from more than 50 per cent to about 30 per cent. Child mortality declined from nearly 14 per cent to 7 per cent. Access to electricity increased by 57 per cent and the share of people using at least basic drinking water and sanitation services increased by 22 per cent and 41 per cent, respectively.

The *World Development Report 2021: Data For Better Lives* shows that due to COVID-19, there is a rise in extreme poverty for the first time in over 20 years. Along with COVID-19, climate change and conflicts have increased the incidence of poverty globally. It is estimated that there are already about 120 million additional people living in poverty due to the pandemic, and the total is expected to rise to about 150 million by the end of 2021. The report further shows that in 2018, four out of five people below the international poverty line lived in rural areas. The report summarizes the following observations of the World Bank:

- Half of the poor are children. Women represent a majority of the poor in most regions and among some age groups. About 70 per cent of the global poor aged 15 and over have no schooling or only some basic education.
- Almost half of poor people in Sub-Saharan Africa live in just five countries: Nigeria, the Democratic Republic of Congo, Tanzania, Ethiopia and Madagascar.
- More than 40 per cent of the global poor live in economies affected by fragility, conflict and violence, and that number is expected to rise to 67 per cent in the next decade. Those economies have just 10 per cent of the world's population.
- About 132 million of the global poor live in areas with high flood risk.

People who had barely escaped extreme poverty would be forced back into it by the convergence of COVID-19, conflict and climate change in 2021. The report further predicts that the 'new poor' probably will:

- Be more urban than the chronic poor.
- Be more engaged in informal services and manufacturing and less in agriculture.
- Live in congested urban settings and work in the sectors most affected by lockdowns and mobility restrictions.

Middle-income countries such as India and Nigeria will be significantly affected; middle-income countries may be home to 82 per cent of the 'new poor'.

The report further predicts that climate change will drive an estimated 68–132 million people into poverty by 2030. Climate change is a particularly acute threat for countries in Sub-Saharan Africa and South Asia. These are the regions where most of the global poor are concentrated. In a number of countries, a large share of the poor live in areas that are both affected by conflict and face high exposure to floods, such as Nepal, Cameroon, Liberia and the Central African Republic.

From the above discussion, it becomes clear that there are vast differences in per capita income and in well-being among countries. Developing countries also do not show a uniform level of development. The convergence theory of levelling up does not work for the developing countries, as we saw in the above discussion, except for some countries like those of the East Asian economies. Uneven development and exclusion exist in the current international economy as there will also exist poverty, illiteracy and high mortality.

As Thomas Piketty shows in his book, *Capital in the Twenty-first Century,* the future of ever-increasing inequality is based on fundamental inequality. Krugman, while explaining Piketty's model, stated that 'a rising share of capital, in turn, directly increases inequality, because ownership of capital is always much more unequally distributed than labour income. But the effects don't stop there, because when the rate of return on capital greedy exceeds the rate of economic growth,' and the 'the past tends to devour the future' they push society inexorably towards dominance by inherited wealth. Therefore, it becomes evident that in the 21st century, inequality has been on the rise in the period of growth as well as in the period of stagnation and recession. Piketty's work tries to find a remedy in the form of a 'progressive global tax on capital' as well as a 'progressive tax on income' and a 'progressive real estate tax'. Given the rise of neo-corporates, the MNCs, the tycoons of business and unbounded accumulation, these remedies would remain as 'ideals' only.

Human Development

Before going into the discussion of human development, it will become easier if we begin with the linkage between economic development and an accelerated pace of globalization. In the 1980s, the wave of globalization engulfed the entire world. The developed countries were already followers of the trends or best described as trendsetters. This was manifested in their pursuance of neoliberal ideology, which itself was an expression of the capitalist mode of production, free trade, free capital flow and the expansion of the activities of TNCs. The developing countries of the Global South also started replicating the capitalist mode of production and the market economy in the belief that this would lead to economic development. In pursuit of economic development, they accepted the conditionalities (SAPs) of the IMF, World Bank and WTO and liberalized their economies, paving the way for the intrusion of foreign capital.

Chapter 6 gives us an idea of foreign direct investment (FDI) and FII from developed countries into individuals or groups of developing countries. Along with these, the activities of the MNCs (see Chapter 3) and the magnitude of their investments began to increase globally in the post-reform era in the developing countries. If the neoliberal belief in the trickle-down effect of globalization were taken as a truth and not a myth, then the Global South would have experienced an enormous pace of economic development that would have been inclusive. The reality, however, is harsh. The widening gap between the rich and the poor countries persists and widens further. The sub-Saharan debt crisis of the 1980s is a reminder of what embracing a free market economy can do, along with rising external borrowing and the balance of payment deficit. Côte d'Ivoire, Morocco, Nigeria, Zaire and Zambia had significant amounts of commercial bank debt outstanding. External debt in relation to GDP or to exports of goods and services has increased more than threefold since the 1980s. In the case of the Sub-Saharan African countries, they exceeded the comparable ratios for other developing countries with debt-servicing problems. Ultimately, the IMF and World Bank came to their rescue with loan packages but with SAPs attached, and how it contributed to their 'lost decade' has been discussed in Chapter 6.

The current economic crisis in Venezuela, which started around 2014 and became worse in 2019, shows that if development is not managed properly, it can cause disaster. Reliance on oil exports and no development of indigenous industries have submerged Venezuela in an economic crisis unprecedented in any Latin American country. The brunt of the economic disaster is being borne by ordinary Venezuelans. As thousands of Venezuelans are crossing the border and seeking asylum as refugees in the neighbouring states of Colombia, Peru,

Ecuador, Chile, Brazil and other countries in Central and North America, as well as some Caribbean islands, are also witnessing an influx of people trying to flee Venezuela. A humanitarian crisis has unfurled with human beings struggling to survive and having the access to food, shelter and medicine. A reminder that Venezuela topped the Latin American countries as far as economic development is concerned and now it has fallen to the lowest rung.

The above examples show the human cost of development. Unsustainable and exclusive development will only multiply the human burden. This leads us to examine whether sheer economic growth can achieve an all-out inclusive development of humans encompassing all sections of society, including gender and providing education, life expectancy, poverty eradication, removal of inequality and the like.

Here, we have to bring in the concept of human development apart from economic development. Purely, the economic concept of development, for example, viewed from the GDP standpoint, would not give a wholesome picture of human development in a state. A high GDP does not ensure a high level of economic development, and this will become clear in the later section of this chapter. Whenever the concept of human development is taken up for discussion, Professor Amartya Sen's concept of human development has to be the starting point. The core idea of his concept of human development is that there is a necessity for the richness of human life rather than the richness of the economy. Economic richness is only a component of development and not the entire one.

Professor Amartya Sen's concept of human development, which later became a pillar of UNDP's creation of HDI, is contained in his seminal works 'Development as Capability Expansion' (1989) and *Development as Freedom* (2000). As pointed out earlier, GDP, industrialization, technological advances and higher incomes do not add up to the richness of human development. Freedom is both the primary end and the principal means of development.

Professor Sen identifies **five types of freedoms.** They are political freedom, economic facilities, social opportunities, transparency guarantees and protective security. Freedom is the 'agency aspect' of an individual. This means that once this freedom is realized, it endows the individual with the ability to help oneself and enhance one's capabilities. Like Adam Smith, he sees social institutions as obstructing enjoyment of individual freedom. He suggests positive role of market and little interventions and regulations that obstruct the freedoms of individuals.

The cornerstone of his concept is the 'capability approach'. Here, he suggests that the basic concern of human development lies in the individual's capability to lead the kind of life that one's reason dictates them to value. Human development cannot be synonymous with GDP, technical progress and industrialization. Professor Sen sees freedom as 'opportunity aspect ... the extent to which people have the opportunity to achieve outcomes that they value and have reason to value.' Therefore, he draws a distinction between human capital and human capability. Human capital is an input in the productive process, whereas human capability, like receiving education, equips an individual with substantive freedom to lead their lives as they reason to value and enhance their choices that they have.

Human development means the removal of major sources of 'unfreedom'. These, he suggests, are poverty, tyranny, poor economic opportunities, illiteracy, lack of access to resources, systemic deprivation, neglect of public facilities, lack of civil and political freedom, as well as intolerance and the overactivity of repressive states. The five freedoms stated above have to be supported by the states. The states, on their part, are to ensure such freedoms. The states must provide public education, healthcare, social safety nets, good macroeconomic policies, productivity and protection of the environment. Professor Sen also opines that GDP/per capita gives us the false picture of development. Higher GDP does produce improved quality of life but not the complete picture. Countries, he points out, such as Sri Lanka, China and the Indian state of Kerala, have higher literacy rates and higher life expectancies despite lower GDP per capita. Their human development rate is much higher than rich countries such as South Africa, Brazil and Namibia. For Professor Sen, 'capability deprivation' can be another measure of poverty other than low income.

In his work 'Development as Capability Expansion', Professor Sen (1989) proposed the concept of human development as the process of enlarging a person's functioning and capabilities to function with regard to the range of things that a person could do and be in life. 'Functioning' refers to the various living conditions one can or cannot achieve. To Professor Sen, 'capabilities' means one's ability to achieve these functioning. In sum, we can conclude that Professor Sen's capability approach encompasses actual attainment of certain goals of standard of living such as income, health and education. This also includes the 'potential' of the person to attain such capabilities. Therefore, he was able to relate freedom/capability to human development. So, on the one hand, there is the pursuit of a person's overall agency goals and promotion of his well-being, and on the other hand, there is the existence of freedom to achieve these goals and achievement attained. Out of these, there are four advantages which an individual can face in their 'agency aspect'. These are (a) well-being achievement, (b) agency achievement, (c) well-being freedom and (d) agency freedom.

Professor Sen and his 'capability approach' towards human development have been a great influence on the thinking of the UNDP on human development. This has been instrumental in the introduction of the HDI in the UNDP report of 1990, as discussed as follows. Professor Sen was also associated with the UNDP on its *Human Development Report 2004: Cultural Liberty in Today's Diverse World*. This report highlighted that an essential element of human development is cultural freedom. This includes the freedom to choose a person's identity and to exercise that choice without fear of being discriminated against or facing disadvantages.

Another significant contribution towards the new vision of human development has been that of the Pakistani economist, Mahbub ul Haq. Under his leadership, the first UNDP Human Development Report was published in 1990. In the UNDP report of 1990, it was argued that growth in national production is a necessity to fulfil essential human objectives, but one thing that has to be pondered upon is how this growth translates or fails to translate into human development in all societies. The report also proposed that the purpose of development is to provide people more options. Access to income is a means but not an end to acquiring human well-being is one of the options. The other options are long life, knowledge, personal security, political freedom, community participation and guarantee of human rights.

In the UNDP report of 1990, it was clearly stated that economic growth is necessary, but the question is how it succeeds or fails to translate into human development in societies. The insight into human development was further made clear by the explanation of the purpose of development on the basis of options offered to the people. There may be many options for well-being, such as life, knowledge, political freedom and human rights, for which another option may be important—access to income. Access to income gives a means of acquiring the other human well-being mentioned above. Therefore, people's first approach is the centre of their thinking about human development. This brand of thinking from the perspective of human well-being is in contrast to the Bretton Woods system or the Washington Consensus, which hammers univocally in favour of neo-liberal economic growth on the basis of a free market economy. The 1990 Human Development Report underpins human development as 'a complex concept of development, based on the priority of human well-being and aimed at ensuring and enlarging human choices which led to equality of opportunities for all people in society and empowerment of people so that they participate in-and benefit from-the development process.' This was an alternative development paradigm to the existing paradigm of economic development. The emphasis is on the building of human capabilities through enabling environments and using those capabilities through planning for growth, empowerment and inclusive and sustainable development. This paradigm human development, therefore, is concerned with building human capabilities through utilizing human capabilities to the full by providing enlargement of human choices and not just GNP and emphasizing the importance of people at the centre of concern for development.

The HDI was designed to measure human development in countries of varying economic development. It was developed by Mahbub ul Haq and has been used since 1993. According to Haq, the concept of human development is to shift the focus of development economics towards people-centred policies from purely national income accounting. The yardstick for measuring human development, that is, HDI, comprises of indices which are used to make a comparative measure of human development. The three basic dimensions of human development used in HDI are (a) a long and healthy life measured by life expectancy at birth, (b) knowledge as measured by adult literacy rate along with combined primary, secondary and tertiary gross enrolment and (c) a decent standard of living as measured by GDP per capita at purchasing power parity (PPP) in the US dollar. Countries are listed and ranked according to their HDI performances annually. HDI values range from 0 to 1. Higher values mean higher human development. Table 8.5 gives an account of the GDP performance and HDI score and rankings of South Asian countries for the year 2018.

On the basis of HDI, there are very high-performing countries, which are usually the developed countries, such as the Scandinavian countries and other European countries, the USA, Russia, Singapore, Saudi Arabia, Bahrain, Hong Kong, Australia and others. The other high-performing countries include Iran, Sri Lanka, Mexico, Colombia, China, Brazil, Indonesia, the Philippines, Vietnam, South Africa and others. The medium human development countries are

Table 8.5 Comparative Analysis of GDP Growth Rate and HDI of South Asian Countries (2019)

Name of the Country	GDP (2019) Growth Rate (%)	HDI Rank	HDI Score
India	4.18	131	0.645
Pakistan	1.90	154	0.557
Bangladesh	8.20	133	0.632
Sri Lanka	2.30	72	0.782
Nepal	7.10	142	0.602
Bhutan	3.90	129	0.654
Afghanistan	2.90	169	0.511

Source: UNDP (2020b).

India, Nepal, Kenya, Cambodia, Syria, Pakistan and others. The low-performing countries include Sudan, Gambia, Ethiopia, Afghanistan, Tanzania and others.

Some might find the human development concept not a wholesome approach, and none of the proponents rejected entirely accumulation-centric growth working on the basis of private ownership and profit-oriented ownership. How such an accumulation-centric growth process negatively contracts the capabilities of the people and generates inequality and depravation has not been discussed at length in this paradigm. However, the concept of human development has emerged as an alternative to the ongoing paradigm of development by putting emphasis on the advancing richness of human life and not the wealth of the economy. As Professor Sen enumerates freedom of choice in making decisions affecting human lives, as well as freedom from restraints on functioning of human beings, such as hunger, illiteracy, unemployment, exclusion, curable diseases and inculcating the ability for social participation, express freely and live socio-economic, political and cultural lives freely, are factors affecting human development. HDI may be limited to three yardsticks, but it gives us an alternative measure to GDP, and it is still under improvisation.

UN Millennium Development Goals (MDGs)

Any discussion on the UN **MDGs** has to fall back on the concept of human development. The lopsided picture of human development across the globe, especially in the Global South, has raised international concern. Certain middle-ranking countries showed high GDP but when measured by HDI (as shown in Table 8.5) and GDI (discussed in Chapter 9), manifested low performance. HDI-wise, Western European countries, especially the Scandinavian countries, showed high performance along the HDI and GDI lines. Therefore, the core issues of development as discussed in the previous section need more serious attention from the international community. By the coming of the new millennium under the aegis of the UN, an initiative was launched to address **eight** core areas of vital importance for human development. In September 2000, the member states of the UN met at the UN headquarters in New York and adopted the **MDGs.**

The MDGs were supposed to bring an assault on the impinging problems which created situations where human capabilities could not be realized. The MDGs are a set of eight goals and corresponding targets to be achieved by the year 2015. Combating diseases, hunger, illiteracy, gender discrimination and environmental degradation were the eight MDGs which were sought to be achieved by the year 2015. The implementation of the MDGs was supposed to begin from 1 January 2001. Every five years, it was agreed upon to hold summits to assess the progress made in the implementation of the MDGs. Table 8.6 gives a brief idea of the eight MDGs and their respective targets.

Evaluation of MDGs

- **MDG1:** There has been some progress under the MDGs over the years. It has been seen that the number of people living in extreme poverty worldwide has come down by more than 50 per cent. In 1990, 1.9 billion people were said to be living in extreme poverty, which is less compared to 836 million in 2015. The number of people living on more than $4 a day—those in the working middle class—has nearly tripled between 1991

Table 8.6 MDGs and Targets Set

Sl No.	MDG	Goal Set	Targets Set
1.	MDG 1	Eradicate extreme poverty and hunger	• To reduce the proportion of people whose daily income is less than $1.25 • To achieve full and productive employment along with decent work for all, including youngsters and women • To reduce the proportion of individuals suffering from hunger by 2015
2.	MDG 2	Achieve universal primary education	• To ensure that children (both boys and girls) universally be able to compete a full of primary education by 2015
3.	MDG 3	Promote gender equity and empower women	• To eliminate gender disparity in primary and secondary education by 2005 and in all levels of education by 2015
4.	MDG 4	Reduce child mortality	• To reduce the under-five mortality ratio by 2/3rd by 2015
5.	MDG 5	Improve maternal health	• To reduce the maternal mortality ratio by 75% • To achieve universal access to reproductive health
6.	MDG 6	Combat HIV/AIDS, malaria & other major diseases	• To halt by 2015 and reverse the spread of HIV/AIDS • To achieve global access to treatment for HIV/AIDS for those who need it by 2010 • To have ceased and started reversal of the incidence of malaria and other major diseases by 2015
7.	MDG 7	Ensure environmental sustainability	• Integration of the principle of sustainable development into domestic laws and policies of the states with an effort towards reversal of the depletion of environmental resources • Reducing loss of biodiversity and achieve a substantial reduction in the rate of loss by 2010 • To reduce the proportion of world population without suitable access to clean and safe drinking water and basic sanitation by 2015 • To achieve substantial improvement in the lives of a minimum of 100 million slum dweller by 2020
8.	MDG 8	Develop a global partnership	• To develop an open, rule-based, predictable, non-discriminatory trading and financial system • To address the special needs of least developed countries • To address the special needs of landlocked developing countries and small island developing countries • To deal comprehensively with the debt problems of the developing countries • To provide access to affordable essential drugs in developing countries in cooperation with pharmaceutical companies • To make available the benefits of new technologies, especially information and communications, in cooperation with the private sector • To monitor aid delivery

Source: Compiled from https://www.un.org/millenniumgoals/ (accessed on 24 November 2021).

and 2015. In 1991, this group made only 18 per cent of the population and rose to 50 per cent in 2015. The proportion of undernourished people in the developing world has dropped by almost 50 per cent since 1990; from 23.3 per cent in 1990–1992 to 12.9 per cent in 2014–2016. However, in India, every day 67,385 babies are born in India, which equals 1/6th of the world's child births. Every minute, one of these new born babies dies. The current gender disparity in child survival is 11 per cent.[2]

- **MDG 2:** Hunger, poverty and illiteracy are difficult to eradicate from the globe. Social protection can, to some extent, ensure education and food security through increased enrolment of students in primary education. The primary school enrolment rate has shown an increase in developing regions that reached 91 per cent this year, up from 83 per cent in 2000.
- **MDG 3:** In South Asia, the number of girls enrolled in primary school was 74 for every 100 boys in 1990. By 2015, there were 103 girls enrolled for every 100 boys. The proportion of women in vulnerable employment compared to total female employment has been reduced by 13 per cent in the period between 1991 and 2015, compared to a 9 per cent decrease for men.

  Political participation of women also shows an increase around the globe. India was ranked 112th among 153 countries in the Global Gender Gap Index 2020. India regressed 13.5 percentage points, with a significant decline in the number of women ministers (from 23.1% in 2019 to 9.1% in 2021).
- **MDG 4:** The global under-five mortality rate has shown a decline by more than half since 1990. This was a drop from 90 to 43 deaths per 1,000 live births, though this falls short of the targeted drop of two-thirds as set by MDG 4. In India, the sex-specific under-five mortality rate, that is, death per 1,000 live births, was 122 males and 131 females in 1990. This declined to 34 males and 35 females in 2019. There was a decrease in the neonatal mortality rate between 1990 and 2019, from 57 to 22. From 1.5 million neonatal deaths, there was a drop to 522,000 deaths in 2019.
- **MDG 5:** Since 1990, the maternal mortality ratio has declined nearly to half. However, this falls short of the two-thirds reduction that was targeted in the MDG. There were an estimated 289,000 maternal deaths in 2013. There was a 64 per cent reduction in maternal mortality ratio in South Asia and 49 per cent in sub-Saharan Africa between the period 1990 and 2013.
- **MDG 6:** There was a 40 per cent reduction in new HIV infections from 3.5 million cases in 2000 to 2.1 million cases in 2013. The universal malaria incidence rate has also declined by an estimated 37 per cent, and the mortality rate by 58 per cent. The TB mortality rate also declined by 45 per cent between 1990 and 2013, while the prevalence rate fell by 41 per cent within the same time period.
- **MDG 7:** Between 1990 and 2015, 2.6 billion people gained access to improved drinking water. This meant the target of halving the proportion of people without access to safe water was achieved. Worldwide, 2.1 billion people have gained access to improved sanitation.
- **MDG 8:** There was a 66 per cent increase in official development assistance from developed countries in real terms during the period 2000 to 2014. It amounted to $135.2 billion. In 2014, the UK, Sweden, Norway, Denmark and Luxembourg continued

[2] https://www.unicef.org/reports/levels-and-trends-child-mortality-report-2019 (accessed on 24 November 2021).

to exceed the UN official development assistance target of 0.7 per cent of gross national income.

In 2015, the UN adopted 17 SDGs to supplement the MDGs. The aim is to achieve decent lives for all on a healthy planet by 2030. The 17 SDGs are as follows:

Goal 1: No poverty
Goal 2: Zero hunger
Goal 3: Good health and well-being
Goal 4: Quality education
Goal 5: Gender equality
Goal 6: Clean water and sanitation
Goal 7: Affordable and clean energy
Goal 8: Decent work and economic growth
Goal 9: Industry, innovation and infrastructure
Goal 10: Reduced inequalities
Goal 11: Sustainable cities and communities
Goal 12: Responsible consumption and production
Goal 13: Climate action
Goal 14: Life below water
Goal 15: Life on land
Goal 16: Peace, justice and strong institutions
Goal 17: Partnerships for the goals

MDGs are novel targets that have been set to achieve human development. Only a little has been achieved. A lot more has to be done to alleviate the sufferings of a billion people. The COVID-19 has revealed the bankruptcy of the health sector around the globe, both in developed countries and developing countries, not to mention the least developed ones. By 7 October 2020, the World Bank had projected extreme global poverty following the outbreak of the pandemic. It is estimated that there will be an increase in poverty from 88 million to 115 million people in extreme poverty in 2020, with the total rising to as many as 150 million by 2021. The World Bank pointed out that the resultant increase in numbers will depend on the severity of the economic contraction globally. The January 2021 updated estimates show that the expected COVID-19-induced new poor in 2020 may be between 119 and 124 million, which is higher than what was predicted earlier. The increase in global poverty in 2020 has been unprecedented in recent history, as reflected in the report. This makes the realization of MDGs and SDGs a more practical goal for countries around the world.

NGOs and Their Role in Development

To begin the discussion about NGOs, it is very important to locate them first in society. For this, we have to fall back upon Friedrich Hegel and his exposition on civil society in his book, *Elements of the Philosophy of Right*, 1820. He stated that civil society is the stage between the family and the state. In the civil society, each member in contact with other members will fulfil their ends and vice versa (Figure 8.2). To him, the whole sphere of civil society is the territory

Figure 8.2 Civil Society (Friedrich Hegel)

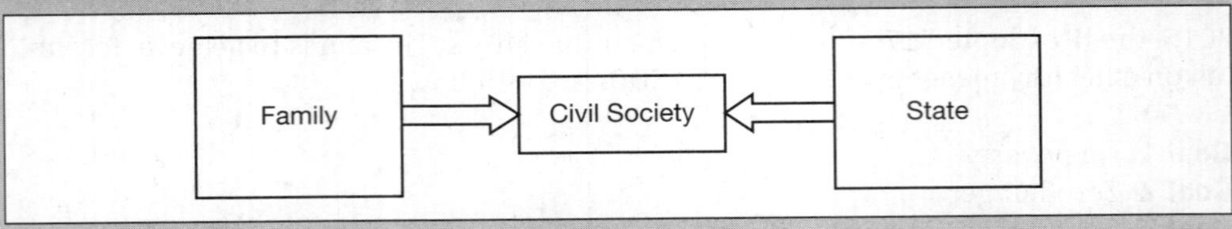

of mediation where there is play for every talent, every idiosyncrasy and every accident of birth and fortune, and every other activity is regulated by reason/particularity. This particularity is restricted by universality, for the dependence on one another creates complete interdependence wherein the livelihoods, happiness and legal status of one are interwoven with the livelihood, happiness and rights of all. Individual happiness is actualized and secured through this.

The concept of civil society has come a long way and instead of pursuing one's individual interests along with others, it has now encompassed to mean pursuing the interests of the masses/particular groups/issues and placing itself between the public and the private. The World Bank gave an explanation of civil society as a wide range of organizations such as community groups, NGOs, labour unions, indigenous groups, charitable organizations, professional associations and foundations. Civil society is thought to be the 'third sector' (first being the state and second commerce). Its activities are increasing day by day, and they try to make an entry into the sphere of public policymaking in order to influence government policies to get the required outcome. Civil societies, as seen above, include a variety of organizations, but NGOs dominate a large part of their activities. Figure 8.3 depicts the location and interaction between society, NGOs and the state.

NGOs are usually viewed as non-profit groups which are independent of the government. They are created around particular goals and work forward to secure them. Social justice, gender issues, transgender rights, environmental concerns and social services may be some of the agenda of many goals which the NGOs pursue. D. Rajasekhar ('NGOs in India: Opportunities and Challenges', 2000) observes that NGOs undertake voluntary action, social action and social movements. He identifies four characteristics that make NGOs distinct

Figure 8.3 Location and Interaction of NGOs

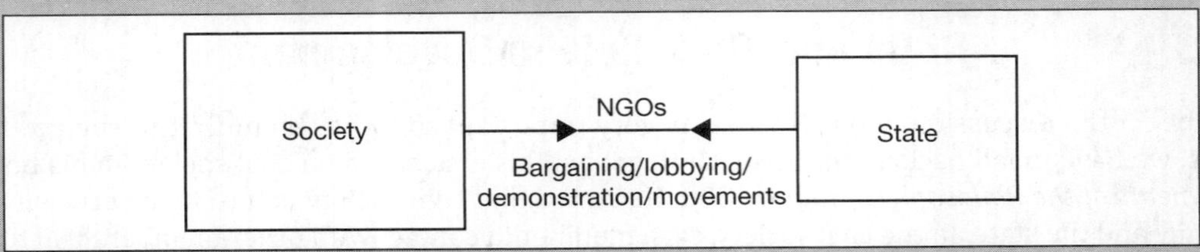

organizations. These can be summed up as voluntary in their formation, working towards development and mitigation of suffering, working on non-self-serving aims and working on the basis of relative independence. The NGOs address issues such as child rights, poverty amelioration, social justice, environment conservation, human rights, care for the elderly, women's empowerment, wildlife conservation, animal rights, sanitation and hygiene, humanitarian relief, health and nutrition-related works, literacy and education, refugee relief, disease control and several others people-related issues.

The World Bank classifies NGOs as (a) community-based organizations, (b) national NGOs and (c) international NGOs. The World Bank defines NGOs as private organizations that pursue activities to mitigate the sufferings of people, promote the interests of the poor, protect the environment, provide basic social services or undertake community development (World Bank Operational Directive 14.70). The Asian Development Bank defines NGOs as organizations that are not based in government and are not created to earn profit. NGOs, therefore, are important in the background of society, social problems and people's interaction with government and government policies. NGOs are created to address various issues, such as environmental concerns, community-based project execution, providing basic social services, awareness-raising, campaigning and advocacy. They are also involved in capacity building through education and training, advocating community development and, most importantly, regional and international cooperation through networking.

There are thousands of NGOs operating at local, national and international levels. It will now be pertinent to discuss their impact on policymaking, which in turn affects the course of development at local, national and international levels. Certain developments around the world have given prominence to NGOs. The impact of globalization and the launching of development projects have led to environmental degradation, market failures, depletion of resources, loss of livelihood, human rights issues, marginalization of women and weaker sections of the population and other issues have led to the emergence of NGOs and NGO movements.

NGOs are able to influence policymaking of the governments in many ways. They may be present in the negotiations on behalf of the stakeholders. The stakeholders concept was introduced at the Rio+20 Summit (Chapter 9). They may make valuable contributions by providing information relating to the cause they are fighting for. NGOs provide suggestions/advice to the government by highlighting the positive and negative aspects of the government policies. They have specific skills and, in many cases, can shape negotiations.

However, what should be considered are the factors which influence the functioning of NGOs. These are size, resources (financial, human resource and sometimes political connections), scope of the NGO (local, national and international), political opportunity, nature of issues and the ability of the NGO to voice its agenda, expertise and technical knowledge. Specifically, if we take some examples of NGOs at international level interacting with prominent international organizations, particularly the UN, the World Bank and the WTO, the functioning of the NGO will become clear.

UN definition of a NGO is that a NGO is a non-profit, voluntary citizens' group, which is organized on a local, national or international level to address issues in support of the public good. About 1,500 NGOs with strong information programmes on issues of concern to the UN are associated with the Department of Public Information. Many NGOs (about 2,700) active in the field of economic and social development have qualified for consultative status with the Economic and Social Council (ECOSOC).

NGO interaction with the UN bodies may assume the character of general consultative status, special consultative status (narrowly focused NGOs working on specific issues) and roster status (very small, often newer NGOs). However, general consultative status is usually enjoyed by large international NGOs working in the areas common with the UN bodies. NGOs can have consultative status with ECOSOC, the International Fund for Agricultural Development, the WHO, the UNDP and the United Nations Commission on Human Rights (UNCHR), among others. NGOs often play a significant role in promoting the various dedications of the UN such as 'days', 'years' and 'decades'. NGOs are also partners with different UN development programmes, such as the WHO, UNHCR and the United Nations International Children's Emergency Fund are actively involved in implementing the UN-led programmes.

NGOs are also involved in negotiations with developmental agencies like the World Bank within the guidelines adopted by the General Counsel of the World Bank in 1996. NGO activities with the World Bank include sharing of information, requesting information, organizing conferences and symposia on WTO-related issues and also making provisions for receiving information. However, NGOs cannot get directly involved in the activities of the WTO. One NGO campaign which is quite noteworthy has been the International NGO Campaign for an Enforceable Labour Standards Clause, led by the International Confederation of Free Trade Unions, focusing on the growing trade liberalization and exploitation of labour and violation of labour rights.

The World Bank is criticized vehemently for its development projects by NGOs and by coalitions of civil society comprising NGOs, indigenous people, churches, international human rights networks and environmental groups. They have come down heavily on the World Bank for sponsoring projects which are having a devastating impact on the environment and the habitats and livelihoods of the people in that area. Further, they have criticized the World Bank for its SAPs (discussed in the case of the sub-Saharan crisis in Chapter 6) which have adversely affected the poor by causing more poverty and unemployment and giving advantage to the political elites. The Narmada Bachao Andolan (discussed below) was one such campaign against the World Bank funding of the dam project which greatly questioned the motive of the World Bank. These criticisms made the World Bank begin its interactions with civil society organizations such as NGOs, social movements, labour unions and other stakeholders in the World Bank-sponsored development projects. There has also been an autonomous NGO working group in the World Bank since 1984. This working group facilitates dialogue with World Bank and the regional NGOs of Asia, Africa, Latin America and the Caribbean.

Some international NGOs which are of great significance are the Green Peace Movement, World Wide Fund for Nature, Amnesty International, the Oxford Committee for Famine Relief, Bangladesh Rural Advancement Committee, Cooperative for Assistance and Relief Everywhere (CARE) International, Médecins Sans Frontières, ActionAid Bangladesh, Anti-slavery International, Congregations around Richmond Involved to Assure Shelter International, Consultative Council of Jewish Organizations, International Federation of Human Rights, International Federation of Red Cross and Red Crescent Societies, World Vision International and so on.

In India, for an entity to become an NGO, it has to register either as a trust, society or a private limited non-profit company under Section 25 of the Companies Act, 1956. Some prominent NGOs in India are HelpAge India, Child Rights and You, Lepra Society, SMILE Foundation, Rural Health Care, Foundation, Goonj, Udaan Welfare Foundation, Deepalaya, Uday Foundation, Sounds of Silence, Sewa, Eklavya, Disha, Environmental Action Group and

Agrani India Foundation and so on. International NGOs like Save the Children works on child rights in India. Save the Children works in 18 states of India. Since the beginning of its journey in 2008 in India and registered as 'Bal Raksha Bharat', they claim to have transformed the lives of more than 11 million (1.1 crore) children in India. Some important international NGOs actively working in India are Save the Children Bal Raksha Bharat, HelpAge India, CARE India, Oxfam, World Vision India, Greenpeace India, ActionAid, Plan India, World Wildlife Fund and World Vision India.

In this contemporary world, where IT has revolutionized the process of communication and there is a growing importance of social media, big data, analytics and artificial intelligence, there will be the growth of more groups and organizations that campaign on issues such as civil liberties, better education systems, combating climate change and fighting diseases. However, they have to build up their capability to create meaningful dialogue as well as influence policymakers and become a voice for the public who are aggrieved, suffering or victims of economic, political, social, developmental or any such reasons affecting their existence and rights.

Culture, Media and TV

Culture is a difficult concept to define. Simply speaking, culture is a system of meanings and values involving certain ways of doing things, conventions, habits, practices (social and religious) and a way of living which are distinct from other cultures. These cultural traits are shared by the members of the same cultural community. However, in the face of globalization, there cannot be a pure culture. Culture keeps on mixing with other cultures and new cultural firms emerge. With the advances in technology and the IT Revolution, which are the drivers of globalization, culture has been impacted, and what we find is the replication of dominant culture and subordination of indigenous culture.

The IT revolution of the 1980s and the invasion of the internet changed the landscape of communication and thereby influenced the process of globalization. The web-based software revolution available on personal computers and mobile phones has revolutionized the ways in which information is exchanged. Therefore, knowledge and information sharing transcended the borders or territorial limits of the states. Information and data sharing at great speed have connected people worldwide who may be linked through their professions or interests. Such information sharing can happen in various fields such as education, business, research, medical sciences, trade, e-commerce, e-governance, e-services and even political communication.

There is an infusion of information capitalism in place. Globalization has led to an increase in the flow of capital across the globe. In the case of capital movement, TNCs/MNCs are the main engines and operate in several countries with the motive of capturing markets and siphoning profit back to their home country. They are the main instruments for embarking on the project of universalization of culture. To create demand for their product, MNCs carry out advertising programmes for popularizing their products and eventually lead to the development of a culture of consumerism which has transformed the tastes, practices and lifestyles of people around the world. A simple example will make things clear. Indigenous dressing styles and clothing patterns have been overtaken by jeans, denim and T-shirts. Food habits have changed from traditional to foods of foreign origin, such as cake, pasta, pizza, McDonalds, KFC, Pepsi, Coke and burgers. Language gets mixed up with alien words and vocabulary. Even attitudes and body languages change. A kind of hybridization of indigenous culture happens which replicates the dominant culture in the world.

Since the USA is a major power, a hegemon (which may be arguably a declining hegemon) and home to the largest of the MNCs, the dominant culture reflects the US consumerist culture. As part of the agenda of the capitalist market economy, consumer culture is posed as the global 'modern'. The control of technology, the control of information flow and the transmission of global culture are in the hands of Western developed countries. The Third-World countries have become the victims of what may be identified as information imperialism, thereby undermining their own indigenous cultures. Culture, therefore, in the Third-World countries is caught in the trap of free trade, market pricing, profit making, demand creation, advertising and the materialistic pursuit of life. Media becomes a powerful tool in the production of the homogenization of culture.

Homogenization of culture is perceived by some as an instrument for the establishment of universal unity and democracy based on a global culture, with its ultimate expression as the 'global village' as perceived by McLuhan (*Understanding Media: The Extensions of Man,* 1964, and *War and Peace in the Global Village,* 1968) due to the expansion of new communication systems. However, there are others who contend that globalization has not resulted in a unified political and economic identity (Rajaei 2001) and has resulted in the destruction of national identities. According to Tomlinson, 'The cultural globalization that we are witnessing today is not the net result of human endeavors and experiences and even it has not equitably benefited from cultural diversities. Rather it is the manifestation of dominance of a certain overpowering culture' (Skelton and Allen 1999).

The most intriguing question at this point is how politics and power structures have been defined or redefined by the media. If the media is the bearer of cultural industries and power is entrusted to the powerful, then production, control and dissemination of information is the realm of the powerful. These powerful centres, then, will be the main drivers of cultural imperialism. The political economy of culture and media is closely linked with the material issues such as capital, infrastructure, and political control which are the key determinants of international communication processes and effects. Here comes the question: Then who are the power bearers of the cultural industries or the media tycoons?

Mediation in development communication plays a significant role. The French theorist, Jean Baudrillard, in his *Simulacra and Simulations,* 1981, saw mediation as a process in which the media alters the relation between representation and reality. This is done through the proliferation of information and images to produce hyper-reality which is a reality far-fetched from the real world.

Mediation has long been seen as a process in which the media, guided by technology, acts as a conduit between the developers and the 'target group'. Mediation has been identified with the aim of utilizing the power of media to impact the minds and consciousness of the target group(s) with the dissemination of specific kinds of knowledge supposedly development or globalization. As we have seen above, the already existing culture of the target group comes into contact with the prescribed views of the stakeholders entrusted with the specific task of intervention on a specific issue. There is no place for reflection in this structure as information is fed to the target and the task of the target/subject is to access the already organized information. There is a cultural value system between those who are making the interventions and those who are receiving them. However, the dominant prevails as it attempts to impose its perspectives on the other. Here, the media is an intermediate agency that enables this process to take place. The print media, the electronic media, television and the internet or social media remain a *meaning-making agencies* of society. Media generates information 24 × 7, which is the mediated information.

The key actors are, of course, TNCs, which are power houses and, more often than not, powerful in economic and political terms and have closeness to the political elites also. If the driver of global capitalism is the process of globalization, then it needs the promotion of the ideology of consumerism. Advertising is a powerful medium for sending messages and setting trends in one's lifestyle worldwide and to cite one of many factors at work to popularize consumer products cutting across all ages and sexes. If we ponder deeply, we will find that Western and, more particularly, American culture and lifestyles are portrayed as the most desirable. The answer to this is not difficult. According to Herbert Schiller and others concerning, this is the dominant position assumed by the American mass-media industry in the post-war period. There is the domination of the global media industry by a small number of powerful transnational media conglomerates such as AOL Time Warner, Bertelsmann, Disney, Viacom and News Corporation, to mention some of the top media companies. They operate globally and determine the trend of production, distribution and selling of their media products.

The global media industry, as pointed out earlier, is a power house and controls the way events are covered and disseminated in the developing world. Global news agencies have selective packages of news from the Third World. The direction or flow of information is from the Global North to the Global South. In relation to the Third-World countries, there is an unequal relation of power that exists between the West and the Third World. The prime objective of the media industry then becomes to distribute the most compelling news, information and entertainment to every corner of the globe, but in a way, it wants to picture/portray/represent the event to appear before the audience with the control of information and power of the media industry with a political or economic agenda.

Therefore, the demand for a New World Information and Communication Order grew simultaneously out of the demand for the NIEO of 1974. The debate that was given birth to was regarding the structure of information flow from developed/industrialized countries to developing countries. The demand was a 'free flow' or 'free and balanced flow' of information between the Western industrialized/developed countries and the developing and underdeveloped of the Global South.

Big Dams and Environmental Concerns

Coronavirus pandemic of 2020 has put a question mark on the entire Western project of development. A virus has done ruckus to the entire world. Even when in 2021 the vaccines have been rolled out, the pandemic shows no signs of ebbing. Seriously, the virus has made human beings question whether development, which started with the advancement of science and technology heralding the period of enlightenment and the paradigm of development, has forced humanity to witness such a crisis.

In the name of progress, human beings have polluted the air and water, led to the depletion of natural resources, destroyed the forests and have threatened the entire flora and fauna. Riding the horses of science and technology, economic development turned out to be a game of exploiting nature beyond limits. The sanctity of life seems to be sacrificed at the altar of science and development. Nature is the part of the support system of the life on this planet.

Harnessing nature negatively will impact human civilization in the long run. The COVID-19 crisis is a testimony to the fact that nature will take its revenge and that may be quite fatal for humankind.

The model of development that has been replicated by the entire world, especially the Third-World countries, is very much a 'Western' model of development. The Third-World countries, first being the colonies of the West and later gaining independence, were made to believe that well-being for all could be achieved through the Westernization of economies. A capitalist mode of production saw nature and natural resources as inputs in the productive process. Therefore, development has created subjugation and subordination of nature. The various development projects have been undertaken by governments of all countries at the expense of nature. Developmental activities tend to disrupt flora and fauna or bio diversity, which affect the survival of human beings too, and many times have a negative impact on their habitat and livelihood.

One such project of development is the construction of 'big dams'. Dams are useful in many ways, especially in meeting the demand for water in times of dry seasons as well as in regulating stream regimes. Dams have become useful for flood control, propelling water for irrigation, providing drinking water and water for domestic use and, most importantly, generating hydroelectric power. Tables 8.7, 8.8, 8.9 and 8.10 give us a list of big dams in Africa, India, China and the USA.

Dams may be built to bring about development, but the debate between dams and destruction has been underway for many years. Resistance to building dams has by far been more vigorous all around the world, including India. Arguments which are forwarded against dams are mostly environmental concerns and loss of human habitat and livelihood. The construction of the dam affects the downstream of the river, and gradually, the river loses its flow and riparian channels lose their natural health. Obstructions to natural flow create oxygen-starved dead zones which hamper natural river life. The effect of large dams is the permanent

Table 8.7 Big Dams in Africa

S. No.	Names of Dams	Country
1.	Grand Ethiopian Renaissance Dam (largest dam in Africa)	Ethiopia
2.	Aswan High Dam (world's largest Embankment dam)	Egypt
3.	Cahora Bassa Dam	Mozambique
4.	Gibe II	Ethiopia
5.	Inga Dams	Democratic Republic of the Congo
6.	Akosombo Dam	Ghana
7.	Kainji Dam	Nigeria
8.	Tekezé Dam	Ethiopia
9.	Bujagali Dam	Uganda
10.	Katse Arch Dam (Africa's second largest double-curvature arch dam)	Lesotho

Source: Compiled by the author from various web sources.

Table 8.8 Big Dams in India

S. No.	Names of Dams	State	Features
1.	Tehri Dam	Uttarakhand	Tallest dam in the world and highest dam in India
2.	Bhakra Dam	Himachal Pradesh	The second largest dam in Asia and the second tallest in India
3.	Sardar Sarovar Dam (Narmada Dam)	Gujarat	One of the largest dams in the world
4.	Hirakud Dam	Odisha	Longest dam in India
5.	Nagarjuna Sagar Dam	Telangana/Andhra Pradesh	World's largest masonry dam
6.	Idukki Dam	Kerala	One of the highest arch dam in Asia
7.	Koldam Dam	Himachal Pradesh	Embankment dam
8.	Ranjit Sagar Dam	Near Pathankot city of Punjab & Kathua District of J&K	Embankment and earth fill
9.	Srisailam Dam	Andhra Pradesh	The second largest capacity working hydroelectric station
10.	Koyna Dam	Maharashtra	Rubble concrete dam and one of the largest dams in Maharashtra
11.	Indira Sagar Dam Reservoir	Madhya Pradesh	Largest reservoir in India
12.	Chamera Dam	Himachal Pradesh	

Source: Compiled by the author from various web sources.

Table 8.9 Big Dams in China

S. No.	Name of the Dam	Region/Province/City	Type of Dam
1.	Three Gorges Dams	Hubei province	Gravity Dam
2.	Jinping-I Dam	Sinchuan	Arch type
3.	Xiaowan Dam	Yunnan	Arch type
4.	Dagangshan Dam	Sinchuan	Arch type
5.	Nuozhadu Dam	Yunnan	Embankment rock-fill

Source: Compiled by the author from various web sources.

destruction of vast expanses of forest, wetlands and wildlife, along with the livelihoods of local people. The routes of migration of wildlife, birds and fishes are lost, which affects biodiversity and the livelihoods of the local people.

Building of dams obstructs the natural course of the river. As a result, the water regime might change. This may affect the natural habitat of the area and even unexpected floods may occur. This will inundate the vegetation and local habitat along the riverbanks. If dams are

Table 8.10 Big Dams in the USA

S. No.	Name of the Dam	State	Features
1.	Oroville Dam	California	The tallest in the USA
2.	Cochiti Dam	New Mexico	One of the largest dams in the USA
3.	Hoover Dam	Arizona/Nevada	The largest by lake volume
4.	Grand Coulee Dam	Washington	The largest power station in the USA
5.	Diablo Dam	Washington	Power-generating dam, Washington
6.	Ashfork Bainbridge Steel Dam	Arizona	First large steel dam in the World and one of the three built in the USA
7.	Fort Peck Dam	Montana	Highest of the six dams built along the Missouri River
8.	Buffalo Bill Dam	Wyoming	Concrete arch-gravity dam
9.	Mansfield Dam	Texas	Dam across a canyon at Marshall Ford on the Colorado River
10.	Roosevelt Dam	Arizona	Arch-gravity dam on Salt River, Arizona
11.	Shasta Dam	California	Eighth tallest dam in the USA
12.	Fontana Dam	North Carolina	The largest dam of the Tennessee Valley Authority system

Source: Compiled by the author from various web sources.

constructed in seismically prone zones, then they can become susceptible to damage. Earthquakes may also be caused by the filling of big dam reservoirs. Changes in the agricultural habits of the people living in this region and also in the flora and fauna might be caused due to building of dams across rivers. The most unfortunate incidents that happened which sparked the anti-dam resistance movement is the displacement of the people who had been residing in the dam area for years but suddenly find themselves dislocated as they lose their land, habitat and way of life.

Huge resistance movements have taken place in India. The Koel-Karo project earned huge resistance from the tribal population. It destroyed 200 tribal villages and 45,000 hectares of arable land. The Narmada Bachao Andolan, under the leadership of activist Medha Patkar, assumed huge proportions and drew international attention. This was a World Bank project, and it questioned the credibility of the World Bank's funding of development projects.

Sardar Sarovar Dam is the second largest concrete dam in the world in terms of the volume of concrete used in its construction. The first is the Grand Coulee Dam across the Columbia River in the USA. The original height of the dam that was approved was 80 m in 1988, and an estimated 66,000 people were to be affected. Later, by 2006, the height had been raised to 122 m and the number of affected people rose to about 300,000. The final plan was to build a reservoir measuring 214 km in length with a capacity of 9,500 Mm^3. The Sardar Sarovar project was caught in national and international debate. The *World Commission on Dams Report* of 2000 referred to it as the cause of environmental and social concern, if not a disaster.

Another dam which is particularly risk-prone is the Tehri dam, which is located in the central Himalayan seismic gap. It is here that the Indian plate crashes into the Asian mainland at a speed of 2 cm per year. Along with this, the Tehri dam will obstruct the natural flow of the massive volumes of sediments. This will contribute to the raising of the river beds upstream and endanger the indigenous settlements there. High chances of inundation of several villages and displacement of its inhabitants from their native places are there.

The World Bank approved the project in 1985 with a loan of $450 million to build a dam on the Narmada River in India. The project was resisted as environmental concerns were raised along with displacement of the indigenous people. After a long resistance movement, the resettlement of the local population was worked out, but without information about the impending settlement, it was not known to all. The name to reckon with the Narmada Bachao Andolan was Medha Patkar. NGOs and activists formed a very powerful coalition with the affected population and demanded from the World Bank access to information about resettlement plans and timetables, results of environmental studies and other basic information. Under virulent protest, the World Bank withdrew from the project. However, the project was completed and the Supreme Court of India, which earlier had given verdicts in favour of the movement, ultimately, in 2000, allowed the construction to proceed as well as gave permission to raise the height of the Sardar Sarovar Dam.

A new dimension in the discourse of dams and their imposition on the environment and the local people is categorized as 'slow' violence' by Nixon (2011). Indigenous peoples who are local inhabitants are identified as victims of the 'slow violence', which is often funded by international financial institutions. They have also been identified as one of the crimes of globalization.

The World Bank, the IMF and their SAPS have proven to be hugely damaging, according to Marfleet (2013), and the funding of mega-dam projects arouses the fear of the invariable damage they can cause to the environment and people. The Asian Development Bank has been sarcastically characterized as the 'dam and bridge' bank as it places priority on such kinds of infrastructural developments. The bank puts its priority on the quick disbursement of big loans, and staff are rewarded for getting these loans out to target clients, mostly developing countries. Whether the project is going to have a negative impact or not on indigenous people of Asia does not come into the consideration.

Dam building on the lower Mekong River is an alarming development project. The 2010 environmental assessment done by the Mekong River Commission announced a 10 year moratorium on the construction of main stem dams, citing their potentially devastating effects on regional food supplies and the likelihood of 'irreversible environmental damage'.

Another development which started under the impact of the anti-dam resistance movement, as well as environmental activists, is the dam removal projects. The USA has undertaken dam removal in a big way under pressure from the environmental lobby. A total of 1,797 dams have been removed in the USA since 1912. The states with the most dam removals in 2020 were Ohio (11), Massachusetts (6) and New York (6).

It is estimated that more than 90,000 dams blocking rivers in the USA affect fish and wildlife habitats and pose threats to ecosystems and communities. The Edenville Dam in Michigan has been identified as the latest threat from an ageing and outdated dam. A recent UN report highlighted the growing risk of ageing water infrastructure. The year 2020 marked the simultaneous removal of the four dams built on the Klamath River, with a combined height of 411 ft (125 m). According to the Klamath River Renewal Corporation, which was to oversee the dam removal project, this was the largest dam removal project in US history. It is also set to be the most expensive, with the project costing about $450 million (£340 million).

From the above discussion, it becomes clear that if the stakeholders are not taken into the ambit of any building dam project and a collective action towards inclusive and sustainable development is not followed, then dams can become the major threats that arise from globalization and the funders of such projects, who are also the drivers of the process of globalization. The anti-dam resistance movements like the Narmada Bachao Andolan are not just without logic but the political economy of funding the dams by international financial institutions have specific agenda of reaping benefits for such loan borne projects. This cannot be stopped or prevented until there is an equitable world order as was the demand of the Third-World countries for the NIEO is established. This is quite impossible a goal to achieve so anti-dam resistance movements will go on if they are not inclusive and sustainable. Now dam removal involving old-aged dams have become a reality which have already destroyed the flora and fauna and human habitat over the years.

Global Arms Industry and Arms Trade

The political economy of the arms industry and the arms trade is quite an interesting point of research and analysis. The question is: Why is there a necessity for arms procurement by states in the world? Here, we have to fall back on political realist thinkers to justify the purpose of armament requirements. If international relations are anarchic, as political realists see it, then each state is up against the other, and as a consequence, there is a security dilemma. Now, to meet the security challenges, there can be two paths—offensive and defensive. According to defensive realists, arming oneself to the extent of survival can be a justification for arms procurement. Offensive realists emphasize military build-up as a way to establish hegemony in international relations. Offensive or defensive, any of these two purposes add up to military build-up, whether on a small or large scale. Military build-up by a particular state can actually create instability in the region of its location as other states can be fearful of its rise and, thereby, start armament procurement and, in this way, destabilize the peace and security of that particular region.

As military preparedness seems to be unavoidable, there seems to be an ever increasing arms sales industry and trade. The Stockholm International Peace Research Institute (SIPRI) provides us with data on the volume of the arms trade annually and the list of top exporters of arms sales and top importers of arms. SIPRI defines arms transfers as including the supply of military weapons through sales, aid, gifts and those made through manufacturing licenses. SIPRI data cover major conventional weapons such as aircraft, armoured vehicles, artillery, radar systems, missiles, and ships designed for military use. SIPRI data excludes transfers of other military equipment such as small arms and light weapons, trucks, small artillery, ammunition, support equipment, technology transfers and other services.

There is a thriving military–industrial complex (MIC). This is a nexus between a country's military and defence industry. In his 1961 farewell address, President Eisenhower sounded a warning bell for the future in which a powerful MIC will manipulate policy to the detriment of American interests. Over the years, the defence budget allocation of the USA is a pointer in that direction. In their analysis, McCartney and McCartney (2015) show that in 1948, the main but not total Department of Defence budget was just over $97 billion. It rose to $444.5 billion in 1952 at the peak of the Korean War, then fell to as low as $216.3 billion in 1955.

This was because the USA maintained a high level of military preparedness during the Cold War between the USA and the Soviet Union. Decline during the 1970s was reversed during Reagan's presidency, up to $551.8 billion in 1985. Then the total again declined and stood at $391 billion in 2000. However, by 2015, they had equalled the size of the Reagan era to the tune of $501.8 billion or, by another calculation, $598.5 billion.

McCartney and McCartney point out that in the post-Reagan years of decline, the US-MIC underwent massive consolidation. The surviving firms won larger contracts after 9/11 and consolidation took place. An example which McCartney and McCartney give is that in 2012, the US defence industry was assigned a budget of $793.9 billion. Much of that amount went to 10 companies whose 2011 contracts earned them huge revenue. The top accumulations were by Lockheed Martin with $40 billion and $46 billion, respectively, Boeing with $21.5 billion and $69 billion, General Dynamics with $19.5 billion and $33 billion, Raytheon with $15 billion and $25 billion, United Technologies with $8 billion and $58 billion, SAIC with $7.4 billion and $11.1 billion, L-3 Communications with $7.38 billion and $15.7 billion, Oshkosh Corporation with $4.94 billion and $7.6 billion, McKesson Corporation with $4.7 billion and $112 billion. The Pentagon, which is the headquarter of the US Department of Defence, is built to house 40,000 military and civilian employees. Over the past two decades since 9/11, there has been a transformation that has brought about new government reliance on private security firms, IT revolutions, a post-9/11 surge in the number of veterans and the creation of the Department of Homeland Security. This is currently the emerging US 'National Security Corporate Complex'.

The SIPRI Fact Sheet March 2020 reveals the trend of arms transfer around the globe. This also provides the list of top exporters of arms and major clients. From March 2020, the SIPRI Arms Transfer Database, which is freely accessible, contains updated data on arms transfers from the period 1950–2019. The summarized fact sheet reveals the following figures.

- The fact sheet reveals that the volume of international transfers of major arms in 2015–2019 was 5.5 per cent higher than in 2010–2014 and 20 per cent higher than in 2005–2009.
- The fact sheet enlists the five largest arms exporters in 2015–2019. They are the United States, Russia, France, Germany and China. Together, they accounted for 76 per cent of all arms exports in 2015–2019.
- The fact sheet shows that during 2015–2019, US arms exports accounted for 36 per cent of the global total, and this was 23 per cent higher than in 2010–2014.
- The fact sheet shows that there has been a decrease in Russian arms exports by 18 per cent between 2010–2014 and 2015–2019.
- The fact sheet shows that French, German and Chinese arms exports in 2015–2019 were higher than in 2010–2014, with respective increases of 72 per cent, 17 per cent and 6.3 per cent.
- The fact sheet reveals that the five largest arms importers in 2015–2019 were Saudi Arabia, India, Egypt, Australia and China. They together received 36 per cent of all arms imports.
- The fact sheet makes a region-wise assessment of arms transfers. It shows that the main recipient region in 2015–2019 was Asia and Oceania that accounted for

41 per cent of global arms imports, the Middle East (35%), Europe (11%), Africa (7.2%) and the Americas (5.7%).
- The fact sheet reveals that between the periods 2010–2014 and 2015–2019, there were increases in arms imports by states in the Middle East by 61 per cent. Other increases were in the states of Europe, by 3.2 per cent. There were decreases in arms imports by states in Africa (–16%), the Americas (–40%) and Asia and Oceania (–7.9%).

The political economy of the arms industry and the arms trade can then be comprehended as a part of trading just like any other commodity and earning a huge profit. If we consider the objectives of sides involved in arms transfer, the exporters as well as the importers, we can find out a number of factors involved in their calculation of selling and procurement of arms. If we take the exporter's point of view, the lobby of MIC is part of the domestic political economy as the jobs and survival of MIC are crucial for them. In most cases, the exporting countries have a highly integrated industry with the government. It is also a part of the foreign policy decisions of countries as they may try to strengthen their allies, balance revisionist power, forge alliances against rivals, retain influence and help to resolve internal conflicts between friends and allies.

There is also an importers' perspective also which can be taken into consideration. Defence is the primary objective amongst others. It can be internal conflict or threat perception from adversaries. The domestic armed industry may lack the capabilities to produce global standard arms. Military lobbying is also a crucial factor in buying arms, and sometimes political leaders make decisions based on defence calculations or a show of might. However, importers can only afford to go on arming themselves depending on their economic performance and budget allocation, likewise. Sometimes, the nexus between client states and their integration into major producer supply chains of other states influences arms transfers.

The December 2020 SIPRI press release shows an upward trend in arms sales and major players located in South Asia. Strikingly, SIPRI's Arms Industry Database shows that arms sales by 25 of the world's largest arms-producing and military services companies amounted to $361 billion in 2019. This represents an 8.5 per cent increase in real terms over the arms sales of the top 25 arms companies in 2018. From this SIPRI database, the names of the largest arms companies can be known. US arms companies top the list, with new entrants from the Middle East among the top 25. In 2019, the top five positions were taken by the US arms companies, namely Lockheed Martin, Boeing, Northrop Grumman, Raytheon and General Dynamics. Taken together, these five amount to $166 billion in annual arms sales. Out of 25, there are 12 US companies in the top 25 for 2019. They account for 61 per cent of the combined arms sales of the top 25 countries. The new entrant from the Middle East was EDGE Group, based in the UAE, and its ranking was 22, with 1.3 per cent of total arms sales in the top 25.

The Chinese arms companies, though they witnessed an increase in arms sale, nevertheless, had the largest share of the arms sales after the USA. In the top 10, three Chinese companies occupied the sixth, eighth and ninth ranks, respectively. They are Aviation Industry Corporation of China (ranked 6th), China Electronics Technology Group Corporation (ranked 8th) and China North Industries Group Corporation (ranked 9th).

However, for the Russian companies, their revenues fell. The revenues of the two Russian companies in the top 25, namely Almaz-Antey and United Shipbuilding, both decreased between 2018 and 2019. They decreased by a combined total of $634 million. A third Russian company, United Aircraft, lost $1.3 billion in sales and was dropped out of the top 25 in 2019.

This SIPRI report also points out the integration of the Global South in the arms industry. They locate the international presence of the 15 largest arms companies in 2019 around the globe, with a presence in 49 countries working out through majority-owned subsidiaries, joint ventures and research facilities. So they have become transnational actors and have acquired the characteristics of MNCs. The report highlights companies with their presence in 24 countries. Thales and Airbus are the two most internationalized companies. Boeing has a presence in 21 countries, Leonardo in 21 countries and Lockheed Martin in 19 countries. The UK, Australia, the USA, Canada and Germany are host countries to the highest numbers of these foreign entities. Apart from the arms industry hubs of North America and Western Europe, the largest numbers of entities of foreign companies are hosted by Australia with 38, Saudi Arabia with 24, India with 13, Singapore with 11, the UAE with 11 and Brazil with 10 arms companies. As in the case of FDI in industrial and financial sectors, countries in the Global South are opening up their defence sectors too. Those who want to reach global standards in arms production are seeking investment, joint venture or any other means to invite foreign arms companies as a means to benefit from technology transfers.

As far as India is concerned, according to SIPRI, India was the second largest importer of arms in 2019 and ranked third in total military spending, just behind the USA and China. India's percentage share in total imports was 9.2 per cent, only to be preceded by Saudi Arabia with a 12 per cent share in total world imports of arms. Next in line are Egypt (5.8%), Australia (4.9%), China (4.3%), Algeria (4.2%), the UAE (3.4%), Iraq (3.4%) and Qatar (3.4%). These are the top 10 global arms importers in 2019.

Export controls include a list of controlled items, licensing procedures, requirements and enforcement mechanisms, which again are determined by the level of transparency, role of decision-makers, control of brokerage and end-user controls and requirements. In the USA, there are arms export controls such as the Arms Export Control Act, 1976, International Traffic in Arms Regulations for implementation of the Arms Export Control Act, Conventional Arms Transfer Policy, presidential directives and arms exports via Foreign Military Sales under the Defense Security Cooperation Agency, which administers the Foreign Military Sales programme for the US Department of Defense or Direct Commercial Sales under Congressional Review. The EU also entails arms export control policies such as common control list, licensing criteria and respect for international obligations, such as UN and EU arms embargoes, weapons of mass destruction treaties, landmines ban and other agreements. The EU denies exporting equipment with a risk factor that might be used for internal repression, or for serious violations of international humanitarian law, among other control measures.

Unfortunately, there is an Arms Trade Treaty of 2014, but arms transfer has seen a steep rise. Amnesty International and the NGO partners of the Control Arms Coalition had lobbied the UNGA for the treaty. Ultimately, the UN General Assembly voted to adopt the Arms Trade Treaty text in April 2013. The treaty entered into force on 24 December 2014. For the first time, this treaty sets prohibitions to stop the international transfer between states of weapons, munitions and related items when it is known they would be used to commit or facilitate genocide, crimes against humanity or war crimes. This is a good step, but the figures cited at the beginning show the sellers and the clients of the arms trade, and it is growing because the arms industry, like any other trading company, seeks profit and market and establishes its reach worldwide.

Knowledge Systems

Before going into the discussion about knowledge systems, let us look at what we can understand by knowledge structure. In her book, Susan Strange (2015) argues that just as the production structure determines what is produced, so too is the knowledge structure, which determines what knowledge is discovered, stored and communicated by whom, by what means and under what terms. Knowledge passes on from generation to generation, and we 'learn' through communication systems. However, who controls knowledge in a globalized world becomes a matter of competition. Obviously, the advanced information technologies possessed by developed countries have come to dominate the world of knowledge. Susan Strange points out the growing asymmetry between states as political authorities in the acquisition of knowledge and in access to it (discussed above under the heading 'Culture, Media and TV'). She points out the domination of the USA in all sectors associated with the knowledge structure. Even Americanized English has become the lingua franca of the global economy as well as of transnational social and professional groups. There is a new brand of 'knowledge workers' who are ruling the service sector. So when the question of development arises, it is obvious that there is a bias towards the Western knowledge structure. The point is that development dilemmas can be solved if a knowledge system can be created by involving stakeholders, executers and policymakers, which can deter environmental impact and also displacement.

In an organizational set-up, knowledge management systems are quite common nowadays. Knowledge management systems here comprise a wide range of strategies and practices used to create, represent, distribute and enable adoption of knowledge. The main objective is to coordinate and collaborate among the people involved in the organization by sharing management solutions and harnessing competitive intelligence. There are various processes of knowledge management by using tools of learning, machines, computer-based software and so on.

Here, in this chapter, the knowledge system has been included because this is an important ingredient when discussing questions of development and, obviously, sustainable development. In matters of development, to make it more sustainable and inclusive, there has to be shared knowledge among the stakeholders involved in the development projects. Science, scientific discoveries and research have set the path of progress since the days of the industrial revolution. However, science cannot always provide inclusive and sustainable development. Policymakers and executers like business groups may have a vision of development quite contrary to the interest of the stakeholders or the people who may lose their habitat and livelihood due to the development project. Linking knowledge and creating a knowledge system become very vital for executing any agenda of development. Rio+22 introduced the concept of stakeholders and coordinated efforts of policymakers, executers, stakeholders and NGOs who can help in mediation and dialogue between stakeholders and policymakers and executers.

Knowledge systems, therefore, comprise agents, practices and institutions that organize the production, transfer and use of knowledge. According to Kerkhoff and Szlezák (2010), when applied to the social goal of sustainability, knowledge systems are 'a network of actors connected by social relationships, formal or informal, that dynamically combine knowing, doing and learning to bring about specific actions for sustainable development'. Science cannot be neglected, but it is not the only one. There are other actors and networks which can play an influential role. However, the question of power cannot be avoided. Who has more power and is in what position to determine the flows of knowledge, credibility and power within the knowledge systems in any societal framework?

Why is there a need to develop knowledge systems? Science and technology have undoubtedly revolutionized lives and have set the course of development, but the pursuit of unsustainable development has led to the loss of biodiversity, ecological imbalances, depletion of resources, loss of flora and fauna, environmental degradation, pollution and, most importantly, climate change. These have again affected the lives and livelihoods of human beings, resulting in their displacement, eviction and even migration from their native places. Science and technology are not to be solely blamed for that. The correct use of science and technology for bringing about sustainable development has not been pursued. The Earth Summit of 1992 highlighted the importance of sustainable development when it upheld 27 principles for sustainable development. So to bring about sustainable development, there is a necessity to link knowledge to action. There is a lack of critical understanding regarding which kinds of programmes and institutional arrangements can create knowledge systems that can most effectively harness science and technology for sustainable development. Knowledge must be translated into action.

Knowledge systems are needed to be like guidelines for executing development projects. Development riding on the progress of science and technology cannot be full proofed. There is no guarantee that it will bring sustainable and inclusive development and will not affect the lives of people and their environment. A linking of the knowledge system of the stakeholders, executers and policymakers is needed to deter environmental impact. Such linking is needed for evolving social responses to public issues involving development project to appear convincing. The stakeholders must feel assured of the credibility, salience and legitimacy of the plan. Credibility is determined by the stakeholders' assessment of the impact of the development project on the environment and their livelihood. *Salience* makes the assessment of the needs of decision makers relevant. The most important is *legitimacy* that reflects the perception that the production of information and technology has been inclusive of the stakeholders' values and beliefs, unbiased in its conduct and accommodative of opposing views and interests.

Here, we again come back to the principles of sustainable development adopted in the Rio Summit of 1992. Principles 9 and 10 in the Rio Declaration on Environment and Development, 1992, contains the importance of interfaces between 'science' and 'policy' and 'science' and 'society' as a whole. This is an uphill task, and bridging the gap between knowledge and action is also difficult. This will involve academicians, researchers, technical experts as well as the stakeholders involving people, polity and business groups/industry. There can be contested knowledge but the success will depend on coordination and accommodation. This is currently being known as 'knowledge democracy'. This signifies that governance is being transformed by knowledge system through mass creation and availability of knowledge. In a concept developed by Veld, knowledge democracy is seen in the production and the use of knowledge could be used to promote a more engaged and reflexive role for science in a 'knowledge democracy' (a concept explored in it Veld, 2010). Society, polity and development strategist and planners must be oriented towards sustainability in the face of accelerating global social environmental change. To bridge the gap between contested interfaces between development and society and polity, developing knowledge systems is crucial.

Here, we must mention UNESCO's Local and Indigenous Knowledge Systems (LINKS) programme. This seeks to promote local and indigenous knowledge and to utilize it in global climate science and policy processes. UNESCO's objective is to link contemporary science-policy-society with local and indigenous knowledge holders and their knowledge. These are now part of the international framework on issues such as biodiversity assessment and management (Convention on Biological Diversity, Intergovernmental Science-Policy Platform on Biodiversity and Ecosystem Services), climate change assessment and adaptation (Intergovernmental Panel on Climate Change, United Nations Framework Convention on Climate Change), natural disaster preparedness (International Strategy for Disaster Reduction) and sustainable development (Rio+20, Future Earth). LINKS programme targets include evolving transdisciplinary engagements with scientists and policymakers and developing newer methodologies to comprehend grave crises like climate change impacts, adaptation and mitigation. Indigenous knowledge has been given a cognizable position in the Rio Declaration as a component of contribution towards climate change policy, SDG 13 on climate action, biodiversity, natural disaster and the like. Figure 8.4 will give a brief idea about creation of knowledge systems that can be change makers in working towards sustainable development.

Figure 8.4 Depiction of Knowledge System

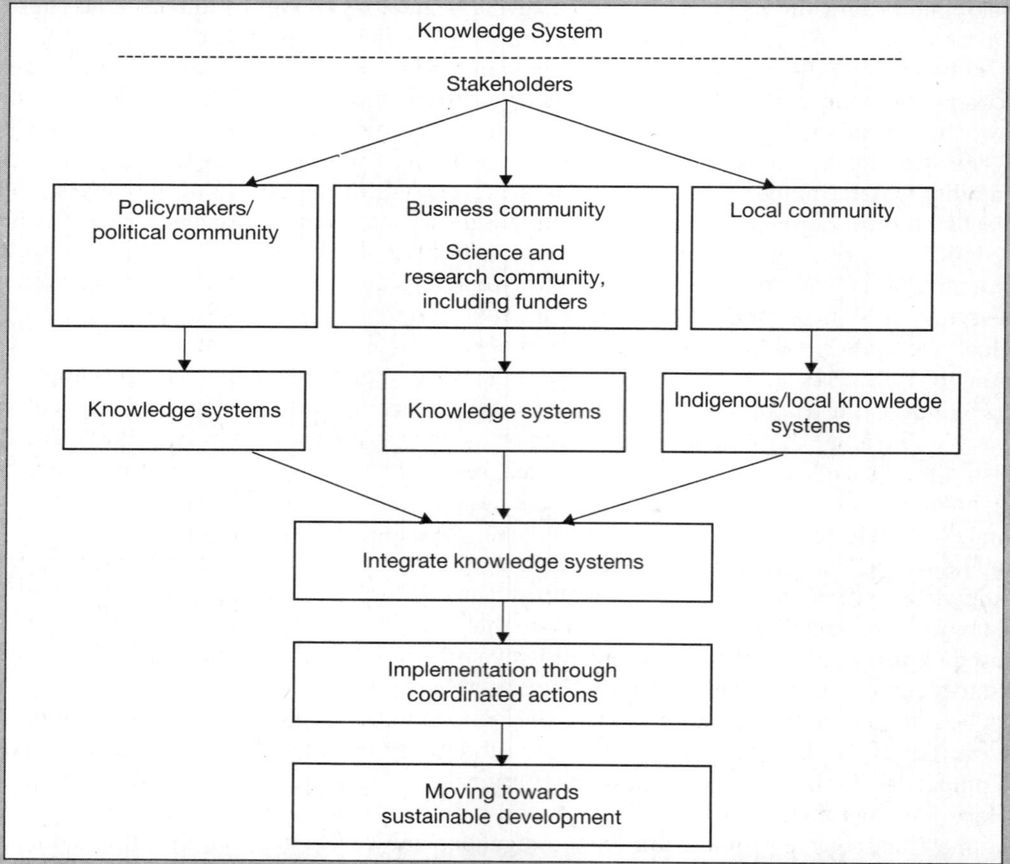

Conclusion

The issues of globalization are plentiful. First and foremost, the debate is around the issue of inequality and uneven growth caused by globalization. As has been examined in this chapter from the perspectives of HDI, poverty and the economic measure of GDP, it is plaintive to see that, despite the promises of neo-liberalism of convergence of income levels across the globe, inequality and exclusion are realities. Such exclusionary development has forced the international community to consider the value of human development. Professor Amartya Sen and Professor Mahbub ul Haq have made important contributions to the development of the HDI. With the aim of inclusive sustainable development, in 2000, the member states of the UN adopted the eight **MDGs.** NGOs also have come to make an important contribution to the projects of development with their advice, expertise and by becoming dialogue partners for bringing in inclusive development.

Apart from this, globalization also challenges the indigenous culture and lifestyle by promoting a universal culture (of consumption primarily) by using the worldwide media. There arises a kind of mixed culture but a culture of domination by the powerful states of the world, for they control the largest media houses as well as the flow of information. The advanced countries, especially the USA, top the list of arms sales, and they have a thriving MIC. The discussion in this chapter showed the growing trend of arms sales around the globe following the SIPRI Reports.

Big dams are also of concern as they may lead to inundation and destruction of ecosystems as well as displacement of people. The environmental and humanitarian concerns have been discussed by bringing the examples of anti-dam movements in India and removal of big dams in the USA. Last of all, to fight climate changes and bring about sustainable development, there is a necessity to link contemporary science, policy and society with local and indigenous knowledge holders and their knowledge, thereby creating a knowledge system.

Summary

The 1990s saw a massive wave of globalization undertake the world. The developing countries got swept by the tide of globalization. The belief in IMF, World Bank or neo-liberal thinking was that unnecessary state intervention would hamper economic growth. Therefore, opening up will help in levelling up the economic development of these countries at par more or less with the advanced countries. The **convergence** theory, therefore, seems to be simplistic.

In long-term growth rates, there are regional disparities. Sub-Saharan African countries are at the bottom of the world income scale. East Asian countries show some growth, such as the ASEAN countries and East Asia such as Japan, Hong Kong, South Korea and Taiwan. South Asian countries, such as India, Bangladesh, Sri Lanka and the Maldives, show increasing growth rates. Eastern European countries previously under the Soviet influence during the Cold War also show higher income.

When we come to human development, then it is evident that the high-income countries rank higher in the HDI ranking. The top 50 positions are occupied largely by high-income countries. So in the case of human development, the disparity, inequality and uneven development become visible between the developed and the developing world. Global poverty is also high in developing and poor countries. Uneven development and exclusion exist in the current international economy, as do poverty, illiteracy and high mortality.

The concept of **human development** is that there is a necessity for the richness of human life rather than the richness of the economy. The HDI was introduced in the UNDP report of 1990. The emphasis is on the building of human capabilities through enabling environments and using those capabilities through planning for growth, empowerment and inclusive and sustainable development.

The three basic dimensions of human development used in HDI are (a) a long and healthy life measured by life expectancy at birth, (b) knowledge as measured by adult literacy rate along with combined primary, secondary and tertiary gross enrolment and (c) a decent standard of living as measured by GDP per capita at PPP in the US dollar.

By the coming of the new millennium under the aegis of the UN, an initiative was launched to address eight core areas of vital importance for human development. In September 2000, the member states of the UN met at the UN headquarters in New York and adopted the **MDGs.** In 2015, the UN adopted 17 SDGs to supplement the MDGs. The aim is to achieve decent lives for all on a healthy planet by 2030.

NGOs are voluntary in their formation, working towards development and mitigation of suffering, working on non-self-serving aims and working on the basis of relative independence. The NGOs address issues related to child rights, poverty amelioration, social justice, environment conservation, human rights, care for the elderly, people, empowerment of women, conservation of wildlife and so on.

Globalization has led to an increase in the flow of capital across the globe. In the case of capital movement, TNCs/MNCs are the main engines and operate in several countries with the motive of capturing markets and siphoning profit back to their home country. They are the main instruments for embarking on the project of universalization of **culture.** The control of technology, the control of information flow and the transmission of global culture are in the hands of Western developed countries. The Third-World countries have become the victims of what may be identified as information imperialism, thereby undermining their own indigenous cultures.

One of the heavy projects of development is the construction of **big dams**. Dams are well known to be useful in many ways. Dams may be built to bring about development, but the debate between dams and destruction has been underway for many years. Resistance to building dams have been by far more vigorous all around the world, including India. Narmada Bachao Andolan is quite well known. Sustainable development of dams by involving stakeholders is therefore necessary.

Military build-up by a particular state can actually create instability in the region of its location as other states can be fearful of its rise and, thereby, start armament procurement and, in this way, destabilize the peace and security of that particular region. As military preparedness seems to be unavoidable, there seems to be an ever increasing arms sales industry and trade. The Stockholm International Peace Research Institute (SIPRI) provides us with data on the volume of the arms trade annually and the list of top exporters of arms sales and top importers of arms. There is a thriving MIC. It is a nexus between a country's military and defence industry. As long as there is military preparedness, the arms trade and arms transfer will persist as a flourishing business.

Knowledge systems are needed to be like guidelines for executing development projects. Development riding on the progress of science and technology cannot be fully proofed. There is no guarantee that it will bring sustainable and inclusive development and will not affect the lives of people and their environment. A linking of the knowledge systems of stakeholders, executers and policymakers is needed to deter environmental impact.

REVIEW AND REFLECTION QUESTIONS

1. Globalization has created uneven development and inequality. Comment on uneven development, inequality and exclusion by giving examples.
2. Social parameters should be included to consider the concept of development in a wholesome way and not just GDP. Discuss the concept of human development in this context.
3. Briefly write on the UN MDGs. Do you think they are necessary to ensure sustainable, inclusive development?
4. NGOs and their role in influencing policy decisions are now quite significant. Comment on the role of NGOs in their activities as civil society organizations.
5. Mediated politics of development: How far do you think media influences culture and creates a mixed culture of dominant culture and indigenous culture?
6. Big dams are necessary, but do you think they are a reason for environmental hazards?
7. The global arms industry is flourishing and growing. Comment on arms transfers and trade and the role of the MIC.
8. Do you think knowledge systems can work to ensure sustainable development?

Bibliography

Beeson, Mark, and Nick Bisley. 2010. *Issues in 21st Century World Politics*. London: Palgrave Macmillan.

Cherunilam, Francis. 2011. *International Economics*. New Delhi: Tata McGraw Hill Education Private Limited.

Chirico, JoAnn. 2014. *Globalization: Prospects and Problems*. Thousand Oaks, CA: SAGE Publications.

Cornell, Sarah E., Frans Berkhout, Willemijn Tuinstra, J. David Tàbara, Jill Jäger, Ilan Chabay, Bert de Wit, Richard Langlais, David Mills, Peter Moll, Ilona M. Otto, Arthur Petersen, Christian Pohl, and Lorrae van Kerkhoff. 2013. 'Opening up knowledge systems for better responses to global environmental change'. *Environmental Science & Policy* 28, 60–70.

Giddens, A. 1999. 'Globalization: An Irresistible Force.' *Daily Yumiuri*, 7, 1999. Available at http://www.globalpolicy.org/ (accessed on 8 October 2021).

Greene, E. Joshua, and Mohsin S. Khan. 1990. 'The African Debt Crisis.' Special Paper 3, African Economic Research Consortium, February. Available at https://idl-bnc-idrc.dspacedirect.org/bitstream/handle/10625/12010/88201.pdf?sequence=1 (accessed on 8 October 2021).

in't Veld, R. J. (ed.). 2010. *Knowledge Democracy*. Berlin: Springer-Verlag.

Krugman Paul, Maurice Obstfeld, & Marc Melitz. 2018. *International Economics: Theory and Practice*. London: Pearson.

Marfleet, P. 2013. 'Mubarak's Egypt: Nexus of Criminality.' *State Crime Journal* 2, no. 2 (Autumn): 112–134. Available at https://www.jstor.org/stable/10.13169/statecrime.2.2.0112#metadata_info_tab_contents (accessed on 8 October 2021).

McCartney, James, and Molly Sinclair McCartney. 2015. *America's War Machine: Vested Interests, Endless Conflicts*. New York, NY: Thomas Dunne Books.

Mukherjee, Aparajita, and Saumya Chakrabarti. 2016. *Development Economics: A Critical Perspective*. New Delhi: PHI Learning.

Nijhuis, M. 2015. 'Harnessing the Mekong or Killing It?' National Geographic, May, 2015. Available at https://www.nationalgeographic.com/magazine/article/mekong-river-dams (accessed on 8 October 2021).

Nixon, R. 2011. *Slow violence and the Environmentalism of the Poor*. Cambridge, MA: Harvard University Press.

Oxford Martin School. 2017. *Our World in Data Report*. University of Oxford.

Piketty, Thomas. 2017. *Capital in the Twenty-First Century*. London: The Belknap press of Havard University Press.

Rajaei, F. 2001. *The Phenomenon of Globalization*. Tehran: Agah Publication.

Sen, A. 1989. 'Development as Capability Expansion.' Available at https://livelihoods.net.in/wp-content/uploads/2020/05/DEVELOPMENT-AS-CAPABILITY-EXPANSION.pdf (accessed on 8 October 2021).

———. *Commodities and Capabilities*. New Delhi: Oxford University Press.

———. 2000. *Development as Freedom*. New York, NY: Anchor Books.

Sinha, Dipankar. 2013. *Development Communication: Contexts for the Twenty-first Century*. Hyderabad: Orient Black Swan.

Skelton, T., and T. Allen. 1999. *Culture and Global Change*. London: Routledge.

Stockholm International Peace Research Institute (SIPRI). Arms Transfers Programme. Available at https://www.sipri.org/media/press-release/2021/global-nuclear-arsenals-grow-states-continue-modernize-new-sipri-yearbook-out-now (accessed on 24 November 2021).

Strange, Susan. 2015. *States and Markets*. New York, NY: Bloomsbury Academic.

Tomlinson, John. 1991. *Cultural Imperialism*. Baltimore, MD: Johns Hopkins University Press.

———. 2003. 'The Agenda of Globalization.' Available at https://core.ac.uk/download/pdf/30648406.pdf (accessed on 8 October 2021).

UNDP. 2020a. 'Latest Human Development Index Ranking.' Available at http://hdr.undp.org/en/content/latest-human-development-index-ranking (accessed on 7 October 2021).

———. 2020b. 'Human Development Index (HDI).' Available at http://hdr.undp.org/en/content/human-development-index-hdi (accessed on 12 October 2021)

United Nations Department of Economic and Social Affairs. 2001. *2001 Report on the World Social Situation*. Available at https://www.un.org/development/desa/dspd/world-social-report/2001-report-on-the-world-social-situation.html (accessed on 24 November 2021).

van Kerkhoff, L., and Nicole A. Szlezák. 2010. 'The role of innovative global institutions in linking knowledge and action.' *Proceedings of the National Academy of Sciences* 113, no. 17: 4603–4608.

World Bank. 1985. *World Development Report 1985*. New York, NY: Oxford University Press. Available at https://openknowledge.worldbank.org/handle/10986/5968 (accessed on 24 November 2021).

———. 2019. *The World Bank Annual Report 2019: Ending Poverty, Investing in Opportunity*. Available at http://hdl.handle.net/10986/32333 (accessed on 8 October 2021).

———. n.d. 'World Bank Country and Lending Groups.' Available at https://datahelpdesk.worldbank.org/knowledgebase/articles/906519-world-bank-country-and-lending-groups (accessed on 7 October 2021).

9 Globalization and Development Dilemmas

LEARNING OBJECTIVES

- Learning about revolution in IT and its impact on sovereignty of state
- Knowing about gender and development and measuring indices of gender development, empowerment and inequality
- Trying to understand racial and ethnic problems through examples
- Comprehending the issue of migration and displacement
- Getting acquainted with environment and sustainability
- Learning about SDGs

Introduction

There has been much enthusiasm for globalization around the globe. With this, a concept of 'global village' has been popularized, that is, the world becoming one. Such universalizing attempts not only have economic fallout but also impact political, social and cultural dimensions. Globalization has brought in risks, reflexivity and paradoxes. The risks are hidden in economic, ecological, political and even social projects. Globalization has set the pace of change in a haphazard fashion. In fact, globalization has ushered in such development dilemmas that risks are becoming out of control. Efforts to bring in convergence, thus, attempting for the creation of a homogenous global culture in the polity and the economy might disrupt the existing fabric of the society. States might just break up like the former Soviet Union or Yugoslavia or Czechoslovakia along ethnic lines. There can be lopsided development when human development is taken into consideration. Even while considering HDI, or in the case of gender, GDI, the figure may be quite pitiable in a particular country which may be showing a high GDP growth. Mismatched paces of globalization and economic policies like SAPs create economic crisis for the indigenous economy and affect the lives of people. There can be extreme poverty due to SAPs as it happened in the Sub-Saharan Africa in the 1980s, which is also known as the lost decade for these countries, when they became victims of vicious cycles of debt trap. The development projects might just lead to displacement of people inside as well as outside the country. Migration and displacement have arisen out of development dilemmas. Ecology is at risk because of development project. Therefore, globalization with its agenda of homogenization and development project may create such dilemmas which affect the common people at large. Even advances in technology, especially IT, not only affects the people but also challenges the sovereignty of the states. This chapter will discuss the challenges which globalization poses before the states and the people.

IT Revolution and Debates on Sovereignty

Sovereignty is the supreme power of a state to control the affairs of ruling and governance both within and outside the state. Therefore, sovereignty entails some sort of territoriality. Sovereignty extends to the territory of a particular state and beyond it, only in matters of foreign relations. Sovereignty has been derived from the Latin word *superanus* which means supreme. It is the supreme power of the state both internally and externally. No individual or group of individuals has the legal right to act contrary to the decisions of the sovereign power internally. Externally, the state is supreme too. Jean Bodin, a French jurist who lived in the days following the Protestant Reformation movement[1] in Europe, was the first to make a systematic study of sovereignty. Bodin (1576) in his *Les Six Liveres de la République* (The Six Books of the Republic) gave an exposition to sovereignty with his objective to establish absolute monarchy of the French monarch which considered sovereignty to be 'the supreme power over citizens and subjects, unrestrained by law'. Thomas Hobbes, a social contract theorist, in his book, *Leviathan* (1651), written in the 17th century during the turmoil of the English Civil War between Parliamentarians and Royalists over the nature of governance in Britain, also gave an exposition of absolute sovereignty. According to Hobbes, 'The sovereign power, whether placed as in monarchy, or in one assembly of men, as in popular and aristocratical commonwealths, is as great as possibly men can be imagined to make it'. Further, Hobbes adds, 'he who considers it too great and will seek to make it less, must subject himself to a power that can limit it, that is to a greater'. Thus, Hobbes professed the sovereignty as absolute, unified, inalienable, based upon a voluntary but irrevocable contract.

Another contribution to the theory of sovereignty is by John Austin in his *Lectures on Jurisprudence* (1875). He writes,

> If a *determinate* superior human superior not in a habit of obedience to a like superior, receives *habitual* obedience from the *bulk* of a given society, that determinate superior is sovereign in that society; and the society (including the superior) is a society political and independent.

Law is the command of the supreme. Austin said, 'Law is the aggregate of rules set by men as politically superior, or sovereign, to men as politically subject'. The determinate superior possesses the power to put compulsion without limit on subjects or fellow subjects.

However, the pluralists contended the absolutist theory of sovereignty. Miss M. P. Follet in her *The New State* (1918) argues, while showing pluralistic tendencies and existence of various groups within the state,

> The ideal unified State is not all-absorptive. It is all inclusive.... The true State must gather up every interest within itself. It must take our many loyalties and find how it can make the one. The home of my soul is in the state.

---

[1] A politico-religious movement of the 16th century which was also a tussle between religious and secular forces. It ultimately came to an end with the 30 years war and the ultimate signing of the Treaty of Westphalia in 1648 and the emergence of the nation state system in Europe.

R. M. Maclver in his *Modern State* (1926) forwards a pluralistic conception of the state which is one of the many associations within a society. State has 'definite limits, definite powers and responsibilities'. 'It stands for the common interest of all individuals and association, but not for the whole of the common interest'. 'The partial interests of a thousand associations, cultural and economic, are also parts of the common interest'.

Robert Dahl (1961), a pluralist thinker, is of the view that pluralists,

> suggest that there are a number of loci for arriving at potential decisions; that businessmen, trade unions, politicians, consumers, farmers, voters and many other aggregates all have an impact on policy outcomes; that none of these aggregates in homogenous for all purposes; that each of them in highly influential over some scopes but weak over many others; and that the power to reject undesired alternatives is more common than the power to dominate over outcome directly.

From the above discussion, it becomes clear that sovereignty is not unrestrained. Sovereignty internally is restricted by the presence of groups/associations and their interests. Externally also, sovereignty cannot be limitless. It is also restricted by the presence of other states in the world as well as international organizations. It is limited from an economic dimension, cultural dimension, political dimension and technological dimension. At the international level, the international organizations like the UN and several regional organizations such as the EU, the Association of Southeast Asian Nations (ASEAN), the North American Free Trade Agreement (NAFTA), the South Asian Association for Regional Cooperation (SAARC) and others limit the absolute sovereignty of the state. In fact, the presence of other states in the world pushes the state to the point to restrain its limitless power vis-à-vis other states. Even international financial institutions such as the IMF and the World Bank and international/multilateral agreements and treaties like the GATT also restricts limitless exercise of sovereignty externally. Culturally also, globalization has set in motion a universalizing tendency around the globe. The culture that is spread usually is the culture of the West, predominantly American. The indigenous culture gets sidelined as the universalizing tendencies of Western culture make a strong foot hold in the minds and lifestyle of the developing world. There is a cultural domination which arises with globalization and it may definitely affect exercise of sovereignty internally and externally. Example can be more civil society activism like in the Western societies which might hinder exercise of sovereign power internally and externally too if the civil society movements align with international civil society organizations. Most importantly, technology has made sovereign existence of state vulnerable. Weapons of mass destruction such as the long-range cruise missiles in the nature of intercontinental ballistic missiles, short-range ballistic missiles, multiple independently targetable re-entry vehicles and host of other nuclear war heads are threatening the sovereignty of states. Terrorists operate sans boundaries. Such non-state actors have really threatened the sovereignty of states. The 9/11 terrorist attack on the World Trade Center is a pointer in that direction.

So a question arises, how globalization and technological advances have affected the sovereignty of the state. With globalization have come technological inventions, innovations, progress in telecommunication system and improvement in manufacturing, transportation and market capabilities. Technology has changed the pace and face of globalization. Transport and communication have become very fast. Manufacturing techniques have been revolutionized. Market stands globalized. Central to such phenomenal changes obviously is the revolution in IT. IT is creating a pool of resources using information. The internet is the core of such data creation. It is a digital world we are living in. The system of governance of a state is highly digitalized today. Government business is more and more dependent on e-governance. Services to public have been digitalized. Digitalization makes services faster and can reach out to a large number of public. However, this digital sovereignty and the internet security of the government of a state can stand compromised/threatened and hacked.

Revolution in the realm of IT has made the world a small space. Connectivity and exchange of information within seconds have made life easier. Cyber revolution undoubtedly helps in faster financial and business transactions, exchange of information, social media activities, entertainment, public relations and advertisement, blogging, tweeting and a host of other engagements. People nowadays live in both the 'real space' and the 'virtual world'. They are both 'citizens' and 'netizens' at the same time.

In one's physical space, one confronts the question of governance and policing as far as matters of law and order, crimes and convictions or even emergency situations like disaster management are concerned. However, in the 'virtual' world, there is a more free play of one's intellect and also one's choices which for long has gone unregulated by authorities of governance. Unregulated activities in the cyber world, which are becoming more encompassing due to the use of social media, sometimes cause problems in maintenance of law and order and often hurt the question of national security. Cybercrimes and cyber terrorism threaten the sovereignty of a state.

Certain common types of cybercrimes include hacking, virus attack, web jacking, mail bombing, theft of internet hours, identity theft, cyber stalking and credit/debit card fraud to mention a few. Another sort of crime which is gradually assuming perilous proportion is cybercrime and victimization of women. Sexual crimes using digital communication technology include online pornography, revenge porn, obscenity, cyber bullying, morphing of images, cyber stalking and hate crimes, among others, which do affect the security in cyber space and may have a repercussion on a person's physical existence also.

A threat to national security involves not only threats to individuals but to the entire country, its defence systems and its critical infrastructure protection. Apart from the cybercrimes referred to above, cyber terrorism is a feature of contemporary times.

IT revolution has strengthened the usual methods of terrorism by giving the terrorist outfits an access into the cyber world. The 9/11 terror attacks on the World Trade Center horrified the world with the revelation of the grave connection and usage of the cyber world by the terrorist outfits. Now, the fear that terrorists in the future might use cheap and unconventional modes of attacks using the cyber space and hacking the national security infrastructure has become a probability and is just a matter of time. It is not just cybercrime in the entire discourse of terrorism. Another category must be added and that is cyber terrorism. The angst of cyber terrorism was so high after the 9/11 attacks that the federal government requested $4.5 billion for infrastructure security, and the FBI has appointed 'cyber investigators'. After the 9/11 attacks, President Bush created the Office of Cyberspace Security in the White House and appointed his former counterterrorism coordinator, Richard Clarke, as the head. Warnings in the US governments were running around the fear of cyber terrorism. The thinking was that, as put in by Tom Ridge, who was the director of the Department of Homeland Security, April 2003, 'Terrorists can sit at one computer connected to one network and can create worldwide havoc' and '[they] don't necessarily need a bomb or explosives to cripple a sector of the economy or shut down a power grid'.

Therefore, with the improvement of IT, there has been a growing threat of not just terrorism but cyber terrorism. Cyber terrorism has given conventional terrorism a new dimension.

There is interaction between the cyber world and the terror outfits. In the case of cyber terrorism, the national security, which is most often the target, now has to combat both physical terrorist assault in the 'real' world and terrorist attacks in the 'virtual' world, sometimes leading to a complete system collapse. The targets mainly are military installations, power plants, air traffic control, banks, trail traffic control and telecommunication networks. They may also target police, medical, fire and rescue systems, among others, with the aim of disrupting public services. It is more dangerous and have the potential to affect a large number of people and often used by terrorists when they want to hit a country's security hard.

Cyber terrorism is the convergence between terrorism and cyber space involving a mixture of cybercrime and misuse of IT. It can also become cyber warfare between a government and terrorist groups. The 9/11 attack was the culmination point of cyber terrorism which found expression in cyberattacks by terrorist outfits against the US government in the form of threat messages, defacing of numerous websites and disruption of internet communication for government as well as civil amenities. In India, the 2008 Mumbai Taj Hotel attack, known as the 26/11 Mumbai attack, and the 2010 blast in Varanasi rocked the country for their intensity and horrific style of operation. The notable points in these two blasts are the usage of cyber space or more specifically cyber communication system for perpetrating such acts of violence. This makes one thing clear and that is wherever acts of cyber terrorism occur, it is done through the acts of gathering information and spreading of the terror through cyber communication for disruption of national security and peace.

On 13 May 2017, there was a Ransom Virus Attack globally. Ransomware is a type of malware that encrypts a user's data, then demands payment in exchange for unlocking the data. This attack used malicious software called 'WannaCryptor 2.0' or WannaCry that exploits vulnerability in Windows. In a computer which is under ransomware attack, the user's files get encrypted. The files can only be decrypted by a mathematical key known only to the attacker. The user is shown a message explaining that the files are now inaccessible and can only be decrypted if the victim sends an untraceable Bitcoin payment to the attacker.

Added to the above dimensions is another space called the social media. *Facebook, Twitter, YouTube, LinkedIn, Instagram, WhatsApp*, to name a few, have changed the way we look at the world. *WikiLeaks* showed the world how powerful the internet can be. Julian Assange's, whose name has become synonymous with *WikiLeaks,* revelations stunned the world with information which the public would have never ever have access to. Since 2006 till now, *WikiLeaks*, used by whistle-blowers, has published anonymous submissions of documents that are generally unavailable to the general public, especially the US diplomatic cable leaks.

In future, there can be other kinds of IT revolution which can undermine the sovereignty of a state. In the digital world, a lot of data moves and hacking those data can put the security of the state at risk, thereby undermining the sovereignty of the state. These may be perpetuated by either another state or non-state actors like the terrorist outfits. Global movements of money, MNCs, satellite communication, nuclear weapons and weapons of mass destruction or even biological and chemical weapons have raised doubts about sovereignty of the states. Besides these, digital sovereignty and the internet security also stand threatened. Still, it can be said that sovereignty might be threatened under changed circumstances but states still continue to be the major actors in the international and domestic scenario. Not only that, globalization is putting several challenges before the states.

It is for these threats that the Government of India passed the new IT Rules, 2021. It contains provisions that digital media platforms now require a larger grievance redressal mechanism that should include a chief compliance officer, a nodal contact person and a resident grievance officer. All social media platforms are to publish such details on their apps and websites and explain to users the mechanism in place to make a complaint against any content on the platform. The complaints are to be acknowledged within 24 hours of receipt and action to be taken within a period of 15 days from the date of receipt.

The exception to this rule is what the guidelines describe as 'any content which is prima facie in the nature of any material which exposes the private area of such individual, shows such individual in full or partial nudity or shows or depicts such individual in any sexual act or conduct, or is in the nature of impersonation in an electronic form, including artificially morphed images of such individual, shall need to be removed or access disabled within 24 hours from the receipt of a complaint via the redressal mechanism'. The social media and digital media platforms are required to take action and immediate redressal of any government notices or court orders. It is almost like a quick response that is required on the part of the social media platforms. Therefore, states are still dominant actors in domestic and international politics and from time to time, they can assert their sovereignty in the interest of the public and law and order.

Gender Including GDI, GEM and GII

Globalization and development have opened up debates about their impact on gender. Gender is a social construct and not a biological one. The biological distinction between male and female is what constitutes 'sex'. The social constructions of 'men' and 'women' or 'boys' and 'girls' is what constitutes gender. Gayle Rubin (1974) a society transforms biological sexuality into products of human activity and in which these transformed talks about the sex-gender system which she sees as a set of arrangements whereby a society transforms biological sexuality into products of human activity and in which these transformed sexual needs are satisfied. Rubin further highlights that sex-gender system creates a compulsory heterosexual relations preferably through the institution of marriages. This entire scheme therefore leaves out the gay, lesbian and event the transgenders whose sexual orientations have been treated as deviant and abnormal.

When it comes to public private dichotomy, women are always pushed into the private and the public domain becomes a space for men only. Within the family, women are subjected to power play and are subjected to a relation of subordination and suppression. It is infused by patriarchy and the patriarchal institutions. Women are subjected to family work of bearing, rearing and caring. Preference for sons over and above a girl child affects the girl child's access to nutrition, healthcare and education. Lack of participation in family decision making and restricting women's role to domestic chores have made women marginalized in the public sphere. Along with the sexual-division of labour within the family, in the public domain, the sexual division of labour places a woman in low-status and low-paid jobs. However, it must be noted that women have to bear the triple burden of work—domestic work, reproductive work and work in productive labour market. In all these three relations, there is a process of domination and subordination involved between men and women.

When we come to the economic concept of work, women are in a more disadvantageous position. Economic theories often make distinction between 'gainful' or 'productive work'/'employment' (work for a salary or wage) and 'unproductive work' (work generating no wage or salary). However, feminist economists have made a distinction between 'work' and 'employment' where doing household chores is 'work' along with a 'gainful employment' that a woman may be engaged with. Women's involvement in domestic work covers works such as housework; family farm work; processing of agricultural products for self-consumption; collection of water and firewood; care of children, elderly and even disabled persons, in fact, care of every person in the family; cooking; cleaning and other routine household work. A point to be remembered is that all these works amount to **unpaid work** and lie outside the market domain. The poorer a household, the more burden of unpaid labour fall upon the women. Affluent families have access to market base substitute for domestic labour. Unpaid work not only covers those works which fall within production boundary but also those outside the production boundary that includes social reproduction.

Academicians working on gender-related issues have time and again tried to relate poverty and gender. They opine that women's lack of access to and control over resources limit their economic autonomy and increase their vulnerability to economic or environmental shocks. Compared to men, lower proportions of women have cash income in the less developed regions. The 'poverty trap', thus, reflects how vertical inequalities of income and wealth are bound up with the multiple and overlapping horizontal inequalities associated with marginalized identities of various kinds to produce entrenched forms of disadvantage which can be referred to as 'chronic poverty'.

Gender inequality cuts across both vertical inequalities and other horizontal inequalities including race and caste and add to 'extreme poverty'. Its intersection with these other forms of inequality means that it is women and girls from the poorest caste, ethnic and racial groups who have poorer levels of health, nutrition and education, and very often, they suffer higher levels of violence than other women, including women from similarly poor backgrounds. This necessitates a researcher to look into the social parameters and not solely the economic one's to assess the status of women in one's own country.

Undoubtedly, women and work—paid or unpaid, gainful or unproductive—have come to occupy the centre stage of debate. There is a need, therefore, to understand women and work beyond the economic framework.

To find out the actual position of women in the society and their contributions to the economy as well as to relate gender to development, mere reference to GDP is not enough. Therefore, apart from GDP, the usual measure of economic progress of any country, a breakthrough came in 1990 with the attempt of the **UNDP** to define development by taking into account certain social factors. The **First Report** on human development tries to define human development 'as a process of enlarging the range of people's choices-increasing their opportunities for education, health care, income and employment and covering the full range of human choices from a sound physical environment to economic and political freedom'. The 1990 report introduced the **HDI** and identified three elements as essential to human life: **life expectancy, knowledge** and **decent standard of living.** HDI gave a new dimension to development by considering factors or indicators other than the economic ones. HDI components include the basic dimensions of human development—health, knowledge and living standards.

HDI, however, does not reveal the disparity of development between males and females. Therefore, keeping the same components of HDI, the UNDP formulated **GDI** in its report in 1995. The GDI is the **ratio of the HDIs calculated separately for females and males** using the same methodology of HDI. It is a direct measure of gender gap showing the female HDI as a percentage of male HDI. Gender gap reveals the percentage of under-development of females in three indicator areas, that is, health, knowledge and living standards, as compared to their male counterparts.

The GDI is calculated, at present, for 166 countries which are grouped into five categories based on the absolute deviation from gender parity in HDI values: (a) very high human development, (b) high human development, (c) medium human development, (d) low human development and (e) other countries or territories.

Along with GDI, another measure which is used to calculate gender inequality is **gender inequality index** (GII). GII was introduced in 2010 Human Development Report in the 20th anniversary edition by the UNDP. It measures gender inequality in three important aspects of human development: (a) **reproductive health,** measured by maternal mortality ratio and adolescent birth rates; (b) **empowerment,** measured by proportion of parliamentary seats occupied by females and proportion of adult females and males aged 25 years and older with at least some secondary education and (c) **economic status,** expressed as labour market participation and measured by labour force participation rate of female and male population aged 15 years and older. The higher the GII value, the more disparities between females and males amounting to low human development gender wise.

Gender empowerment measure (GEM) was also introduced by UNDP Human Development Report of 1995. This uses estimated earned income based on non-agricultural wages, percentage of parliamentary seats by gender, percentage of technical positions held by women and percentage of legislators, senior officials and managers who are women as indicators. The three dimensions considered in GEM are: (a) political participation and decision-making, (b) economic participation and decision-making and (c) power over economic resources. The index runs from 0 to 1, with 1 being the maximum. A higher score is always desirable.

The GDI reveals that gender gaps in human development are pervasive. On average, at the global level, female HDI value is about 8 per cent lower than male HDI but disparities do exist across countries, human development groups and regions. Across countries, gender gaps in HDI values range between 0 per cent and 40 per cent. Gender gaps in HDI values tend to be lower in the 'very high human development index group' and widens as one moves towards the 'low human development index group'. On average, the six regions assessed by the **Gender Gap Report 2020** have witnessed a reduced gender gap. Western Europe has the least gender gap (76.7%), followed by North America (72.9%), Latin America and the Caribbean (72.1%) and Eastern Europe (71.5%). The East Asia and the Pacific region (68.5%) ranks before Sub-Saharan Africa (68%). South Asia has closed 66.1 per cent of its gender gap and is ahead of the Middle East and North Africa. These regions are with the lowest performance (61.1%).

The GDI, GII and GEM help the researchers to map the gender disparity and actual position of women in the developing countries.

Table 9.1 is the summary of India's record of gender development based on the Human Development Reports published by the UNDP. Table 9.1 shows India's HDI ranking as well as GII ranking. It also gives GDI value.

Further, a majority of the countries worldwide show a positive trend in female workforce participation, which is the proportion of working age population in paid employment or looking for paid work. The sharp reduction in India and China has been held responsible for the drop in global averages. Yet China, where the percentage for female labour participation is 63.9 as against the male rate of 78.3 per cent, has a better figure when compared to India's dismal figures of 27 per cent for women versus 79.9 per cent for men (World Economic Forum

Table 9.1 GDI and GII of India (2010–2019)

HDI Reports Year	HDI Value	HDI Ranking	GDI Value	GII Value	GII Ranking
2010	0.519	119	*	0.748	122
2011	0.547	134	*	0.617	129
2013	0.554	136	*	0.610	132
2014	0.586	135	*	0.563	127
2015	0.609	130	0.795	0.563	130
2016	0.624	131	0.819	0.530	125
2017	0.638	130	0.841	0.501	122
2018	0.647	129	0.828	0.524	130

Source: Compiled from Human Development Reports, UNDP, 2010–2019.

Note: *GDI value could not be accessed.

Table 9.2 Gender Gap Index 2012–2015, Position of India

Gender Gap Indices	Rank 2012	Value 2012	Rank 2013	Value 2013	Rank 2014	Value 2014
Economic participation and opportunity	123	0.4588	124	0.446	134	0.410
Educational attainment	121	0.8525	120	0.857	126	0.850
Health and survival	134	0.9612	135	0.931	141	0.937
Political empowerment	17	0.3343	9	0.385	15	0.385
Overall index	105	0.6442	101	0.655	114	0.646

Source: Compiled from World Economic Forum, *Gender Gap Report*, 2012–2019.

2015). Tables 9.2 and 9.3 show the dismal picture of gender gap in India over the period 2012–2019, and it seems it is getting worse.

If the gender gap rankings of India and SAARC countries are considered for the year **2015,** it will be as follows in the ascending order: Bangladesh (64), Sri Lanka (84), India (108), Nepal (110), Maldives (113), Bhutan (118) and Pakistan (144). The gender gap ranking of India and SAARC countries in the year **2016** in ascending order has been: Bangladesh (72), India (87), Sri Lanka (100), Nepal (110), Maldives (115), Bhutan (121) and Pakistan (143). The gender gap ranking of India and SAARC countries in the year **2017** in ascending order has been: Bangladesh (48), Sri Lanka (100), Nepal (105), India (108), Maldives (113), Bhutan (122) and Pakistan (148). In the year **2018,** the rankings were as follows: Bangladesh (48), Nepal (105), Sri Lanka (100), Bhutan (122), India (108) and Pakistan (148). In the year **2019,** the gender gap rankings for SAARC countries are as follows: Bangladesh (50), Nepal (101), Sri Lanka (102), Bhutan (131), India (112) and Pakistan (151). In the year **2020,** the ranking of SAARC

Table 9.3 Gender Gap Index 2016–2019, Position of India

Gender Gap Indices	Rank 2015	Value 2015	Rank 2016	Value 2016	Rank 2017	Value 2017	Rank 2018	Value 2018
Economic participation and opportunity	139	0.383	136	0.408	142	0.385	149	0.354
Educational attainment	125	0.896	113	0.950	114	0.953	112	0.962
Health and survival	143	0.942	142	0.942	147	0.940	150	0.944
Political empowerment	9	0.433	9	0.433	19	0.382	18	0.411
Overall index	108	664	87	0.683	108	0.665	112	0.668

Source: Compiled from World Economic Forum, *Gender Gap Report, 2012–2019.*

countries are as follows: Bangladesh (65), Nepal (106), Sri Lanka (116), Bhutan (130), India (140), Pakistan (153) and Afghanistan (156).

This, however, should not impair us in taking an optimistic image of globalization and increased participation of women in various sectors. Globalization, which has led to more integration on the economic front, has also brought people together, especially to the civil society movements (discussed in Chapter 8). The globalization also has knitted the gender-based groups as well as struggles for gender equality around the globe. It is feminization of the movements on women issues which have led to greater sensitization about women's issues and policies and strategies to close the gender gaps in different countries; for example, in India, there are programmes like *Beti Bachao, Beti Padhao* and several Acts to prevent sex determination at birth and foeticides. Globalization has helped through the internet facilities to establish intertwined communitarian, associative or transnational associations and their interactions to fight for gender issues from local to global. Therefore, there has arisen the debates related to women and work (paid versus unpaid) which still continue. This cannot be denied as a positive impact of globalization.

Globalization has opened up new opportunities for both the genders—male and female. Free market and trade openness and the diffusion of new ICT have created different genres of jobs. Many women have accessed the job markets for and sought economic opportunities. This is facilitated by greater access to information about life and mores of global requirements and likewise developing skills for seeking the jobs which are outsourced. There is also an argument that MNCs seek female labour in developing countries because they can offer 'cheap labour' and thereby high profit and are engaged mostly in unskilled job. This creates a job hierarchy in workplace. The World Development Report of 2019 shows that the service sector currently is the largest employer from 2000s and accounts for 45 per cent of global employment. The Report says that women hold greater proportion of service sector jobs than men (55% versus 45%). However, an overall of 48 per cent of the women participated in the workforce in 2018, while men accounted for 75 per cent of workforce participation.

The *Global Gender Gap Report 2021,* published by the World Economic Forum, contends that the COVID-19 crisis has put the gender equality much behind. The Report says that another generation of women must wait for gender parity as an extra 36 years are added to the time remaining to close the gender gap. The Report observes that despite progress in education and health, women face economic hurdles, low political participation and workplace challenges or, in other words, fail to meet GDI parameters. Like earlier years, Iceland remains the world's most gender equal country, followed by Finland, Norway, New Zealand and Sweden. The Report says if the current trend in political gender gap continued, then it is to be expected to take 145.5 years to close, compared to 95 years in the 2020 edition of the Report, an increase of over 50 per cent. As far as economic gender gap is concerned, it is seen that only a marginal improvement has been made since 2020 and is expected to take another 267.6 years to close. In education, while 37 countries have reached gender parity, for others, it will take another 14.2 years to completely close this gap due to slow progress for the causes mentioned above. In health, over 95 per cent of this gender gap has been closed, registering a marginal decline since 2019. The Report suggests that strategies and policies should be devised that should emphasize investment in the care sector, equal hiring practices and skill development.

The picture is quite bleak worldwide except some high-performing countries, mostly the developed countries showing high HDI. Yet in the SDGs, Goal 5 has made gender equality a prime objective to be achieved. It has also set targets to achieve the SDG Goal 5. They include targets to end all forms of discrimination against all women and girls globally, stop violence against women in public and private spheres including trafficking and sexual exploitation, eliminating practices such as child marriage and female genital mutilation, giving value to unpaid care work, ensuring women's participation in decision-making and leadership in political, economic and public sphere, ensuring reproductive rights and access to sexual and reproductive healthcare, giving equal rights to economic resources and ownership and control over land and property, making women skilled in technology, especially IT and communication technology and adopting gender-sensitive reforms and legislation, thus ensuring more gender equality.

Racial and Ethnic

Inequalities are present in every society. There can be seen a hierarchy existing in a given society. These divisions within the society can be based upon class, caste, race and ethnicity. Each has a specific role to play when it comes to the political, economic and social processes. If it is thought that globalization has set in such a progress in motion that these dividing lines will vanish, then it will just be a figment of imagination. On the other hand, such divisions have been reinforced by the process of globalization and resulting development dilemmas.

Du Bois in an article, 'World of Color', published in the journal, *Foreign Affairs*, showed that the actual problem is the colour line. He opined that it was a relation between the darker races and lighter races. The former could be found in Asia, Africa and America and the latter, he says, in the islands of the sea. Even this journal began as the *Journal of Race Development*. It can be seen as a project of maintaining the supremacy of lighter race or the Whites and their mission to uplift underdeveloped races.

Earlier during the days of European colonialism, race became a tool or differentiation between the colonizers and the colonized as well as the civilized and the barbaric ones. It was kind of a construct which testified the standards of civilizations. Imperial masters, therefore, justified their expansion as a mission to civilize the barbaric indigenous people. Their lives can only be improved through the process of colonization. The Global South, identified as the Third World, has a history of colonial past and how the colonial masters perpetuated a difference of superior and inferior, which was translated into the power relation of domination and subordination. Indians have experienced 200 years of British rule and extreme racial segregation and abuses.

The 19th-century racism saw a new turn in the guise of 'racial hygiene' where preservation of purity of race became the main consideration. This was the policy which was implemented by the Nazis who propagated the racial superiority of the Aryan race. Working on this history has witnessed the crime against humanity when almost six million Jews were killed. The German concentration camps and the methods of torture and killing are notoriously known. Among the concentration camps, the ones at Auschwitz in Poland had been the most horrifying and scariest of all.

Coming to the post-Second World War era, South Africa had implemented the policy of 'apartheid' which meant separate treatment for the Whites and the Africans. Development agenda was also designed in that way. The African National Congress and personalities like Nelson Mandela had fought a long battle against apartheid. Ultimately, during the Presidency of F. W. de Klerk, a series of negotiations with the African National Congress in the 1990s process to end apartheid was carried on. Ultimately, in the elections of 1994, with a landslide victory of the African National Congress with Nelson Mandela as the President, apartheid came to an end in South Africa.

The USA had a long legacy of plantation slavery which was perpetuated along the lines of race. The huge Black population belongs to an impoverished group. The presidential Emancipation Proclamation by the then president, Abraham Lincoln, in 1862, which became effective in 1863, freed a large number of people from slavery. The Thirteenth Amendment to the US Constitution ratified in 1865 by the Senate abolished slavery in the USA. Martin Luther king Jr had fought relentlessly against racial inequality by following the path of non-violence. He received the Nobel Peace Prize for his struggle against racism.

From the perspective of IPE, the neo-Marxist schools of thought show the creation of dependency of the Third-World countries by the Euro-American policies of exploitation and extraction. Though the dependency theory and world systems theory did not emphasize upon race, we can translate the interconnection of colonization of the Third-World countries by the colonizers who belonged to the lighter race and used race as an ordering principle with a mission to civilize the indigenous people. Race has been central to the imperialist nature of capitalism.

Globalization has brought an end to such kind of consciousness of 'the other' is not true. It has reinforced such divisions. Refugees, migrants, asylum seekers, labourers and terrorists to mention a few have reinvigorated such divisions. Former French president, Valéry Giscard d'Estaing, in 1992, stated that the country was facing an invasion of dark-skinned immigrants. Therefore, he suggested that the 'right of blood' be incorporated into citizenship legislation. On the face of rising number of asylum seekers from countries such as Iraq, Somalia, Sudan, Nigeria, Syria, Yemen and Afghanistan to mention a few, with their preferred destinations being European countries, the EU faces tough challenges of managing the asylum seekers and refugees. These are mostly illegal immigrants often entering European countries by sea. They face strict immigration laws and sometimes deportations and depravations. The presence of this 'other' again in a veiled manner reinforces the issue of race as well as religion. There is now an *Islamophobia* that is working at the heart of strict immigration policies since the 9/11 terror attacks. Developed countries need cheap labour from the Third-World countries but immigration laws have become very tough and often guided by parochial choices of the political system and their vision towards 'the other'. There has been an increase in racist and xenophobic activities throughout the developed world such as in Europe, Australia and USA. They are targeted at the immigrant population—'the other'—who are very different from the mainstream people of the land. The current policy of former US president, Donald Trump, of refusing entry of persons from certain Islamic states and tougher visa regulations for immigrant workers, H-1B visas, building wall between the USA and Mexico border as well as separating children from their migrant families, which are part of his 'zero-tolerance' immigration policies, have earned negative criticisms.

Maybe now race is not used in common parlance but now more often one encounters with the term ethnicity. It is again another term used for differentiation among groups of people. These groups of people share certain commonalities like a common culture, language, religion, customs and mores, food and physical features. They may inhabit a certain territory also or may be linked to a historical territory. However, these very facts create a sense of 'otherness' among groups. Ethnicity might create a sense of nationalism and arouse the spirit of self-determination. This might create ethnic tensions, conflicts and even ethnic cleansing. Rwanda, Burundi, Chechnya, former Yugoslavia, Sri Lanka and even India are a few countries riffed by ethnic crisis which sometimes gives rise to demand for separate statehood. Once there is an outbreak of ethnic crisis, undoubtedly, there are gross human rights violations, genocide, failure of state mechanisms, economic distress, environmental harm and even mass exodus of people as internally displaced persons or as refugees.

If one looks at Rwanda, an impoverished country, it witnessed massive genocide along ethnic lines during 1994. Ethnic tensions had persisted even during the colonial rule between the Hutu and the Tutsi, which had often led to ethnic clashes. However, in 1994, soon after the death of the Rwandan president, Habyarimana (a moderate Hutu leader), in a plane crash, genocidal killings started. The Tutsis were ethnically cleansed. The civil war and killings continued till the end of the 1990s. Burundi also faced civil war which persisted till 2006. Here also, the clash was along ethnic lines and between the Hutus and the Tutsis. In Rwanda, if the ruling elites, the Hutus, systematically tried ethnic cleansing, in Burundi, it was the Tutsis who did the same. The Hutu–Tutsi ethnic dichotomy was at the centre of ethnic tensions.

Sri Lanka witnessed an ethnic strife where demand for Tamil Eelam or Tamil homeland in the north and east of the country was raised. It was long civil war fought between the Liberation Tigers of Tamil Eelam and the Sri Lankan government. It was in 2009 that the civil war came to an end. However, there was mass displacement of Sri Lankan Tamils as refugees, and most moved to the southern part of India, as well as internally displaced persons. The economy and the environment both were affected. According to UN estimates, civilian casualties have been around 40,000. Yet this figure seems to be incomplete.

India's Northeast has been disturbed for long due to ethnic problems in the seven sisters or seven states. Assam, Nagaland, Manipur, Arunachal Pradesh, Mizoram, Tripura and Sikkim have experienced different scales of conflict over years. Several militant outfits such as the Dima Halam Daogah and the United Liberation Front of Asom in Assam; the National Socialist Council of Nagalim, based in Manipur and Nagaland; and the United National Liberation Front, based in Manipur, have grown up. In Assam, there is an Assamese nationalism, targeting foreigners who are primarily the Bengalis/Bangladeshis in Assam, and a Bodo nationalism demanding a separate Bodo land. Nagaland also witnessed massive insurgencies in their effort to establish a separate state. Such insurgency percolated into the neighbouring state of Manipur and ethnic clashes with Kuki tribals began, creating their own guerrilla groups in order to protect their interests from alleged Naga violations. The 1990s show a peak of such clashes. The Paite, Pangals, Hmars and Vaiphei also got entangled in ethnic skirmishes and formed militant outfits. These are only few examples of ethnic conflicts in Northeast India. They also had a spillover effect as the insurgents took shelter in the forests of southern Bhutan. These called for actions by the Royal Bhutan Army to oust the insurgents from southern Bhutan. The most significant among them was Operation All Clear taken up in 2003.

Yugoslavia split into five sates along ethnic lines in 2003 after terrible ethnic clashes between Serbs and Croats. The five states created were Slovenia, Croatia, Macedonia, Bosnia-Herzegovina and Serbia-Montenegro. Kosovo declared independence from Serbia in 2008 after intense civil war. NATO bombings in Kosovo to retaliate Slobodan Milosevic's repressive policies including ethnic cleansing attracted international attention too. Milosevic faced trial before the International Criminal Tribunal for the former Yugoslavia till his death in 2006 as perpetrator of crimes against humanity, genocide and war crimes.

Czechoslovakia had been a case of tensions between the two prominent ethnic groups, the Slovaks and the Czechs. There has been allegation of economic disparity by the Slovaks against the Czechs. The country was bifurcated on 31 December 1992 but unlike Yugoslavia, this transition was peaceful and a result of rounds of negotiations between the political leaders representing the two ethnic groups.

Chechnya tried to break away from the Russian Federation as the Chechens considered themselves as a separate ethnic group. Every effort in this direction has been met with Russian suppression when the Russian army embattled to thwart the rebellious activities of the Chechens. The fallout has been terror attacks in Moscow and other cities of Russia. The Chechen problem still continues and ethno-nationalism in Chechnya will go on creating problem for Russia in future too.

Ethnic differences have resurfaced in the post-Cold War era as those divisive factors lay hidden in the wider spectrum of Cold War between the USA and the USSR. Globalization acting along the neoliberal ideology of capital accumulation and wealth creation often result in imbalanced economic growth. Such situations perpetuate inequality, create poverty, arouse sense of depravation and thereby fan the ethnic differences which might take a toll on a country's law and order and even its security situations. As we discussed in the case of race, here also the sense of 'otherness' works. Ethnic factor along with religion have now come to be determining criteria in the case of seeking asylum or refugee status and even immigration.

Migration and Displacement

Migration and displacement both involve movement of people. If these two concepts are considered from the perspective of states, then the territorial boundaries of the states have to be considered. Movement of people can be inside the territory of a state or may be across borders. If we look at the causes of migration within the boundary of a state, then one of the factors can be rapid urbanization and the attraction of better life. There can be a pattern of out migration from the villages to the cities in search of better livelihood. There can be migration from one city to another city and the cause may be again better livelihood or occupational requirement. For women, marriages are sometimes cause of migration. Family unification sometimes becomes a reason for migration. Education is also a reason for national migration sometimes. These are cases of voluntary migration within the territory of a state. There can be migration across the boundary of a state too. The destination may be another country. When these migrations take place through proper procedure, they are categorized as legal migration and when such migrations happen without proper documents and following immigration laws, then they are treated as illegal migration.

Some examples of voluntary migration include migrant workers, students, professionals, permanent settlers, but all with valid documents of immigration. Sometimes migration across border can be a result of forced eviction from one's country of origin due to political, religious, ethnic, economic, environmental causes and sometimes due to human trafficking. Such migrations can happen in groups or individually. However, they are often classified as irregular migration. It is the status of migration that renders the migration as irregular. Migration laws might change turning an individual into an illegal immigrant in the destination country. The status can change during the course of the journey or even during transit.

Everett Lee (1966) has conceptualized the factors that may be associated with the decision to migrate and the purpose of migration. He divide them into four categories. They are as follows:

- Factors associated with areas of origin
- Factors associated with the areas of destination
- Intervening obstacles
- Personal factors

To explain Lee's theories, there is the combination of two or three factors that may induce to migrate or not to migrate. One set of factors attract and are called the pull factors. The other set of factors might compel to leave and are known as push factors. There may be other factors which might repel to migrate. There may be other factors to which people may be indifferent.

Intervening obstacles may prevent migration from taking place or may reduce the number of people moving away. The intervening obstacles or factors may be negative or positive as well as neutral. These can be religion, services, political factors, misinformation, government policies, travel cost, immediate job opportunity and language, among others. Lee found that in the place of origin as well as destination, intervening obstacles, life cycle, social as well as personal characteristics of individuals are the main factors leading to migration or spatial mobility. Migration takes place on the comparative strengths of positive/plus and negative/minus factors at the origin and destination. It is represented schematically in Figure 9.1. Comparative strengths of the plus and minus factors may influence the decision to migrate.

The plus and minus may be too simplistic to cause migration because sometimes intervening factors may be such that they will dissuade the people/individuals to migrate. Push and pull factors are also crucial in the case of migration. Push factors are impelling or compelling factors which may be poor economic condition, lack of economic and other opportunities or, in other words, search for livelihood or better opportunities. Pull factors usually refer to those factors which encourage migration to a particular area such as the presence of economic opportunities, facilities and safety.

The UN data shows that in mid-2019, North America had presence of estimated 58.6 million migrants; Europe, 82.3 million migrants; Asia, 83.6 million; Latin America and the

Figure 9.1 Lee's Model of Migration

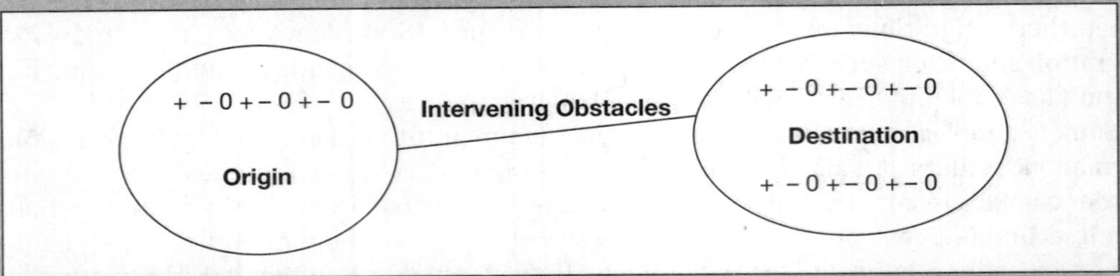

Source: Lee (1966).

Caribbean, 11.6 million; Africa, 26.5 million; and Oceania; around 8.9 million migrants. Estimated total number of international migrants is about 272 million (mid-2019). When compared to the figures of previous years, it can be seen that there is an upward surge. In 2015, it was 248 million, in 2010, it was 220 million, 191 million in 2005 and in 2000, the figure stood at 173 million. These figures are provided by the United Nations Department for Economic and Social Affairs Report 2019.

Labour migration has been one of the largest migrations around the globe. It is obvious that economic motivations are behind such movements. Either economic hardships or lucrative economic destination, both might cause migration of labour force. The push and pull factors work behind labour migration like migration of unskilled labour of the developing countries to the oil-rich Middle East countries. Wage difference is a pull factor and absence of it may be the push factor.

The available estimates from International Organization for Migration and UNHCR Migration (2020) indicate that there were roughly 164 million migrant workers around the world in 2017. This accounted for nearly two-thirds (64%) of the 258 million global stock of international migrants of that time. In 2017, 68 per cent of migrant workers were residing in high-income-level countries which were around estimated 111 million people. A total of 47 million migrant workers (29%) were living in middle-income countries. And 5.6 million (3.4%) were in low-income countries. Male migrant workers outnumbered female migrant workers. Male migrant worker figures were 28 million in 2017, with 96 million males (58%) compared to 68 million females (42%).

Forced migration causing displacement can assume the forms of refugees, asylum seekers, stateless people and even internally displaced persons. There is an element of compulsion or force to leave one's place of residence. Displacements can be caused by disasters or it may be conflict induced. When such forced migration results in crossing the international boundary or a territory of a state, then such migrants can be classified as refugees and when borders are not crossed, that category of migrants is classified as internally displaced persons (IDPs).

The 1951 Refugee Convention relating to the Status of Refugees defines a refugee as a person who

> as a result of events occurring before 1 January, 1951 and owing to well-founded fear of being persecuted for reasons of race, religion, nationality, membership of a particular social group of political opinion, is outside the country of his nationality and is unable or, owing to such fear, is

> unwilling to avail himself of the protection of that country; or who, not having a nationality and being outside the country of his former habitual residence as a result of such events, is unable or owing to such fear, is unwilling to return to it.

Those who have committed crimes against peace, war crimes, crimes against humanity or serious non-political crimes abroad are exempted from the category of refugees.

A timeline and a geographic location are present along with causes of moving out of one's country as this was in the heyday of the Cold War and people were fleeing East Europe out of fear of Communism. Thus, political opinion was added as one of the causes for granting refugee status. Later, the Protocol Relating to the Status of Refugees of 31 January 1967 removed the timeline of 1 January 1951. It also stated that the present Protocol should apply without any geographic limitation as the 1951 Convention by 'events occurring before 1 January, 1951' referred to events occurring in Europe and elsewhere.

However, persons may not be accorded refugee status but might be seeking asylum from another country or from the UNHCR will fall in the category of asylum seekers. Once they have been given refugee status, they will be recognized as refugees and avail the rights emanating from the refugee status. The UN reports show that there were estimated 3.5 million people seeking international protection and those who are commonly referred to as asylum seekers were awaiting determination of their refugee status by the end of 2018.

Let us now consider some refugee situations in the world. Syria caught in the civil war since the Arab Spring of 2011 has displaced, according to the UN data, 12 million people. As of October 2020, there were about 2.6 million Syrian children living as refugees and about 2.5 million children living as internally displaced people. Another major migrant-generating country due to political instability and hardships is Venezuela. To date, about 4.6 million Venezuelans have left the country as a result of an unprecedented humanitarian crisis. The UNHCR recognizes 143,665 as refugees and over 800,000 as asylum seekers. Afghanistan suffering from a two-decade long conflict, economic hardship and climate-related challenges has generated refugees of more than 2.7 million people who have fled to other countries, mostly to Iran, Pakistan and countries in Europe. Another refugee-generating country is South Sudan. It was born in 2011. From 2013, a conflict broke out, engulfing South Sudan into a condition of violence, economic crisis, hunger and disease. Millions of South Sudanese have fled their homes and have created the largest refugee crisis in Africa. Of the estimated 2.3 million South Sudanese refugees, over 80 per cent are women and children.

The largest refugee problem in the Southeast Asia is that of the Rohingya refugees. The Rohingya people belong to an ethnic minority group in Myanmar. It was from the 1990s that they have been facing discrimination and violence, forcing many to flee Myanmar. The government considers them illegal immigrants from Bangladesh. In August 2017, more than 720,000 Rohingya refugees fled due to the escalation of violence in Myanmar's Rakhine state. A vast majority of the Rohingyas settled in refugee camps in Cox's Bazar, Bangladesh. The majority of the Rohingya refugees are women and children and an estimated 40 per cent are children under 12 years of age. In 2018, even though an agreement was reached for the Rohingyas to return home but the Rohingyas did not return without the guarantee of safety and citizenship. Most recently, in December 2020, the Bangladeshi government started relocating groups of Rohingya refugees to settlements on an island in the Bay of Bengal. It is hoped that this would offer the families better quality of life and security as they await repatriation to Myanmar.

Some other examples of refugee-generating countries are Democratic Republic of Congo (estimated refugees, 918,000, and number of internally displaced people, 5.01 million). Somalia has a long history of refugee crisis emanating from political crisis and instability of a failed state. The number of refugees is around 750,000 living in neighbouring countries of Kenya, Yemen and Ethiopia. The number of IDPs is estimated to be 2.6 million. Central African Republic has generated 623,400 refugees and 684,004 IDPs. Burundi which has almost become a forgotten crisis started with the presidential election of 2015 and has generated 312, 615 refugees and 104,191 IDPs. Matters have been made worse with conflict, economic hardship, food insecurity and disease. Iraq experiencing an escalated violence in 2014 in its northern part with attacks launched by the Islamic State (ISIL) gave rise to a conflict. This conflict forced millions of families to flee their homes and seek refuge elsewhere. The number of Iraqi refugees is estimated to be 260,000 and number of IDPs is estimated to be 1.3 million. Since 2015, as conflict erupted in Yemen, 200,000 people have fled the country and 3.6 million have become internally displaced. More than 24 million are people in need. Yemen is facing the worst humanitarian crisis in the world today while it also hosts more than 200,000 refugees from neighbouring Somalia and Ethiopia.

Now if we look at the case of IDPs, there were no criteria for classifying group/s of people as internally displaced. It was only in 1993 that the Commission on Human rights requested Mr Francis M. Deng of the Brookings Institution to prepare the guiding principles regarding the international standards of IDPs. According to the Guiding Principles on Internal Displacement, E/CN.4/1998/53/Add.2, internally displaced persons are

> persons or groups of persons who have been forced or obliged to flee or to leave their homes or places of habitual residence, in particular as a result of or in order to avoid the effects of armed conflict, situations of generalized violence, violations of human rights or natural or human-made disasters, and who have not crossed an internationally recognized State border.

Disaster-induced migration was clearly stated by the UN Office for Risk Reduction in 2009 as the displacement of people as a result of

> a serious disruption of the functioning of a community or a society involving widespread human, material, economic or environmental losses or impacts, which exceeds the ability of the affected community or society involving widespread human, material, economic or environmental losses or impacts, which exceeds the ability of the affected community or society to cope using its own resources.

Deng found the doctrine of sovereignty as the most suitable conceptual framework for dealing with internal displacement. Sometimes called the Brookings doctrine, it highlights that states have primary responsibility for the security and well-being of their populations. If they are unable to provide protection and life-supporting assistance, they are expected to request and accept outside offers of aid.

From the gravest world refugee crisis, as shown above, we have also got the UN estimates of IDPs. In the past years, as also in the present, the African continent has generated refugees as well as IDPs due to humanitarian crisis, civil war, as in the 1990s, the Hutu Tutsi rivalry in Burundi along ethnic lines. Roberta Cohen and Francis M. Deng in *Masses in Flight: The Global Challenge of Internal Displacement* pointed out how conflict and displacement in African countries can create IDPs with the potential to result in refugee outflow. They give the example of the Great Lakes region of Africa which can also call for military invasions of other countries. Similarly, they gave examples of the Horn of Africa and West Africa where conflict and internal displacement can quickly spill over borders and help destabilize neighbouring countries.

According to The Water Project (n.d.), in November 2010, thousands of people were internally displaced from villages in Central Somalia due to conflict between two sub-clans fighting over the right to control the area's grazing pasture and water. Many of the people who were displaced were nomads who were forced to flee their water sources and have landed in areas where there are no water points. These people have to travel to find a new supply of water and to make new homes for themselves in order to survive.

In 2008, when drought occurred in Yemen, thousands were displaced. The main areas that were affected were the mountainous regions. Almost waiting for a year for water, these people had to abandon their homes and move to the main cities (The New Humanitarian). The drought disabled the farmers to irrigate their crops and they were forced to move from their homes to find new means of life and livelihood.

According to the UNHCR reports, around 70.8 million people forcibly displaced as a result of persecution, conflict, generalized violence or human rights violations. Among them, 58 per cent or 41.3 million were IDPs. The remaining 42 per cent comprised 25.9 million refugees and 3.5 million asylum seekers. The highest number of displaced people was recorded in the Syrian Arab Republic, which was around 6.1 million. Next was Colombia with 5.8 million displaced people and the Democratic Republic of the Congo with 3.1 million displaced people. The number of stateless persons globally in 2018 was 3.9 million. Bangladesh had the largest number of stateless persons (around 906,000). Côte d'Ivoire with 692,000 stateless people and Myanmar with 620,000 stateless people came next in line.

Whatever may be the reason of migration or displacement, if they are forced, then there is an element of vulnerability regarding the migrants or displaced. Children, young migrants, trafficked persons and women, especially, might face abuse, exploitation and discrimination. Women and girls face double risk—as women and as migrant also. What is overlooked is the forced displacement of persons belonging to LGBT community who might face gender-based violence and, therefore, become vulnerable during migration as well as after reaching the country of destination. Anti-immigration laws are also on the rise. The boat people from Syria, Iraq, Somalia and other countries in European countries face tough screening and stiff immigration laws. There are also suspicions around these people because of their religion. *Islamophobia* is now on rise in Europe as well as in the USA and other countries since 9/11 terror attacks as well as terror attacks in European countries such as the UK and Paris. There is also the fear of demographic character change as the immigrants bring in different ethnic, racial and religious identities with them. Therefore, 'the other' label is stuck on the refugees, asylum seekers or migrant population.

Therefore, migration is a process involving temporary or permanent movement of people producing changes in both the areas of origin and destination. The socio-economic, demographic, age–sex structure and political and cultural fabric of the country of origin and destination changes depending upon the rate and volume of migration. Even the ethnic, racial and cultural composition of the population may change through the continued in-migration and out-migration of people with different culture, ethnic traits and lifestyle. Migration is an ongoing process. The fact of the matter is whether it is forcible or voluntary and how the states react to the population/individuals migrating.

However, the SDGs, Agenda 2030, identified migration as a part of sustainable development. 10 out of 17 goals contain targets and indicators that are relevant to migration or mobility. 'Leave no one behind' is the core principle of the SDGs which addresses migrants. This also requires data disaggregation by migratory status in order to improve migration data compilation.

Environment, Sustainability and SDGs

The buzzword in the current times is environment. However, in the discursive of development, environment has been the last and the least important issue to be included. Only for around 70 years or so, environmental concerns have come to the fore. Still, it is much debated and much politicking goes around it, be it at the national level or at the international level. Environment involves not only the nature, oceans, hills, mountains, biodiversity but also lives dependent on them, be it humans or animals. Environment is a broad concept and it is not easy to define or demarcate it. Added to this is the huge natural resources present in the nature and harnessing these natural resources is at the centre for all environmental problems. Exploiting the environment and reshaping the environment having consequential effect in the form of environmental degradation, erosion, depletion of resources, pollution, contamination and the like have currently captured the thinking of academia as well as world leaders. Therefore, sustainable development and inclusive development are becoming more pervasive rather than development in strictly economic sense.

Development in economic sense means improvement or progress according to economic criteria such as GDP, GNP and per capita income. Nowhere one finds the mention of environmental factors. Like labour, environment is seen as an input in the production process. There is no calculation of natural green stock capital. Therefore, no clear picture of the amount of natural resources left. There may be high rate of development but the level of environmental degradation can be high also. Such a situation definitely will put our future generations at peril.

It is quite noteworthy that the Supreme Court of India has broadened the scope of Article 21. Article 21 which pertains to right to life and liberty was interpreted to include the right to wholesome environment. In the *Rural Litigation and Entitlement Kendra* case (1983), the Supreme Court of India upheld that any disturbance in the natural process was bound to affect human life and society. In *Subhash Kumar vs. State of Bihar* case, the Court held that the right to life includes unpolluted air and water. It further held that if anything endangers or impairs the quality of life in derogation of law, a citizen has a right to move the Supreme Court under Article 32 of the Constitution. In various PIL petitions, the Supreme Court has given judgments which have become cardinal principles of environmental protection in India. Green Benches in Madhya Pradesh, Kolkata, Punjab and Haryana have been constituted to hear environment-related petitions.

Development is considered to be brought about by building much-needed infrastructure, setting up of industrial production units, constructing dams and even nuclear installations. Development is also seen as increasing the income of the people, creation of employment opportunities and reduction of economic inequalities. Development to be inclusive has to look into social and human inputs other than the above. The GDP growth rate of a country can be high but the human development growth rate can be quite low. The UNDP in 1990 developed the HDI to measure the social factors of development. The criteria chosen were life expectancy, knowledge and decent standard of living. Even in the Millennium Development Goals, the targets included eradication of poverty and hunger, reduction of child mortality, achieving universal primary education and, most importantly, ensuring environmental sustainability.

Sustaining the natural resources through usage in such a way that the future generations are not deprived from their benefits should be the objective of the present generation. Not only must this but the interests of the stakeholders also be made compatible to sustain development and making development sustainable. The question is how to do this. Only in 1972, environment came into the thoughts of world leaders when they realized the pitfalls of high population growth, too much of exploitation of the Earth, extraction of non-renewable natural resources, industrialization, urbanization, usage of chemicals and fertilizers in agriculture and effects of technological progress in the form of depletion of resources, pollution, contamination, greenhouse effect, climate change and global warming. The 'Club of Rome' in 1972 first underscored the importance of environmental issues vis-à-vis development. The United Nations Conference on the Human Environment or the Stockholm Conference (5–16 June 1972) highlighted the critical issues of resource depletion and ecological crisis. Report of the Bruntland Commission, *Our Common Future* (1987), highlighted the essence of sustainable development that meets the needs of the present without compromising the ability of future generations to meet their own needs. However, the United Nations Conference on Environment and Development or the Rio Summit, also known as the Earth Summit, underpinned the principles of sustainable development.

The **Agenda 21: Green Paths to the Future** or the **Rio Declaration** contain 27 guiding principles which are not only lofty ideals to work towards achievement but also a set of instructions for states to bring about sustainable development. Article 1 presses on the importance of human beings as at the centre for sustainable development. States have sovereign rights over exploitation of their resources but not at the expense of the environment of other states (Article 2). Eradicating poverty was stressed upon as a necessity to reduce disparities in standards of living as central to bring in sustainable development (Article 5). The states were urged to cooperate in a spirit of global partnership to conserve and protect Earth's ecosystem (Article 7). Developing endogenous capacity building through scientific rigour for attaining sustainable development was to be encouraged by states (Article 9). Developing requisite national legislation was stressed upon to address matters of liability and compensation for victims of environmental damage (Article 13). Role of women was also upheld in environmental management and development (Article 20). The Guiding Principles also acknowledge the role of indigenous people and their communities in environmental management and development on the basis of their knowledge and traditional practices (Article 22). Article 25 emphasizes peace, development and environmental protection as interdependent and indivisible. All environment-related disputes should be resolved peacefully in accordance with the Charter of the United Nations (Article 26). Article 27 re-emphasized the cooperation among states in good faith and in a spirit of partnership in order to fulfil the guiding principles as enumerated in the Declaration. Further, the states should take a pledge to develop international law for the implementation of sustainable development (Article 27).

However, there have been decades of non-action except for the United Nations Framework Convention on Climate Change (1992 onwards) or signing of the Kyoto Protocol (1997). After 20 years, there was the Rio+20 United Nations Conference on Sustainable Development (13–22 June 2012). This conference envisioned a green economy towards building sustainable development. The most important concept that was highlighted was the inclusion of stakeholders who will be involved or affected by the development projects. The conference document was titled, 'The Future We Want by, for and with All Stakeholders Redefining the Multi-stakeholder Partnership Contract'. Stakeholders were for the first time given a focus. There are primary stakeholders and secondary stakeholders. Primary stakeholders include those who carry out the development projects, such as the investors, employees, customers, clients and suppliers. Secondary stakeholders are the most crucial ones. They are those which might be affected or they may affect the development projects, such as the local communities, indigenous groups, social activist groups and local governments.

Ultimately, there was no breakthrough. Sustainable development seemed to be an unattainable goal. In 2015, the 2030 Agenda for Sustainable Development (SDGs) was adopted which aims at attaining sustainable development by the year 2030. Heads of states and governments adopted the **Transforming Our World: The 2030 Agenda for Sustainable Development** on 25 September 2015 at the UN Summit on Sustainable Development. Four years down the line, there was no progress towards attaining Agenda 2030. So in 2019, the international community gave a call for a decade of action to achieve the goals. There are 17 SDGs and 169 targets.

The **SDGs** include:

- Eliminate poverty
- Erase hunger
- Establish good health and well-being
- Provide quality education
- Enforce gender equality
- Improve clean water and sanitation
- Grow affordable and clean energy
- Create decent work and economic growth
- Increase industry, innovation and infrastructure
- Reduce inequality
- Mobilize sustainable cities and communities
- Influence responsible consumption and production
- Organize climate action
- Develop life below water
- Advance life on land
- Guarantee peace, justice and strong institutions
- Build partnerships for the goals

If these goals are realized, then the world can move towards a greener Earth and social equity. That it is a hard target to achieve has become evident from the Climate Change Conference only. The Paris Climate Change Agreement 2015 pledged to keep the average global temperature rise below 2 degrees Celsius. However, the USA has pulled out of the Paris Agreement in 2017. There has been bitterness over the global warming issue of reducing it to 1.5 degree Celsius and also regarding climate finance. The stumbling blocks are the USA and China. Therefore, the question before the current generation is that can a green economy be built to secure our future generations. It surely has to bank upon technologies which lessen environmental risks and ecological imbalances. The SDGs can be the guiding principles in that direction.

Conclusion

Globalization has brought many changes but has also created crisis in the traditional forms of political, economic and social processes. It can be good. It can also be bad. If we look at IT revolution, it has made the mode of communication speedier and seamless. It has, therefore, facilitated faster economic activities and business processes. On the other hand, the virtual world challenges the digital sovereignty of a state. Globalization has also raised awareness about gender-related issues and problems. Therefore, the talk about gender disparity is on the rise. It is of concern obviously whether globalization has hit the gender hard and created impoverishment among women more than men. It has been discussed in this chapter also. How racial and ethnic factors still remain a divisive force and can be reinforced by the development dilemmas of globalization is at the core of concern of IPE as well as international relations. The development dilemmas, particularly unequal development, economic depravations and mega development projects, can cause migration and displacement. As in Venezuela, once a flourishing economy, now a country with acute economic crisis, from 2015, has caused influx of refugees into neighbouring countries such as Colombia, Peru, Ecuador, Chile, Argentina and Brazil. When one looks at the 'Narmada Bachao Movement' or 'Chipko Andolan' in India, one is reminded of the fact that environment is a reality and a part of our 'self'. Environment needs to be protected. Globally, initiatives have been taken. SDGs is one such initiative. However, action backed by political goodwill is needed to turn ideals into reality. What is needed is balanced and inclusive development by adjusting the challenges posed by economic forces set rolling by globalization.

Summary

Revolution in the realm of IT has made the world a small space. Cybercrimes and cyber terrorism threaten the **sovereignty** of a state. Certain common types of cybercrimes are hacking, virus attack, web jacking, mail bombing, theft of internet hours, identity theft, cyber stalking and credit/debit card fraud to mention a few. In the case of cyber terrorism, the national security which is most often the target now has to combat both physical terrorist assault in the 'real' world and terrorist attacks in the 'virtual' world, sometimes leading to a complete system collapse. Further, weapons of mass destruction also have circumscribed the sovereignty of states.

Gender inequality cuts across both vertical inequalities and other horizontal inequalities including race and caste and add to 'extreme poverty'. Its intersection with these other forms of inequality means that it is women and girls from the poorest caste, and ethnic and racial groups who have poorer levels of health, nutrition and education, and very often, they suffer higher levels of violence than other women, including women from similarly poor backgrounds. GDI, GEM and GII are measures to calculate gender inequality.

Earlier, during the days of European colonialism, **race** became a tool for differentiation between the colonizers and the colonized as well as the civilized and the barbaric ones. It was kind of a construct which testified the standard of civilizations. More recently, it has been ethnicity more than race that has been a concern for differentiation, conflict and displacement. **Ethnic** differences have resurfaced in the post-Cold War era as those divisive factors lay hidden in the wider spectrum of the Cold War between the USA and the USSR. Globalization acting along the neoliberal ideology of capital accumulation and wealth creation often results in imbalanced economic growth. Such situations perpetuate inequality, create poverty, arouse sense of depravation and thereby fan the ethnic differences which might take a toll on a country's law and order and even its security situations.

Migration and **displacement** both involve movement of people. There can be voluntary or forced migration. Voluntary migration can be in search of jobs, education and so on. Refugee movements are examples of forced migration and displacement across borders. Displacement can be internal also, commonly identified with environmental degradation, development projects and even natural disasters.

Sustaining the natural resources through usage in such a way that the future generations are not deprived from their benefits should be the objective of the present generation. Not only must this but the interests of the stakeholders should also be made compatible to sustain development and make development sustainable. **Sustainable development** is exploitation of their resources but not at the expense of the environment of other states. **Transforming Our World: The 2030 Agenda for Sustainable Development** was adopted on 25 September 2015 at the UN Summit on Sustainable Development. It includes 17 SDGs and 169 targets.

REVIEW AND REFLECTION QUESTIONS

1. Sovereignty of states has now been circumscribed by revolution in IT. Examine the impact of IT revolution and the limits of sovereignty.
2. Gender becomes an issue in development. How does gender inequality pervade development?
3. Discuss the various measures of gender inequality—GDI, GII and GEM.
4. How does forced migration cause refugee problems across the world? Give examples to explain your view on this perspective of migration.
5. IDPs have no international regime to protect them. Examine how Francis Deng brought out certain guidelines for the protection of IDPs.
6. Examine racial and ethnic factors and development problems.
7. Sustainable development is the truest way to inclusive development. Examine the concept of sustainable development. In this connection, briefly discuss the SDGs.

Bibliography

Bala, Krishnamoorthy. 2018. *Environmental Management: Text and Cases*. Delhi: PHI Learning.

Baylis, John, Steve Smith, and Patricia Owens. 2017. *An Introduction of World Politics: An Introduction to International Relations*. Oxford: Oxford University Press.

Brookings. 1999. 'New Challenges for Refugee Policy: Internally Displaced Persons.' Available at https://www.brookings.edu/on-the-record/new-challenges-for-refugee-policy-internally-displaced-persons/ (accessed on 11 October 2021).

Cavusgil, S. T., Gary Knight, and John R. Riesenberger. 2018. *International Business: The New Realities*. New Delhi: Pearson.

Cherunilam, Francis. 2011. *International Economics*. New Delhi: Tata McGraw Hill Education Private Limited.

Chirico, JoAnn. 2014. *Globalization: Prospects and Problems*. Thousand Oaks, CA: SAGE Publications.

Colum, Lynch. 2011. 'UN: Sri Lanka's Crushing of Tigers May Have Killed 40,000 Civilians.' *The Washington Post*. Available at https://www.washingtonpost.com/world/un-sri-lankas-crushing-of-tamil-tigers-may-have-killed-40000-civilians/2011/04/21/AFU14hJE_story.html (accessed on 15 March 2020).

Dahl, Robert A. 1961. *Who Governs? Democracy and Power in an American City*. New Haven, CT: Yale University Press.

Gayle, Rubin. 1974. 'The Traffic in Women: Notes on the Political Economy of Sex.' In *Towards an Anthropology of Women*, edited by Rayna R. Reiter. Boston, MA: Beacon Press.

Giddens, Anthony. 2008. *Sociology*. 5th ed. New Delhi: Wiley India Pvt. Ltd.

ILO. 2018. 'New ILO Figures Sho 164 Million People Are Migrant Workers.' Available at https://www.ilo.org/global/about-the-ilo/newsroom/news/WCMS_652106/lang--en/index.htm (accessed on 15 March 2020).

IOM and UNHCR Migration. 2020. *World Migration Report: 2020*. Geneva: IOM.

Kabeer, Naila. 1994. *Reversed Realities: Gender Hierarchies in Development Thought*. London: Verso Publications.

———. 2010. *Can the MDGs Provide a Pathway to Social Justice? The Challenge of Intersecting Inequalities*. Brighton: IDS/UN MDG Achievement Fund.

Lee, Everett S. 1966. 'A Theory of Migration'. Demography 3, no. 1 (1966): 47–57. https://doi.org/10.2307/2060063.

Marx, Karl. 1867. *Das Kapital*. Available at https://www.marxists.org/archive/marx/works/1867-c1/ (accessed on 20 March 2017).

Mark, Beeson, and Nick Bisley. 2010. *Issues in 21st Century World Politics*. New York, NY: Palgrave Macmillan.

Mukherjee, Aparajita, and Saumya Chakrabarti. 2016. *Development Economics: A Critical Perspective*. PHI Learning Pvt. Ltd.

Murthy, R. K., and Lakshmi Sankaran. 2003. *Denial and Distress: Gender, Poverty and Human Rights in Asia*. London: Zed Books.

UNDP. 2010. *The Human Development Report*. New York, NY: United Nations.

———. 2011. *The Human Development Report*. New York, NY: United Nations.

———. 2012. *The Human Development Report*. New York, NY: United Nations.

———. 2013. *The Human Development Report*. New York, NY: United Nations.

———. 2014. *The Human Development Report*. New York, NY: United Nations.

———. 2015. *The Human Development Report*. New York, NY: United Nations.

———. 2016. *The Human Development Report*. New York, NY: United Nations.

———. 2017. *The Human Development Report*. New York, NY: United Nations.

———. 2018. *The Human Development Report*. New York, NY: United Nations.

———. 2019. *The Human Development Report*. New York, NY: United Nations.

Weimann, Gabriel. 2004. 'Cyberterrorism, How Real Is the Threat?' United States Institute of Peace, Special Report. Available at https://www.usip.org/sites/default/files/sr119.pdf (accessed on 11 October 2021).

World Economic Forum. 2012. *Global Gender Gap Report*. Geneva: World Economic Forum.

———. 2013. *Global Gender Gap Report*. Geneva: World Economic Forum. Available at http://www3.weforum.org/docs/WEF_GenderGap_Report_2013.pdf (accessed on 11 October 2021).

———. 2014. *Global Gender Gap Report*. Geneva: World Economic Forum. Available at http://reports.weforum.org/global-gender-gap-report-2014/press-releases/ (accessed on 11 October 2021).

———. 2015. *Global Gender Gap Report*. Geneva: World Economic Forum. Available at http://reports.weforum.org/global-gender-gap-report-2015/economies/#economy=IND (accessed on 11 October 2021).

———. 2016. *Global Gender Gap Report*. Geneva: World Economic Forum. Available at http://reports.weforum.org/global-gender-gap-report-2016/rankings/ (accessed on 11 October 2021).

———. 2017. *Global Gender Gap Report*. Geneva: World Economic Forum.

———. 2018. *Global Gender Gap Report*. Geneva: World Economic Forum.

———. 2019. *Global Gender Gap Report*. Geneva: World Economic Forum.

———. 2020. *Global Gender Gap Report*. Geneva: World Economic Forum. Available at http://www3.weforum.org/docs/WEF_GGGR_2020.pdf (accessed on 11 October 2021).

The Water Project. (n.d.). 'Water Scarcity and Internally Displaced Person.' Available at https://thewaterproject.org/water-scarcity/water-scarcity-internally-displaced-persons (accessed on 11 October 2021).

10 Regional Economic Formations

LEARNING OBJECTIVES

- Knowing about the concepts of a region and regionalism
- Learning about the processes of regional economic integration through various trading arrangements
- Knowing specifically about ASEAN
- Familiarizing with SAARC and SAFTA
- Knowing about APEC
- Learning about NAFTA
- Knowing about the latest economic formation—the BRICS

Introduction

Regional organizations are now a phenomenon in IPE. They are nothing new. Earlier, some security organizations like NATO (4 April 1949) and Warsaw (14 May 1955, later dissolved in 1991) were formed during the Cold War. Both corresponded to the requirements of the two superpowers engaged in the Cold War. They had their strategic calculations behind such security pacts and that was to balance off each other and hold onto their spheres of influence by the show or use of military might. Council for Mutual Economic Assistance or COMECON was formed in 1949 (dissolved in 1991) to provide aid to Eastern European countries belonging to the Soviet Bloc to counter the expansion of the US influence. Apart from these, there are at present the Shanghai Cooperation Organisation which was formed as a security organization to counterbalance the US expansion in the Central Asian region using NATO.

However, apart from the above strategic and security organizations, there are also other kinds of regional formations which have economic interests as prime motivating factors. The EU, NAFTA, ASEAN, SAARC, Asia-Pacific Economic Cooperation (APEC) and, more recently, BRICS are current regional economic formations or extra-regional emerging economic groupings. Preservation of economic interests, bargaining at international economic forums, cooperating among themselves and deepening of economic relations become primary objectives of such regional economic formations. Other than these mentioned here, the example of somewhat successful regional integration is the EU. The EU is not only an economic powerhouse but also a political federation. BREXIT or the UK's exit from the EU has put the organization into a difficult situation but it is still working sans Britain. The advent of coronavirus has taken its toll on the international market. Recession has set in globally. It is to be seen how these blocs/organizations perform or protect themselves from a slump in the market. This chapter will deal with some of the regional formations to give an idea of the growth of regionalism and regional economic formations.

These regional organizations are quite expansive in scope. They include regional issues as well as areas of cooperation in political, social, cultural, health, education, environment among a host of other issues. One thing which is important about the regional grouping is trade and tariff issues. The trade liberalization set by globalization with the universalizing agenda being prescribed by multilateral groupings and arrangements such as the IMF and the GATT/WTO has also made economic regional integration quite meaningful. Sometimes, to cushion the effects of the multilateral approach to global free trade, regional organizations have emerged to have regional trading arrangements and thereby increased volume of trade among the countries of the region. In this chapter, we will discuss the evolution of several regional organizations formed around the globe in several continents.

Regions and Regionalism

What constitutes a region and how does it lead to the growth of regionalism have always been topics of debate. There must be something which leads to the coming closer of some countries and forming regional formations. If what constitutes a region is considered theoretically, then several definitions can be found. Usually, by a region what is meant is that a few countries sharing a common geographical space by means of their proximity. Sometimes they may be contiguous and are placed so near to one another geographically that they constitute a region. These states might be further tied to one another by common interests. Sometimes ties among states transcend geographic limits and are just determined by common interests. It is then these common interests that strive these states to come together and form regional arrangements. So regional arrangements are either political or economic 'constructs'. They go beyond the division of continents. They may be said to be sub-divide of continents.

However, sometimes it has been seen that members not belonging to a particular region are incorporated into a regional formation and sometimes excluded. Examples can be APEC, where India is not included, whereas its membership includes Russia, Papua New Guinea and Peru. SAARC region was extended to include Afghanistan in the year 2007. ASEAN extended its region by including Vietnam, Myanmar, Laos and Cambodia to the original six founding members of this regional grouping. BRICS is such an economic arrangement which does not belong to one particular region and it is trans-continental. Nevertheless, it is an important emerging economic grouping.

This then brings us to the discussion of what are then the reasons behind regional formations. There can be a number of factors such as common interests; common problems; shared visions; economic, political and social interests; and security concerns. There can be interdependence and cooperation as driving factors for the regional cohesion. Integration can be also another factor for regional cooperation. There is difference between the two. When we talk about cooperation, this can live up to creation of certain arrangements mutually worked out among states on political, security, economic and commercial areas. These may include energy, health, transport, trade, foreign policy and cooperation at international fora. However, these are limited to normal obligations arising out of agreements and treaties under international law. When we talk about integration, it becomes quite a comprehensive process, especially if we are talking in terms of economic integration. It involves setting up of FTA, PTAs, custom unions and so on, addressing trade and tariff issues as well as movement of goods and services.

The theory of neo-functionalism propagated by Ernst Haas (*Beyond the Nation State: Functionalism and International Organization and the Uniting of Europe: Political, Social, and Economic Forces, 1950–1957,* 1964) has been a guide to understand regional organizations from the perspective of integration. Whereas functionalism, as its main proponent, David Mitrany (*A Working Peace System*, 1943), talked about, is a process of building international organizations on the basis of shared sovereignty. Neo-functionalism, on the other hand, emphasizes the possibilities of formation of regional arrangements. However, both emphasize on functions or functional sectors of cooperation by which sovereignty can be transferred to a supranational body. David Mitrany forwarded functionalism with the creation of functional organizations at international level. On the other hand, Haas who forwarded the theory of neo-functionalism based on his study of process of European integration was more eager towards voluntary creation of larger political units by creating a supranational organization among a group of states.

Regional integration may not always be the European type. There can be economic integration for establishing free trade area (FTA), CU, common market and economic and monetary union (EMU). This can happen the EU way where there are CU, EMU, common market and so on, as well as political integration in the form of the EU. There can also be just FTA, CU, common market and EMU without political integration.

Regional arrangements are regional groupings formed with countries occupying a particular region with particular objectives. When such regional arrangements are formed for economic cooperation, they can be classified as regional trading bloc or regional trade arrangement. These are formed to coordinate trade policies among the member countries vis-à-vis global trade practices. Regional economic cooperation can also arrive at PTA which aims to lower tariff and non-tariff barriers among member countries while they can keep them high for other countries outside the economic arrangement.

PTAs are based on arrangements of lower trade barrier among the states participating as trading partners. FTA is based on removal of all trade barriers among members while retaining the same by each state in their dealing with non-members. Examples include the European Free Trade Area, NAFTA, South Asian Free Trade Area (SAFTA) and ASEAN–India FTA. There are also CU under which the participating countries fulfil the requirements for FTA along with a common external tariff and non-tariff barriers on imports by member countries from countries outside CU. Some examples can be Caribbean Community and Common Market, the Gulf Cooperation Council and MERCOSUR. The EU CU had its origin in the European Customs Union in 1968 created by the six founding states, France, Germany, Italy, Belgium, the Netherlands and Luxembourg, to harmonize trade, customs duties on goods among European countries and trade with non-European countries. This was nothing but the foundation of what is now called the EU, which is actually a CU. The EU had also established an EMU on 1 January 1991 by adopting a common currency—the Euro. Earlier in 1957, the European Economic Community (EEC) also known as the European Common Market was established by France, West Germany, Italy, the Netherlands, Belgium and Luxembourg by signing a Treaty in

Rome to provide unrestricted movement of goods among them. This can be seen as the stepping stone towards the process of European integration which moved through several phases and treaties finally to take the shape of the EU by the signing of the Maastricht Treaty in 1992 that came into effect on 1 November 1993 and the EU was born. The EU could make quite a good progress to a great extent but got a jolt after BREXIT. The EU is a unique example of regional integration in all senses that it encompasses single currency, tariff and non-tariff issues, a common market and so on.

The gains from such regional arrangements can be manifold. It can lead to increase of trade among participating countries due to removal of trade barriers (FTA) or lowering of tariff and non-tariff barriers (PTA) and creation of trade from non-member countries to member countries. This is also known as, according to Jacob Viner (*The Customs Union Issue,* 1950), *trade creation* effect. FTA diverts trade from non-member countries to member countries also as tariffs are lowered so goods imported from non-member countries are now diverted to imports from member countries. This is known as Viner's *trade diversion* effect. According to Viner, trade creation can have welfare-improving effects, whereas trade diversion may reduce welfare for member countries. Besides these static gains and losses, there is always a probability of larger markets to increase the rate of product innovations and growth of member countries. CUs, on the other hand, may lead to gains from the market power in international trade which they confer upon their smaller member countries juxtaposed to its non-member countries. Regional arrangements also provide with other benefits like reciprocal market access by linking non-trade issues such as labour standards, TRIPS and environmental standards with trade gains.

If the EU is an example of economic integration, then ASEAN and SAARC are regional economic formations. NAFTA, SAFTA and so on are examples of economic cooperation with integration of FTA. For our discussion in this chapter, we will restrict ourselves to regional economic formations and focus on the EU, ASEAN, SAARC and SAFTA, APEC, NAFTA and BRICS.

European Union

The EU is an example of economic integration as well as political integration in stages. The origin of the EU is from functional cooperation and then its journey towards integration and finally BREXIT. The Organization for European Cooperation can be seen as a first step towards European integration with its primary objective of channelizing Marshall Plan[1] aid among the West European countries. The European Payments Union was established in 1950 by the Organization for European Economic Co-operation (OECC) to coordinate trade and economic transactions among the member countries. However, it came to an end in 1951.

The next step was Schuman Plan (1950) where the French foreign minister, Robert Schuman, proposed the formation of a community which would cooperate in two key sectors, that is, coal and steel, as an initial step towards building a federation of Europe. This culminated in the creation of European Coal and Steel Community (ECSC) in 1951 vide the Treaty

[1] The **Marshall Plan,** also known as the European Recovery Program, was a US programme providing **aid** to Western Europe following the devastation of the Second World War.

of Paris (1951). France, Italy, West Germany and the BENELUX countries signed the Treaty. ECSC created a common single coal and steel market without export and import duties.

The next big step came with the signing of the Treaty of Rome in 1957 by West Germany, France, Italy, Belgium, the Netherlands and Luxembourg which came into effect on 1 January 1958. This created the EEC. A common external tariff at the current average of all member states was fixed and gradually free trade of industrial goods within the EU and a common price for agricultural products.

In 1960, the European Free Trade Association (EFTA) was established as an intergovernmental organization comprising Iceland, Liechtenstein, Norway and Switzerland for the promotion of free trade and economic integration between its members. The EFTA Convention was signed on 4 January 1960 which was last amended on 1 July 2013. The objectives for EFTA were to promote a continued and balanced strengthening of trade and economic relations between the member states. This should be done keeping in mind the fair conditions of competition and the respect of equivalent rules, within the area of the association.

EFTA convention upheld other objectives as promotion of the free trade in goods, progressively liberalize free movement of persons, trade in services and investment, as well as provide fair conditions of competition affecting trade between the member states. EFTA also aimed at opening of the public procurement markets of the member states and provide appropriate protection of IPR in accordance with the international standards. EFTA provides the member states to negotiate free trade agreements with partners outside the EU. Currently, EFTA has 29 free trade agreements with 40 countries and territories outside the EU.

In 1968, the Customs Union was established. At the Lomé Convention in 1975, there was elimination of most trade barriers on imports from 46 developing countries of Africa, the Caribbean and the Pacific region that were former EU colonies. Every five years, this Treaty got renewed till 2000. Lomé IV expired and was replaced by a new agreement, the Cotonou Agreement (2000). This was replaced by the EU by the New Partnership Agreement in 2008. In 1979, the European Currency Unit (ECU) was formed which was replaced at parity in 1999 by the Euro.

In 1985, the Schengen Agreement created a seamless Europe with mostly open borders without passport controls between most member states. In 1986, the Treaty of Rome was amended and Single European Act (SEA) was signed which set 1 January 1993 as the date by which full internal market was to be established. The SEA removed the remaining barriers regarding flow of goods, services and resources among EU members. The EU was finally established by the Maastricht Treaty on 1 November 1993. Euro was named in 1995 in Madrid. The Euro was introduced to world financial markets as an accounting currency on 1 January 1999, replacing the former ECU.

The EU enlarged largely in 1973 to include Denmark, the UK, the Republic of Ireland and Norway. In the 1980s, Greece, Spain and Portugal joined the EU. In 1995, a further expansion of the EU took place with the joining of Austria, Sweden and Finland. In 2009, Slovakia joined the EU. A further expansion of EU eastwards took place to include countries of Eastern Europe. Malta, Cyprus, Slovenia, Estonia, Latvia, Lithuania, Poland, the Czech Republic and Hungary joined the EU and this constituted the largest expansion of the EU. Croatia joined in 2013.

The EU comprises the Commission of the European Communities, Council of European Union, European Parliament, Court of Justice of the European Communities, Courts of Auditors and European Economic and Social Committee.

Commission of European Communities is the executive wing of the EU. It is composed of one appointee/representative from each member state. Currently, there are 27 commissioners. The commissioners are nominated by the European Council and are confirmed by the European Parliament. It is led by a commission president. It is headquartered in Brussels, Belgium, and Luxembourg City, Luxembourg.

The Commission has the duty of daily running of the EU's business as well as setting up of proposals for new European legislation, and implementation of the decisions of the European Parliament and the Council of the EU. This body manages EU policies, enforces EU laws and allocates EU funding. Above all, the Commission represents the EU internationally.

Council of European Union is the main decision-making body of the EU. It consists of 47 countries which includes 27 members of the EU. It is composed of Secretary General and Deputy Secretary General elected by the Parliamentary Assembly for a five-year term separately. The Parliamentary Assembly consists of 324 members of Parliament from the 47 member states. The Committee of Ministers is the Council's decision-making body. It comprises the ministers of foreign affairs of each member state or their permanent diplomatic representatives in Strasbourg, the headquarter of the Council. The Committee of Ministers decides policies of Council of Europe and also approves its budget and programme of activities.

European Parliament is the only body which comprises directly elected members. The Members of the European Parliament (MEPs) are directly elected by voters in all member states. This body is entrusted with supervisory, legislative and budgetary responsibilities. Along with the Council, the European Parliament is an important legislative body of the EU. Under the Lisbon Treaty, the number of seats allocated to each state is according to population and the maximum number of members is set at 751. Since 1 February 2020, the number of members has reduced to 705 MEPs (including the President of the Parliament). With the BREXIT, there has been a reduction in size. The Parliament has its headquarter in Strasbourg, France, and has its administrative offices in Luxembourg City.

Court of Justice of the European Communities is the highest court of the EU. The principal function of this body is to foresee that the EU's law is uniformly interpreted and enforced effectively. It also has jurisdiction in disputes involving the member states, EU institutions, individuals and other matters well within its jurisdiction.

Courts of Auditors merely functions to provide audit report for each financial year to the Council and the Parliament.

European Economic and Social Committee is an advisory committee in matters of economic and social importance. It is composed of 344 members who are appointed by the Council for a term of four years.

The EU has other important bodies such as the European Central Bank, the European Investment Bank and the European Investment Fund.

Britain went for a referendum in 2016 for BREXIT. Approximately, 51.9 per cent voted for BREXIT and approximately 48.1 per cent voted against it. This was preceded by sovereign debt crisis in Greece and the Eurozone faced severe shocks emanating from sovereign debt crisis. Greece accounted for 3 per cent of Euro area's output. In reality, global assets of internationally active banks grew in 2007–2009 for not only European banks but banks in Eurozone too. Their asset sides grew through purchases of US credit-backed products as well as lending to other eurozone countries including purchases of government debt and lending to other consumption spending, housing investment and mortgage lending. The prime factor that worked was very low global interest rates that induced banks to take greater risks in search of profit. The banks' credit expansion was higher than the home countries' GDPs. With the elimination of exchange rate risk, government bond yields moved closer to equality. For example, spreads between the governments of most creditworthy like Germany (according to Moody's) and the least creditworthy like Greece became small. This led to spending and borrowing in countries such as Greece, Portugal and Spain. With higher inflation than Germany, the eurozone peripheral countries such as Ireland, Portugal, Spain, Italy and Greece saw their currencies appreciate in real terms relative to Germany as well as with their trading partners within and outside EMU.

With higher inflation rates than Germany but equal bond rates, the peripheral countries had lower real interest rates in mid-2000s that led to increase in spending and inflation. Whereas Germany had growing account surpluses, these peripheral countries had growing deficits. The 2007–2009 global economic crisis sent shocks in the eurozone as some banks had their exposure in US real estate markets. European housing markets began to fall just like in the USA. Ultimately, Greece's fiscal problems became apparent in late 2008. Greece's government under George Papandreou ultimately unveiled radical reforms to rescue Greece's public finances on 14 December 2009. The austerity plans were met with strikes over coming months.

Other Euro countries such as Germany, Finland and the Netherlands were not willing to underwrite the borrowing of countries like Greece. The critical state of each government's credit in turn weakened the solvency of domestic banks. Banks were heavily invested in government's bonds and when the price of bonds fell, bank assets and bank capital were reduced. There was a lack of trust of the banks' lenders that if government itself cannot obtain cash, then it might be unable to inject public capital into the banks. The prospects that some governments might default their debts hurt the banks and banks' weakness forced governments into expensive bailouts in a self-reinforcing doom loop. This resulted in soaring government borrowing rates and capital flight from fiscally stressed countries. The crisis was met by the European Central Bank becoming a lender of last resort of support to peripheral banks as money fled. There was also requirement of loans from other EU member countries. The IMF extended loans on conditions of fiscal austerity and structural reforms. Eurozone plunged into a deep crisis. This was followed by Britain's decision to exit from the EU and it was confirmed by the referendum of 2016.

BREXIT was a long process and could not be completed before four years. This was followed by a trade agreement between the UK and the EU that retains their tariff-free status. Former Prime Minister Theresa May negotiated the exit vide Article 50 of the EU in 2017 but could not get approval from the Parliament. The next prime minister, Boris Johnson, coming to power with a majority in 2019 could get Parliamentary approval for his exit deal. Royal assent was received on 23 January 2020 and with Queen's formal assent the bill turned into law. The UK formally left the EU on 31 January 2020 and entered into a transition process which ended on 31 December 2020. The EU–UK Trade and Cooperation Agreement was agreed on 24 December 2020 and was signed on 30 December 2020. From 1 January 2021, Britain ceased to be a member of the EU and exit was sealed. The Trade and Cooperation Agreement also comes to effect from this date and underlies three main pillars of trade, cooperation and governance but not defence and foreign policy.

The agreement between Prime Minister Boris Johnson and Irish Premier Leo Varadkar could remove the stumbling block in the exit deal regarding the sensitive land border issue between Ireland and Northern Ireland. Prime Minister May could not resolve it finally Boris Johnson could do it. The two agreed to shift the border checks to between Northern Ireland and the rest of the UK and BREXIT could be worked out. Under the BREXIT withdrawal agreement, that day could be delayed until 2022 or 2023, but Johnson has ruled out any extension of the transition period. It is to be seen how much BREXIT affects the EU, Britain, Ireland and Scotland.

Association of the Southeast Asian Nations

Southeast Asia location wise is at the southernmost tip of South Asia, south of China and north-west of Australia. It is encircled by Bay of Bengal, the Indian Ocean in the south, the South China Sea, the Philippine Sea and the Pacific Ocean in the east. It is also home to diverse geography, society, culture, religion, political systems and demography. However, this region comprises economies that have quite impressive performances over the time.

Five countries initially came together on 8 August 1967 in Bangkok, namely Indonesia, Malaysia, Singapore, Thailand and Philippines, and formed ASEAN. It was a move towards regional integration. Later, Brunei joined in 1984, Vietnam in 1995, Laos and Myanmar in 1997, and Cambodia in 1999. The membership, therefore, rose to 10 from 5. In 2019, the total population of all ASEAN states amounted to an estimated 655.51 million inhabitants. The current population of **South-eastern Asia** is **674,063,633** as of Friday, 30 April 2021 (latest UN estimates). The population of Southeast Asia is **8.58 per cent** of the total world population. The total land area of this region is 4,340,700 sq. km (1,675,953 sq. miles).

The estimated total GDP of all ASEAN states amounted to approximately 3.11 trillion US dollars in the year 2020. This is quite a significant rise from 2019. In fact, the GDP of the ASEAN region has been skyrocketing for a few years now, reflecting the region's growing economy. ASEAN was the fifth largest economy in the world with a GDP of around 3 trillion US dollars in 2018.

The dialogue partners are Australia, Canada, China, the EU, India, Japan, the Republic of Korea, New Zealand, Russia and the USA. ASEAN has enlarged the Treaty of Amity and Cooperation (TAC) by opening up of ASEAN's TAC to the dialogue partners in order to safeguard the peace and security of Southeast Asia.

China was the first dialogue partner to sign the TAC followed by India at the Bali Summit in 2003. ASEAN also extended TAC to the ASEAN Plus Three partners, Japan and the Republic of Korea, to sign the TAC in order to coordinate relations in East Asia. Japan became a party to TAC in 2004. ASEAN continues to pursue the signing of the Treaty of Southeast Asia Nuclear Weapon-Free Zone) with the five nuclear powers to ensure the peace and security of Southeast Asia. Russia became a party to the TAC in 2004. The USA signed the TAC in 2009. France signed the TAC in 2006. The UK signed the TAC in 2012. This is quite a significant step towards more than regional integration and economic cooperation. ASEAN is moving towards strategic partnerships for ensuring peace and security vis-à-vis China.

The objectives behind the formation of ASEAN have been an effort to promote economic, social and cultural development of the people of Southeast Asia. Further, as this region witnessed political instability from colonial domination and overwhelming Chinese presence, the members wanted to establish political stability through collective action to work as bulwark against the Cold War politics. ASEAN had its predecessor as Association of Southeast Asia in

1961 and Maphilindo in 1967. However, these initiatives could not materialize and finally ASEAN came into existence in 1967.

ASEAN is an intergovernmental organization oriented towards economic growth, political stability through active collaboration and mutual assistance fostered through educational and cultural integration of member countries. To foster the regional integration, the ASEAN members signed the TAC in Southeast Asia in 1976. This treaty enshrines the fundamental principles in the path of regional cooperation. Working towards economic cooperation, ensuring gaining greater market access for ASEAN exports and facilitating trade, tourism and investments to foster more regional integration are chief objectives of ASEAN countries.

The strengthening of economic cooperation has been achieved through the number of Comprehensive Economic Partnerships (CEPs) that ASEAN has entered into with its dialogue partners. China, India and Japan have concluded CEPs with ASEAN and are working towards FTAs for a long time. ASEAN–China Free Trade Area came into effect as of 1 January 2010. The ASEAN–India FTA final agreement was signed on 13 August 2009. This FTA came into effect on 1 January 2010. These will not only address trade in goods but also trade in services, investments and abolition of non-tariff barriers. ASEAN is also working on economic cooperation with the USA, the EU, Australia and New Zealand.

The other effort of the regional organization has been the ASEAN Community that constitutes the three main pillars of ASEAN Security Community, ASEAN Economic Community (AEC) and the ASEAN Socio Cultural Community. The AEC is to bring in more economic integration through the building blocks comprising ASEAN FTA, ASEAN Investment Area and the ASEAN Framework Agreement on Services. ASEAN has to gain advantage from the FTAs with its dialogue partners and strengthen the AEC. However, the ASEAN countries have to gain competitive edge for greater share of its exports from the ASEAN to the markets of its dialogue partners.

ASEAN is not only an economic bloc but it has, as pointed above, worked towards cooperation in the political and security area which has been expressed in the realization of the ASEAN Regional Forum in 1994, engaging the major players of the world and preserving peace and security and ASEAN countries' interest in the region. Other landmark achievements have been the ASEAN Plus Three process involving China, Japan and South Korea, Asia–Europe Meeting, ASEAN–Russia Summit and East Asia Summit, which have helped to build rings of security around ASEAN countries, bolstering peace, security and prosperity of the region.

More efforts will be required to facilitate investments into ASEAN and promote tourism as well as to dismantle non-tariff barriers. In 2014, the USA and the 10 ASEAN nations traded more than $250 billion in goods and services, representing about 8 per cent of all US trade and making ASEAN USA's fourth largest trading partner.

ASEAN's achievements are quite remarkable in all sectors—political, security and economic. Its achievements can be summarized as follows:

- ASEAN has adopted two conventions to counter transnational crime. They are the ASEAN Convention on Counter Terrorism in 2007 and the ASEAN Convention against Trafficking in Persons in 2015.
- The AEC has established a single and open market with many economic opportunities since 2015.

- ASEAN is working to integrate the association with the world economy and has developed free trade agreements with several partners including Australia, China, Japan, India, South Korea and New Zealand.
- The ASEAN Coordinating Centre for Humanitarian Assistance on Disaster Management is seeking to develop regional disaster risk management and climate change adaptation capabilities.

It is predicted that the rise in the ASEAN economy will continue to rise despite the outbreak of the pandemic named COVID-19. There was a contraction in real GDP in 2020 due to lockdown restrictions after the outbreak of the pandemic. The ASEAN countries are expected to experience a sharp V-shaped recovery in 2021. From mid-September 2020, most of the ASEAN countries started to see a declining trend of COVID-19 cases. The fatality rate declined to 2.7 per cent in Indonesia, followed by the Philippines (2.1%), Malaysia (0.4%), Thailand (0.3%) and Singapore (0%) as of February 2021.

Indonesia, Malaysia, the Philippines, Singapore, Thailand and Vietnam, which are the six largest ASEAN countries, are expected to have positive real GDP growth rates in 2021. With continued expansion of trade and gradual recovery in tourism sector and construction activities, Singapore's GDP growth is forecasted to increase to 5.8 per cent in 2021. Malaysia is set to witness a growth of 7.1 per cent in 2021 after experiencing a negative (–)5.2 per cent in 2020. Therefore, ASEAN will play an important role in regional economy quite significantly.

Asia-Pacific Economic Cooperation

APEC is the acronym for Asia-Pacific Economic Cooperation. Asia-Pacific is a huge area. It stretches from the Americas, almost the countries situated on the Eastern Pacific region, to Australia and also encompasses Asia including South, East and Southeast Asia and the Oceania and Pacific Islands. It is too difficult to exactly identify or define the Asia-Pacific region. Economic performance of the Asia-Pacific is quite impressive. In terms of GDP in 2019, China had the highest in the Asia-Pacific region. China had a turnover of 14.34 trillion US dollars, followed by Japan, India and South Korea. South Asia, Southeast Asia and Southwest Asia are home to the leading economies of the region with comparably higher GDP growth rates. Developed countries including Australia, New Zealand and Japan are also high-performing economies. The Corona pandemic undoubtedly has hit hard the economic performance of the countries of Asia-Pacific region.

APEC was formed in 1989 as a regional economic organization. APEC was established with the objectives to achieve economic prosperity and balanced, inclusive and sustainable growth in the region through economic integration of member countries. As an economic grouping, APEC members seek to ensure easy movement of goods and services as well as investment among the member countries. In the way ahead, APEC seeks to work out customs procedure through mutually agreed procedures.

APEC comprises 21 members. They are the USA, Australia, Brunei Darussalam, Canada, Chile, China, Hong Kong, Indonesia, Japan, Malaysia, Mexico, New Zealand, Papua New Guinea, Peru, the Philippines, Russia, Singapore, the Republic of Korea, Chinese Taipei, Thailand and Vietnam. However, it does not include all the states of this region as it does not include India or any other South Asian states.

In 1995, the APEC leaders adopted a declaration on specific objectives to be achieved by the grouping. At Blake Island, the ground vision of APEC community was established and at Bogor, APEC worked out its goals in order to coordinate and reap collective advantage. The members sought to establish free and open trade and investment in the Asia-Pacific by 2010 in the case of industrialized economies and 2020 in the case of developing economies. They further envisioned expanding trade and investment facilitation programmes, and intensifying development cooperation to attain sustainable growth, equitable development and national stability.

The future roadmap was adopted in the Osaka Action Agenda. It comprised three pillars of working out economic cooperation by evolving efforts of voluntary liberalization, collective actions to advance liberalization and contributing to global liberalization.

The 30th anniversary of APEC was celebrated in the Chile Summit in 2019. The theme of the Summit was **connecting people, building the future.** The 2019 Chile Summit worked out the priorities of APEC such as digital society, integration 4.0, women, small and medium-sized enterprises and inclusive growth, and sustainable growth. The other future agenda of APEC which it wanted to materialize was regarding marine debris and unregulated fishing aiming at maintaining the biodiversity and sustainable development in the Asia-Pacific. The Free Trade Area of the Asia Pacific is a framework for APEC members to build collective ability to enhance trade cooperation. For sustainable regional economic cooperation, the **People and Prosperity: An APEC Vision to 2040** was adopted. It has a long way to go to realize its full potential.

North American Free Trade Agreement

NAFTA is a free trade agreement among the three countries—the USA, Canada and Mexico. However, Mexico belongs to Latin America but as discussed above, regions can be made flexible as per economic interests involved. The three countries signed the NAFTA in September 1993 which came into effect on 1 January 1994. This is the largest FTA agreement in any part of the globe. Three US Presidents negotiated the trade agreement to finally make it a reality. President Ronald Reagan (1979) floated the idea of such trade negotiations for creation of a large North American market. The Congress passed the Trade and Tariff Act in 1984 which gave the president authority to negotiate free trade agreements, although it permits the Congress the power to approve or disapprove without changing the terms of negotiation. In 1992, President George H. W. Bush signed the NAFTA before the end of his term, finally to be ratified by the legislatures of the member countries. President Bill Clinton signed it in 1993. NAFTA came into effect on 1 January 1994. So it was a long journey ultimately, which took shape in 1994.

The USA already had a free trade agreement with Canada. It was the Canada–United States Free Trade Agreement (CUFTA) which was signed in 1989. The objective of the pact was elimination/removal of tariff and non-tariff trade barriers between Canada and the USA by 1998. The other highlights of the pact were guidelines for trade in services, reducing red tapism for accountants, lawyers, engineers and other professionals crossing borders. Some other restrictions pertaining to energy and investments were eliminated. Some of CUFTA's provisions were incorporated.

Thereafter, NAFTA came to place. This was an agreement signed by two developed countries with a developing country. However, NAFTA has been renegotiated in November 2018. It is now United States–Mexico–Canada Agreement (USMCA). It is subjected to ratification by the three countries. The US Senate passed the implementation Act in January 2020 and was signed by President Donald Trump. Canada is yet to ratify the USMCA.

The highlights of NAFTA had been the MFN status to the parties to the agreement. It also eliminates all sorts of tariffs on imports and exports among these three co-signatories. NAFTA upholds that the three countries should respect patents, trademarks and copyrights. NAFTA also had established procedures for resolving disputes. The NAFTA Secretariat plays an important role in resolving the disputes. The NAFTA Secretariat has three sections in three countries. The US Section in Washington DC, the Canadian Section in Ottawa and the Mexican Section in Mexico City.

The principles which work behind NAFTA cooperation aim to remove tariff barriers as well as barriers to services and investment capital. The areas covered by NAFTA chiefly encompass market access, trade rules, services, investment, intellectual property and dispute settlement. Unlike other free trade agreements, NAFTA not only includes rules for trade liberalization but also labour standards and environment standards. The labour lobby in the USA and Canada feared loss of jobs to cheaper labour from Mexico which almost forced upon the adoption of labour standards under NAFTA.

NAFTA like the EU does not have an elaborate administrative structure. The two main structures of NAFTA are the Secretariat and the Free Trade Commission (FTC). It is composed of the US Trade Representative, Mexican Secretary of Commerce and Industrial Development and the Canadian Minister for International Trade. The FTC is the principal organ to oversee the performance of NAFTA, supervise works of different committees of NAFTA and resolve disputes. The FTC operates on the basis of consensus and Cabinet-level meetings are held annually.

The Secretariat is the administrative wing of the NAFTA and is entrusted with the day-to-day affairs of the bloc like assisting the FTC and other committees, working groups and panels constituted from time to time by NAFTA. A trilateral Secretariat since 14 January 1995 has been located in separate national offices in Mexico City, Ottawa and Washington DC. However, this body is restricted in its activities in the absence of proper regulations and guidelines and prevalence of clash of interests of member countries, business elites, labour bodies and environmental groups.

The objective of NAFTA like any other free trade agreement was to increase cross-border commerce in North America. This free trade agreement created regimes by lowering or eliminating tariffs and reducing some non-tariff barriers among member countries on various grounds like in accordance with local content requirements of a particular country like Mexico. Most of the increase came from USA–Mexico trade that amounted to $481.5 billion in 2015, and USA–Canada trade which was to the tune of $518.2 billion. Trade between Mexico and Canada between the period of 1993 and 2015 totalled just $34.3 billion.

However, NAFTA led to the 30 per cent drop in manufacturing employment, from 17.7 million jobs at the end of 1993 to 12.3 million at the end of 2016. NAFTA also led to shifting of lower-wage jobs to Mexico. An example that can be cited is the case of Mexico which became a car manufacturing hub. The big automobile companies such as General Motors, Fiat Chrysler, Nissan, Volkswagen, Ford Motor, Honda, Toyota and other countries shifted their manufacturing unit to Mexico. These and other industries owe their growth in part to the more than a four-fold real increase in US FDI in Mexico since 1993.

The uneasiness in the unequal returns from the NAFTA, especially on the part of the USA, led the leaders of the three member countries to renegotiate the deal in November 2018. It came to be known as the USMCA or NAFTA 2.0. The three member countries will also review the deal every six years and will decide whether they want to extend the deal or not. The new provisions inter alia included that automobiles must have 75 per cent of their parts manufactured in North America in order to qualify for no tariffs. People who are involved in the manufacture of 40–45 per cent of car parts must earn at least $16 per hour. Copyright terms will be extended to 70 years beyond an author's life. There would be more access for American farmers to the Canadian dairy market ensuring that farmers can sell their products in Canada without pricing provisions.

There were other two larger trading regimes which were planned out which could have been larger than NAFTA. They were the Trans-Pacific Partnership and Transatlantic Trade and investment partnership. However, the USA under President Donald Trump pulled out of such trading arrangements.

South Asian Association for Regional Cooperation, SAPTA and SAFTA

South Asian neighbours got interested in regional integration from the success stories of the EU and ASEAN. South Asia is a huge area with almost 4.7 million sq. km. The total land area of South Asia is 6,400,127 sq. km (2,471,102 sq. miles). It comprises high economic performers like India. The market size is huge and in terms of population, the region has a population of almost **1,958,894,343** (as of Wednesday, 5 May 2021), based on the latest UN estimates. The population of South Asia is equivalent to **24.89 per cent** of the total world population. South Asia ranks number 1 in Asia among subregions ranked by population. South Asia comprises India, Bangladesh, Sri Lanka, Pakistan, Afghanistan, Nepal and Bhutan.

In 2020, the GDP growth compared to the previous year was forecasted to be the highest in Bangladesh with 3.8 per cent. Comparatively, the GDP in the Maldives was forecasted to decrease by 18.6 per cent in 2020. In 2019, India had a GDP of US$2.87 lakh crores, while Bangladesh has a GDP of US$30,257.13 crores and Sri Lanka, US$8,400.88 crores. The Maldives and Nepal were among the countries with the lowest GDP in the Asia-Pacific region. In terms of poverty, Bangladesh had the highest share of people living below the poverty line. However, the Maldives and Sri Lanka appear to be the richer South Asian countries, exhibiting the highest and second highest GDP per capita among the South Asian countries. The recent data show that Bangladesh's GDP per capita will exceed that of India's in 2021 despite India having a 25 per cent lead just five years ago because of India being destabilized due to the second wave of coronavirus.

However, the economic disparity is noteworthy. South Asia includes almost 29 per cent of the people living in extreme poverty worldwide (216 million extreme poor in South Asia out of the estimated 736 million extreme poor worldwide). The *Poverty and Shared Prosperity Report* (2018) provides the following highlights of 2015 which says that 4 out of 5 extreme poor in the South Asia region resided in India. With a poverty rate of 13.42 per cent, India's large population of 1.3 billion constitute a high absolute number of poor (175.7 million). Bangladesh with a large population is at second place within the region in terms of absolute number of poor (24.4 million extreme poor). Pakistan is at the third place with a smaller amount of extreme poor (9.9 million extreme poor). Bhutan and Sri Lanka are considered to be successful in the sense that extreme poverty has gone down although a large share of the population lives on slightly more than the extreme poverty line. Maldives is an example of a country where extreme poverty is nearly non-existent according to this report.

The estimates from the 2018 Global Multidimensional Poverty Index[2] released by the UNDP and the Oxford Poverty and Human Development Initiative report that high incidences of poverty are present in Nepal (35.3%), Bangladesh (41.1%) and Pakistan (43.9%). India with a poverty incidence of 27.5 per cent has to take care of the multidimensions of poverty and make efforts towards poverty eradication. On the whole, South Asia accounted for 29 per cent of the people living in extreme poverty globally. Out of the 736 million extreme poor globally, South Asia accounted for 216 million as suggested by the *Poverty and Shared Prosperity Report* (2018).

Specifically coming to the countries of South Asia, India, Pakistan and Bangladesh are large economies followed by Nepal, Bhutan and Maldives. So is Afghanistan. On the basis of income, the World Bank classifies the South Asian countries as given in Table 10.1.

The major economies of the region embraced liberalism in the economic sphere in the early 1990s. While India is making economic progress, the other economies cannot catch up to it. This is the crux of the fear psychosis among the South Asian neighbours. The sheer size of India, both physical and economic, creates a picture of a dominant power—a big brother among countries of South Asia.

Despite such diverse economic and political background under the enthusiasm of Bangladesh, SAARC was formed with the adoption of SAARC Charter on 8 December 1985. The founding members were Bangladesh, Bhutan, India, Maldives, Nepal, Pakistan and Sri

Table 10.1 South Asian Countries as per Income Level

S. No.	Countries	Income Level
1.	Afghanistan	Low income
2.	Bangladesh	Lower-middle income
3.	Bhutan	Lower-middle income
4.	India	Lower-middle income
5.	Maldives	Upper-middle income
6.	Nepal	Lower-middle income
7.	Pakistan	Lower-middle income
8.	Sri Lanka	Lower-middle income

Source: World Bank.

[2] The multidimensional poor refers to individuals who are deprived of more than one dimension such as health, education and living standards.

Lanka. The first SAARC Summit was held on 7–8 December 1985. Afghanistan became the eighth member of SAARC on 13 November 2005. Australia, China, the EU, Iran, Japan, Mauritius, Myanmar, South Korea and the USA are Observers to SAARC.

The broad objectives laid down in the SAARC Charter underpin the rationale behind the formation of regional cooperation. The Charter upholds that the member states would strive to promote welfare of the peoples of South Asia. They would work towards accelerating economic growth, social progress and cultural development. They will also try to promote and strengthen collective self-reliance among countries of South Asia. The member states would promote active collaboration and mutual assistance in the economic, social, cultural, technical and scientific fields. They would strive to strengthen cooperation among developing countries, international forums and cooperate with international and regional organizations.

However, the general provisions of SAARC have proved to be a stumbling block in achieving cooperation among SAARC members. Bilateral and contentious issues are excluded from the deliberations of SAARC. India–Pakistan bitterness has many times prevented the organization from delivering positive results. Total 18 Summits of SAARC had been held but the 19th SAARC Summit could not be held due to Uri attacks by Pak-sponsored terrorists. Further, China vies for a permanent position in the organization. Pakistan, Bangladesh, Sri Lanka and Maldives insisted on greater interaction with observer states. India has been expressive about its disagreement with this entire idea of enhanced role of the observers as well as adding members to this regional organization.

Some notable outcomes of these Summits have been the adoption of the SAARC Preferential Trade Agreement (SAPTA), which came into force on 7 December 1995, SAFTA (2004), South Asian Regional Standards Organization (2008), SAARC Development Goals, adoption of SAARC Regional Convention on Suppression of Terrorism (1987) and SAARC Convention on Narcotic Drugs and Psychotropic Substances (1990).

The decision to convert SAARC into a FTA was taken in the 9th SAARC Summit in May 1997 in Malé. SAFTA was signed on 6 January 2004 in the 12th SAARC Summit. SAFTA aimed at accelerating the pace of regional economic integration through promotion of preferential trade among member countries. Earlier, SAPTA was signed in Dhaka on 11 April 1993, which came into force in December 1995. There was a necessity to move beyond the preferential trading arrangement towards higher levels of trade and economic cooperation in South Asia. This could only be achieved by removing tariff barriers for facilitating cross-border flow of goods. Therefore, SAFTA came into force on 1 January 2006. This Agreement superseded SAPTA. Afghanistan as the 8th member state of the SAARC ratified the SAFTA protocol on 4 May 2011.

Article 7 of the SAFTA provides for tariff liberalization in phases. Under this, in two years, Non-Least Developed Contracting States (NLDCS) would bring down tariffs to 20 per cent and Least Developed Contracting States (LDCS) should bring them down to 30 per cent. NLDCS will then bring down tariffs from 20 per cent to 0–5 per cent in five years with only exception of Sri Lanka which has been given the time frame as six years, while LDCS will do so in eight years. NLDCS will reduce their tariffs for LDCS products to 0–5 per cent in three years. This tariff liberalization programme would cover all tariff lines except those kept in the sensitive list (negative list) by the member states.

SAFTA aims to involve free movement of goods, between countries through, inter alia, the elimination of tariffs, para tariffs and non-tariff restrictions on the movement of goods, and any other equivalent measures. The special needs of the LDCS are to be given recognition by adopting concrete preferential measures in their favour on a non-reciprocal basis.

The institutional arrangements for implementation of SAFTA were worked out. The Contracting States established the SAFTA Ministerial Council (SMC). The SMC has been designed to be the highest decision-making body of SAFTA and shall be responsible for the administration and implementation of this Agreement and all decisions and arrangements made within its legal framework.

All countries completed the respective Trade Liberalization Programme (TLP) under Phases I and II of SAFTA. In terms of Article Rule 7(3)(a) of SAFTA, the TLP of SAFTA would not apply to the tariff lines included in the sensitive lists. The member states brought down tariffs to a level between 0 per cent and 5 per cent on all products keeping aside the respective Sensitive Lists. Sri Lanka has been accorded a special treatment in Rules of Origin under SAFTA. Further relaxation of tariff on and reduction of SAFTA Sensitive List was in the offing under Phase III of SAFTA to be achieved by 2020.

The economic achievement of the SAARC has been the least. According to the World Bank assessment in comparison to the ASEAN, SAARC has failed to meet its target economic achievement. It reports that for ASEAN, from 1992 to 2017, intraregional imports as a share of global imports increased from 17 per cent to 24 per cent, and exports from 21 per cent to 27 per cent. For South Asia, these shares were largely stagnant since SAFTA came into effect, at 3 per cent for intraregional imports and 6–7 per cent for intraregional exports. The intra-regional trade in South Asia has been recorded as the lowest among world regions. It has been approximately around 5 per cent of its overall trade with the world.

The failure of SAFTA has been pointed out by the World Bank Report, *Glass Half Full: The Promise of Regional Trade in South Asia* (2018), and can be summarized as follows:

- The Report puts the onus of unsuccessful tariff free trade among the SAARC countries despite SAFTA on opaque 'para tariffs' levied by some countries in the region. Such tariffs are nothing but import duties in disguise and in reality, there are very substantial duties on a wide range of products traded within South Asia.
- The costs of trading which include transportation and logistics infrastructure and the efficiency of customs and border procedures are considerably higher within South Asia. The average level of trade costs is 20 per cent higher between country pairs in South Asia than between country pairs in East Asia.
- Unclear non-tariff measures restrict the opportunities of market access granted by South Asian countries to each other. For example, Pakistan allows only 138 items to be imported from India over the Attari–Wagah land route which is the only land port between the two countries. There is a long shared land border between the two but that is denied of access. This makes bilateral trade to be conducted along the sea route and this in reality is not cost-effective for two countries which can overcome this by trade along a long shared land border. Bangladesh and India also impose some restrictions on imports from each other at certain ports.
- The Report further shows that SAFTA is compromised and the goal of duty-free trade cannot be reached because of long Sensitive Lists that are created by all member countries. The Report says that as much as 35 per cent of the value of intraregional trade in South Asia is subject to Sensitive List tariffs. Around 44–45 per cent of the imports from other SAFTA members fall under Sensitive Lists in Bangladesh and Sri Lanka. Over

39 per cent of India's exports to the region fall under the Sensitive Lists of various partners. There is no proper guideline under SAFTA for phasing out the Sensitive Lists.
- There is also trust deficit among the partners, especially India and Pakistan. Bilateral relations and bitterness in it get reflected in the overall cooperation in the SAARC and its sectoral areas.

SAARC Summit has been postponed over India–Pakistan face-off. The future of SAARC is not as bright as the ASEAN so is of SAFTA as has been discussed above about the obstacles in establishing a free trade regime in South Asia.

Brazil, Russia, India, China and South Africa

If the above economic/trading arrangements have a common geographical location occupying a same region and have some common features, history, culture and political and strategic interests, BRICS is a little different from them. Initially BRIC and later BRICS is an upcoming economic forum of emerging economies. BRICS is the acronym taking the first alphabet of the constituting countries. BRIC was composed by Brazil, Russia, India and China. Later, in the Third Summit of BRIC held in 2011, Sanya, China, South Africa joined the grouping and BRIC became BRICS.

The striking feature of the BRICS countries is that they are all emerging economies of the world and BRIC countries amounted to an estimated 3.12 billion inhabitants of the world in 2019 and GDP of an estimated 20.81 trillion US dollars in 2019. In 1990, BRIC countries accounted for 11 per cent of global GDP. By 2014, this figure rose to nearly 30 per cent. These figures include a high in 2010, following a plunge in value, surrounding the 2008 financial crisis. Together, BRICS accounts for about 40 per cent of the world's population and about 30 per cent of the GDP, making it a critical economic engine.

Taking a cue from Jim O'Neill of Goldman Sachs who referred to the investment opportunities of the rising emerging economies of the BRICS, the initiative to form this grouping was borne. However, this grouping is not merely an economic grouping nor a regional grouping but a very important emerging group undoubtedly. BRICS focus on a wide array of subjects such as trade, agriculture, health, global governance, sustainable development, peace and security, science and technology and national security, energy and climate change, and social issues, among others.

The efforts for forming this bloc began in 2006 where four foreign ministers of BRIC met on the sidelines of the United Nations General Assembly. This was followed by meetings of heads of states in Sapporo before the G8 Summit in 2008 and another one in Yekaterinburg, Russia, in 2009. Meetings were also held at several official levels such as foreign affairs, economy, finance, agriculture, trade and health. The 2009 BRIC Summit at Yekaterinburg, Russia, laid down the foundation of the grouping. This grouping is truly international across continents. Asia-Africa-Latin America connected by common objectives pointed above. BRICS comprises countries which are emerging investment markets and constitute global power bloc.

There is however no formal institutional framework of BRICS. Usually, annual summits are held among the heads of states. The chairmanship rotates annually among the members, in accordance with the acronym BRICS. Besides summit meeting, sectoral meetings are also held around various global issues over the year.

The objectives of the BRIC/S were underpinned in the first Summit at Yekaterinburg, Russia. In a joint statement issued at the end of the Summit, certain points of the grouping were upheld. They stressed on reform of international financial institutions so as to change the working of the global economy and recognize the increasingly significant role that emerging markets now play. They foresaw that a reformed international financial and economic architecture should be based on the principles of democratic and transparent decision-making as well as implementation process at the international financial organizations. This should be based on legal basis, compatibility of activities of effective national regulatory institutions and international standard-setting bodies and strengthening of risk management and supervisory practices. The other areas identified for cooperation were sustainable development, energy sector, disaster management, science and education, and development of advanced technologies. BRIC/S reaffirmed its faith in multilateral diplomacy through the UN. Promoting dialogue and cooperation among BRIC/S countries in an incremental, proactive, pragmatic, open and transparent way was also other identified objective. Over the years, BRICS has evolved its areas of cooperation with primacy of economic cooperation. Areas of cooperation now include people-to-people exchanges such as the **Young Diplomats Forum, Parliamentarian Forum, Trade Union Forum, BRICS Civil Forum** and the **Media Forum.** Another area of cooperation is political and security aimed at achieving peace, security, development and cooperation for a more equitable and fair world.

The latest 2020 Summit was hosted by Russia and it was held during the COVID-19 pandemic outbreak. Therefore, it had to be conducted virtually. In this Summit, the heads of states adopted the Moscow Delectation which commemorated the 75th anniversary of the

Table 10.2 BRICS Summit (2009–2020)

Year	Host Country
16 June 2009	Yekaterinburg, Russia
15 April 2010	Brasilia, Brazil
14 April 2011	Sanya, China
29 March 2012	New Delhi, India
25–27 March 2013	Durban, South Africa
15–16 July 2014	Fortaleza, Brazil
8–9 July 2015	Ufa, Russia
15–16 October 2016	Goa, India
3 September 2017	Xiamen, China
25–27 July 2018	Johannesburg, South Africa
14 November 2019	Brasilia, Brazil
17 November 2020	Moscow, Russia[a]

Source: Compiled by the author from BRICS website.

Note: [a]Originally scheduled to be held in St Petersburg on 21–23 July 2020; postponed indefinitely on 27 May 2020 and finally held virtually on 17 November 2020.

founding of the UN and the 75th anniversary of the end of the Second World War. BRICS also reinforced its commitment to a world of peace, stability and prosperity, mutual respect and equality, faith on international law as well as the purposes and principles as enshrined in the Charter of the UN. BRICS states reaffirmed their commitment to multilateralism and the principles of mutual respect, sovereign equality, democracy, inclusiveness and strengthened collaboration. The leaders pledged to continue to work towards strengthening and reforming international governance in order to make it more inclusive, representative and democratic by ensuring greater participation of developing countries in international decision-making bodies. The countries congratulated India on its election as a non-permanent member of the UN Security Council for the term 2021–2022. BRICS leaders reiterated the necessity of strengthening international cooperation to increase shared capacities in order to jointly fight the emerging worldwide threats like the COVID-19 pandemic and its adverse impacts effectively.

BRICS reiterated the importance of open, stable and secure global markets and acknowledged the building of more resilient global supply chains for increased production of critical health, food and other industrial and agricultural products at the national level and in their respective regional contexts along the lines of WTO rules. It urged the WTO members to ensure that all COVID-19-related measures are targeted, proportionate, transparent and temporary and do not create unnecessary barriers to trade or disruption to global supply chains. Several initiatives and documents were also signed such as the BRICS Counter Terrorism Strategy (17 November 2020) and Strategy for BRICS Economic Partnership 2025 (17 November 2020).

BRICS has a long way to go and for that it has to take a calibrated approach. A major breakthrough made by the BRICS countries was in the 6th BRICS Summit at Fortaleza in 2014. BRICS member countries signed the Agreement that established the New Development Bank (NDB) with its headquarter in **Shanghai.** In the **Fortaleza Declaration,** it was pledged that the NDB will strengthen cooperation among BRICS that will supplement the efforts of multilateral and regional financial institutions for global development. This will contribute to sustainable and balanced growth. NDB has its key areas of operation as clean energy, irrigation, transport infrastructure, sustainable urban development and economic cooperation among the member countries.

However, the bilateral stand-off between two major partners, India and China, affect the possibility of peaceful political relations amongst the member countries of BRICS. Earlier, Doklam stand-off and in May 2020, the Ladakh incursions by China hamper the political atmosphere of BRICS. Further, China's economic clout alone and its policies of Belt and Road Initiative (BRI), China–Pakistan Economic Corridor and Maritime Silk Road further dampen China's relations with India. It can only be hoped that bilateral antagonism is able to bypass the necessity of economic cooperation side by side. The other challenges include the dominance of the trio over the other members. They are the big three, Russia–China–India, which enjoy a dominant position in the grouping. China's efforts to induct its friendly countries which are integral to its BRI into BRICS can cause a crisis and conflict in the grouping. This will further increase the bitterness between India and China. The future road ahead of BRICS includes their collective effort to meet their commitments under the Paris Agreement on climate change and the UN's SDGs. The idea of setting up a BRICS Credit Rating Agency, as proposed by India, opposed to Western agencies such as Standard & Poor's and Moody's, can be on BRICS future agenda.

Conclusion

From the above discussion, now we have a clear idea about regional economic integration. Countries of a region come together to form groups or blocs for free trade, free flow of goods and services, removal or reduction of tariff and non-tariff barriers and so on. There can be FTAs, PTAs, CU or simply economic cooperation. The leading economic blocs are the EU, ASEAN and NAFTA. SAARC has not been able to produce positive results mainly because of bilateral tensions. Success of regional economic blocs may contribute to increase in market size by integrating the economies of a region. This also increases the economies of scale and factor productivity among firms in member countries. If the economies are able to make great progress, then the economic bloc can attract FDIs. Still there can be economic crisis as the Southeast Asian economic crisis, the eurozone crisis and even events like BREXIT. Bilateral tensions can also obstruct regional cooperation. Rajat Acharyya (2014) has shown that either the regional integration can be like a spaghetti bowl effect (Jagdish Bhagwati) or may be juggernaut and domino effects (R. Baldwin, 'Multilateralizing Regionalism: Spaghetti Bowls as Building Blocs on the Path to Global Free Trade', 2006). The former shows that regional organizations may not be the best way of organizing world trade. The latter, however, says that spaghetti bowls can be transformed into building blocks through juggernaut and domino effect. Still the boost to this juggernaut is tariff rates through multilateral negotiations but is not incorporated through unconditional MFN clause in many regional initiatives. So regional integrations have a long way to go to achieve full success. Even the EU has suffered the BREXIT; after remaining for so long within the EU, Britain decided to exit. Therefore, political and economic factors also are behind the success of regional organizations.

Summary

A **region** is meant to be a few countries sharing a common geographical space by means of their proximity. Sometimes, they may be contiguous and are placed so near to one another geographically that they constitute a region.

There can be a number of factors such as common interests, common problems, shared visions, economic, political and social interests and also security concerns among the countries of a region. There can be interdependence and cooperation as driving factors for the regional cohesion. Integration can be also another factor for regional cooperation.

Integration becomes a comprehensive process, especially if we are talking in terms of economic integration. It involves setting up of FTA, PTAs, CU and so on, addressing trade and tariff issues as well as movement of goods and services.

The **EU** is an example of economic integration as well as political integration in stages. It moved through stages over the year. The EU was finally established by the Maastricht Treaty on 1 November 1993. Euro was named in 1995 in Madrid. The Euro was introduced to world financial markets as an accounting currency on 1 January 1999, replacing the former ECU.

BREXIT has jolted the European unity and how far EU countries and the UK manage their deal and economies is to be watched carefully.

ASEAN is an intergovernmental organization oriented towards economic growth, political stability through active collaboration and mutual assistance fostered through educational and cultural integration of member countries. The objectives behind the formation of ASEAN have been an effort to promote economic, social and cultural development of the people of Southeast Asia. Indonesia, Malaysia, the Philippines, Singapore, Thailand and Vietnam, which are the six largest ASEAN countries, are expected to have a positive real GDP growth rates in 2021 even as the pandemic is on. Therefore, ASEAN will be a big regional player undoubtedly.

APEC is the Asia-Pacific Economic Cooperation organization. APEC was formed in 1989 as a regional economic organization with the objectives to achieve economic prosperity and balanced, inclusive and sustainable growth in the region through economic integration of member countries. To achieve sustainable regional economic cooperation, the **People and Prosperity: An APEC Vision to 2040** was adopted. APEC has a long way to go to realize its full potential.

NAFTA is a free trade agreement among three countries—the USA, Canada and Mexico. The three countries signed NAFTA in September 1993 which came into effect on 1 January 1994. The principles which work behind NAFTA cooperation aim to remove tariff barriers as well as barriers to services and investment capital. The areas covered by NAFTA chiefly encompass market access, trade rules, services, investment, intellectual property and dispute settlement. Unlike other free trade agreements, NAFTA not only includes rules for trade liberalization but also labour standards and environment standards.

SAARC was formed with the adoption of SAARC Charter on 8 December 1985. The objectives laid down in the SAARC Charter uphold that the member states would strive to promote welfare of the peoples of South Asia. They would work towards accelerating economic growth, social progress and cultural development. SAFTA was signed on 6 January 2004 in the 12th SAARC Summit. SAFTA aimed at accelerating the pace of regional economic integration through promotion of preferential trade among member countries. However, the general provisions of SAARC have proved to be a stumbling block in achieving cooperation among SAARC members. Bilateral and contentious issues are excluded from the deliberations of SAARC. The SAARC economic cooperation has stumbled due to unsuccessful tariff-free trade among the SAARC countries despite SAFTA mainly because of 'para tariffs'.

BRICS comprises countries which are emerging investment markets and constitute global power bloc. The 2009 **BRIC** Summit at Yekaterinburg, Russia, laid down the foundation of the grouping. BRIC became BRICS in 2011 when South Africa joined the grouping. BRICS emphasizes the importance of open, stable and secure global markets and acknowledges the building of more resilient global supply chains for increased production of critical health, food and other industrial and agricultural products at the national level and in their respective regional contexts along the lines of the WTO rules. BRICS has to go a long way and for that it has to take a calibrated approach. A major breakthrough made by the BRICS countries was the in the 6th BRICS Summit at Fortaleza in 2014 with NDB.

REVIEW AND REFLECTION QUESTIONS

1. What do you think of a region? If you are aware of what is a region, then what is regionalism?
2. Regionalism gives rise to cooperation and integration, be it political or economic. Here, argue your case for economic cooperation and integration with examples of regional organizations.
3. ASEAN is growing economically even in the post-pandemic world. Trace the evolution of this regional economic organization.
4. SAARC is also an economic cooperation forum of the South Asian countries. Comment on its progress and obstacles to cooperation.
5. Trace the evolution of APEC as an economic organization of the Asia-Pacific region.
6. NAFTA is a free trade regime. Comment on its evolution and future prospect.
7. BRICS is emerging as a trans-continental economic bloc. Summarize its evolution, achievements and future prospect.

Bibliography

Acharyya, Rajat. 2014. *International Economics: An Introduction to Theory and Policy*. New Delhi: Oxford University Press.

Baylis, John, Steve Smith, and Patricia Owens. 2017. *An Introduction of World Politics: An Introduction to Introduction to International Relations*. London: Oxford University Press.

Bose (Das), Anuradha. 2011. *SAARC: A Quest for Unity—Problems and Prospects*. Kolkata: Minerva Associates (Publications).

Cavusgil, S. Tamer, Gary Knight, and John Riesenberger. 2018. *International Business: The New Realities*. London: Pearson.

Cherunilam, Francis. 2011. *International Economics*. New Delhi: Tata McGraw Hill Education Private Limited.

Kathuria, Sanjay, ed. 2018. *A Glass Half Full: The promise of Regional Trade in South Asia*. World Bank Group. Available at https://openknowledge.worldbank.org/bitstream/handle/10986/30246/211294ov.pdf?sequence=3&isAllowed=y (accessed on 9 October 2021).

Krugman, Paul, Maurice Obstfeld, and Marc Melitz. 2018. *International Economics: Theory and Practice*. London: Pearson.

Mukherjee, Aparajita, and Saumya Chakrabarti. 2016. *Development Economics: A Critical Perspective*. New Delhi: PHI Learning Private Limited.

11 The Political Economy of India: Post-reform Period

LEARNING OBJECTIVES

- To know about India's planned development decades
- Learn about the necessity for economic reforms in India
- Knowing about the reforms brought about in different sectors
- Understanding the economic performance of India in the post-reform period
- Trying to figure out the performance of the Indian economy during the COVID-19 pandemic

Introduction

India started its planned economic growth in the year 1951 with the establishment of the Planning Commission. At the time of Independence, India was at a low level of economic growth as it was a post-colonial state. India's journey began with the initial plans—the Nehru–Mahalanobis plans—aimed at the creation of heavy industries and state intervention in most of the sectors of the economy. The aim was that key industries would be built up by the state and be under the control of the commanding heights of a new modern industrial economy for India by the state. In this scheme, the private sector was to play a complementary role in the 'mixed economy'. Initially, this meant heavy dependence on imports and foreign aid, but ultimately, it would move the country towards import substitution and ultimate self-sufficiency.

The Mahalanobis planning strategy initially recorded rapid growth of 10 per cent in the industrial sector. Heavy industries grew at a rate of 22 per cent annually, while basic industries such as iron, steel, fuel and electricity grew at a rate of 19 per cent per annum. Agriculture output also recorded a growth of almost 3 per cent on average annually. Food shortage could almost be overcome to feed a growing population. Overall, however, the economy could not record a high growth rate till 1965–1980. It was sluggish at the rate of 3–4 per cent. Industrial growth rate slowed around 5 per cent between 1965 and 1980, from a high of 10 per cent between 1955 and 1965.

It was felt that time has come for reform and to encourage the private sector to play an important role. The need to shift from planning the economy to the management of the economy was thought to be the need of the hour. The trend from state-directed development towards liberalization of the economy was first initiated under Mrs Indira Gandhi and then followed by Rajiv Gandhi. Ultimately, the acute economic crisis of 1990 that saw an increase in public expenditure and heavy external debt, flight of capital, oil shocks after the Gulf War and the depletion of foreign reserves which forced India to approach the IMF and the World Bank. Following the SAPs of the IMF and the World Bank, India carried out economic reforms under the New Economic Policy (NEP) of 1991. India's economic performance post-reform period has been discussed in this chapter. India's economic performance during the pandemic years 2020–2021 has also been discussed in this chapter. The chapter begins with the discussion of India's planned economic journey to the post-reform years.

Phases of Economic Development in India (1947–1991)

India gained its independence in 1947. Since then, India has tried to walk down the path of economic development. From a phase of planned economic growth since 1951 with heavy state intervention, India moved to a phase of economic reforms in 1991. From 1991 onwards, it has been India's tryst with reforms.

At the time of independence, the Indian economy exhibited signs of underdevelopment. The cause was almost 200 years (1757–1947) of British colonial domination and exploitation. It contributed to 'the guided underdevelopment' of India because of the export of raw materials and profit to Britain. The underdevelopment of India and the Third World at large was caused by the development of the 'core' countries. So India inherited an economy pegged with stagnating per capita income, a low standard of living, poor industrial development and an agrarian based economy predominantly. Only a significant achievement can be seen in the form of growth of indigenous industries such as soaps, chemicals and textiles. With such a background, India embarked on the path of planned economic development.

The Planning Commission was created in 1950 to design the Five-year Plans for economic development with proper utilization of available resources, human and material and capital. This was a Nehruvian vision inspired by Fabian socialism through public control of services, largely by the municipalities.

Jawaharlal Nehru was the first chairman of the Planning Commission of India. The Planning Commission was formed with the objective of accelerating economic development through balanced utilization of resources through proper plans. It was to make an assessment of the available resources and identify the obstacles to economic development. The Planning Commission was supposed to play an integrative role in the adoption of a holistic approach towards formulation of policies in critical areas of economic as well as human development. Nehru placed the First Five-year Plan before the Indian Parliament on 8 December 1951.

In this planned development, the state was to play a significant role. The aim was to raise the domestic savings rate, which was thought to be putting India's economic growth at 5 per cent. Growth was central to the thinking of planning. The central responsibilities of alleviating poverty and removing existing inequalities through the expansion of economic and social responsibilities can be achieved through the pivotal role of the state. This necessitated the existence of both the nationalized and private sector.

Now let us look at the five-year plans we can estimate India's attempts towards economic development. Table 11.1 gives the timeline of Five-year Plans in India.

Table 11.1 Five Year Plans: Targets and Achievements

Plan	Target Growth (%)	Actual Growth (%)
First Five-year Plan	2.9	3.6
Second Five-year Plan	4.5	4.3
Third Five-year Plan	5.6	2.8
Fourth Five-year Plan	5.7	3.3
Fifth Five-year Plan	4.4	4.8
Sixth Five-year Plan	5.2	6.0
Seventh Five-year Plan	5.0	6.0
Eighth Five-year Plan	5.6	6.8
Ninth Five-year Plan	6.5	5.4
Tenth Five-year Plan	8.0	7.7
Eleventh Five-year Plan	9.0	8.0

The **First Five-year Plan** was launched for the period 1951–1956. It was based on the Harrod–Domar model (Figure 11.1). As pointed out earlier, there was an attempt to increase domestic savings, which was thought to spur economic growth. The same was reflected in the Harrod–Domar model. This model was followed in many developing countries. The basic assumption of this model, to put it simply, is that developing countries suffer from low-economic growth because of low savings rates. To overcome this, it is important to increase savings either domestically or from abroad. The thinking goes that higher savings create a virtuous circle of self-sustaining economic growth.

Figure 11.1 Harrod–Domar Model

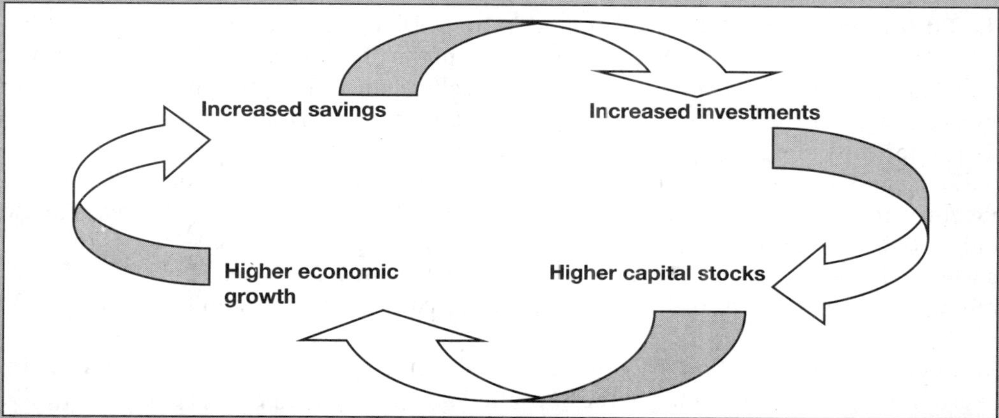

Overall, the **First Five-year Plan** was successful and it achieved more than the target growth rate of 2.1 per cent. The growth rate that was achieved was 3.6 per cent. The total plan allocation was ₹2,069 crore. This amount was distributed among different sectors. Priority was given to agriculture and community development. Other emphasis areas were irrigation and power, transport and communications, industry, social services including rehabilitation and other miscellaneous sectors. The huge dam projects of Bhakra Dam and Hirakud Dam were quite an achievement of the First Five-year Plan. A good harvest helped to boost exchange reserves and per capita income.

The **Second Five-year Plan** (1956–1961) was based on the Mahalanobis plan, as Prasanta Chandra Mahalanobis was the chief architect of the Second Five-year Plan. The Mahalanobis model aims to achieve a rapid long-term rate of growth through encouraging basic heavy industries. The assumption was that by increasing production of capital goods, encompassing electricity, machinery, steel and so on, productive employment would follow. Another objective was import substitution for both foreign capital equipment and machines. Later, he modified his model and introduced a four-sector growth model. Heavy industry's sector was not disturbed, but he added consumer goods sector, which he divided into three more sectors: factory enterprises producing consumer goods, household and small-scale enterprises also producing consumer goods and the provision of services. These are known as C-sectors, which are divided into C1, C2 and C3 sectors. A total of ₹4,600 crore and was focused on power and irrigation, social services, communications and transport and miscellaneous sectors. A 4.3 per cent growth rate could be achieved, although the target was 4.5 per cent.

The **Third Five-year Plan** (1961–1966) got a jolt due to the 1962 Sino-Indian War which exposed the weakness of the economy. Defence, which was neglected, also came into focus. However, the Indo-Pak war and severe drought pushed the Five-year Plans into failure. Till 1969, the Five-year Plans were put on hold due to the excruciating crisis from external aggression that India was suffering. There were three annual plans in place of the Five-year Plan.

The **Fourth Plan** (1969–1974) took off at the behest of Smt. Indira Gandhi as the prime minister. The major achievement was the nationalization of banks, and the Green Revolution boosted the economy. However, agricultural production was harmed due to the poor monsoon. There was an additional burden of refugees from Bangladesh due to the Bangladesh Liberation War. Therefore, the growth rate achieved 3.3 per cent although the target set was 5.7 per cent.

The **Fifth Plan** (1974–1979) was drafted by D. D. Dhar, who was also closely associated with the Bangladesh Liberation War. The objectives of the plan were quite lofty. It aimed at the removal of poverty or '*garibi hatao*' and attaining 'self-reliance'. The growth rate achieved was 4.4 per cent against the target of 4.5 per cent. The plan was terminated in 1978 instead of 1979, as after the Emergency period, the Janata government came to power.

The subsequent Sixth Plan implemented in two phases, as the first was suspended after the Janata government lost the elections to Congress in 1980. So the first Sixth Five-year Plan was for only 1978–1979. The second was for the entire five-year term (1980–1985). The objectives were to increase national income, ensuring a continuous decrease in poverty and unemployment, modernization of technology, population control through family planning and so on.

The **Seventh Five-year Plan** for 1985–1990 was implemented against the backdrop of the success of the Sixth Plan. Volume I of the Seventh Plan upholds the positive points of the Sixth Plan. It upheld that the Sixth Plan growth target of about 5 per cent had been achieved.

Agricultural performance was also good, especially in food grains. The rate of inflation has been kept under control and the balance of payments has been successfully managed despite the fact that the world economy is experiencing the worst recession since the 1930s. Most developing countries, and even industrialized countries, face severe economic hardships.

The Seventh Plan was thought to be reinforcing these strong foundations. The objectives of the plan were to maintain the momentum of growth in the economy, removal of poverty, economic growth to be accompanied by social justice and removal of age-old social barriers that oppress the weak. The plan also sought to push the process of economic and technological modernization of the economy further to achieve self-reliance. It means the building of a strong, independent national economy which will be dealing extensively with the world on equal terms.

The Seventh Plan also upheld that development is not just about factories, dams and roads. Development was also about people. The goal, therefore, was people's material, cultural and spiritual fulfilment. This plan focused the human factor and the human context as being of supreme value. The plan emphasized that policies and programmes in education, health and welfare must be restructured to provide a fuller life to the people. The public sector outlay was of ₹180,000 crores which was a massive volume. It was a success and the economy recorded a 6 per cent growth rate against the targeted 5 per cent.

The **Eighth Plan** was postponed as India was going through an acute balance of payments crisis, and after the crisis was managed, the Eighth Plan was launched in 1992. It was for the period of 1992–1997. The target growth rate was 5.6 per cent. This would be worked out with financial discipline from all levels of government and private enterprises. The plan also sought to evolve a consensus and fruitful cooperation among all the 'social partners' in development, including the government, farmers, trade unions, businesses and the like.

Human development was the ultimate goal of the Eighth Plan. Volume I of the plan upholds the objectives such as the generation of adequate employment opportunities to achieve near-full employment by the turn of the century, the building up of people's institutions, control of population growth, universalization of elementary education, eradication of illiteracy, provision of safe drinking water and primary health facilities to all, growth and diversification of agriculture to achieve self-sufficiency in food grains and generate surpluses for exports.

This plan envisaged that development was to be achieved by freeing them of unnecessary controls and regulations and withdrawing state intervention, while keeping in mind that the growth and development of the country could not be left entirely to the market mechanism. Planning is required to strike a balance or an 'equilibrium' between 'demand', backed by purchasing, power and 'supply'.

The **Ninth Five-year Plan** was launched for the period 1997–2002 in the 50th year of India's independence. The plan's objective states that as the millennium draws to a close, it is the time to re-dedicate and consolidate the developmental efforts, especially in the social and economic spheres. This will lead the country to realize its full economic potential so that the poorest and the weakest will be able to shape their destiny in an unfettered manner. As this will require not only higher rates of growth in output and employment but also a special emphasis on all-round human development, this plan is therefore envisaged to focus on social sectors and the eradication of poverty.

The plan was based on the concept of cooperative federalism, which was supposed to give greater freedom to states so that they could determine their own priorities and also the modalities of public intervention and the provision of goods and services. The Ninth Five-year

Plan placed its objectives as giving priority to agriculture and rural development, generating adequate productive employment and eradicating poverty, accelerating the growth rate of the economy with stable prices and ensuring food and nutritional security for all. The plan puts emphasis on the upliftment of the vulnerable sections of society by providing the basic minimum services of safe drinking water, primary healthcare facilities, universal primary education, shelter and connectivity to all in a time-bound manner. The planned growth rate was 6.5 per cent but was attained at 5.4 per cent.

The **Tenth Five-year Plan** (2002–2007) has been prepared against a backdrop of high expectations arising from some aspects of the recent performance. India's GDP growth in the post-reform period has improved from an average of about 5.7 per cent in the 1980s to an average of about 6.1 per cent in the Eighth and Ninth Plan periods, making India one of the fastest-growing countries in the world. Encouraging progress has also been made in other dimensions. The percentage of the population in poverty has continued to decline, even if not as much as was targeted. Population growth has decelerated below 2 per cent for the first time in four decades. Literacy has increased from 52 per cent in 1991 to 65 per cent in 2001 and the improvement is evident in all states. Sectors such as software services and IT-enabled services have emerged as new sources of strength, creating confidence about India's potential to be competitive in the world economy.

The target that was set to be achieved was GDP growth at the rate of 8 per cent. Further, poverty ratio should be reduced to 20 per cent by 2007 and to 10 per cent by 2012. The plan among others upheld the following objectives: providing gainful high-quality employment to the addition to the labour force over the Tenth Plan period, reduction in gender gaps in literacy and wage rates by at least 50 per cent by 2007, universal access to primary education by 2007, increase in literacy rate to 72 per cent within the plan period and to 80 per cent by 2012, reduction in decade rate of population growth between 2001 and 2011 to 16.2 per cent, increase in literacy rate to 72 per cent within the plan period and to 80 per cent by 2012, increase in forest and tree cover to 25 per cent by 2007 and 33 per cent by 2012, reduction of infant mortality rate to 45 per 1,000 live births by 2007 and 28 by 2012, all villages to have sustained access to potable drinking water by 2012 and cleaning of all major polluted rivers by 2007 and other notified stretches by 2012. The growth rate achieved of 7.7 per cent.

The **Eleventh Plan** was for the period 2007–2012. The main aim was to accelerate the growth rate of GDP from 8 to 10 per cent. By the beginning of the Eleventh Plan, India had emerged as one of the fastest-growing economies in the world. The objectives of the Eleventh Plan were to increase agricultural GDP growth rate to 4 per cent per year, create 70 million new job opportunities, reduce educated unemployment to less than 5 per cent, raise the real wage rate of unskilled workers by 20 per cent and reduce the headcount ratio of consumption poverty by 10 per cent. The Eleventh Five-year Plan for education also aims to reduce the number of children dropouts, develop minimum standards of educational attainment in elementary school, increase literacy rate for people aged 7 years or up to 85 per cent and reduce gender gap in literacy to 10 per cent. The Eleventh Five-year Plan for health also aimed to reduce infant mortality, provide clean drinking water for all and reduce malnutrition and anaemia. Increasing the sex ration for age group 0–6 to 935 by 2011–2012 and 950 by 2016–2017 was one of the Eleventh Plan's other targets. The plan also ensures that at least 33 per cent of the direct and indirect beneficiaries of all government schemes are women and girl children and that all children have a safe childhood, without any compulsion to work. The plan also addressed infrastructural and environmental issues. Due to a global slowdown due to the sovereign debt crisis in Europe and domestic constraints such as tight monetary policy and supply-side bottlenecks, which resulted in decorated growth, it could not achieve its target of 9 per cent but achieved 8 per cent.

The Twelfth Five-year Plan (2012–2017) was envisioned for 'faster, more inclusive and sustainable growth', with a growth rate target 8.2 per cent. Other objectives include reducing poverty by 10 per cent more than the rate at end of the Eleventh Plan, achieving agriculture growth at 4 per cent, increasing mean year of schooling to seven years and creating 20 lakh seats for each age bracket in higher education. The Twelfth Plan also aimed to close the gender gap and social gap in school enrolment, reduce infant mortality ratio to 25, maternal mortality ratio to 1, increase the sex ratio to 950, provide 40 litres of drinking water per capita per day to 50 per cent of rural population and provide Nirmal Gram status to 50 per cent of all gram panchayats and achieve environmental sustainability.

The Twelfth Plan is the last plan executed by the Planning Commission. The Planning Commission has been replaced by the NITI Aayog. It was formed on 1 January 2015. The NITI Aayog has been constituted to evolve a shared vision of national development priorities, sectors and strategies with the active involvement of states.

Indian Economy: Reform Period (1991 Onwards)

India started its journey of economic reforms in 1991. Now, let us look at the reasons which almost compelled India to embrace economic liberalization through economic reforms. As we have seen in the previous section, India has been following an import-substitution industrialization model followed by regimes of high tariffs, import controls, an overvalued exchange rate and industrial licensing policies. As Vivek Chibber pointed out, a democratic political system like India faces difficulties in opening up its economy through industrial deregulation, privatization, disinvestment in public sectors and the selling of public sector assets, increased taxation and tight money policy. On the other hand, East Asian countries such as Taiwan and Korea, which are authoritarian regimes at ease implemented economic reforms and have implemented trade-led growth. Even democratically, the elected governments of South Korea and Indonesia were quite autocratic in introducing economic reforms that redefined the role of the state vis-à-vis labour and business interests. Chile, Bolivia, Ghana and even Turkey belong to other part of the globe that, along with other Latin American, African and Middle Eastern countries, tightly carried out economic reforms.

India going for economic reforms in the 1990s needs to be discussed, as this is the main thrust of this chapter. India followed the import-substitution industrialization model, but it created low productivity since it was adopted. Although the Second Five-year Plan crafted by P. C. Mahalanobis stressed on heavy industries using internal economies of scale rather than trade, it failed to foster higher economic growth. Figures showed that the public sector accounted for 27 per cent of the GDP, but in terms of turnover investment ratio, it was a meagre amount. It was 0.79 in 1971, 2 in 1981 and declined to 1 in 1991. India was lagging behind in the race for 'catch-up' with the US economy. India's international competitiveness became low, and its share of exports in manufacturing to developing countries fell from 22.1 per cent in 1962 to 3.4 per cent in 1990. India's global share of manufacturing exports also fell down from 0.84 per cent in 1962 to 0.54 per cent in 1990.

On the social front, there was a demand for better living standards, protectionism and subsidies. Agriculture received a huge subsidy. Fertilizers and electricity were subsidized, leading to huge government expenditure and losses in revenue. Revenue from agriculture vis-à-vis recurrent expenditure fell from 22 per cent in 1980 to 7.5 per cent in 1989. In 1988, V. P. Singh's National Front government waived the debts of small farmers, causing pressure on the exchequer. At that point, the foreign exchange reserves of India were at just $3.7 billion, which could support two months of imports.

Non-economic and non-developmental government expenditure rose at an alarming rate. In the case of state and central government, the percentage of subsidies rose from 3.3 per cent in 1960 to 12.1 per cent in 1989. Non-development expenditure rose from 6.5 per cent of the GNP in 1960 to 15 per cent in 1989. The overall growth rate of government expenditure rose from 6.9 per cent during 1979–1983 to 9.5 per cent during 1983–1987. This was a mismatch with the productivity rate. The productivity rate was low and the high level of expenditure created an unsustainable fiscal situation. The fiscal deficit till 1983 was within 6.4 per cent of the GDP mark, but from 1983 to 1990, the fiscal deficit fluctuated between 7.5 per cent and 9 per cent of the GDP.

Prime Minister **Indira Gandhi in the 1970s** and, to some extent, **Rajiv Gandhi in the 1980s,** tried to tide over the economic crisis through pro-trade policies but faced political obstacles. Indira Gandhi, after her return to power post-Emergency, embarked on a new model of development. She moved away from the statist model of the Nehruvian era towards an alliance of state and business. Mrs Gandhi was also committed towards '*garibi hatao*'. During the 1980s, Mrs. Gandhi prioritized economic growth and sought alliances with big businesses, and to some extent, she also adopted some anti-labour laws along with diverting attention from the public sector industries, which lessened the importance of the Planning Commission. There were three components of the new model of development from the 1980s by Mrs. Gandhi. They were prioritizing of economic growth as a state goal, supporting big business to achieve this goal and taming labour as a necessary aspect of this strategy.

Mrs Gandhi constituted high-powered committees to recommend the process of this transformation of the economy. The L. K. Jha Committee was entrusted with studying the overhaul of the economic administration. The Abid Hussain Committee was constituted to review trade. The M. Narasimham Committee was formed to consider financial reforms. Thus, a long-term process was put into motion. External situations in 1981 forced India to enter into a loan agreement with the IMF for nearly $5 billion over a few years. There was a petroleum price hike in 1981, and the import of machinery and technology for industrial growth led to an anticipation of a foreign exchange squeeze and the seeking of a loan from the IMF.

Rajiv Gandhi, after Mrs Gandhi, continued the policy changes. He started a new 'liberal' beginning. His economic advisors included people such as L. K. Jha, Manmohan Singh, Montek Singh Ahluwalia and Abid Hussain. Manmohan Singh and Montek Singh Ahluwalia played a significant role in the policy shift in 1991 also. Rajiv Gandhi called these reforms a 'judicious combination of deregulation, import liberalization and easier access to foreign technology'. This was a total break from Nehru and Indira Gandhi's emphasis on socialism, planning and self-reliance.

After Rajiv Gandhi, with a few years of India's experience with coalition governments, it was a minority government of P. V. Narasimha Rao that introduced the economic reforms due to a foreign exchange crunch, leading to borrowing from international financial agencies, namely the IMF and the World Bank. External factors also pushed the Indian economy into a terrible crisis. The Gulf War of 1991 led to an increase in the price of oil, which led to the depletion of foreign exchange reserves. The balance of payments of India deteriorated in the worst possible way. The current account deficit rose from $3 billion, which was 1.7 per cent of GDP in the first half of the 1980s, to $7 billion, which was 3 per cent of the GDP in the latter part of the 1980s. The oil price rise of 1990 made the current account balance stressful. There was, on the one hand, a huge fiscal deficit and, on the other hand, a savings–investment gap. Twenty tons of gold were sold to the Union Bank of Switzerland in April 1991, and 47 tons of gold were shipped to the Bank of England. In 1991, India was on the verge of a liquidity crisis, as India had foreign reserves to last for about a fortnight. India approached the IMF to tide over the crisis.

This loan was tied to SAPs to fully go for out and out liberalization. Commentators such as Prabhat Patnaik, C. P. Chandrasekkhar and Rahul Mukherji have observed a synergy between pro-trade executives in India and the IMF and the World Bank. So at the behest of Prime Minister Narasimha Rao and Finance Minister Manmohan Singh, India's tryst with reforms started.

The objectives were fiscal stabilization, internal liberalization and integration with the global economy. The 1991 India was a set of economic policy reforms that included, among others things, de-licensing, the removal of monopolies and restrictive trade practices (MRTP) constraints, tax concessions, the opening of new areas kept reserved for public sector and taming of labour. India's two chambers of commerce, the Federation of Indian Chambers of Commerce and Industry (FICCI) and the Associated Chambers of Commerce and Industry of India (ASSOCHAM), as well as the emerging Confederation of Indian Industry (CII), according to Stanley Kochanek, in his 'Liberalization and Business Lobbying in India' (1996), showed how these business groups lobbied for and against opening up the economy. While the first two were wary of external opening, the third supported the pro-liberalization policies.

The reforms were introduced in all sectors. We will discuss how the reforms brought about changes in trade and industrial sectors. The structural reforms since 1991 in the industrial sector could be summarized as follows.

- New Industrial Policy, 24 July 1991.
- Changes in the industrial investment regime.
- Industrial licensing policies regarding industrial investment were abolished, except for five industries which were to be regulated to avert environmental hazards, national security or social considerations. Among the industries reserved for being exclusively belonging to public sector were atomic energy and railways. Other industries, including infrastructural ones such as riads, telecommunications, power and ports, were opened up for privatization; even FDI entry was permitted.
- Public private partnership was encouraged, especially in infrastructural development.
- 'Industries reserved for the public sector' were dismantled and opened up for privatization, including the foreign private sector.
- Repeal of MRTP (1969) permitted opening up of large industries. The amendment carried out in 1991 permitted the MRTP Act to be extended to the public sector and government-owned companies, which was erstwhile not applicable to government companies and undertakings owned by the government. With this amendment, the large private players in the market no longer needed to take special permissions from the government before undergoing any reconstruction of the corporate nature. Therefore, the License Raj was abolished. It was replaced by the Competition Act, 2002.

- In 2014, the list reserved for small-scale industries was reduced to 20, and even the definition of a small-scale industry was changed. Now, manufacturers, even big ones, can also manufacture the items previously reserved for small and medium-sized enterprises.
- The foreign equity investment threshold of 40 per cent was removed and increased to 51 per cent in the 34 'priority' industries as enlisted in Annex III of the New Industrial Policy.
- FDI in the defence sector was permitted up to a maximum of 26 per cent. In the 2014–2015 budget, it was increased to 49 per cent. In 2020, it was raised to 74 per cent under the automatic route.
- To encourage FDI in the manufacturing sector in 2019, the government permitted 100 per cent FDI in contract manufacturing through the automatic route.
- A phased programme of disinvestment in the public sector was launched, which is still on.

In the trade policy regime since 1991, the reforms can be summarized as follows.

- Import licensing system was abolished.
- Non-tariff barriers phased out from all tradables except consumer goods.
- Commitment to liberalization under the WTO Agreement.
- Non-agricultural tariffs were reduced from 150 per cent to 5.8 per cent.
- Agricultural tariffs have subsequently fallen from 19.3 per cent in 2007–2008 to 4.2 per cent 2008–2009 and 2.5 per cent in 2009–2010.

In the financial sector since 1991, the reforms can be summarized as follows.

- In 1993, a package of reforms were introduced.
- Permission to new private sector banks.
- Permission for foreign joint ventures in the banking sector.
- New regime for non-banking finance companies.
- Flexibility and functional autonomy to banks and other financial institutions.
- Merger of public sector banks.
- The Capital Issues Control Act repealed.
- The Securities and Exchange Board of India was established on 12 April 1992 to monitor the functioning of capital markets.
- Online trading and dematerialized trading have been introduced.
- The 1992 guidelines for FII were introduced. FII could enter into all types of securities with full repatriation benefits. FIIs were allowed to invest in India's primary and secondary capital markets only through the country's portfolio investment scheme. This scheme allows FIIs to purchase shares and debentures of Indian companies on the country's public exchanges.

The recent reform includes *note bandi* or demonetization that was introduced on 8 November 2016. It scrapped the ₹500 and ₹2,000 notes. Another reform that took place was the goods and services tax (GST), which was passed on 29 March 2017 by Parliament. It came into effect from 1 July 2017. GST is supposed to be a uniform indirect tax.

Performance of the Indian Economy Post Reform

Table 11.2 shows that India's rate of growth accelerated from the 1980s onwards. Although it was not markedly very high, it was a departure from the sluggish growth rate of the 1950s. Atul Kohli calls it a significant improvement over the decade of stagnation that India experienced before. It represents a break from India's 'Hindu growth rate'.[1]

In the post-reform period, during 1990–2004, growth in investment improved as public investments declined with a simultaneous increase in private investments. Private corporate investment shot up post-reforms and peaked in the mid-1990s. Since then, it has remained at a level generally higher than the earlier level, though less than the peak. Capital formation in the household sector also increased by the mid-1990s. The industrial sector reform, as Atul Kohli suggests, helped big businesses rather than small businesses. He points out that the big businesses were comfortable with the gradual opening of the economy. A high proportion of private investment also propelled steady growth in industry, although it was not that remarkably high. He observes that the pro-growth and pro-business drift of the state, which began with Indira Gandhi and Rajiv Gandhi in the 1980s and moved beyond the 1990s, were mainly responsible for the respectable performance of the Indian economy. Table 11.3 gives us a picture of growth GDP-wise, industrial growth, capital formation and international trade.

Table 11.4 shows a spurt in economic growth with a GDP at factor cost (at constant prices base 2004–2005) for the year 2003–2004 of 8.1 per cent. This more or less continued, only to be disturbed by the global meltdown of 2008. Data from 2010–2011 also shows a high, at 8.4 per cent. The reason shown by Ghosh and Ghosh is large inflows of foreign capital. Reliance on foreign capital to sustain economic growth has made India's reliance on credit rating agencies inevitable. In 1991, it was the SAPs, but now, it is economic policies. To make ease of doing business for foreign investors, India has to follow the terms of credit rating agencies. The relative autonomy of India may have been lessened in the field of economic policymaking.

Another round of liberalization took place again in 2012 to gain the confidence of foreign investors. As in 2011–2012, India's assessment by credit rating agencies was downgraded, and

Table 11.2 Growth Data of India (1950–2004)

	1950–1964	1965–1979	1980–1990	1991–2004	1980–2004
GDP growth	3.7	2.9	5.8	5.6	5.7
Industrial growth	7.4	3.8	6.5	5.8	6.1
Agricultural growth	3.1	2.3	3.9	3.0	3.4
Gross investment/GDP	13.0	18.0	22.8	22.3	22.5

Source: Kohli (2009).

[1] *Hindu growth rate:* This was the annual growth rate of the economy of India before the economic reforms were introduced in 1991. From the 1950s to the 1980s, it stagnated around 3.5 per cent. Aggregate growth in the 1970s was even lower than what used to be termed the 'Hindu rate of growth', at an average of 2.4 per cent per year.

Table 11.3 Post-reform Economic Indicators

Year	GDP Growth (%)	Industrial Growth (%)	Capital formation (GDP in %)		International Trade (% GDP)	
			Private Sector	Public Sector	Exports	Imports
1990–2001	5.6	7.0	13.9	9.0	6.2	9.4
1991–2002	1.3	-1.0	12.9	9.2	7.3	8.3
1992–2003	5.1	4.3	14.2	8.2	7.8	10.2
1993–2004	5.9	5.6	13.4	8.0	8.1	9.6
1994–2005	7.3	10.3	13.2	8.8	8.1	10.9
1995–2006	7.3	12.3	16.7	7.7	8.9	12.0
1996–2007	7.8	7.7	15.9	6.9	8.6	12.3
1997–2008	4.8	3.8	15.3	6.4	8.5	12.2
1998–2009	6.5	3.8	15.1	6.5	8.3	11.5
1999–2000	6.1	4.9	15.6	6.2	8.4	12.4
2000–2001	4.0	7.0	15.9	6.0	9.9	12.7
2001–2002	4.4	3.7	16.2	5.9	9.4	11.8
2002–2003	5.8	6.3	16.6	5.6	10.6	12.7
2003–2004	8.5	6.6	16.8	6.0	10.8	13.3
Average	5.7	5.9	15.1	7.2	8.6	11.4

Source: Kohli (2009).

Table 11.4 Growth Rate of India, Net FDI and Foreign Portfolio Investment

Year	Growth Rate of GDP at Factor Cost (at Constant Prices Base 2004–2005)	Net FDI ($ Million)	Net Portfolio Investment ($ Million)	Total ($ Million)
2000–2001	5.3	3,270	2,590	5,860
2001–2002	5.5	4,734	1,952	6,686
2002–2003	5.0	3,157	944	4,101
2003–2004	8.1	2,388	11,377	13,765
2004–2005	7.0	3,712	9,291	1,303
2005–2006	9.5	3,033	12,492	15,525
2006–2007	9.6	7,693	6,947	14,640
2007–2008	9.6	15,891	27,434	43,325

Year	Growth Rate of GDP at Factor Cost (at Constant Prices Base 2004–2005)	Net FDI ($ Million)	Net Portfolio Investment ($ Million)	Total ($ Million)
2008–2009	6.7	22,343	–14,032	8,311
2009–2010	8.4	17,965	32,396	50,361
2010–2011	8.4	11,305	30,292	41,597
2011–2012	6.5	22,006	17,171	39,177
2012–2013	4.5	19,819	26,891	46,710
2013–2014	4.7	21,564	4,822	26,386

Source: Ghosh and Ghosh (2016).

there was a huge current account deficit with an impending currency crisis due to a sudden large increase in the exchange rate. The reforms included liberalized FDI norms for the retail, insurance and pension sectors, a road map for fiscal consolidation and an increase in FII limits in the corporate and government debt markets. It was also declared that subsidies on diesel prices would be removed and prices would be raised. In 2012–2013, the government cut down on subsidies and raised indirect tax rates in order to neutralize the adverse impact produced by the fall in the net fall in the net inflow of foreign capital that happened in the first quarter of 2012–2013. However, foreign investment bounced back in the second quarter of 2012–2013. In 2012–2013, GDP at factor cost was at 4.5 per cent. This shows that the recession which started in 2011–2012 continued into 2012–2013. The RBI observed that the recession was due to slackening of export growth owing to a slowdown in external demand.

There was a revised definition of GDP and the new base year which pushed up India's economic growth in 2012–2013 and 2013–2014 when compared to the older series. This was partly on account of the movement of indirect taxes and subsidies. Manufacturing increased by 5.3 per cent in 2013–2014, compared to a contraction in the previous series because some services promoted factory production by large corporates were only included in this output.

Therefore, by the new definition of economic growth, GDP is estimated at market prices, which includes indirect taxes but excludes subsidies. Earlier, GDP growth was estimated at factor cost, which excludes indirect taxes but includes subsidies. Therefore, taking factor cost with base year of 2004–2005, India had a GDP growth of 4.5 per cent in 2012–2013 and 4.7 per cent in 2013–2014. With the new series, GDP growth stood at 5.1 per cent for 2012–2013 and 6.9 per cent for 2013–2014. GDP at factor cost has been abandoned, and in place of GDP at factor cost, gross value added (GVA) at basic prices[2] will be used now.

India's growth at 7.6 per cent in 2015–2016 was the fastest in five years as against 7.2 per cent in 2014–2015. According to the data released by the Central Statistics Office (CSO) on 31 May 2016, the growth in manufacturing and farm sectors during the fourth quarter accelerated to 9.3 per cent and 2.3 per cent, respectively. The core sector data in April 2016

[2] The difference between GDP at factor cost and GVA at basic prices is that production taxes are included and production subsidies are excluded from the latter. Production taxes and subsidies are different from product taxes and subsidies.

also indicated momentum in the economy as it grew at a rate of 8.5 per cent in the month, the highest in the last four years. On 1 February 2017, the Economic Survey 2016–2017 by Chief Economic Adviser, Arvind Subramanian, observed that the demonetization exercise could slow GDP growth by 25–50 basis points in 2016–2017 on the baseline growth assumption of 7 per cent. One basis point is 0.01 per cent. For 2017–2018, the survey projected the economy to grow in the wide range of 6.75 per cent to 7.5 per cent.

The Economic Survey highlighted that demonetization will have both short-term costs and long-term benefits. 'Briefly, the costs include a contraction in cash money supply and subsequent, albeit temporary, slowdown in GDP growth, and benefits include increased digitalization, greater tax compliance and a reduction in real estate prices, which could increase long-run tax revenue collections and GDP growth'.

The GDP at current prices for 2015–2016 was estimated at ₹135.76 lakh crore, showing a growth rate of 8.7 per cent over the first revised estimates of GDP for the year 2014–2015 of ₹124.88 lakh crore. The real GDP, or GDP at constant (2011–2012) prices, was now estimated at ₹113.50 lakh crore for 2015–2016, showing a growth rate of 7.6 per cent over the first revised estimates of GDP for 2014–2015 of ₹105.52 lakh crore.

There was a significant increase in growth estimates for the industrial and services sectors. While the industrial sector is estimated to have grown by 8.2 per cent against the earlier estimation of 7.4 per cent, the services sector is estimated to have grown by 9.9 per cent against 8.9 per cent earlier. The farm sector growth rate was, however, cut to 0.76 per cent from 1.2 per cent estimated earlier.

In the fiscal year 2016–2017, GDP growth is estimated at 7.1 per cent in 2016–2017, lower than the 7.6 per cent growth in 2015–2016. The fall in growth rate may be due to slower growth in the manufacturing and construction sectors. There has been a growth in GDP over the past few years, from 5.3 per cent in 2012–2013 to 7.3 per cent in 2014–2015. The agriculture sector, which has been witnessing low growth over the past few years, was estimated to grow by 4.1 per cent in 2016–2017. Growth in the manufacturing sector was estimated at 7.4 per cent, and in the services sector, at 8.8 per cent.

Retail inflation has been declining over the past few years. It has dropped from 8.3 per cent in 2012–2013 to 4.9 per cent in 2015–2016, owing to a fall in the prices of food and oil. The Index of Industrial Production (IIP) measures the level of production in sectors such as manufacturing, electricity and mining. IIP has increased over the past few years, from 1.1 per cent in 2012–2013 to 3.1 per cent in 2015–2016. *The fiscal deficit was estimated at 3.5 per cent of GDP in 2016–2017, the revenue deficit at 2.3 per cent and the current account deficit was on a decline, from $88 billion in 2012–2013 to $22 billion in 2015–2016.*

For the fiscal year 2017–2018, according to the CSO estimate, the real GDP or GDP at constant (2011–2012) prices for 2017–2018 and 2016–2017 stood at ₹131.80 lakh crore and ₹122.98 lakh crore, respectively, showing a growth of 7.2 per cent during 2017–2018 and 8.2 per cent during 2016–2017. Earlier, the CSO, in its advance estimate, had estimated the GDP growth rate for 2018–2019 at 7.2 per cent. During 2017–2018, the growth rates of primary (comprising agriculture, forestry, fishing and mining and quarrying), secondary (comprising manufacturing, electricity, gas, water supply and other utility services, and construction) and tertiary (services) sectors have been estimated as 5 per cent, 6 per cent and 8.1 per cent as against a growth of 6.8 per cent, 7.5 per cent and 8.4 per cent, respectively, in the previous year.

The period following the years 2018–2019 witnessed a low in the performance of the Indian economy. It had a growth rate of 6.8 per cent (2018–2019) and had fixed a target of 8 per cent per annum. India was experiencing a decline in the core sectors such as agriculture, manufacturing, infrastructure, construction and power. India's GDP rate also got reduced each quarter in 2018–2019. It fell from 8 per cent in the first quarter to 7 per cent in the second quarter, 6.6 per cent in the third quarter and 5.8 per cent in the fourth quarter. The ultimate result was 6.8 per cent for the whole year and brought down its forecast for 2019–2020 to 7 per cent from its earlier forecast of 7.3 per cent (by 0.3%).

Factors which were found to be decreasing the growth rates can be summarized as follows.

- Decline in domestic demand
- Fall in savings from 30.5 per cent in 2017–2018 to 28 per cent in 2018–2019
- Rise in inflation beyond 4 per cent
- Destabilizing influences on the monetary and fiscal sides
- Slow growth in manufacturing
- A decline in agriculture growth
- Shrinking share of labour force
- Fall in exports
- Unfavourable foreign capital flows

K. P. Kannan and G. Raveendran pointed at the findings of the employment survey. The Periodic Labour Force Survey (2017–2018) highlighted that the two biggest issues in the Indian economy were the shrinking share of the labour force and rising unemployment. An earlier survey revealed that **labour force participation rate (LFPR),** that is, per cent of people working or seeking work above 15 years of age, was 55.5 per cent in 2012. There was an absolute decline in the number of workers from 467.7 million in 2012 to 461.5 million in 2018. **The overall unemployment rate** at 6.1 per cent was 2.77 times the same figure for 2012. The rate of unemployment (of the severe type) was highest among urban women at 10.8 per cent, followed by urban men at 8.7 per cent. The rural unemployment rate was high among men at 5.8 per cent, followed by women at 3.8 per cent. If the location of residence is ignored, unemployment was higher among men at 6.2 per cent than among women at 5.7 per cent. The fall in women's LFPR from 31.1 per cent to 25.3 per cent (decline by 7.8% points) proves that India is among the countries with the lowest LFPR among women in the labour force. **The unemployment rate among young people** (those in between 15 and 29 years of age) shot up to a high of 17.8 per cent, which is a matter of concern to the economy. Gender-wise, women face more disadvantages than men, specifically urban women. The unemployment rate for urban young women reached 27.2 per cent (peak level), which is double the percentage (13.1%) in 2012. The rate for urban men was equally high at 18.7 per cent. The 2018 survey observed that the trend of 'jobless growth', which was earlier confined to the organized sector, has now spread to other sectors of the economy and has become a generalized situation.

The annual growth in output that is measured by GVA is close to 6.91 per cent, whereas employment growth is negative and that leads us to characterize the period as one of 'job-loss growth'. The job-loss growth is due to the net decline in jobs in five sectors of the economy which account for 65 per cent of total employment (in 2011–2012). Agriculture, given its high share in employment, emerges as the biggest loser in terms of the absolute number of jobs lost.

K. P. Kannan and G. Raveendran also point out that men's share of employment in the primary sector (mostly in agriculture) declined from 43.1 per cent in 2011–2012 to 38.7 per cent in 2017–2018. For women, the decline was from 62.3 per cent to 55.3 per cent. They also point out that this trend shows that a major share of the women workers whose total size is also shrinking are those who continue to be dependent on the primary sector. It has registered a GVA growth rate of a little more than 3 per cent.

Manufacturing, despite high growth in output, has also been one of the jobs that have affected men. Table 11.5 shows that there was growth in many sectors, except construction. A number of these failed to generate employment and provide more jobs for those seeking to enter the labour force. Two sectors among these were real estate and trade and repair services. The data shows that seven sectors, all of which are services, have registered impressive employment elasticities ranging from 0.43 to 0.65. However, their combined weight in total employment was only 10.6 per cent in 2011–2012, rising to 13.9 per cent in 2017–2018.

Table 11.5 Employment Elasticity with Respect to Growth by Industry in India (2011–2012) and (2017–2018)

Sl No.	Industry Group		Annual Growth Rate		Employment Elasticity
			GVA	Employment	
A.	**High Growth in Output and Employment**	**Sectoral Share of Total Employment (2011-2012)**			
1.	Professional & technical activities	0.6	10.94	7.07	0.65
2.	Information & communication	0.8	7.41	4.60	0.62
3.	Administration & support services	0.7	16.54	10.32	0.62
4.	Transport	4.2	6.57	3.18	0.48
5.	Health & social work	1.0	9.33	4.44	0.48
6.	Education	3.1	8.25	3.83	0.46
7.	Arts & recreations	0.2	10.08	4.33	0.43
Sl No.	**Industry Group**		**Annual Growth Rate**		**Employment Elasticity**
			GVA	**Employment**	
B.	**High Growth in Output & Moderate Employment Absorption**	**Sectoral Share of Total Employment (2011-2012)**			
8.	Electricity, gas & water supply	0.5	6.19	2.43	0.39
9.	Finance & insurance	0.9	7.15	2.75	0.38
10.	Construction	10.6	3.74	1.30	0.35
11.	Accommodation & food services	1.7	6.09	2.16	0.35

Sl No.	Industry Group		Annual Growth Rate: GVA	Annual Growth Rate: Employment	Employment Elasticity
C.	High Growth & Low Employment Absorption	Sectoral Share of Total Employment (2011–2012)			
12.	Real estate	0.2	12.70	2.06	0.16
13.	Trade & repair services	9.7	9.92	1.31	0.13
Sl No.	**Industry Group**		**GVA**	**Employment**	**Employment Elasticity**
D	High Growth (except Agriculture) with Job Displacement	Sectoral Share of Total Employment (2011–2012)			
14.	Manufacturing	12.6	7.51	−0.16	−0.02
15.	Public administration & defence	1.8	5.67	−0.76	−0.13
16.	Other service activities	2.2	9.49	−1.67	−0.18
17.	Agriculture	47.8	3.09	−2.32	−0.75
18.	Mining & quarrying	0.6	5.78	−4.67	−0.81
E.	**Whole Economy**		**6.91**	**−0.22**	**−0.03**

Source: Government of India (2019).

COVID-19 and Indian Economy

The year 2020 began with the outbreak of the pandemic. The article, **'The Economic Impact of COVID 19 with Special Reference to India'** (as on 01 May 2020), showed the first case on 30 January 2020. Since then, the cases have increased. The first wave was followed by the second wave in March–May 2021. The number has increased manifolds, and as of 15 June 2021, the number of cases for infection is 2.95 crore. The outbreak of the pandemic hit the economy hard due to lockdowns and closures to break the chain.

The FICCI report, ***Impact of COVID 19 on Indian Economy*** **(March 2020),** highlighted the condition of the economy due to the pandemic, lockdown and shut down. The economy was experiencing a growth rate at a six-year low rate of 4.7 per cent. Economic recovery was hoped for the business sector, but the corona pandemic made it difficult. The reports, the earlier one and this FICCI report, showed that closures hit the demand side. Tourism, hospitality and aviation were the worst affected sectors that are at a complete loss because of travel restrictions and lockdown. The closing of cinema theatres as well as declining footfall in shopping complexes have affected the retail sector by declining consumption of both essential and discretionary items. Job losses and decline in income levels of people, particularly the daily wage earners, due to slowing activity in several sectors, including retail, construction, entertainment and so on, have affected consumption also.

On the supply side, the shutdown of factories and the resulting delay in the supply of goods from China has affected many Indian manufacturing sectors which source their intermediate and final product requirements from China. Some sectors such as automobiles, pharmaceuticals, electronics and chemical products, among others, are facing raw material and component shortages.

Agriculture and allied activities have been adversely hit by the coronavirus scare. The poultry sector has been severely affected. It is the fastest-growing subsector of India agriculture ecosystem. India is the third largest producer of eggs and fifth largest producer of broilers, but because of the pandemic and massive losses, it would push back in its economic ranking.

The informal workers and daily wage earners already facing problems with low wages and incomes in the pre-COVID-19 period are worst hit by the pandemic. With almost no economic activity, particularly in urban areas, the lockdown has led to large-scale losses in jobs and incomes for these workers. The estimated number of seasonal migrant workers in India is about 40–50 million who are engaged in the construction of urban buildings, roads, factory production and participate in several service activities. Shutdowns, closures and lockdowns have led to a large-scale exodus of interstate workers (migrant workers).

The May 2020 report also showed that the MSMEs sector would be badly hit by reduced cash flows caused by the nationwide lockdown. Not only would their supply chain be disrupted, but they would also be affected by the exodus of migrant workers. They will suffer due to restrictions in the availability of raw materials, the widespread travel bans, the disruption to exports and imports, closure of malls, hotels, theatres and educational institutions and the like.

The data from the Consumer Pyramid Household Survey of the Centre for the Monitoring of the Indian Economy shows an increase in unemployment rate in urban areas by 30 per cent in the week ending 29 March, which is about 3.5 times the rate of 8.7 per cent for the week ending 22 March. For rural areas, the unemployment figures were 21 per cent and 8.3 per cent for the same period. The overall unemployment rate increased from 8.4 per cent to 23.8 per cent. In the data for the week ending 5 April 2020, the estimated rate of unemployment was at 30.9 per cent for urban areas, 20.2 per cent for rural areas and 23.4 per cent at the all-India level.

The Government of India's response was the formation of the COVID-19 Economic Response Task Force led by the Finance Minister, Nirmala Sitharaman. On 24 March 2020, in his address to the nation, the prime minister announced a ₹15,000 crore fund for the health-care sector. The Pradhan Mantri Garib Kalyan Yojana was to provide, among many components, a free additional 5 kg of wheat or rice per person for three months, 1 kg of free pulses per household for three months, free LPG for *Ujjwala* beneficiaries for three months, ₹2,000 to 87 million farmers under the *Pradhan Mantri Kisan Yojana* in 10 days, an increase in Mahatma Gandhi Employment Guarantee Act wages to ₹202 from ₹182 and so on. More than 33 crore poor people have been directly given financial assistance of ₹31,235 crore (as on 22 April 2020) under the Pradhan Mantri Garib Kalyan Package.

The RBI in April 2020 announced more measures to deal with the economic fallout of COVID-19. These were like an increase in ways and means advances and short-term liquidity to provide relief to state governments and relief to exporters in the form of relaxed repatriation limits. The World Bank in April 2021 approved $1 billion emergency financing for India to tackle coronavirus under the label 'India COVID-19 Emergency Response and Health Systems Preparedness Project'. The central government released ₹17,287 crore to different states to help combat coronavirus. The Ministry of Home Affairs approved ₹11,092 crore for states as relief under the State Disaster Risk Management Fund. These were also followed by other kinds of economic assistance measures throughout 2020.

Let us look at **GDP growth** now. The IMF slashed India's growth estimate for financial year 2021 to 1.9 per cent from 5.8 per cent estimated in January 2020. It gave the warning that the 'worst recession since the Great Depression' will dwarf the economic damage caused by the global financial crisis a decade back. However, it also predicted that India and China would be the only two major economies likely to register growth while others would be contracting. Domestic rating agency CRISIL's projections for India's economic growth rate is to be 1.8 per cent, from 3.5 per cent it had earlier predicted for 2020–2021. Moody's Investors Service slashed India's growth forecast for the calendar year 2020 to 0.2 per cent, from 2.5 per cent projected in March. For 2021, the rating agency expects India's growth to rebound to 6.2 per cent.

The Economic Survey 2020–2021, published in January 2021, also predicted a 'V-shaped' economic recovery for the nation, spurred by the COVID-19 vaccination programme. The survey also cautioned that it would take at least two years to revert to pre-pandemic gross domestic levels.

As of 31 May 2021, the OECD raised its 2021 global GDP growth forecast but warned that 'too many headwinds persist' because enough COVID vaccines are not reaching emerging economies, thereby making the world vulnerable to variants. The world economy will, however, expand by 5.8 per cent this year, up from a previous estimate of 5.6 per cent.

On 31 May 2021, while unveiling the revenue expenditure data of the union government for 2020–2021, the Controller General of Accounts (CGA) said that the revenue deficit at the end of the fiscal was 7.42 per cent. India's fiscal deficit for 2020–2021 was at 9.3 per cent or ₹18.21 lakh crore of the GDP, lower than 9.5 per cent estimated by the Finance Ministry in the revised budget estimates, according to the CGA data. On 1 February, the government revised its fiscal deficit target to 9.5 per cent of GDP or ₹1,848,655 crore for the financial year 2020–2021, instead of its original target of 3.5 per cent of GDP as the coronavirus pandemic led to lower tax collection and higher spending.

According to Moody's prediction, India's economy rebounded quickly from a steep contraction in 2020. However, a severe second wave of the coronavirus has increased risks to India's credit profile, including a persistent slowdown in growth, weak government finances and rising financial sector risks. Moody's expects a decline in economic activity in the April–June quarter but followed by a rebound, resulting in real, inflation-adjusted GDP growth of 9.3 per cent per cent in the fiscal year ending March 2022 (fiscal 2021) and 7.9 per cent in fiscal 2022. Moody's forecasted a 13.7 per cent growth in current fiscal year earlier in February. As the country battled the first wave of COVID, the Indian economy contracted by 7.3 per cent in fiscal 2020–2021, as against a 4 per cent growth in 2019–2020.

By June 2021, India's trade deficit hit an eight-month low in May at $6.32 billion as per preliminary trade data released by the Commerce Ministry on 3 June 2021. While rising external demand kept exports robust, the second wave of the pandemic led to a decline in domestic demand with a dip in imports. (As of May 2021, the trade deficit stood at $15.1 billion.)

India's average agricultural tariff rose from 36.4 per cent in the financial year 2015 to 36.5 per cent in the financial year 2021. Average non-agricultural tariff increased from 9.5 per cent to 11.1 per cent in 2020–2021. The most important increase in non-agricultural goods included clothing (from 10% to 19.6%), oilseeds, fats and oil and their products (from 26.7%

to 35.1%), and sugar and confectionary (from 35.4% to 47%). In the case of non-agricultural products, the average tariff increased mainly as a result of a hike in duties levied on leather, rubber, footwear, and travel goods from 12.8 per cent to 15.4 per cent. India's average tariff increased to 14.3 per cent in the financial year 2021 from 13 per cent in the financial year 2015. The WTO has urged India to reduce tariffs.

In June 2021, the Reserve Bank of India (RBI) cut its forecast of real GDP growth to 9.5 per cent in the current financial year (2021–2022). The RBI predicted that the economy is likely to grow at a rate of 18.5 per cent in the first quarter, 7.9 per cent in the second quarter, 7.2 per cent in the third quarter and 6.6 per cent in the fourth quarter. The RBI had earlier forecasted 10.5 per cent GDP growth for financial year 2022. The RBI had expected growth at 26.2 per cent for the first quarter, 8.3 per cent for the second quarter, 5.4 per cent for the third quarter and 6.2 per cent for the fourth quarter.

In June 2021, the Wholesale Price Index inflation was a record high of 12.94 per cent. This is thought to be pushed by higher fuel and commodity prices, and a low base effect. This led to higher retail inflation of 6.30 per cent in May 2021, which was a six-month high. With this, retail inflation has breached the inflation target of +4/−2 per cent set by the RBI.

In the Union Budget 2021–2022, the Finance Minister, Nirmala Sitharaman, proposed an outlay of ₹2.23 lakh crore towards health and well-being. This represents a 137 per cent increase over the ₹94,452 crore budgeted expenditure on healthcare in the ongoing fiscal year. The health scheme is an addition to the existing National Health Mission that focuses on three areas: preventive, curative and well-being.

Prime Minister Narendra Modi announced a free vaccine policy in an address to the nation on 7 June 2021. The centre, by June 21, will take over the existing COVID vaccination drive that has been partly done by the states since 1 May 2021. The centre is to provide free vaccines to all states for vaccination of those above 18 years of age from June 21. The main points of this policy are as follows.

- Every individual above 18 years of age in the country gets free vaccines at government facilities.
- The centre will buy 75 per cent of jabs from vaccine manufacturers and provide them to the state governments.
- Private sector hospitals will continue to procure 255 of the vaccine directly from manufacturers.
- Service charges in private hospitals are capped at ₹150 per dose over the fixed price of the vaccine.

On the same day, on 7 June, in his address to the nation, Prime Minister Modi announced under the centre's free food programme which will be extended for five months till November that the government has decided that the Pradhan Mantri Garib Kalyan Anna Yojana (PMGKAY) will now be extended till Diwali. In this time of pandemic, the government is standing with the poor in their every need as their partner. That is, free food grains will be available in fixed quantity every month to more than 80 crore countrymen till November.

More than 800 million beneficiaries will get an additional 5 kg of wheat or rice per person free during July and November 2021. The current population of India is estimated to be

1,392,642,289 as of 8 June 2021 as based on Worldometers[3] elaboration of the latest UN data. So 800,000,000 million people, or 57.4 per cent of the population who are poor, have to be fed, which is quite a huge number of poor. Reaching out to them will need proper execution of policy. However, a robust policy can make India sail through the pandemic and lead it towards economic recovery. An economically strong, healthy, sustainable, self-reliant and inclusive India is a vision to be achieved in the future.

Conclusion

India started its journey with a mixed economy model and planned economic growth from 1951 to 2015. From the 1950s to the 1980s, India had a sluggish economic growth rate. The oil shock of the 1990s due to the Gulf War and a rising fiscal deficit took India to the verge of a liquidity crisis in 1990. India had to borrow from the IMF and the World Bank. Therefore, India had to implement economic reforms as per the SAPs imposed by the IMF and the World Bank. India adopted a NEP in 1991. The NEP's objective was to achieve economic growth combined with economic efficiency. The other features were a reduction in state intervention, liberalization, privatization, removal of restrictions on foreign ownership, equity holdings, repatriation of profit and abandonment of laws such as Foreign Exchange Regulation Act, MRTP and many more. Implementation of NEP gave a spurt to India's economic progress discussed above. If we take into account the trajectory of India's development, we will see unprecedented growth from 2003–2004 to 2010–2011, with the exception of 2008–2009, when there was a global melt down. The recession hit in 2011–2012. In the financial years 2015–2016, India witnessed unprecedented GDP growth of 8.3 per cent (World Bank estimate), though after that there was a decline (discussed above). However, the COVID-19 pandemic that overtook the world in 2020 and is still continuing in 2021, first wave and second wave, has hit the economy hard. The only hope is that by mid-2021, if the recovery starts, India will have a growth rate of 8.3 per cent, according to the World Bank's *Global Economic Prospects, June 2021.*

Summary

India travelled through 12 plans. The Twelfth Plan could not be completed because the Planning Commission was abolished and replaced by NITI Aayog.
India experienced a sluggish growth rate, the 'Hindu growth rate', over the period from 1951 to 1980.

The external situation after the Gulf War of 1991 and the oil price hike put India into difficulties, and there was a foreign exchange reserve crunch as well as a mounting fiscal deficit that forced India to approach the IMF and the World Bank for loans, which imposed SAPs. Following this, India introduced NEP in 1991 and carried out economic reforms, thereby initiating liberalization of the economy.

---

[3] Population of India, availabe at https://www.worldometers.info/world-population/india-population/ (24 November 2021).

Following the economic reforms, India's economy recovered quickly. Since 2003–2004, India has recorded a high growth rate, with the exception of 2008–2009, when there was a global melt down. Since 2012–2013, there has been a recession in the economy. In the financial year 2015–2016, India witnessed unprecedented GDP growth of 8.1 per cent. In the following years, there was a reduction in the GDP growth, but with the outbreak of pandemic, the first and second wave, economic recovery is suffering. If the recovery starts by the mid-2021, India will have a growth rate of 8.3 per cent, according to the World Bank's *Global Economic Prospects, June 2021.*

REVIEW AND REFLECTION QUESTIONS

1. Planned economic growth started in India in the year 1951. In this light, discuss the different plans.
2. What compelled India to introduce economic reforms in the economy?
3. The NEP, 1991, introduced economic reforms in India. Examine the economic reforms that were introduced in the economy in 1991.
4. Examine the economic performance of India in the post-reform era.
5. COVID-19 has made economic progress difficult. Examine the economic scenario in India during COVID times.

Bibliography

Bardhan, Pranab. 1998. *The Political Economy of Development in India.* New Delhi: Oxford University Press.

Chibber, Vivek. 2006. *Locked in Place, State-Building and Late Industrialization in India.* Princeton, NJ: Princeton University Press.

Ghosh, Chandana, and Ambar Ghosh. 2016. *Indian Economy: A Macro-theoretic Analysis.* New Delhi: PHI Learning.

Government of India. 2019. 'GAV at Basic Prices.' CSO, National Accounts Statistics, Unit Level Data of 68th Round of NSS & PLFS 2017–2018.

IANS. 2018. 'India's GDP Growth Fell to 7.1% in 2016–17 from 8.2% in 2015–16.' Available at https://www.business-standard.com/article/news-ians/india-s-gdp-growth-fell-to-7-1-in-2016-17-from-8-2-in-2015-16-118013101255_1.html (accessed on 12 October 2021).

Kannan, K. P., and G. Raveendran. 2019a. 'Jobless Growth Becomes More Systemic.' *The Hindu*, July 12. Available at https://www.thehindu.com/opinion/op-ed/jobless-growth-becomes-more-systemic/article28391822.ece (accessed on 12 October 2021).

———. 2019b. 'From Jobless Growth to Job-loss Growth: India's Employment Performance during 2012–18.' Available at file:///C:/Users/lenovo/Downloads/KP_Kannan_GRaveendran_Jobloss Growth_EPW2019.pdf (accessed on 12 October 2021).

Kapila, Uma. 2019. *Indian Economy: Performance and Policies.* New Delhi: Academic Foundation.

———(ed.). 2019. *Indian Economy since Independence: A Comprehensive and Critical Analysis of India's Economy, 1947–2019.* New Delhi: Academic Foundation.

Kohli, Atul. 2009. *Democracy and Development in India.* New Delhi: Oxford University Press.

Lakshman, S. 2021. 'India Expected to Grow at 8.3%, Says World Bank.' *The Hindu,* 2021, June 8. Available at https://www.thehindu.com/business/Economy/india-expected-to-grow-at-83-says-world-bank/article34762989.ece (accessed on 12 October 2021).

Magazine, Aanchal. 2021. 'Pushed by Rising Fuel and Food Prices, Retail Inflation Breaches 6% Comfort Zone of RBI.' *The Indian Express*, 2021, June 15. Available at https://indianexpress.com/article/business/economy/india-wpi-wholesale-inflation-rises-12-94-per-cent-in-may-2021-commerce-ministry-data-7358271/ (accessed on 12 October 2021).

Ministry of Finance. 2021. *Economic Survey: 2021.* Government of India, Ministry of Finance, Department of Economic Affairs. Available at https://www.indiabudget.gov.in/economicsurvey/doc/echapter_vol2.pdf (accessed on 12 October 2021).

Mint. 2021. 'India's Fiscal Deficit at 9.3% of GDP for FY21, Down from Revised Estimate of 9.5%.' Available at https://www.livemint.com/economy/indias-fiscal-deficit-at-9-3-of-gdp-in-fy21-down-from-revised-estimate-of-95-11622459720813.html (accessed on 12 October 2021).

Mishra, Asit Ranjan. 2017. 'India's GDP Growth Rate for 2015–2016 Revised to 7.6% from 7.9%.' Available at https://www.livemint.com/Industry/fOtMe4T3PN8CtLaeoO3E8M/Indias-GDP-growth-rate-for-201516-revised-to-79-from-76.html (accessed on 12 October 2021).

Mishra, Asit Ranjan. 2021. 'WTO Urges India to Reduce Tariffs.' Available at https://www.livemint.com/news/india/india-frequently-using-trade-policy-measures-to-encourage-local-production-wto-11610006956392.html (accessed on 12 October 2021).

Mukherji, Rahul (ed.). 2010. *India's Economic Transition: The Politics of Reforms*. New Delhi: Oxford University Press.

PRS India. 2016. 'PRS Legislative Research, State of the Economy 2016–17.' Available at https://prsindia.org/policy/vital-stats/state-economy-2016-17 (accessed on 12 October 2021).

PTI. 2016. 'India's Growth at 7.6% in 2015–16 Fastest in Five Years.' *The Economic Times*, May 31. Available at https://economictimes.indiatimes.com/news/economy/indicators/indias-growth-at-7-6-in-2015-16-fastest-in-five-years/articleshow/52522153.cms?utm_source=contentofinterest&utm_medium=text&utm_campaign=cppst (accessed on 12 October 2021).

———. 2019. 'GDP Growth Rate for 2017–18 Revised Upwards to 7.2%.' *The Economic Times*. Available at https://economictimes.indiatimes.com/news/economy/indicators/gdp-growth-rate-for-2017-18-revised-upwards-to-7-2-/articleshow/67775487.cms?from=mdr (accessed on 12 October 2021).

Ray, Meenakshi. 2021. 'Free Ration to 800 Million People till Diwali, Announces PM Modi.' *Hindustan Times*. Available at https://www.hindustantimes.com/india-news/free-ration-to-800-million-people-till-diwali-announces-pm-modi-101623071436210.html (accessed on 12 October 2021).

Saha, Suhrita. 2016. *Political Responses to the New Economic Policy in India*. Kolkata: Readers Service.

The Times of India. 2021. 'Centre to Give Free Vaccines to States from June 21: PM Announces New Policy.' Available at http://timesofindia.indiatimes.com/articleshow/83308354.cms?utm_source=contentofinterest&utm_medium=text&utm_campaign=cppst (accessed on 12 October 2021).

Index